AUGUSTUS HERVEY

Augustus Hervey in 1768. From the picture at Ickworth by Thomas Gainsborough, reproduced by courtesy of the National Trust.

Augustus Hervey

A Naval Casanova

M. R. J. HOLMES

The Pentland Press
Edinburgh – Cambridge – Durham – USA

First published in 1996 by
The Pentland Press Ltd
1 Hutton Close,
South Church
Bishop Auckland
Durham

ISBN 1-85821-384-3

Typeset by Carnegie Publishing, 18 Maynard St, Preston
Printed and bound by Bookcraft (Bath) Ltd., Midsomer Norton, Somerset

Contents

Illustrations

Maps

Acknowledgements

I am particularly grateful to the Honourable David Erskine, who edited the published edition of Hervey's *Journal,* for much information and advice and for permission to quote from the *Journal.* Dr N A M Rodger gave me encouragement and advice on sources. I am also much indebted for advice and assistance to the keepers of the many manuscript and other sources on which I have drawn, including the staff of the Public Record Office, the National Maritime Museum Library, Cambridge University Library, the Suffolk Record Offices at Ipswich and Bury St Edmunds, Suffolk Library Services and the British Library.

.

Preface

For 150 years after Augustus Hervey's death in 1779 his place in history was a small one. Experts in eighteenth-century naval history knew him for his brave and resolute exploits as a naval commander, while the many biographers of his unpredictable wife blackened his name by describing his marital behaviour from a standpoint of prejudice and ignorance. Horace Walpole combined praise for his naval achievements with witty but far-fetched comments on his political aspirations and marital imbroglio.

It was not until Hervey's *Journal* was published in 1953 that a broader picture of his life, his character and his attitudes began to emerge. Covering only thirteen years of his life, in midcareer, it describes his life as a ship's captain in the Mediterranean and elsewhere. There emerges from it a scenario of unashamed good-living and pleasure in peacetime, balanced by courage, resolution and ingenuity in time of war. His comments provide insights into the lackadaisical way in which the navy employed its ships in time of peace and of the unsure hand with which administrators and commanders controlled their squadrons in time of war. His accounts of his philandering in Mediterranean ports draw a fascinating picture of the freedom open to a ship's captain to enjoy his opportunities to the full and rank him with the most promiscuous men of his age. They also show an open and generous character bent on enjoying the social round while peace lasted and a zealous proponent of meaningful action when the guns began to fire.

The *Journal,* however, says little about his earlier life and nothing about his last twenty years, during with he was successively a naval captain, an aspiring politician, a Lord Commissioner of the Admiralty and a scourge of government and particularly Admiralty policies. It is these 'unknown' periods that have never previously been described and which emerge in some detail from his own few surviving writings, writings which include a delightful youthful account of his part as a 16-year-old lieutenant in the attack by Admiral Vernon on Cartagena, his letters to and correspondence with contemporaries including two prime ministers, his naval correspondence with the Admiralty and other Admiralty records. Though most of his private naval papers on which he drew to compose the *Journal* disappeared from view within a decade or so of his death, enough documentation is to be found to delineate a man of vital and sometimes contentious character and to demonstrate Hervey's attitudes to and interactions with many of the great men of his time.

It would be a dubious extravagance to describe Hervey himself as a great man. Anyone, however, who served in the navy with distinction in two world wars, who aspired to the highest position that the British naval establishment had to offer, who made love almost as a hobby to women of all degrees in most countries of western Europe, who was actually married to the notorious Elizabeth Chudleigh (best known as the bigamous Duchess of Kingston), and who is mentioned eighty times in Horace Walpole's correspondence, cannot be satisfactorily described as either uninteresting or negligible.

CHAPTER I

Origins

A silver spoon

Augustus Hervey was a man of many parts. The persona by which he would undoubtedly wish to be remembered is that of Captain the Honourable Augustus Hervey, who was described by one of his naval superiors as a 'gallant and deserving officer', while another wrote that he 'never saw a more complete exact officer since I had the honour of being in His Majesty's sea service'. Amongst his achievements were command of the inshore squadron during the long blockade of Brest in 1759, and the distinguished part he played in the capture of Havana in 1762. But he was also the contentious and inconsistent politician who eventually succeeded to the family title of Earl of Bristol and the man who was actually married to the notorious Elizabeth Chudleigh, known to history as the bigamous Duchess of Kingston.

Perhaps it was the failure of his injudicious early marriage that turned him into the promiscuous man-of-the-world who seduced or was seduced by women of all positions in life at home and abroad, in most countries of western Europe. Until his journal was published earlier this century his activities in this field were virtually unknown. In it, however, he conceals little, giving an account of sexual liaisons that rank him with the greatest of philanderers and justify those who have called him the English Casanova.

The second son of John Lord Hervey of Ickworth and his wife the former Mary Lepel, Augustus John Hervey was born in London on 19 May 1724, about one o'clock of the afternoon. His paternal grandfather was John Hervey, 1st Earl of Bristol, and it was his membership of this great Whig family that opened to him almost every door in Europe and enabled him to make the most of his undoubted talents, in the navy, in the political life of the reigns of George II and III, and in the pursuit of women.

The Herveys had first emerged as substantial landowners at Ickworth, near Bury St Edmunds in Suffolk, when in the fifteenth century Thomas Hervey of Thurleigh in Bedfordshire married Jane Drury, heiress to the Ickworth estate. From the sixteenth century they became the pre-eminent family in local politics and from the seventeenth controlled one and sometimes both of the two St Edmundsbury seats in Parliament. Herveys were regularly returned to the Commons until the early years of the twentieth century. With a seat also in the Lords successive heads of the family thus had considerable influence in national politics and the opportunity to place their relatives in positions of power and reward.

It was John Hervey, Augustus's grandfather, who raised the status of the family from that of important landed gentry to make it one of the grand Whig dynasties of the eighteenth century. It was a remarkable achievement, for he did this without providing any special service to his country, though he and his second wife were strong supporters of Queen Anne and the Protestant succession. Both his wives were in fact wealthy heiresses, bringing with them extensive estates in Lincolnshire and Suffolk, and providing him with the money to support the lifestyle of a grandee. In 1703 Queen Anne raised him to the peerage as Baron Hervey of Ickworth. In this ennoblement Sarah Duchess of Marlborough appears to have had a principal hand, certainly if her own words on the subject are to be believed. That at this date she had the power to influence the Queen in such matters is not to be doubted and in a later letter she wrote:

> I had made a promise to Sir Thomas Felton [father of John Hervey's second wife], when the Queen first came to the crown, that if Her Majesty should ever make any new Lords I would certainly use my interest that Mr. Hervey should be one of them.

Felton (who had no son to succeed him) was Master of the Household to Queen Anne. Thus it may be that the new peer owed his noble status not solely to any merit of his own, but at least equally to the Queen's desire (or Sarah's) to reward the father-in-law's services by making the son-in-law a peer and the daughter a peer's wife.

The new Baron's continued enthusiasm for the Protestant settlement and Hanoverian succession persuaded George I, shortly after his accession in 1714, to advance him to the Earldom of Bristol. Perhaps the assurance that at least one of the members elected for St Edmundsbury would for the foreseeable future vote in the Whig (and therefore Hanoverian) interest was sufficient justification for this honour. Certainly the new Earl took little part in politics, living quietly at Ickworth until his death in 1751. His wife, however, was much involved in court affairs, being for many years Lady of the Bedchamber to Caroline of Anspach (wife of George II), both as Princess of Wales and as Queen.

In the eighteenth century the family seat at Ickworth was infinitely less palatial than the idiosyncratic mansion that stands there today. The ancient manor house had been demolished in 1710 and though the 1st Earl consulted more than one architect he never succeeded in building the intended replacement. He and the three grandsons who succeeded him in the title had as their country residence Ickworth Lodge, an upgraded farmhouse on the estate, of whose inadequacy he complained bitterly. However, the family also had a town house in Bury and a large London house in St James's Square. The building of today's great house at Ickworth was not started until the 1790s when Frederick, Augustus's younger brother, 4th Earl of Bristol and Bishop of Derry, planned it as a home for his vast collection of works of art.

If the 1st Earl of Bristol brought the family to a place of influence in the

John, Lord Hervey. From the picture at Ickworth by John Fayram, reproduced by courtesy of the National Trust

nation's affairs it was his children whose behaviour led Lady Wortley Montagu – or did Lord Chesterfield beat her to the post? – to say that the human race was divided into three sorts – men, women, and Herveys. His offspring by his two wives numbered twenty, of whom fourteen pre-deceased him. Many of them were wild and unpredictable, and the inability of their father to build at Ickworth has been attributed to the financial stringencies caused by his reluctant efforts to support them or pay their debts.

John Lord Hervey, the eldest son of the 1st Earl's second marriage, was one of the least unruly, and after his half-brother Carr Hervey died in 1723 was heir to the title and estates – though because of his death in 1743 at the age of 47 he never enjoyed them. Lord Hervey was a man in whom it is easy to be interested but with whom it is difficult to become enthralled. He is best known as the close friend and confidant – though nothing improper is implied in this description – of Queen Caroline, and for his memoirs of the reign of George II, in which he describes in embarrassing detail the goings-on of the Court and the unpleasant disagreements and quarrels that scarred the life of the first family in the land.

In politics Lord Hervey was a Whig and a manipulator of the first water. Elected for St Edmundsbury in 1725 he was at first a supporter of the group around William Pulteney, later Earl of Bath. But when Pulteney split with Sir Robert Walpole in 1728 Hervey chose to back the latter. In 1730 he was appointed Vice-Chamberlain of the Household and in this position was able to help Walpole in his relations with Queen Caroline, who until her death in 1737 had a controlling influence on George II and his policies. In 1733 he was called to the Lords in his father's barony, an elevation that made his second son the Honourable Augustus.

Lord Hervey was a contentious man in both public and private affairs, and spiteful to his enemies. After a spate of truly eighteenth-century pamphlet writing in 1730/31 he fought a duel with Pulteney in Green Park, while his unpleasant quarrel with Alexander Pope was fought out in verse characterized by vicious sexual innuendo. Pope's caricature of him as 'Sporus', who was one of the Emperor Nero's favourites, imputed to him a homosexual bent, and indeed he had a certain effeminacy of bearing and speech. Yet Lord Fanny, another of Pope's inventions, was a successful father of a family of eight and the only recorded infidelities – and there were a number – were all with members of the opposite sex.

One of these infidelities appears to have been a factor in Lord Hervey's break with Frederick Prince of Wales, George II's son, who came to London from Hanover in 1728, and to whom he was at that time very close. But the friendship did not last and in 1731 they parted company. The parting was effected in uncharacteristically subfusc style and Hervey's memoirs do not describe it, so that some surmise is necessary as to the details. In view of

Frederick's differences with his father, which were both political and personal in nature, it would in any case have been difficult to maintain such a friendship alongside Hervey's position at Court and as a supporter of the government. But a second and perhaps overriding difficulty resulted from rivalry between the Prince and Lord Hervey for the favours of Miss Anne Vane, one of the Queen's Maids of Honour. Undoubtedly the Prince and Hervey had contemporaneously enjoyed these favours and when the lady gave birth to a son whose paternity the Prince publicly acknowledged Hervey and the Earl of Harrington also laid claim to that honour. As his memoirs show, Lord Hervey continued the liaison after the Prince had discarded her.

Lord Hervey suffered from ill health and in particular was subject to epileptic fits. Though a man of charm and wit when he so desired he had a sharp tongue and a cynical view of life. His travels in the twenties and his duties at court in the thirties took up much of his time and by no stretch of the imagination could he be described as a loving husband and proud father. His wife, the former Mary Lepel, was a very different character. She was the daughter of a Danish army officer of German extraction who had come to England in 1683 as an attendant on Prince George of Denmark, Queen Anne's husband, and had subsequently become an English subject. Aided by her father's courtly connections Mary, often known as Molly, was appointed a Maid of Honour to Caroline of Anspach soon after the future Queen and her husband arrived in London from Hanover. In this position she soon gained a reputation for beauty, wit and common sense, as well as for virtue, and turned the heads of men as disparate as John Gay, Voltaire, Pope and Lord Chesterfield. Nicholas Rowe, Poet Laureate in the time of George I, gives a marvellous picture of a young and flighty maiden – Miss Lepel cannot have been more that 18 at the time – who was more than a match for the men around her at court:

> I counted o'er the long long score
> Of laughing Chloe's lovers:
> Which sad to see, besides poor me
> Full forty-nine discovers.
> But Cupid cries, her nimble eyes
> Will quickly end your sorrow:
> Fifty a day, for that's her play,
> She kills – you'll die tomorrow

Gay, in his verses on Pope's completion of his translation of the Iliad, refers to 'Youth's youngest daughter, sweet Lepell'. Voltaire's only surviving poetry in English, referring to Mary Lepel in her married state begins:

> Hervey, would you know the passion
> you have kindled in my breast?

She was intelligent, spoke French and understood Latin (the latter an exceptional accomplishment for a girl at that time) and in her widowhood corresponded on equal terms with that great letter writer Horace Walpole. The marriage, performed in secret on 24 April 1720, was a love match, marked by the publication of a lengthy ballad to the tune of John Gay's Molly Mog, the principal authors of which were Lord Chesterfield and William Pulteney. Its general tone is given by the following verse:

> Bright Venus yet never saw bedded
> So perfect a beau and a belle
> As when Hervey the handsome was wedded
> To the beautiful Molly Lepell.

But however intense the romantic euphoria that surrounded the early months of the marriage, the groom was in two senses a wanderer. He travelled much, ostensibly for his health, and he was unfaithful, though not more so than many husbands of the time. His wife, however, appears to have put up with his infidelities with resignation and composure. They had eight children, of whom Augustus was the third and the second son. He was undoubtedly the one she loved most, and was the principal comfort and support of her old age.

The time into which Augustus Hervey was born could hardly, for a young Englishman of good family, have been more propitious. Britain had begun the long climb which took her through the industrial and agricultural revolutions to the economic and financial leadership of the world. Her position on the edge of Europe enabled her to move out with confidence along the ocean trade routes to North America, to the West Indies, to India and to China. The wealth accumulated from accelerating economic activity at home and from trade abroad, while welcome in itself, also underpinned the country's foreign policy and her recently acquired stature as one of the great European powers. The wars of William III and of Marlborough had placed her for the first time in a position of confident equality and fervent competition with France and of dominance – at least outside continental Europe – over Spain, Holland and the rest. Wealth was available, so long as reluctant Parliaments could be persuaded that the need existed, to build and man a navy commensurate with the nation's new-found status in the world and to support with British regiments or with subsidies to allied countries such military activities as were vital to British interests.

At home, however, the different strata of society were as unevenly rewarded as ever. The benefits of economic well-being may have filtered down to the labouring poor, but only as long as they were fit for work, and could find it. For many life was still short, hard and brutalizing. The weakest went to the wall and there were few to help them. In contrast, at the other end of the scale the great landed families enjoyed the dual advantages of money and of influence, or 'interest' as it was called. Though in theory the Sovereign's powers were still absolute, in effect the country was ruled only with the consent of the landed aristocracy, who controlled Parliament either as members of the House of Lords or by their mastery of borough seats in the Commons. To be a peer and to control a seat or two in the Commons as Lord Bristol did, and in addition to have a wife with the ear of the Princess of Wales or the Queen, was to have power and influence beyond present day imagination. Places and sinecures were available at attractive salaries to royal favourites, to those whose support was important to the government of the day and to members of their families. When the second Earl of Bristol, Augustus Hervey's elder brother, was made Minister to the kingdom of Sardinia in 1755 he was only appointed on condition that he left his proxy vote in the Lords with the Duke of Newcastle, the Prime Minister of the day. Worse than that were numerous practices bordering on corruption, in which the most upright felt it acceptable to indulge. To name a single case, Augustus's mother Mary Lepel was entered at birth as a cornet in her father's regiment and a cornet's pay was drawn on her behalf throughout her childhood.

The eighteenth-century establishment was small, its members forming an oligarchical society in which all were on speaking acquaintanceship. Augustus Hervey was one of them from birth, so, for example, when he returned from the West Indies in 1746 as a young naval lieutenant, he could go with letters straight to the two leading ministers of the day and sit down to a pleasant chat with them on the state of Jamaica. When he wanted a ship there were Lords of the Admiralty who were family friends or acquaintances to whom it was natural for him or his family to make application.

Where the young Mr and Mrs Hervey (John did not come to the title of Lord Hervey until the death of his half-brother Carr Hervey in 1723) lived in the first year or so of their marriage is not recorded – possibly at the Hervey town house in St James's Square. In 1724, however, the new Lord Hervey took the lease of 31 Old Burlington Street, north of Piccadilly, and this seems to have been the family home until he sold it to Stephen Fox, 1st Lord Ilchester, in 1733. It was a gracious house and writing in 1936 Mary Lady Hervey's biographer Dorothy Stuart could say[1] 'Neither internally nor externally has it been drastically altered. The original door has been replaced . . . but the ponderous chain and the massy key still hang beside the doorpost . . . extraordinarily fine staircase of oak, with balustrades of three different designs, two spiral and one fluted, to each tread, and a gracefully curving handrail . . . the dining room, its walls soberly rich with carving and panelling, its ceiling with moulded plasterwork . . . a not less stately morning room with a seascape of Monamy let into the carved framework of the mantlepiece, above a row of three staring, inscrutable human faces, skilfully sculptured in wood.' Though today the house is no longer in single domestic occupation much of the splendour remains, certainly to the extent that its eighteenth-century occupants would have no difficulty in recognizing it, both externally and internally.

Augustus's birthplace is not known but it seems likely that much of his childhood was spent in this magnificent new house, replete with the fashionable embellishments of the age, though the young Herveys with their nurses and tutors in the nursery and the schoolroom probably saw little of the beautiful principal rooms described above. In the fashion of the day, however, his parents moved from one family home to another and also spent much time at Bath or at the great country houses of their friends. It is unlikely that the children moved about with them all the time, but they were certainly very familiar with Ickworth – the 1st Earl's 'sweet Ickworth' – whose park with its oaks and its cool East Anglian breezes played such a part in the memories and reflections of every member of the family.

Augustus was christened on 18 June 1724. The three sponsors were consistent with the infant's position in life: George, Prince of Wales (the future George II), the Earl of Godolphin, son of Queen Anne's Lord Treasurer and son-in-law of the first Duke of Marlborough and his Duchess, and his father's favourite sister Betty, wife of the Hon. Bussy Mansel.

There is no record of Augustus's early schooling; like his brothers he probably had a tutor at home. In January 1733, however, he entered Westminster School, then the leading school in the country, its alumni including his three brothers, his father and most of his uncles. He was probably there until he entered the navy in 1735. Certainly he emerges as an intelligent and well read but not intellectual young man who could put together a fine, ranting pamphlet, who had a confident command of written and spoken English and an acquaintance with poets such as John Milton, and who spoke adequate French. Whatever their faults the Hervey's seldom lacked intelligence and in the light of his relative lack of formal education Augustus could claim to be as good in this respect as his brothers, his father and mother, and his grandfather. Lord Hervey was not a rich man and while Lord Bristol was ready and willing to subsidize his immediate heir similar liberality did not necessarily extend to the needs of younger sons and grandsons. In such circumstances the navy provided an attractive career for the scions of the aristocracy, because relative to the army entry was cheap and because of the prospect of prize money, which was the source of many eighteenth-century fortunes. At the age of 11, therefore, Augustus was sent to sea. Thus we can imagine a young but self-confident boy, for Augustus was never anything but positive about his own capabilities, leaving a comfortable London home for the rigours and privations of life in an eighteenth-century ship of the line, with its discomforts, its monotonous and unsuitable diet, its risks of disease and death, and its periods of hard routine studded by short bouts of hectic activity, all overlain by the stiff and often cruel discipline needed to sail and fight these engines of war.

The navy which Augustus entered was still far from achieving the standards of professionalism and efficiency that it reached in Nelson's day. Since the defeat of the Spanish Armada its track record had been a mixed one. There had been victories, mostly of a secondary nature, and there had been failures. British sea power could be exerted round Britain's coasts, in the Mediterranean, in the West Indies and in Indian and North American waters. But for much of the two wars in which Hervey was at sea (the War of the Austrian Succession and the Seven Years War) the fleets of France and Spain were very much in being, had always to be taken into account and at times constituted a threat to the homeland itself. It was not until Admiral Sir Edward Hawke's great blockade of the French Biscay ports in 1759, in which Hervey played a not inconsiderable part, and which culminated in the destruction of the French fleet in the storm-wracked wars of Quiberon Bay, that Britannia really ruled the waves, even in the Channel and its western approaches.

The problems were many. Naval officers emerged and were promoted largely through family influence and it was to an extent a matter of luck whether a ship's captain or a squadron commander was really competent to fulfil the duties entrusted to him. In wartime a high proportion of the lower deck were pressed men, some of whom were experienced seamen, but many were landsmen dredged by the press gangs from the lowest strata of society, or even convicts. Whichever category they came from, unwilling hands seldom make good workers. Further disincentives to high morale were that pay was always much in arrears and shore leave almost non-existent. The royal dockyards were inadequate, corrupt and run for the most part by political nominees many of whom were of doubtful competence and even more doubtful honesty. In peacetime, expenditure on the navy was cut to the bone and few ships remained in commission. In wartime, Parliament could more easily be persuaded to provide funds, but it took time and organisation to bring ships to a state of readiness for sea and to find crews for them.

Control of naval affairs was in the hands of an Admiralty Board made up for the most part of civilians appointed for political convenience rather than administrative ability and for much of Augustus Hervey's active naval career the Admiralty was controlled by a cabinet more concerned with politics than with providing the right ships in the right place at the right time. Not until Captain George Anson (later Admiral of the Fleet Lord Anson) was made a Lord of the Admiralty in 1744 was there an effective professional input into naval strategy and naval administration. And even as late as 1757 when Anson had been First Lord for six years he found it impossible to have Hawke appointed to a vacancy on the Board, because the Duke of Newcastle (then

Prime Minister) preferred Hans Stanley, one of his time-serving lackeys, who once appointed was notable for his indifference to naval affairs.

When the young Hervey joined the navy, however, he was not interested in politics. Also, he was fortunate in being sheltered from the worst discomforts, for *Pembroke*, the ship he joined at Portsmouth in May 1735* was commanded by his uncle, William Hervey; he was entered in the ship's books as captain's servant, a standard rating for a boy of good family at his age and in practice implying a cadetship, preparatory to rating as a midshipman. William Hervey was to be his mentor and patron for the next eight years.

Reference

1. Stuart, 1936.

---

* There is some conflict of evidence on this date, the DNB and Stuart stating that he entered as a midshipman in 1736, by which time he was serving under Captain John Ambrose in the frigate *Greyhound*. Entry in 1735 is supported by the movements of *Pembroke* and *Greyhound*. In May 1735 *Pembroke* was at Spithead, where Hervey could easily have joined her, while in the spring of 1736 both ships were with the fleet at Lisbon − an unlikely location for a new midshipman to join his first ship, but providing a logical opportunity for him to be transferred from one ship to the other. Furthermore, the log which he immediately started to complete in *Greyhound* shows from its first page every sign of previous instruction and experience.

CHAPTER II

Midshipman and Lieutenant

A sound foundation

When Augustus joined *Pembroke* at Spithead Britain was at peace and her captain, his uncle William Hervey, was one of the fortunate few to enjoy a command. Though Augustus gained considerable advantage from starting his naval career under his uncle's eye, that uncle though a fine seaman was in many ways a far from satisfactory officer. Though more normal in his relationships and behaviour than some of his brothers, he had gained a reputation in the service as a harsh and cruel man, irrational and unbalanced in the way that he treated his subordinates and hard in the punishments that he inflicted on his crew. His marital misfortunes cannot have helped to soften him. He married in November 1729 Elizabeth Ridge of Portsmouth, but his wife died in childbirth less than two years later leaving him with an infant daughter. He did not remarry until just before his death forty years later and his affairs while at sea were managed for him by his father.

Pembroke had been commissioned at Woolwich in 1733 and since then her crew had had an unexciting time. William Hervey had taken her round to Portsmouth and with few calls on the services of the peacetime navy there she had remained. There was, however, chronic and gradually increasing tension with Spain, largely arising from trading antagonisms in the Caribbean, and in the spring of 1735 it was decided as a precautionary measure to get together a fleet under Admiral Sir John Norris. In May of that year, therefore, *Pembroke* was under orders for sea and when Augustus joined was moored at Spithead, in the throes of victualling and taking in stores. She sailed with the fleet on 27 May, arriving at Lisbon and anchoring in the Tagus on 9 June. She stayed at Lisbon with most of the fleet until February 1737, and for the first twelve months Augustus stayed with her. For the active and intelligent boy it cannot have been a stimulating experience. The ship shifted her moorings a number of times, but apart from that her routine must have been very similar from day to day and week to week; taking in stores and water as needed; painting ship and routine maintenance; checking from time to time the condition of masts and spars, rigging and sails; exercising the guns; maintaining discipline among a bored and restless crew. All this, however, was new to the young Hervey and provided a useful introduction to many aspects of shipboard life. It may be expected also that he took part in the schooling and training of the midshipmen on board; schooling in the sense of a continuation of their education; training particularly in navigation and all forms of sea-manship.

On 24 May 1736 Hervey reached his twelfth birthday and it was shortly after this milestone that he was rated midshipman and taken onto the books of the frigate *Greyhound*, Captain John Ambrose. Whatever his own feelings on the subject, and the view of the Lisbon riverfront must by then have become over-familiar, only his uncle could have arranged this move, presumably because he knew *Greyhound* was under orders for sea and that *Pembroke* was not. *Greyhound* in fact sailed from Lisbon on 5 June, on passage to Gibraltar and then Genoa.

It is at this point that Hervey's midshipman's log[1] begins and provides an almost daily record of his movements for the next forty-three months. In keeping it he was following the usual course of training. When at sea he was required to take the ship's position at noon, in which he was not at first as accurate as would be required in a navigating officer; the first entry, when *Greyhound* was off the Portuguese coast just south of Lisbon, places the ship in the Mediterranean off Oran. As a general rule, however, he was reasonably accurate and the general tenor of the entries suggests that he had benefitted by his year in *Pembroke*. The log also required him to be alert to, and to record, the ship's course, wind speed and direction, bearings and distances of coastal features and the sail the ship was carrying from time to time. When out of sight of land he had to estimate the ship's position by dead reckoning. His spelling at this early age was unpredictable, but perhaps not more than that of his adult contemporaries. He soon picked up the naval spellings (and presumably pronunciations) of foreign place names. Indeed the first entry records Cape Espichel, south of Lisbon, in the normal naval form of Cape Spitchell. The whole exercise was of course designed to keep him alert and raise his nautical awareness, and to make him the first class seaman that he was in due course to become.

Greyhound had a slow passage to Gibraltar in light winds, anchoring in Gibraltar Bay on 13 June. Hervey had his first view of the Rock but did not go ashore. The ship sailed the next day, coasting along the Spanish littoral and then across the open sea to Genoa and later Leghorn, both ports that he was to become very familiar with later in his career. The return passage took *Greyhound* past Minorca and Cabrera in the Balearics and then continued to Lisbon, arriving on 8 August.

The next day Hervey returned to *Pembroke* where the slow uneventful life at anchor in the Tagus continued until February 1737. His feelings about such a stationary and confined life are not recorded, but those of his uncle

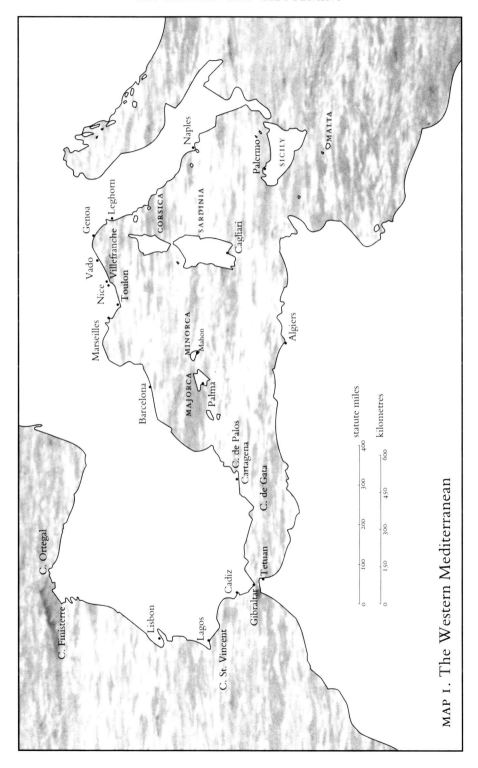

MAP 1. The Western Mediterranean

emerge from a letter William Hervey received from his father Lord Bristol, who on 18 August 1736 wrote commiserating with him:[2]

> . . . I am truly concerned you are like to continue so much longer on a station both expensive and disagreeable to you . . . I am glad to hear so good an account of Augustus; God for ever prosper and protect you and him . . .

When Augustus was in his turn captain of a ship that called at Lisbon he was to find it a much more pleasant and pleasurable port of call, of which he took full advantage.

Pembroke, and Augustus in her, then had her one Mediterranean voyage of the commission. On 3 February she set sail from Lisbon and made a very similar circuit to that which he had enjoyed in *Greyhound*, spending a few days in Genoa harbour and three days in Malaga Bay, where the ship watered, and returning to Lisbon on 28 March. On 5 April she left Lisbon with the fleet under Norris and set course for home, anchoring at Spithead on the 24th of the month. Four days later she made sail again and on 2 May moored at Blackstakes in the Medway, the point in the river at which the ship's guns were put ashore so that she could proceed upstream. Two days later she sailed up to Chatham and was unrigged; on 6 May *Pembroke* was put out of commission and the ship's company went ashore.

Augustus now had a month's leave before joining his next ship. No record of his activities during these weeks survives, but undoubtedly he saw his family for the first time for nearly two years and perhaps went down to Ickworth to see his grandfather. But on 6 June 1737 he joined his next ship and saw no more of them for another five years. The ship was *Gloucester*, a ship of the line then moored at the Nore under the command of the Honourable George Clinton.

Clinton had taken command of *Gloucester* at Sheerness two months previously. Six days after Hervey joined her she sailed for Spithead, spending a fortnight there before going on to Plymouth, where she moored in the Sound on 2 July. Clinton's orders were for the Mediterranean and *Gloucester* left Plymouth for Gibraltar on 6 July in company with the sloop *Grampus*, arriving fifteen days later. There she stayed until the following February. The log which Hervey kept in *Gloucester* shows nothing out of the ordinary until the ship reached Gibraltar. It then gradually becomes less complete, less carefully entered and the writing deteriorates into a scrawl; on 1 September entries cease. They do not start again until 3 November, by which time Hervey had left *Gloucester* and was back in *Greyhound*. The frigate, still under the command of John Ambrose, had arrived a few days before and the only mention of contact between the two ships was in *Gloucester's* log:[3]

Received from his Majesty's ship *Greyhound* a 14 inch cable.

There is no reason to expect that the transfer of a midshipman in the other direction would be noted in either log, but clearly the two captains agreed on it. The reason is not obvious. Illness might have been sufficient explanation for Hervey's deteriorating log but would not explain the transfer. It seems likely that he found *Gloucester* an uncongenial environment, or that there was a clash of personalities on board, or that he was suffering from home-sickness after his brief visit to his family. If so, Clinton, faced with the problem of what to do with the son of the Queen's intimate adviser (and probably having given assurances to Lord Hervey that he would act *in loco parentis* to the boy) would have found Ambrose's arrival providential and the transfer would have satisfied all parties; Clinton was rid of a problem; Ambrose was happy to take on board a boy of whom he had a good opinion; and Hervey was glad to be back with shipmates known to him – and a frigate to boot, with the prospect of much more sea time and much less idling in port. Whatever the reasons, the move seems to have been a success, for the entries in his log return immediately to their previous high standard.

Hervey now served in *Greyhound* for over two years, during which she spent much of her time at sea and saw the transition from uneasy peace to war with Spain. For the remainder of 1737 and the whole of 1738 she was engaged in the usual activities of the peacetime Mediterranean squadron – showing the flag, keeping an eye on the North African corsairs, providing a means of communication between the British bases at Gibraltar and Minorca, and the freightage of coin and bullion for all and sundry – the last a remunerative perquisite for her captain, as both governments and individuals paid him the going rate, in peacetime usually one per cent.

These preoccupations took *Greyhound* round the western Mediterranean, in the sea area from Lisbon past Gibraltar and Minorca to Genoa and Leghorn. Very few incidents seem to have been worth recording in either the captain's log or that of his new midshipman. Hervey's entries under 'Remarkable Observations' when at sea are mostly fairly mundane, for example: 'Little wind and clear weather. At 5 spoke with a Brig from S Luca [San Lucar] with salt bound for Norway' and 'Fresh gales and squally. At 11 am struck yards and topmasts.' When *Greyhound* was in port he noted the arrival and departures of other craft, especially His Majesty's ships, and recorded the work going on on board, for example 'Imployed (*sic*) about the mainmast in overhauling the rigging' or 'The carpenters imployed in fixing a fish for the mainmast'. Deaths on board are mentioned, as occasionally are punishments – 'Jsh Grimes seaman on board Run the Gauntlet for theft'.

By the beginning of 1739 relationships with Spain were becoming less amicable. In the previous year Rear-Admiral Haddock had been sent out with a considerable fleet and *Greyhound's* movements became more limited and more purposeful. In January of the new year she made a short reconnaissance eastward as far as Fuengirola and Malaga Bay and then cruised in the sea area west of Gibraltar as far as Lisbon. On 28 February relations were still good enough for Ambrose to send his barge ashore at Malaga, but on 3 April his log and Hervey's both report the first hostile acts by the Spanish. *Greyhound* was cruising off Cape Spartel when they sighted an unidentified ship. Hervey's is a far more lively account of the incident than that in the ship's log:

> . . . At 9 a.m. [saw a ship] who gave us chase. She fired two guns to larboard, when she came very near up with us we attacked and stood to her; when we hoisted our colours he hoisted a Spanish man o' war's Colours; and run her lower Tear (sic) of guns out and when we were very near up with him he crowded all the sail he could and put before the wind and hauled down his colours.

Later that month, however, it was still possible for *Greyhound* to anchor in Cadiz bay and water there, after which she returned to Gibraltar, where she was refitting until the beginning of June. On 7 June and thereafter she was cruising between Gibraltar and Cape St Vincent, in close association with Haddock's fleet, stopping and examining ships, if necessary by firing a gun.

On 9 July Hervey came under fire for the first time. *Greyhound* had come up with a ship off the Portuguese port of Lagos and Hervey records the course of events in the following words:

> Saw a sail at 8 am and sent a boat after her to chase, in which I went and when we chased her the Fort on point of Lagos fired 1 gun and 2 shotts – 1 fell over us and 2 short of us. The Ship made our signal to leave chasing and come on board. Came aboard and boat was hoisted in.

Though Portugal was Britain's firm ally the proprieties were to be observed and the commander of the fort was not prepared to let Portuguese territorial waters be abused so flagrantly.

Three days later *Greyhound* took a tartane* flying French colours and put a prize crew into her – presumably on examination she was Spanish – and on 13 August made a prize of a Spanish barque bound from Vigo to Cadiz and took her into Lagos bay. During August and September *Greyhound* continued to stop any vessel she came up with. Most were neutral or friendly. On 30 September, however, she stopped a Genoese ship which had been flying British colours and was bound for Cadiz. The boarding party found Spanish passengers on board and took away property belonging to them – wearing apparel, twelve barrels of honey and 300 coconuts. The last two items must have been a welcome addition to the ship's fare.

---

* Tartane: a single-masted lateen-rigged vessel with a foresail.

Greyhound had already been overhauled or refitted four times in the last two years but her condition continued to give trouble. In October she was overhauled, caulked and refitted again at Lisbon and then in December took a convoy northwards to Oporto and Viana do Castello, in northern Portugal. On her return to Lisbon she was inspected by carpenters from *Newcastle*, *Adventure* and *Seaford*, the customary way of coming to an unbiased decision on a ship's state; they recommended her for complete overhaul in one of His Majesty's dockyards. Early in February 1740, therefore, Ambrose took her to Gibraltar. There Hervey found *Superbe,* a 60-gun ship commanded by his uncle, William Hervey. Captain Hervey had taken command of her at Chatham in June 1739 and after service in the Channel had arrived at Gibraltar on 13 January. She was now refitting and taking on stores for sea.

Augustus now transferred once more to serve in his uncle's ship. His midshipman's log ends on 15 February with the words 'Discharged into the *Superbe*'. The reason this time cannot have been the prospect of more time at sea, for *Greyhound* was to leave Gibraltar several weeks before *Superbe*. It is possible that it was the doubtful position in which Ambrose now found himself, with the threat of a court martial hanging over him. This hazard had arisen in a not unusual way, from dissatisfaction felt by the Lisbon merchants at the degree of protection offered to their ships. After *Greyhound* had taken the convoy from Lisbon up the Portuguese coast the previous December some of them began to accuse him of demanding money for this service, and laid information to that effect. Eventually he was court-martialled on this charge, but the wealth of evidence in his support, including that from many Lisbon merchants, resulted in his acquittal. Or perhaps the standard of Hervey's performance in *Greyhound* was falling away, for there exists a comment in a letter from his grandfather to his father later in the year (when he had been in *Superbe* several months) to the effect that he was glad to see such a sudden reformation in his grandson:[4]

> I am as glad as I can be for most things to hear of so sudden a reformation in Augustus, God prosper and protect him.

The implication of poor previous performance in this sentence is one of the very few unfavourable comments on Hervey's professional behaviour that has survived. William Hervey had many faults as a ship's captain, but he seems to have had an eye at critical times for his nephew's well being.

Superbe was at Gibraltar until 19 April, the only excitement during this period being when her boat went out and took a Spanish settee* laden with wine and fruit.

William Hervey was then sent with a small squadron to cruise for two

---

* Settee: A small lateen-rigged vessel with two or three masts, a very fast sailer.

months off the coast of the Algarve and in June back to Gibraltar. By this time the threat of a French invasion was causing great concern in London and a number of ships including *Superbe* were recalled to home waters as part of the concentration against it. *Superbe* arrived at St Helens on 9 July and served in the Channel fleet under Sir John Norris until September. Sir John was in effect waiting for the French to come out and in a stormy summer the fleet spent most of its time in Torbay, with short sorties into the western Channel.

Superbe at this time cannot have been a happy ship. Her log records many deaths among the crew, more than would be expected even in those days of ill health at sea; seven men died, for example between 24 June and 5 July 1740, when the ship was only a few days out from Gibraltar. The disciplinary situation was no better. Quarrelling among the officers seems to have been endemic and came to a head at Spithead on 15 September, the captain being out of the ship at the time. According to the evidence at the subsequent court martial Lieutenant Rosewell, the third lieutenant, was the watchkeeper and ordered the topmasts to be struck. While the hands were doing this the first lieutenant, Lieutenant Sibrell, came on deck and countermanded the order before the operation had been completed. His reason for doing so does not emerge from the depositions, but as the senior officer on board he may well have thought such a matter should have been referred to him; alternatively he was drunk. Rosewell, however, sent for the second lieutenant and the master, and together they put Sibrell under arrest and confined him to his cabin. Augustus was present during these events, which were witnessed with ribald delight by most of the lower deck. He was ordered to stand guard with drawn sword before the door of the first lieutenant's cabin and did so until a marine sentry arrived, having at one stage to restrain the prisoner physically from coming out.

When Captain Hervey came on board he sent the second and third lieutenants and the master to be court-martialled. The Court met ten days later in *Victory*. Augustus gave evidence, confirming the course of events and saying that the first lieutenant's order had caused utter confusion. Others gave evidence that both the Captain and the first lieutenant habitually beat and ill-treated petty officers and men. Nevertheless, all three accused were found guilty and dismissed from the ship.

Superbe's officers were a quarrelsome collection. Augustus's position as the Captain's nephew may have sheltered him at times from the worst of the squabbling, but he was certainly not immune from it. When Lieutenant Sibrell gave evidence at the court martial he said that on a previous occasion Lieutenant Rosewell had struck Augustus and so many high words and such ill-language passed between them that he called out to the master to come out and help him quell the disturbance. Drink probably played a part, but

William Hervey seems to have been completely unable to control his officers; later events show that by this time he was himself a completely unreasonable man and that his mental state was deteriorating. Within a few days of the court martial, according to the ship's log, he had come aboard and confined to his cabin the first lieutenant whom he had previously supported.

In September *Superbe* was ordered to the West Indies as one of a substantial squadron escorting a large fleet of transports and merchantmen under the overall command of Rear-Admiral Sir Chaloner Ogle. The twenty-five of the line and 9,000 troops that Ogle took with him were intended as a reinforcement for Vice-Admiral Edward Vernon, who with a much smaller force – he only had six of the line – had recently taken Porto Bello by a determined surprise attack. He was now under orders to attack Carthagena in present day Colombia, the troops being under the command of General Wentworth. In the squadron went *Superbe*, carrying uncle and nephew. After delays through contrary winds Ogle got away from St Helens on 26 October and by the 31st was about half-way between the Lizard and Cape Finisterre.

In *Superbe* steps had been taken to fill the vacancies resulting from the September court martial. A third lieutenant had been appointed and it can be deduced from Augustus's log that since 22 September he had been serving as acting fourth lieutenant. Ogle now set out to regularize the position and *Superbe's* log for 31 October includes the following entry:[5]

> Moderate gales and cloudy, at 4 pm 110 sail in sight. At noon the Admiral made signal for our ship. Sent our yawl and came on board Lord Newberry and Lord Augustus [Fitzroy] to examine the Hon. Augustus Hervey for a Lieutenant.

The two captains did their duty, disregarding the fact that Augustus was over three years short of the minimum age of twenty for a lieutenant's certificate, and that he was six months short of the stipulated six years sea service. No doubt the urgency of the need and the fact that they were examining, at their Commander-in-Chief's direction, the son of the Lord Privy Seal provided sufficient justification for what was not in the practice of the times an act of unusual latitude.

It was not intended, however, that Augustus should stay as a lieutenant in his uncle's ship, but that he should transfer into *Shrewsbury* in exchange for one of her officers. On the morning of 1 November he duly did so, in half a gale of wind, but then returned to *Superbe* for his belongings. And in *Superbe* he stayed, for before he could return to *Shrewsbury* the elements took over and events moved beyond the control of Captain or Admiral. As the day wore on the moderate gale became a great and violent storm from the north west and the sea rose accordingly. Worse was to come, for the fleet was in the grip of perhaps the greatest storm of the century, a storm which brought with it maritime disaster in all the waters of north west Europe. Ogle gave the signal to lie to on the starboard tack and most of his ships came through with only minor damage, though the fleet and its convoy were left dispersed over a wide area of the North Atlantic. On *Superbe*, however, the situation worsened hourly. The ship laboured in the heavy seas and the rigging stretched so that by the next day, 2 November, it gave little support to the masts. During the morning the mainmast broke about one-third of the way up and brought down with it the fore and mizzen masts; and in the fall of the mainmast William Hervey's left leg was broken. There was soon six feet of water in the hold, a critical state of affairs which was accentuated by the breaking of both the pump chains.

By late afternoon they had managed to get the pumps working, to cut away the wreckage and to set a cross jack and small sail on the stump of the mizzen mast. It took several days to set up jury masts and it was 9 November, having in the meantime been driven south by the strength of wind and sea, before the ship was under sail again. With an injured captain and a shortage of experienced officers it seems a feat of some magnitude to have achieved so much so quickly in the prevailing heavy weather. For Augustus it had been the first experience that he had had of maritime disaster, of the ingenuity and exhausting labours required to make the ship seaworthy and of the threat of a watery death if they did not manage to do so.

Though *Superbe* had lost touch with the fleet *Cumberland* had seen the difficulties that she was in and remained with her, recommending William Hervey to take his ship to Lisbon. The two ships remained in company and anchored in the Tagus on 13 November. The Falmouth packet left Lisbon five days later taking with her the news of the ship's safe arrival; but news of the disaster, though not of the recovery from it, had already reached England and caused alarm in London, especially among the Hervey family with two of their number on board. Having heard with relief the news of their safe arrival in port, Lord Bristol wrote from Ickworth to his son on 7 December as follows:[6]

Judge how great my concern and that of all your friends here must have been upon the report that you and your ship were all lost, when the news of your being gott to Lisbon, tho' with a broken leg and shattered ship, proved no small relief to us. As I have been credibly assured that the bone was well sett, I hope this will find you out of pain. Should you have any occasion for any money where you are, I need not tell you what ample assets I have of yours in my hands to answer any draughts you make upon me. As I understand your former agent, Jasper, hath been and still is under some difficulties, I hope you had early notice enough of his embarrassments not to have suffered much by him. Lord Privy Seal [John, Lord Hervey] tells me he had a letter from Augustus (who methinks or young Oliver, might have given themselves the trouble of a line or two to me also) who it seems is made a Lieutenant, and going in another ship to America; if he should be still with you, give him my blessing however, which with my fervent prayers for your safety and better success shall constantly attend you also . . .

The *Prince Frederick* packet sailed from Falmouth on 12 December, making Lisbon in seven days, so that the letter reached William Hervey on 19 December, twelve days after it was written.

At Lisbon *Superbe* in her shattered state was something of a nine days wonder. The British Minister, Lord Tyrawley, came on board to see the shambles and congratulate the crew, as did the British Consul and his wife. Two members of the Portuguese royal family visited and were entertained on board. Neither William Hervey nor Augustus were new to the Portuguese capital and William in particular had had every opportunity to establish a circle of acquaintances there. He was, of course, the son of an English Earl and his nephew, now a lieutenant and able to spend time ashore, was an Earl's grandson and therefore yet another English milord.

It was during this spell in the Tagus that Augustus enjoyed his first known sexual encounter. There is no record of how he met Ellena Paghetti, an Italian singer of repute, renowned also for her beauty, but the opera or musical entertainment at one of the great houses of the Portuguese capital could readily have provided the opportunity. Neither is there any record of how the association developed. Hervey was 16, the lady appreciably older, and it therefore seems likely that, however forward the young lieutenant may have been, it was 'the Paghetti' (in which form he doubtless referred to her, following the custom of the times with respect to compliant singers and actresses) who with much experience of such matters and a young daughter to show for it made the running. Whatever the circumstances of this liaison, a liaison it certainly was, for on a subsequent visit to Lisbon, in 1748, he describes her as his 'old acquaintance', with whom he 'had formerly been very intimate', and duly returns to her bed.[7]

William Hervey, however, had much more on his mind than the social round. *Superbe's* condition was desperate and it needed the full co-operation of the Portuguese authorities to refit, rerig and caulk her, and to make good her water, victuals and stores. These repairs took three months and it was 17 February 1741 before she was able to sail from the Tagus for Port Royal. Augustus, however, was no longer one of William Hervey's officers and arrangements were quickly made for him to transfer to *Cumberland*, which sailed from Lisbon for the West Indies on 29 December. She joined Vernon's fleet off the western end of Hispaniola on 8 February. It cannot have been a pleasant crossing. If *Superbe* was a madhouse inhabited by an irrational Captain and a set of quarrelsome officers, Cumberland had even direr problems.

By the time she made Port Royal in Jamaica on 23 February eighty-seven of her crew were dead of shipboard diseases, while over 200 others were on the sick list and had to be sent ashore.

Though the great storm in November had left Ogle's fleet and convoy in disarray most ships had arrived in the West Indies by the end of 1740. By the time *Cumberland* arrived preparations for the attack on Carthagena were well advanced. Hervey was transferred to the 60-gun *Tilbury*, Captain Robert Long, where he was appointed third lieutenant, and in *Tilbury* he was to serve for the next seven months. He took an active part in the attack on Carthagena and shortly afterwards wrote an account of his experiences.[8] Much has been written about this controversial campaign, in which the initial successes were gained under the guns of the fleet, while the eventual failure was a consequence of unsuitable military tactics in a location where naval power could not readily be exerted. Hervey's account is given with the freshness of his sixteen years and provides a straightforward report, as viewed from a rather lowly position, though a position in which he had a good sight of events and of the commanders' difficulties; he makes no attempt to allocate the blame for the ultimate failure of the operation.

He begins with the arrival of the fleet and transports off the town. On 9 March the naval bombardment began, though *Tilbury* was not one of the ships directly involved. While the action was generally a success *Shrewsbury* was much damaged and Hervey was one of those sent in boats to help in warping her off. For several days he was one of the lieutenants in command of boats landing men, guns and stores for an attack on the forts and on 18 March he took part in a night attack from the ship's boats on a troublesome battery. He paints a picture of much confusion, of losing their way in the woods, of wading knee-deep for a considerable distance, though eventually reaching the battery and destroying it.

On 23 March the attack on the forts at the harbour mouth was launched by sea and land, *Tilbury* taking a full part in the bombardment, and by 26th of the month the fleet had broken into the outer harbour. There followed a long period of preparation for the attack on the town itself, requiring much boat work to move the army from one side of the harbour to the other. On 9 April the army mounted a grand onslaught on Fort San Lazaro, immediately before the town. It was repulsed with heavy casualties and this reversal of fortune, together with accelerating losses from disease, appears to have had a depressing effect on the morale of all ranks. The attack was abandoned and from 12 April the ship's boats were in demand again, this time to embark the army, a process which took several days and was accompanied by the destruction of all the captured Spanish forts and defences. In early May the fleet and transports sailed for Port Royal.

The outcome was a desolate one, and led to much ill-feeling between the navy and the army, and indeed to a campaign of true eighteenth-century pamphlet writing. For the 16-year-old Hervey, however, the experience must have been both exciting and educational, and must have taught him lessons which he would put to good use during the more successful West Indian campaigns in which he took part twenty years later.

Tilbury was at Port Royal until 11 June when she left to cruise north east of Jamaica and as far as Nassau in the Bahamas. She made several calls at Cumberland Harbour, the British base on the south coast of Cuba, and on 20 September she found *Superbe* there. Hervey now returned to his uncle's ship, in which he was appointed second lieutenant, the incumbent transferring to *Tilbury*.

Superbe had been at Port Royal until the end of June and during this time her captain's mismanagement resulted in another court martial, this time of Eber Elwall, the first lieutenant. William Hervey, having just refused this officer leave to go ashore, went ashore himself. The depositions show that Elwall, left in command, then ordered the boat to take him ashore, where he remained for several hours, leaving the boat's crew waiting in continuous rain. When the captain came on board and heard of this he put his second in command under arrest and asked for a court martial for disobedience of orders. He also sent the master, William Shackerley and the Lieutenant of Marines, Lieutenant Marshall, for court martial on charges of using disrespectful language. The court sat in *Boyne* on 5 June, under Ogle's presidency. The first lieutenant's defence was that he had had to go to Kingston to deal with the will of a previous second lieutenant, who had died on passage from Carthagena, and that in the Captain's absence he was entitled to take the decision to do so. No evidence was offered against the others and all three were found not guilty. The first lieutenant shortly left the ship, and his successor Richard Kempenfelt stayed in her only five months.

On 4 November 1741 *Superbe* left for home, passing through the Crooked Island Passage in the Bahamas and having her last sight of land, Watling Island, when fourteen days out. A week later, when somewhere to the south east of Bermuda, all on board had the only stroke of luck of the whole commission. The ship's log gives the following account:

> Saw a sail bearing ENE and gave chase to him at ½ past eight came up alongside him. He hoisted Spanish colours and fired a broadside at us which went through our main topsail and sprit sail and cut our fore and mainstay tackle falls in pieces. We returned two broadsides with double rounds after which he struck and brought to. We brought to likewise and sent our second lieutenant aboard with men and took part of their men aboard of us. She proved to be the *Constant* of 24 guns and 64 men from Caracas bound to the Canaries loaded with coco.

The prize was undoubtedly valuable and was reported at the time to be worth £200,000. A letter dated 24 September 1746 from Lord Bristol shows, however, that Hervey's share of the prize money* amounted to something more than £1500. If this was one-fifth of the lieutenant's share the total value realized becomes about £60,000. Even his share of this lower estimate was sufficient to keep him in funds for several years.

Hervey was put aboard *Constant* with a prize crew of twenty-nine men and *Superbe* struggled on with the prize in company. After six months in the West Indies the condition of her hull was appalling and in the troubled seas of the North Atlantic winter she was making water fast, while her crew became weaker by the day. The two ships shortly became separated and did not make contact again until they were approaching soundings (the western approaches to the English Channel). By 23 December *Superbe* was in such poor condition and the wind so unfavourable that on the advice of all his officers William Hervey put the helm up and bore away for Ireland. On Christmas Day the two ships were in sight of the Irish coast near Cork and signalled for a pilot to take them into Kinsale harbour; in the case of *Superbe* it was in the nick of time. There were, however, no dockyard facilities at Kinsale and much to be done to make her fit for sea. The Admiralty ordered *Ruby*, which had been cruising in the Bristol Channel, to proceed to Kinsale to bear assistance. It was, however, 10 March before she reached port, to find that *Superbe* and her prize had sailed for Plymouth on the 6th. They made the Sound a week later, anchoring in the Hamoaze.

Soon after *Superbe* arrived at Plymouth William Hervey left the ship. It is likely that Ogle had made an unfavourable report on his performance, though his court martial, which took place later in the year, was on a complaint by Lieutenant Hardy, *Superbe's* first lieutenant during the voyage home. The court sat on *St George* at Spithead on 19 August under the presidency of Admiral Philip Cavendish. The brief report of the proceedings that has survived reads in essentials as follows:

> A complaint from Lt Hardy, late 1st Lt of *Superbe* against William Hervey for his ill treatment of the said Lt and desiring his own and the captain's conduct might be enquired into. At the same time the court enquired into

* Prize money was divided as follows:
Captain – three-eighths of which one-eighth was payable to the Flag Officer, if one was present.
Lieutenants and Master – one-eighth
Warrant Officers – one-eighth
Petty Officers – one-eighth
Lower Deck – one-eighth
In addition head money was paid by the Admiralty at the rate of £5 for every member of the enemy crew alive at the start of the action.

the aforesaid Captain's complaint against the lt for using the Spanish prisoners ill and forming a scheme to try the aforesaid Captain for the murder of a man. And having heard the evidence . . . and what each had to say in his own proper defence and maturely considering the same were unanimously of the opinion that Captain Hervey had extremely ill-used Lt Hardy and the other lts by frequent abusive and reproachable language, and treated the warrant officers and ship's company with great inhumanity by ill language and beaten both one and the other with great cruelty. As likewise that he omitted to put all things in the ship in a full posture for fight, when he met with the Spanish ship (which he afterwards took) tho' it was represented to him by her officers to be absolutely necessary.

William Hervey was found guilty and cashiered, while the first lieutenant was acquitted.

But by the time of the court martial Augustus was far away. On 3 April the ship's company was given a month's leave and he travelled to London. It must early have been realized that with *Superbe* at Plymouth and his uncle likely to be court-martialled, his position as one of her officers and a potential witness was a delicate one. Fortunately this was a period during which the Hervey interest was strong, with Lord Hervey as Lord Privy Seal in these the last months of Sir Robert Walpole's administration and the Earl of Winchilsea, a family friend, as First Lord. The right things were said in the right places and Augustus was sent back to Plymouth armed with a letter[9] from the Admiralty addressed to Captain John Byng, who was under orders to sail as soon as possible for Newfoundland in the fifty-gun *Sutherland*:

[Admiralty 2nd May 1742]

Sir

This will be delivered to you by the Honble Lieut. Augustus Hervey, son of the Lord Privy Seal.

As he is very desirous of serving abroad, and as no immediate opportunity happening here to give him a commission in a ship bound abroad, the Earl of Winchilsea desires that if any of your Lieutenants chuses to decline the voyage you are going upon you will give him leave to resign, and appoint Mr Hervey Lieutenant in his room according to his rank; and the Lieutenant who lays down shall be provided for in some other ship.

But if no such vacancy can be made you are then desired to receive him on board as a Midshipman extra, and appoint him to rank and do duty as a Lieutenant.

If you meet with any ship of Vice-Admiral Matthew's squadron when you go to Portugal, or that yourself or the *Bridgewater* do go up the

Mediterranean you are then desired to order him a passage to Vice-Admiral Matthews who will take care of Mr Hervey when he comes to him.

Hervey made good time back to Plymouth, arriving there on 5 May, just in time to sail with Byng the next day for St John's Newfoundland.

Newfoundland at that time was at the very edge of civilization, its fisheries conducted with little control, the fish collected and dried on unsupervised beaches open to every kind of abuse, and its merchants as free-wheeling in search of profit as any in the western hemisphere. The cod fisheries were indeed a lucrative business, supplying much of the dried fish for winter consumption in Catholic Europe. French-held Louisburg on Cape Breton Island was not far across the water and the French had a much resented concession allowing them fishing rights in Newfoundland waters and landing rights on certain beaches in the colony. To protect the British fisheries and British sovereignty in the colony a naval governor was appointed annually, crossing the Atlantic in early summer and returning via Lisbon in the autumn. In 1742 the man appointed was Byng. He had already collected the fishing boats from the Channel ports – Poole, Weymouth, Lyme, Dartmouth and the Cornish ports – preparatory to escorting them across the Atlantic. Then with the 50-gun *Sutherland* and the sloop *Bridgewater* he was to spend the summer months supervising these activities to the best of his ability and to see that the fishermen came home and did not abscond to the American colonies. In autumn, following the usual practice he was to escort the fishing boats and the trade with their cargoes of fish back across the Atlantic to Portugal, returning then to England by the end of the year.

On passage Byng combined his escort duties with chasing any vessel which came his way. His first success came on 12 May about 150 miles west south west of Scilly, when early in the morning *Sutherland* sited two ships and chased, coming up and firing two guns at one of them. *Sutherland's* log entry continues:

> I sent Mr Harvey [*sic*] on board her who sent me word she was an English brig that a privateer had taken 3 days before.

Sutherland made both of them prize and then sighted and chased the privateer herself. But although he began to overhaul her Byng found that the chase was taking him away from his convoy and was forced to desist. By 15 June they were on the Grand Banks and saw an 'island of ice' and on the 18th, after losing the convoy in thick fog and feeling their way to a landfall near Cape Spear *Sutherland* anchored in the harbour at St John's.

The summer was comparatively uneventful, *Sutherland* remaining the whole time in harbour at St John's. Byng sent *Bridgewater* round to Placentia and the southern ports to regulate affairs while his first lieutenant in a hired vessel went northwards on similar duties. *Sutherland* left on 6 November with a small convoy for Lisbon. After a month in the Tagus, which may well have allowed Hervey to renew his acquaintance with Ellena Paghetti, Byng sailed with a convoy for home, mooring at Sheerness on 1 February 1743.

Hervey's time with Byng in *Sutherland* had been important for him in a rather special way. During their time together a friendship grew up between them which was to last until Byng's execution fourteen years later. Perhaps it was a friendship of opposites. Byng was not a companionable man, while Hervey seems to have had no difficulty in quickly making himself comfortable with his fellows. Byng, though brave was indecisive and prone to see all the difficulties in every situation, while Hervey said what he thought without fear or discretion, and in his private life as well as professionally acted promptly to grasp the opportunities that offered themselves. Indeed in his actions ashore he was often too forward for his own good, as will become apparent later; his hasty marriage is perhaps the most disastrous example, while his forwardness in supporting unpopular causes – opposition to the Navy Act of 1749 and support for Byng during the latter's court martial in 1757 are two prominent examples – made him an uncomfortable and unpredictable figure in the eyes of many in the establishment. But in his professional life, once he was captain of his own ship, can be found many instances in which he followed with advantage the reliable advice to 'engage the enemy more closely', and his high reputation as a sea officer persuaded successive First Lords to overlook his record as a 'difficult' man. But whatever the motivation for the relationship, for the rest of Byng's life Hervey regarded him as a friend as well as a patron and Byng did much to further Hervey's career.

Soon after her arrival in England *Sutherland* was paid off and Hervey had two months or so of leave. Of how he occupied it there is no record, though it may be expected that he made a point of seeing his mother and father, the latter for the last time. But Byng was shortly appointed to the 70-gun *Captain,* then on the stocks at Woolwich, and early in April Hervey was appointed her fourth lieutenant.

Captain was launched later in the month and then began the lengthy process of fitting her out, bringing on board stores and victuals and getting a crew together. Byng was provided by the Navy Board with a tender called *Charming Joan* – given the vessel's nature she is unlikely to have lived up to her name – and on 13 May he put Hervey in command and sent him off to the northward pressing whatever men he could find. On 15 May Hervey was at Harwich writing to Byng that he was about to take station off Orfordness and was then minded to make for Yarmouth Roads, which was a great crossroads for east coast shipping.

Once at Yarmouth he took *Charming Joan* into harbour, and it was during this visit that he first came across Mrs Artis. She was the wife of the ageing postmaster of the town, Samuel Artis, who had found and married her in London as his second wife in 1736, when he was well over 50 and she 15. She was now 22 and had many attractions, while Hervey was 19. From subsequent comments in Hervey's *Journal* there was clearly a liaison between them, though no details have survived. But Hervey obviously made an impression that was to remain in the lady's mind and lead her more than once to attempt to renew it.

Hervey had been given full instructions on whom he could press and who was protected. In practice, however, it was not easy for an inexperienced young officer to find his way though the web of prevarication with which the captains of merchantmen tried to protect their crews and he was soon in trouble. Before the end of May Byng received a letter from the Admiralty enclosing a petition for the release of John Selandas, an apprentice whom Hervey had taken out of the *Elizabeth and Mary;* and 8 June the Admiralty wrote again about James Christy, who the Master of the ship *Industry* claimed was a protected mate. When Hervey returned and all relevant information was sent to the Admiralty Selandas was judged to be an apprentice protected from pressing by Act of Parliament, but Christy was not so lucky and was kept in *Captain.*

On 18 June Hervey brought twenty-one pressed men back to *Captain,* by this time anchored in the Thames, among whom may have been the three good seamen whom, according to enquiries from the Admiralty, the constables of Beccles in Suffolk had undertaken to deliver to him. The numbers may be thought to be small, but they were double those brought by a second tender which had been sent up the Thames on the same business.

In June Byng was ordered to cruise with three other ships off Belleisle and the Gironde, and in particular to watch for a number of Spanish merchant ships making for the French Biscay ports. He took *Captain* round to Spithead and finally got to sea on 17 July. Two days later Hervey was being sent on board a ship they had come up with off Ushant, finding her to be a Dutchman bound for Amsterdam with a cargo of logwood from Honduras. This was the pattern of life for the next seven weeks, the lieutenants taking turns to board suspected blockade runners. However, they took only one prize, when Hervey went on board and found her to be a Frenchman carrying Spanish cargo from Vera Cruz and Havana.

Captain was back at Spithead in early September and Hervey found that while he had been at sea his father had died unexpectedly at the age of 47. John Lord Hervey had gone out of office with Walpole the previous year but still remained at the centre of affairs in London. There is no evidence that Augustus was especially close to him, though his death was undoubtedly a bitter blow to Lord Bristol, and in spite of her husband's infidelities to

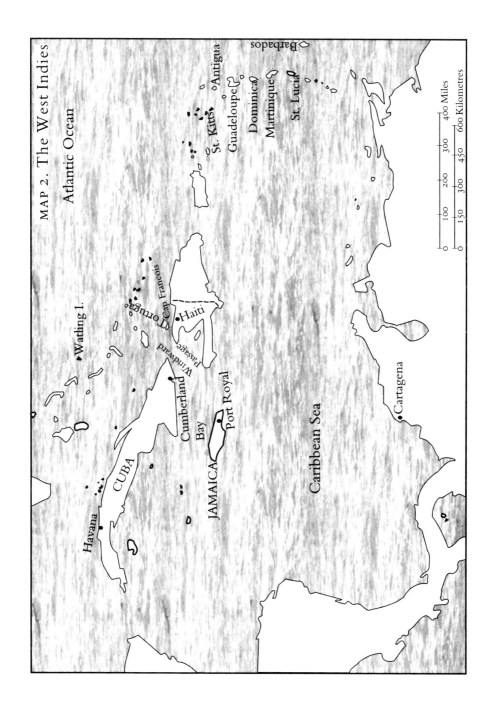

MAP 2. The West Indies

Atlantic Ocean

Antigua
Barbados
St. Kitts
Guadeloupe
Dominica
Martinique
St. Lucia

Cap Francois
Tortuga
Wading I.
Haiti
Windward Passage

Havana
CUBA
Cumberland Bay
Port Royal
JAMAICA

Caribbean Sea

Cartagena

0   100   200   300   400 Miles
0   150   300   450   600 Kilometres

Mary Hervey also. And in practical terms it removed from the scene the man able to bring the most interest to bear on the young lieutenant's future in the navy.

Byng left *Captain* in November 1743 but Hervey stayed in her. The reason he stayed behind seems to have been that he was hoping for better things. He was now 19 and thus at an age when the sons and grandsons of the aristocracy could begin to expect a command and the promotion that went with it.* The age at which an officer could hope to reach the rank of commander or post-captain depended essentially on the degree of interest that he could command. The age rules on these promotions were ignored as readily as those for the step to lieutenant, and ability was far from the criterion; for example, the ineffective Archibald Clevland, son of John Clevland the long serving Secretary of the Admiralty, was captain at 18, while Edward Hawke, who had few connections in high places but ability that was to make him one of the most successful fleet commanders before Nelson, had to wait until he was 29.

In Augustus's case his father's early death meant that the family's influence in London was temporarily eclipsed. Though Lord Bristol took up the cudgels on behalf of his grandson, the best he could do was to approach Captain Thomas Davers, a senior captain who was about to receive his flag. This he did in October 1743, shortly before Byng left *Captain*. Davers was a neighbour, his home at Little Horringer Hall adjoining Ickworth Park. Not always, however, had there been good blood between the families. In 1722 His Lordship had accused Sir Jermyn Davers, brother to Thomas, of bribery and corruption in a matter arising from a disputed election for the St Edmundsbury seats. In response Sir Jermyn had challenged Lord Bristol to a duel, though it was never fought.

The copy of Lord Bristol's letter in his letter book is in his usual flowery and dated style, and may be thought to be somewhat lacking in sincerity or depth:[10]

> As I hope that the time has now come which has been long wished for by all your friends and particularly myself, when justice will be done to your rank and merit in the service of your country by giving you a flag, and the bearer, my grandson Augustus, being more ambitious of being your Captain (in that event) than of any other present preferment, if you would be so good as a neighbour and relation to think him worthy of that honour, the obligation would be too great ever to be forgott, by, Sir, your most

---

* At this time promotion beyond the rank of lieutenant depended entirely on appointment to a command. Command of a sloop or other small vessel brought promotion to master and commander (with the courtesy title of captain), while command of a frigate or ship of the line resulted in promotion to post-captain.

affectionate friend & humble servant,
    Bristol.

The request was ineffectual, the reason unclear. The family background may be enough to explain Davers' lack of enthusiasm, but he may also have had a better candidate in mind or taken against the young man. Certainly when they were together later the association was entirely unfruitful. He did not make Hervey his captain, though the First Lord, the Earl of Winchilsea, did propose to appoint him as master and commander into the sloop *Grampus,* a move that would have presaged early promotion to post rank. Politics intervened, however, in the person of the ineffable Duke of Newcastle, Secretary of State and the Government's manager of parliamentary affairs. The problem was that Hervey's elder brother George, now Lord Hervey in his father's place and like his father called to the Lords as the heir to the earldom, had not yet expressed the unmistakable support for the Government that was a prerequisite for preference to be shown to his relations.

So Hervey remained in *Captain* for a further uneventful six months. Under the command of Thomas Griffiths she formed one of a squadron of three which cruised off Cape Finisterre until the second half of January, stopping and examining all shipping. By early February she was at Spithead and on the 15th sailed to the eastward in the fleet assembled in the Downs under Sir John Norris to counter the French attempt at invasion. The French fleet from Brest came up Channel and on 24 February the two fleets were in sight of each other off Dungeness. There were all the makings of a great and decisive fleet action. The adrenalin must have begun to flow in all on board, the faint hearts − and in a crew many of whose members were not there from choice there must have been more than a few − must have trembled while the courageous looked forward to the laurels to be won. No comment on Hervey's feelings has survived, but in the light of his subsequent attitude to passages of arms there is little doubt that he was one of those who had no reservations about the impending battle. But the weather intervened; on the 24th the wind was very light and that together with the easterly tide prevented Norris bringing the French to action; and by the next morning a hard northeasterly gale had blown up. Its violence prevented the fleets from coming to action, the French making their way in disorder back to Brest. The British fleet was driven westward but maintained its integrity and on the 26th *Captain* was off Beachy Head with twenty-seven sail in company.

After this disappointment Hervey spent a further three unexciting months in *Captain,* most of the time in the western Channel, until on 23 May she went into Portsmouth dockyard for a lengthy refit. This was his opportunity to leave her and to look elsewhere for a more promising future.

References

1. British Library, Add. MS 12129
2. Hervey S H A, 1894, no. 1033
3. PRO, ADM51/401
4. Hervey S H A, 1894, no 1136
5. PRO, ADM51/933
6. Hervey S H A, 1894, no 1140
7. Erskine, 1953, p74
8. British Library, Add. MS 12129
9. PRO, ADM2/58
10. Hervey S H A, 1894, no 1184

CHAPTER III

Marriage and the West Indies

'If he has his faults, it is not want of spirit'

In May 1744 Hervey, just turning 20 and a lieutenant of three years seniority, was becoming even more frustrated by what he regarded as the lack of progress in his naval career. A number of his contemporaries, including Augustus Keppel son of the Earl of Albemarle and Richard Howe son of an Irish viscount, were already post-captains, and in the captains' list would always enjoy seniority over him. Hervey's own position as the grandson of an earl and the son of a minister who, though now deceased, had served George II well seemed to him to justify similar early promotion, and his journal shows how despondent he was becoming. But the Hervey name was still under a cloud and no attractive plum from the Admiralty came his way. So to get to sea he was constrained to fall back on the good offices of Admiral Davers, the neighbour who had rebuffed his grandfather's efforts on his behalf the previous autumn. The best Davers was willing to offer, however, was to take him as second lieutenant of his flagship, *Cornwall,* which was being made ready at Portsmouth for service in the West Indies, where Davers had been appointed Commander-in-Chief, Jamaica.

This was a better offer than at first sight appears. A Commander-in-Chief abroad had the gift of any command that fell vacant in his station, such promotion almost always being confirmed by the Admiralty. It was the custom for the vacant command to be given to the first lieutenant of the flagship, with promotion to commander (or even to post-captain, if the vacancy was in a post ship). The second lieutenant would then move up to first lieutenant and so on down the line. Thus serving on a station in which the death of a ship's captain from disease was not an infrequent event Hervey would be only two lives away from promotion, a macabre outlook which he may be thought to have looked upon with considerable interest.

While the ship was fitting out some periods of leave came Hervey's way and he spent as much of the summer as possible enjoying life in and around town, no doubt running through most of his remaining funds from the prize *Constant of Teneriffe.* Some time in June or July he went to Winchester races and there met − many would say was unfortunate to meet − Miss Elizabeth Chudleigh, later known as the Duchess of Kingston, one of the most remarkable and unpredictable women of the time. Miss Chudleigh came of an old Devon family with estates near Chudleigh in that county and is thought to have been born there in 1720. She was the daughter of Colonel Thomas Chudleigh who was a former Lieutenant-Governor of Chelsea Hospital and who by 1744 had been dead for many years. She appears to have been brought into London society by William Pulteney, the politician, though the terms on which their relationship was conducted are obscure. Pulteney was by this time in his sixties and did not have a reputation for the seduction of young women.

Whatever their relationship Pulteney introduced her to the court of the Prince and Princess of Wales at Leicester House and early in 1744 she was appointed a Maid of Honour to the Princess. She was then 24 and clearly a young woman of considerable beauty, endowed also with wit and a lively manner, and intent on making a good marriage to a husband with prospects. At the same time she gained a reputation for easy virtue, though specific incidences of promiscuity are hard to come by. In the Leicester House circle she was introduced to the 19-year-old Duke of Hamilton, nephew of the Prince's current mistress Lady Archibald Hamilton. The relationship prospered, though whether on Miss Chudleigh's part it was driven by love or by the prospect of money and high rank is not clear. With little delay they entered into a secret engagement to marry. Soon after, however, the Duke went off on the Grand Tour, professing his undying love and intent on marriage on his return.

When Hervey met Miss Chudleigh she was staying with her aunt Mrs Hanmer at the house of another relative, Mr Merrill, at Lainston, two miles from Winchester. He was immediately attracted to her and his feelings were reciprocated. Within weeks they were married. So unexpected and imprudent was this outcome that the motivations of those involved remain an enigma. Hervey by this time had had a number of sexual encounters, of which those with Mrs Artis at Great Yarmouth and Ellena Paghetti at Lisbon are well documented. It is doubtful, however, if at the age of 20 and having spent all his adolescent life at sea he had had anything that could be described as an affair of the heart. It is thus entirely credible that he should have been bowled over as he had never been before by the attentions of this beautiful and intelligent young woman. On a lieutenant's pay, however, supplemented only by small allowances from his grandfather and from his father's estate, and by the prospect of prize money, there was no way in which he could expect to support a wife. But young men of 20 are not remarkable for their prudence or for taking care for the future. Hervey would not be alone in being attracted by feminine charms into a reckless marriage, nor alternatively would he be the only one to find marriage the only route to the loved one's favours. And a reckless marriage is entirely in accord with his lifelong reputation for precipitate and impetuous action.

Miss Chudleigh's actions are more difficult to explain, and so are those of her aunt. Mrs Hanmer seems to have been more than doubtful of the reliability of the young Duke of Hamilton's good intentions. She knew nothing of the secret engagement and had no reason to believe that a young man so much higher in rank and so richly endowed with material things had any serious intentions towards her niece. Thus it is said that when letters addressed to Miss Chudleigh arrived from abroad she opened them and kept them from her; Miss Chudleigh, naturally expecting letters from her affianced lover, became disenchanted when they did not reach her and allowed her glance to wander. Though unproven, so much is entirely credible, and so is the next stage along the pathway to disaster. Augustus Hervey in his naval lieutenant's uniform and with the persuasive charm that he was always able to exert towards women, and with the remnants of his prize money burning a hole in his pocket, must have made a fine figure and have been easy to fall in love with. Miss Chudleigh duly lost no time in doing so.

The real mystery is why what started as a wholly understandable affair escalated within weeks to engagement and then marriage. Miss Chudleigh may be regarded as 'on the rebound' from the lover who appeared to have failed her. Such a state of mind is well known to induce perverse and often irreversible decisions, though a decision to marry a man who was shortly to depart for the West Indies for an unforeseeable period and indeed would have every statistical chance of perishing in that deadly climate, would seem particularly obtuse. Furthermore, her situation was such that no marriage could take place without the willing co-operation of Mrs Hanmer, and it is perhaps in Mrs Hanmer that the key to the puzzle lies. She may have been a rather stupid, romantically minded woman like Trollope's Mrs Roby,* to whom an intrigue was meat and drink, so that she encouraged and even persuaded the couple into marriage without regard for the consequences. Or perhaps she was more purposeful but misjudged matters. Hervey at this time was only two lives away from the Bristol titles and the Bristol estates. Moreover, the Earl his grandfather was nearly 80 and his heir, Augustus's elder brother George, was already well known for his poor health (after his accession he was known as the 'delicate earl') and lived from one crisis to another. George never married so that for the rest of his life, another thirty-one years, Augustus's expectations and financial stock fluctuated wildly with his brother's state of health. Mrs Hanmer may well have expected John Lord Hervey's eldest son to follow his father to an early grave.

The marriage was performed in secret, a precaution for which there were very good reasons. The bride's £400 a year as a Maid of Honour, her essential means of support in the fashionable world, would be forfeit if she was known

* in *The Prime Minister*

to be married, while Hervey could not expect his family's approval for the undertaking and could not himself support an acknowledged wife. Only five people, excluding the bride and groom, were privy to the ceremony, which took place at 11pm in Lainston church. They were Mrs Hanmer, Mr Merrill, Mr Mountenay (a guest in the house), Miss Chudleigh's maid Anne and the vicar, Mr Amis. The parish was small and apart from Mr Merrill's house and the vicarage the church was isolated. The situation was therefore ideal for a secret marriage, though precautions had to be taken to keep Mr Merrill's domestic staff in the dark. It is reported 'that Mr Merrill and Mrs Hanmer dined at a friend's house and went directly to the church, where the vicar was waiting; Hervey and Miss Chudleigh ostensibly went for a walk shortly before the appointed time and made their way to the church; Mr Mountenay and Anne followed them. At the church Mr Mountenay lighted a taper and stuck it in his hat, providing the only illumination for the short ceremony. Afterwards the party did not proceed to the vestry to sign the register, for the good reason that Mr Amis did not have one, not having found it necessary in his tiny parish.

When Anne had assured them that the coast was clear Lieutenant and Mrs Hervey crept quietly into the house by the back door and went to the nuptial bed. They had only a few days together before the groom, his leave expired, was due to rejoin *Cornwall* at Portsmouth. That for this short time the marriage was a real and happy one is shown by Anne's evidence at the bride's famous trial for bigamy (she had in the meantime 'married' the Duke of Kingston) thirty-two years later. Answering the Solicitor-General she said:

> I saw them particularly in bed the last night Mr Hervey was there, for he was to set out in the morning at five o'clock; I was to call him at that hour, which I did, and entering the chamber, I found them both fast asleep; they were very sorry to leave.

There is no evidence that they met again before Hervey left for the West Indies. Indeed they were never to live openly as man and wife, though for a short period after Hervey's return from Jamaica in 1746 they cohabited surreptitiously in London. From that period of intimacy a son was born in the following autumn but died in infancy. By this time Hervey was serving in the Mediterranean and he did not see his wife again until December 1748; after a few ill-humoured meetings at this time they separated, though legally the marriage was to remain in being until Hervey's death in 1779.

After this interlude of roses and wine Hervey perforce turned to his other love, the sea. Davers, now a Vice-Admiral, was under orders to take over the Jamaica command from Admiral Sir Chaloner Ogle, who had been there since the unsuccessful attack on Carthagena. He was intended to sail in late summer, taking with him replacements for some of Ogle's ships and escorting the merchant shipping for Jamaica and also for the Leeward Islands, which at this time formed a separate command. However, conflicting reports on the whereabouts of the French Brest squadron led to a series of changes in his orders, all of which were in turn frustrated by delays due to unfavourable winds or the state of readiness of his ships. It was not until 18 November that he sailed with a large convoy of sixty-one merchant ships, making Madeira roads on 8 December. After a week replenishing stores they got to sea again, and with calls in the Windward and Leeward Islands arrived at Port Royal on 11 March 1745.

Davers had only a weak squadron to oppose the West Indian forces of France and Spain. Though he brought with him *Cornwall, 80, Strafford, 60, Enterprise, 44,* and the sloop *Grampus,* Ogle took home three ships of the line and a frigate, leaving the squadron weaker than ever, consisting of five of the line, two frigates and some smaller vessels. Moreover, a severe hurricane had hit Jamaica in October 1744, sinking one ship and badly damaging several others, and the dockyard had by no means made good the damage when Davers arrived. The climate was bad for both men and ships, the various tropical diseases that were endemic in the region leading to a steady loss of men and the high temperatures causing ships to become foul and their woodwork to deteriorate more rapidly than in home waters. Thus there was a continual need to refit and any major effort by the squadron exhausted its powers for months to follow.

The squadron's primary function was the protection of British trade. Its heavier ships were available for use as convoy escorts and the frigates and sloops went in search of French and Spanish privateers. Though offensive action against enemy trade and their ports in Cuba and Hispaniola might have been desirable the small numbers and poor state of the squadron's ships made such forays difficult to mount; in any case Davers was not an enterprising or aggressively minded commander. Thus there can have been little opportunity for the officers of his flagship to exercise their initiative or military propensities, and not much more to practise their seamanship.

Davers, however, had much to contend with. In addition to sickness, foul ships and leadership of a squadron which was inadequate for the many duties pressing on it, he was faced with the selfishness and quarrelsome behaviour of the planters. This was a cross that he shared with his predecessors and followers in the Jamaica command, and indeed with all senior naval officers who served in the Caribbean, but his difficulties were compounded by his background, for his family had been planters themselves. The last word in private enterprise, many planters had no thought except for the furtherance of their trade and their profits, they were prepared to trade with the enemy if there was money to be made from it and they placed the furtherance and protection of their own trade before any thought of destroying that of the enemy. On one occasion the Barbados planters opposed the capture and planting of St Lucia on the grounds that it would result in competition with their own produce. The planters had the ear of home government and one Leeward Islands commander, Commodore Lee, was court-martialled at their initiative in 1747 for not doing enough to safeguard local trade. All this was common experience for an admiral commanding in the West Indies, but Davers appears to have taken the line not just of non-resistance but of active co-operation and intrigue with the most troublesome of the planters.

As flagship, *Cornwall* tended to remain in Port Royal. Hervey says in his *Journal* that in the sixteen months or so that he was on the Jamaica station she went to sea for only fourteen days, and that during this excursion the sole excitement he had was to be landed at Leoganne bay to destroy an insignificant settlement. Her log, however, shows that while Hervey was in the flagship she was at sea for two months, from 8 August to 17 October 1745, that she went out with the squadron escorting a homebound convoy northward and after that remained out for several weeks cruising for enemy shipping.

Whether *Cornwall* was out for two or nine weeks Hervey had a miserable time on the Jamaica station, a state of affairs to which climate, conditions on board *Cornwall,* lack of sea time and a deteriorating relationship with the Commander-in-Chief all contributed. No promotion or preferment of any kind came his way. He later complained that Davers had used him as a go-between in his business with the Governor, Edward Trelawney, but had continually failed to honour the commitments which he had instructed him to give. Eventually Hervey asked to be relieved of these liaison duties, to which Davers agreed with a bad grace. From then on he was kept busy with duties on board and seldom given shore leave. In June 1746 he fell ill and asked to be sent ashore for the good of his health. There he concluded that no good could come of continuing in such frustrating and unproductive circumstances, resigned his appointment as second lieutenant of *Cornwall* and determined to return home.

He had wasted two years, from the time he left *Captain* in May 1744 to this low point in his career in 1746. No promotion had come his way and even worse he had fallen out with his naval superiors on the station. But the latter misfortune was less distressing than it would be today, for there was no system of reporting on officers' performance, and Davers' dislike of him had in the event no adverse effect on his future progress. Indeed, it may be said that there was a silver lining to the *débâcle*, though Hervey did not recognize it. By shortening his period of service in the West Indies he may well have avoided the fate of so many who served there, who died of one or other of the endemic and incurable diseases which afflicted the region. Davers himself was one of the unfortunates, dying at Port Royal before the year was out.

There was, however, another and more pleasant side to Hervey's time on the Jamaica station. He met and became friendly with many members of the official and commercial communities, including Governor Trelawney and James Ord, one of the more important merchants, and his wife Anne-Petronilla. Mrs Ord and her family, the Elletsons, appear to have treated him with much kindness and on his return to England he sent her a present which he describes as 'a very pretty onyx toothpick-case with a picture of me in the top.' This friendship with a young married woman was, it may be said, one of the few in which there was no element of impropriety and no suggestion on Hervey's part that he wished matters otherwise. It continued for many years.

Hervey arranged his passage home in the frigate *Seahorse,* which sailed from Port Royal on 23 June with a convoy of merchant shipping. The social standing that he had established in Jamaica is shown by the company at his farewell stag party the day before his departure. It was given by Mr Manning, another important merchant, at his plantation near Kingston. The guests included the Governor, Mr Price the Speaker of the Assembly, Mr Ord and many gentlemen of the island. Trelawney himself escorted him to the quayside that evening. Hervey did not, however, consider it necessary to take leave of the Admiral, who remained at Port Royal with *Cornwall,* sending the rest of the squadron to escort the convoy through the Windward Passage.

The boredom of the nine-week voyage home gave Hervey the opportunity to compose a lengthy pamphlet on affairs in Jamaica, a pamphlet which was in effect the genesis of his first foray in public contention. It was entitled 'A Letter from a Friend at Jamaica to a Friend in London, giving an impartial account of the violent proceeding of the faction in that island'[2] and was published in September, a few weeks after his arrival home. In anything touching his personal convictions, however, Hervey was seldom capable of being impartial and the manuscript that has survived is verbose, obscure, factional itself and often abusive. There was of course more than one faction or group in Jamaica. The one that Hervey abuses contained 'the mean blundering kind of wretches' who Admiral Davers supported and gave comfort to, while the other included 'one of the best of men', the Governor, Edward Trelawney. The strength of Hervey's invective is shown by his description of Mr Rose Fuller, one of the leaders of the 'faction':

He has no judgement, he has neither fixt principles, nor any steady affections, I think 'tis certain he loves no one, and much to be questioned whether he hates any but as they thwart him on his mighty passion, the love of power . . . As he will flatter in the servilest manner the meanest and worst of men to their faces so he will abuse the best in the most scurrilous & indecent manner behind their backs . . .

Readers of any of John Lord Hervey's diatribes against his personal or political enemies will be struck by the facility with which Augustus had picked up his father's vituperative style.

One of the incidents described in the pamphlet may well have crystallized Hervey's developing dissatisfaction with the Admiral's behaviour. During the summer of 1745 two French prizes were taken by *Strafford* and brought into Port Royal. The ships were saleable but there was no market in Jamaica for their cargoes. A scheme was therefore devised whereby the captains of the prizes bought the cargoes (which they did with loans from banks in Jamaica) on condition that they could take them to Leoganne in a hired ship under flag of truce; the hired vessel would then return to Jamaica with a cargo of saleable indigo. The Admiral concurred with this peculiar arrangement (the more willingly perhaps because it enhanced his flag officer's share of the prize money), the Governor also endorsed it and it was put into effect.

In the meantime, as mentioned above, Davers was escorting a home convoy through the Windward Passage and then stayed out cruising with four of the line until October. On his return passage to Port Royal Davers met the bomb vessel *Basilisk*, Captain Dudley, on her way to escort the hired vessel with its cargo of indigo. In spite of the Admiral's formal approval for the exchange to take place he appears to have given Dudley private and verbal orders to apprehend the hired vessel and take her back to Port Royal as a prize, thus expecting to receive twice over his flag officer's share of prize money. This Dudley duly did.

Back in Jamaica Davers was accused of breaching the agreement and not honouring the flag of truce to which he was a partner. In response he tried unsuccessfully to throw the blame on Dudley. The Agent-Victualler, John Gray, who was one of the Admiral's subordinates and a supporter of the 'faction' then entered the fray. As with so many in his position he had made a fortune by defrauding the Government, and had gone on to use the Admiral's greed to embroil his superior in his dishonesty. Gray now accused the merchants (including Hervey's friends Manning and Ord) who had had a hand in arranging the sale of the cargoes back to the French of trading with the enemy and laid a charge of treason against them. Trelawney, however, with the advice of the Attorney-General threw the accusation out. From this time, according to Hervey, the Admiral reduced his contacts with the Governor to a minimum, sat sulking at Port Royal and became a tool of the 'faction', which became known as the Admiral's party.

Hervey's pamphlet goes on to assert that Davers then began to indulge in excessive pressing, and that he picked on ships belonging to Ord and Manning, taking key men from them so that they could not sail. In November the merchants petitioned the Governor to lay their grievance in this respect before the King. Trelawney told Davers that he was minded to do so, with no effect.

Indeed, the 'faction' went on to make an accusation of spying against a Spanish merchant who had long been resident in the island with the Governor's approval. He was brought before the Assembly and Davers produced as witness a pilot taken from one of Manning's ships, who had been imprisoned without charge on *Cornwall* for several months. Once off *Cornwall* and out of Davers' hands, however, the pilot refused to testify and the case failed. Hervey as one of *Cornwall's* officers must have known the truth of the matter, and such behaviour by the Commander-in-Chief was certainly enough to provide the final incentive for him to leave the ship.

Such is Hervey's description of the relations between the Admiral and the Governor, a parlous state of affairs and a minefield for junior officers from which he had managed to extricate himself without undue damage. The voyage home was uneventful, its tedium somewhat alleviated by visiting between *Seahorse* and the other escort, *Falmouth,* both of which were carrying passengers. Hervey landed at Dover with Captain David Hamilton, a passenger in *Falmouth,* on 19 August and reached London at 2 pm the next day, having slept at Canterbury. He found none of his family in the capital and took lodgings with Mr Volls, his tailor, in Pall Mall.

He now had two problems to address. One was to inform himself on the whereabouts of Elizabeth his wife and the state of his marriage, the other to find himself a sea appointment consistent with his age and station in life. But first he had more immediate duties – reunion with members of his family after nearly two years away, and delivery of official letters entrusted to him by Governor Trelawney. He made these deliveries in person and the account in his journal is written with the mature judgement of his forty-odd years at the time of writing rather than the relative naivety of his twenty two years on the actual occasion.

The first visit was to the Duke of Newcastle, then Chancellor of the Exchequer, who he found at a wedding dinner for Lady Caroline Fitzroy at her father the Duke of Grafton's house: 'The Duke received me with all that civility that ministers can put on, and with all that falseness natural to his Grace . . .'

The Duke made the mistake of expressing surprise that Hervey was not a captain, a misfortune due entirely to his own refusal to give him *Grampus* in 1744. They exchanged polite platitudes and Hervey then went down to Greenwich to the Duke's brother Henry Pelham, Prime Minister from 1742 to 1754, for whom he had a verbal message from Trelawney as well as letters. Pelham kept him talking about his experiences in Jamaica and conditions in the colony for several hours but did not appear likely to act on any of Trelawney's suggestions.

That evening he returned to London, to his brother George Lord Hervey's house, where he found George at home with their brother William. After

Mary, Lady Hervey. From the picture at Ickworth by Alan Ramsay, reproduced by courtesy of the National Trust

the first generalities of welcome had been completed George Hervey began to ask questions about Miss Chudleigh, saying that the family had been told that Hervey was engaged (or even married – the manuscript of the *Journal* is ambiguous) to the lady and that if this was so he had persuaded Lord Bristol to receive her. Hervey was less than explicit in reply and the question was not pressed. He dined that evening at White's Club with his reprobate uncle Thomas Hervey. The next few days he spent in delivering letters and visiting friends in London and found no difficulty in taking his place in society. Lord Waldegrave took him to Court at Kensington and presented him to the King his godfather, who was characteristically ungracious to him. The same evening he went to an assembly at the Duchess of Richmond's and played cards with her and the Venetian Ambassador's wife 'who was beautiful'. He made various naval contacts, including Lord Vere Beauclerk, one of the Lords of the Admiralty, and his patron John Byng who had by then received his flag.

Nothing definite came of these contacts and on 26 August Hervey went down to Ickworth with brother George. The usual route from London followed the London-Norwich road as far as Newmarket and the journey normally involved an overnight stop at Harlow, Newport or Chesterford. On this occasion they stopped at George's insistence to look at Audley End, the great house near Saffron Walden which had been the home of the Howard family, from which they were both descended through their great grandmother Lady Elizabeth Howard. At Ickworth Hervey found his mother, his grandfather and his sister Mary, who lived there, and in addition his sister Lepel, now married to Constantine Phipps, later Lord Mulgrave. The next day was Lord Bristol's birthday, marked according to custom by a dance attended by all members of the family in residence and by all the indoor staff. Ickworth Lodge was hardly adequate for such entertainments, and this one was held in a very small room, in hot August weather, 'enough to stew us all'.

Hervey stayed at Ickworth only a few days. A sea appointment was very much in his mind and the family did what they could to support him. Brother George provided him with a letter to the Duke of Bedford, now First Lord, and Mary, Lady Hervey one addressed to George Grenville, one of the Lords of the Admiralty, and later to be Hervey's political mentor. Lord Bristol was characteristically careful in his send-off, giving his grandson his blessing and, according to his account book, ten guineas – though Hervey gives a figure of eight guineas in his *Journal,* written twenty years later, a discrepancy that may serve as a reminder of the uncertainty of memory and a warning against taking everything he wrote as gospel.

In London he saw Grenville, who promised to do all he could to help, but the Duke of Bedford was in the country. London was empty at this uncomfortable time of year and Hervey had no funds to maintain himself in the capital. He therefore went to stay with his uncle William, who had been living quietly at Rickmansworth since his court martial and had been looking after his nephew's financial affairs while he was at sea. By this time the windfall of prize money from *Constant of Teneriffe* had been spent and Hervey had to give his uncle a note of hand for £68–12–7.

Returning to London Hervey looked around for financial support, not only to pay the debt to his uncle but also to meet the expense of fitting out a ship, for by this time he had heard that he would shortly be given a sloop. His Uncle Harry, one of the wicked uncles who had so much troubled Lord Bristol's mind and pocket, was kind enough to take him to the family bankers, who were unhelpful. Eventually he raised £120 on the strength of expectations from various unsold prizes in which he was due a share.

Uncharacteristically, with money in his pocket, Hervey went back to Rickmansworth, as he says 'to keep out of town'. London may well have been empty of his friends, as well as expensive to live in, but a further reason for this seclusion may be found in a desire not to be troubled with questions about his wife, still absent in the west country. He did, however, receive a letter from an earlier acquaintance, Mrs Artis of Great Yarmouth, but felt unable financially and unwilling personally to take up with her again.

On 15 September Lord Vere Beauclerk breakfasted with Hervey and told him that he was being appointed Master and Commander into the sloop *Porcupine,* then on the stocks at Taylor's shipyard at Deptford. This preferment seems to have been largely a result of Lord Vere's support. He had written to Bedford on the 9th suggesting *Porcupine* for Hervey, adding 'I am told that, if he has faults, it is not want of spirit nor knowledge in his profession.' *Porcupine* was launched on the 20th, Hervey being sworn in three days earlier. Later George Grenville told him that he might have choice of station, home or abroad, and Hervey chose the latter, on the grounds (which presumably he kept to himself) that service in home waters was too much open to interference from the Admiralty, and that advancement to post rank was more likely away from such influences.

Taking up a new command was liable to be expensive for the captain, especially when he had been appointed to a new ship; his quarters had to be furnished and provisions obtained for his personal use, all at his own expense. Hervey's funds being very low there was yet another financial crisis and he wrote to his grandfather asking for money. The letter has not survived, neither is it known how much he asked for – though Lord Bristol clearly thought it too large. He immediately wrote back to his grandson:[3]

> I have received yours of the 27th instant, and am much concerned to find you are still in want, tho' upon your stating of the case I must own I think you ought to have lived upon much less; for what would you have done if fortune, as you call it (but I more justly call it Providence) had not thrown upwards of £1500 into your lap? One thousand of which I would

have saved, had I been you, for future exigencies, one whereof it seems has now arrived, but what that is you do not at all explain, but I must in the meantime so far do so as to let you know that my finances were never lower, nor taxes and my expenses never higher than at this time, and therefore if your present demands will not be suitable to my circumstance, I must not think of concerning myself at all with yours; therefore for your own sake let your next demands not exceed whatever is absolutely necessary, which I think might well be contrived to come within the compass of one hundred pounds more to that already given you by your affectionate grandfather,

Bristol.

This somewhat curmudgeonly response may be explained by His Lordship's view of his grandson's undoubted ability to spend money, but the reference to what he had given already is unfair, as far as his account book shows, the only gift Hervey had received from him being the ten guineas for pocket money in August. Hervey replied with an itemized and priced list of his requirements and on 6 October was sent £100, which Lord Bristol recorded as follows: 'Gave to my Grandson Captain Augustus Hervey One Hundred Pounds more to fitt him out, in his new Sloop, for the sea'. Hervey, finding this quite insufficient, borrowed again on the security of his prize expectations in his new command.

Now that he was in funds again Hervey stayed in London and went about in society and in the *demi-monde*. He enjoyed the favours of two Italian singers, Signora Galli and Signora Campioni, but preferred the latter partly because of her beauty but also because she took no payment, being kept by the Imperial Ambassador, Count Hasslang. So his only expenditure on her account was for a diamond ring as a leaving present.

All this time Miss Chudleigh, as Hervey described her, or the Honourable Mrs Augustus Hervey as we should call her in conformity with the result of her trial by the House of Lords in 1776, had remained in Devon, but on 16 October she arrived at her aunt Mrs Hanmer's house in London. She had been no more faithful to him since they parted in August 1744 than he had to her, and was at this time again enjoying an alliance with the Duke of Hamilton. Acquaintances in London had told Hervey enough about her activities for him to be much disillusioned and to be wary of admitting the existence of their marriage. So he went to see her and they quarrelled. She rebuked him for not going down to Devon, while he considered that she should have come to London to see him, as well as to carry out her duties as Maid of Honour to the Princess of Wales, a position of which her clandestine marriage had not deprived her. After a brief quarrel, however, the physical attraction between them took charge and they did not let their differences break into their pleasures. Mrs Hanmer was away and many nights Hervey came to her house about midnight and stayed until four or five o'clock. All was not roses, however, for on other evenings his wife would not receive him. Though not meeting her in public Hervey gave her money to pay her debts and bought presents for her, including an onyx watch set with diamonds, up to the limit of tradesmen's credit that he could obtain – for now that he had a ship of his own he had expectations of future prize money and was an acceptable financial risk.

In early November, according to an entry in his *Journal* which has been partially obliterated, he had an intriguingly baffling experience entertaining a mystery woman overnight at his lodgings. The entry reads: 'I was surprised the 10th in the evening at my lodgings in Pall Mall, as I was to go away in a day or two . . . chair and insisted on staying there all night . . . 5 in the morning and then . . . where she had left her . . .'. It is commonly supposed that these erasures and others were the work of Hervey's nephew Frederick William, the 5th Earl and 1st Marquess of Bristol, as an act of prudery or to save the family name. It is not easy, however, to find a name for this strange visitor, who insisted on staying all night because (on the simplest interpretation) she could not get a chair. Hervey appears not to have welcomed her presence and his nephew would not have erased the name of one of his known current or past lady friends. The best fit to the evidence seems to be a woman of good family who had become infatuated with him, and whose reputation the 1st Marquess was at pains to protect.

Porcupine was two months fitting out at Deptford and no doubt Hervey's frequent absence from his ship on visits to London did not escape the notice of the Admiralty, nor did he escape the Lords' displeasure. On 20 October the Secretary wrote to him[4] emphasizing the need for all despatch and pointing out that he should report progress daily. He went on to convey Their Lordships 'directions to you to do so for the future . . . and they hope you will be able to fall down to Longreach without any delay'. He was quick to supply a reason for his remissness.[5]

> *Porcupine* at Deptford Oct 21st 1746
> . . . and am sorry to find . . . their Lordships should imagine I should neglect any part of my duty, therefore must beg you to acquaint them, that the reason for my not sending my daily progress before was the *Porcupine*'s being in the wet dock and in the charge of the Officers of the Yard . . . '

Progress letters followed regularly but not daily – eight in the twenty-seven days before *Porcupine* left Deptford. During this time Hervey gave a lavish dinner on board his ship at the dockyard, attended by several of the Admiralty. The festivities lasted until two o'clock in the morning, when the guests returned to London much the worse for drink. Perhaps this was intended to show that progress was being made and to smooth over any lingering dissat-isfaction in some of Their Lordships' minds.

The Admiralty had decided that *Porcupine* should join the squadron com-manded by Hervey's friend Captain Harry Legge, at that time Commodore on the Leeward Islands station. With this Hervey was very satisfied, for he expected Legge to give him post rank at the first vacancy. His orders, which were quickly overtaken by events, were to take a convoy round from the Thames to the Downs, and then under Captain Pigot in *Centaur* to form part of its escort down channel to Spithead. After that *Centaur* and *Porcupine* were to collect a convoy from southern Ireland and escort it to the West Indies.

November 17th 1746 was a day Hervey is unlikely ever to have forgotten, the day on which he made sail for the first time in his first command, taking her downstream to Galleon's Reach. The next day, in spite of a drunken, abusive and incompetent pilot, of whom he complained to the Admiralty, he took her on to the Nore, where the agent came on board to pay the crew. While this was going on Hervey himself slipped off back to London -it may be thought to one of his current ladies, though he does not say so – in doing so surely risking the wrath of the Lords Commissioners for being out of his ship without their leave.

After a few days *Porcupine* and her convoy got round to the Downs, where contrary winds prevented further progress for several weeks. While waiting, Hervey had many conversations with a Captain Huish, who seems to have known his old acquaintance Mrs Artis rather well, and told him much about her. It was five years since any recorded meeting that Hervey had had with the lady, and it may be that he took due note from these conversations not to repeat the experience. At about the same time he heard from Mrs Hanmer that his wife was still consorting with the Duke of Hamilton, and that nothing she could do would stop her. More welcome news came in the form of a letter from Rear-Admiral Byng, who was staying with his aunt Mrs Masters at Brook in Kent, and who was about to go out to the Mediterranean as second-in-command to Vice-Admiral Medley. Byng proposed taking Hervey with him as his flag captain and in support wrote to the Admiralty that he 'never saw a more complete exact officer since I had the honour of being in His Majesty's sea-service'. Hervey wrote to the First Lord and others, but there were counter-proposals and objections, especially from Lord Vere Beau-clerk, who opposed Byng's choice. The basis of the Admiralty's coolness to Byng's nomination of Hervey as his flag captain has not survived, though Byng was to go out overland and Lord Vere asked him if he expected to carry his flag captain out in his pocket.

Confirmation of the appointment that Hervey was so eagerly awaiting did not come through and on 18 December he sailed down-channel with the convoy, ninety-three sail in all. It was not long before he had an opportunity to show his enterprise and his mettle. On the 21st, still off the Kent coast, contrary winds allowed a French privateer to get among the convoy. Hervey took *Porcupine* in pursuit and followed her for seven hours. *Porcupine's* log [6] gives a graphic description of the effort he put into the chase:

> . . . Wind NW moderate and clear every sail out I could spread after the chase. He threw French colours out, which I returned with the same – less wind – he rather gained of me – but just out of gunshot, sometimes in – I stove 4 tunns of water and then gained of him – but being little wind growing cloudy, and night coming on a lee shore, and very near in (to) Étaples – I gave over chase at five and hauled off – saw several things float by me in his wake, among which was a gun carriage.

The log makes no claim about the fate of the privateer, indeed it leaves the suggestion that she got into Étaples. In contrast Hervey's *Journal* states 'I run her on shore on the coast of Boulogne, she having throwed everything overboard . . .'. Perhaps the verdict should remain open.

Out of touch with the convoy, Hervey made his way westward to rejoin *Centaur* and on 23 December, when off the Dorset coast, he found that he was himself being chased. Judging the pursuer to be another French privateer he decoyed her by making away from her, but used the well worn device of trailing objects over the side to make *Porcupine* appear to be a slow sailer. There then followed a complex succession of deceits; first Hervey showed a Dutch ensign and the Frenchman replied with Danish colours; then *Porcupine* showed a French ensign and pretended to be in distress by firing a gun and putting a weft (a knot) in the French flag. Considering how near the English coast this minuet was being enacted the French captain seems to have been easily deceived, approaching *Porcupine* and coming well within gunshot. At this Hervey showed his real colours, whereon the Frenchman fired a broadside, without doing material damage. On receiving *Porcupine's* broadside in return her captain surrendered. She was a notorious privateer, the *Bacquencourt* out of Cherbourg. Under her captain, de la Mer, she had for two years beset the English coast between Portland and the Start and by her fast sailing qualities had taken a great number of prizes.

To have destroyed one enemy, or at least come near to it, and taken another on his first voyage in command was a commendable first step. Hervey was already showing the courage, the ability in handling his ship and the tactical ingenuity for which his name became a byword. Whether his regard for orders was equally commendable must be doubted, for it was one of the more vital precepts of the day that a convoy escort should stay with her sheep. But he never caught up with *Centaur* and thus cannot have been the recipient of the rough edge of Captain Pigot's tongue; and he went out of his way in reporting to the Admiralty to emphasize and justify his reasons for losing contact.

The wind was strong from the east and Hervey took his prize into Plymouth, where he arrived on Christmas Day. It blew so fiercely that before he could get into the Sound he was carried westward and narrowly escaped the clutches of the Dodman, the prominent headland thirty miles along the coast. Hoping as he was for a ship of the line he must have welcomed this fortuitous but justifiable last contact with the British mainland. There were, however, no orders for him and the next day he sold the prize, receiving £149 as his share of the proceeds. The same day he made haste to follow *Centaur*, but as he got under way the Port Commissioner's yacht was seen coming out to him. On board were orders for him to leave *Porcupine* to his lieutenant and proceed to London to take command of *Princessa*, a ship of the line of 74 guns, which was due to join the Mediterranean squadron, where Byng would raise his flag in her. He lost no time in getting ashore, rejoicing that at last he had received his due and was within reach of the coveted rank of post-captain.

References

1. Pearce, 1910
2. SRO (B), F941/50/5, p9
3. Hervey S H A, 1894 no 1216
4. PRO, ADM2/695
5. PRO, ADM1/1886
6. PRO, ADM51/793

CHAPTER IV

Post-Captain

'They'll tell thee, sailors when away,
In ev'ry port a mistress find' – John Gay.'

With his appointment to *Princessa* Hervey was at last on the ladder which could be expected to convey him, accidents excepted, to flag rank. That he had achieved this at the age to 22 was due to a combination of family 'interest' and perhaps in the end more important the influence of his friend and patron John Byng. His service under Byng in *Sutherland* and *Captain* from May 1742 to October 1743 had clearly made a most favourable impression on the older man – though it must be admitted that Byng's judgement of men was not always of the highest order, and that he had favourites and followers, as all admirals did in that age. Hervey's subsequent career, however, suggests that Byng's assessment of his abilities was a sound one; that Byng should wish to have him as his flag captain was essentially a professional judgement, and he no doubt felt that here was a man of competence and promise with whom he could work in harmony. In the end, however, the co-operation came to nothing. Because *Princessa* was far from ready for sea Byng went out in *Superbe*; and by the time *Princessa* arrived in the Mediterranean circumstances had altered and Byng chose not to transfer his flag to her.

However, for a young man of his station in life Hervey was two years or so late in reaching post rank, a delay that gave many of his contemporaries seniority over him in the navy list. The fact that his place in the list was fixed until such time as he might be promoted to flag rank continued to rankle for many years, particularly when he saw younger men in senior commands or reaching flag rank before him.

Hervey left Plymouth for London and his new command on 4 January 1747. There were as yet no post-chaises, so he had before him an uncomfortable horseback journey, riding a succession of hired horses on the poorly maintained roads of the West Country, rough and muddy in winter, in January weather that ranged from tolerably cool to wet, cold and windy. The journey took five days and one night, with stops overnight at Ashburton, Exeter, Dorchester, Salisbury, and Basingstoke. On the last day, impatient to reach the capital, he continued through the night, arriving in London at 6 am on 9 January.

The new captain was sworn in on 16 January and soon went down to Portsmouth where *Princessa* was fitting out. She had been taken from the Spaniards in 1740, her original name being *Princesa*. Like most Spanish ships she was well built and Hervey described her as 'a glorious ship . . . but rather too large for my wishes for cruising'; certainly for Hervey as a flag captain in expectation the reverse of the medal was that the flagship would have few opportunities to cruise for prizes, and that he (unlike his admiral) would have no share in prizes taken by other detached ships of the fleet.

Princessa was already fitted out as a flagship but in spite of Hervey's efforts to expedite matters getting her ready for sea was a slow business, doubtless because of dockyard inefficiencies, and Hervey had been sworn in for five months before she sailed from Portsmouth. For the first three months of waiting he spent much of his time in London. His wife was also in town, enjoying her position as a Maid of Honour. Hervey knew she had again been deceiving him with the Duke of Hamilton and possibly others, but preferred to ignore the fact and determined to enjoy the marital rights which she seemed to him quite prepared, even eager, to offer. There are, however, differing accounts of her attitude to him. In his *Journal* Hervey says that he was with her 'every evening'. Miss Chudleigh, on the other hand, is on record as bruiting it about that he was continually pestering her, much to her annoyance, and even that he had forced her into intercourse against her will. Forward he may have been, but virtual rape was never his style.

Whatever her degree of assent, later that year she bore a son who on 2 November was baptized Augustus Henry Hervey at Chelsea. It has been assumed that the infant was the outcome of these meetings, though in view of its mother's reputation for promiscuity there can be no certainty that this was so. But whether it was so or not, in the event of Hervey becoming Earl of Bristol Augustus Henry would be the heir to the title. It may be noted that his mother made sure of the infant's rights, even if by doing so she laid the secret of her marriage open to anyone who scrutinized the Chelsea register. All came to nothing, however, for the baby died shortly after the christening.

There is no indication that Hervey knew of his wife's pregnancy or of the birth of his son. While abroad he received few letters. In June 1748, when he and *Princessa* had been in the Mediterranean nearly a year he wrote to Lady Townshend that he had had no letters from his family in that time, apart from his mother, who wrote frequently, and one from his Uncle Aston. Whether 'his family' in this context included his wife is unclear, but there is no evidence elsewhere that he ever heard from her. For his part as late as September 1747 his thoughts were certainly directed to retaining her goodwill. As soon as *Princessa* took her first valuable prizes he wrote to her from sea telling her of his good fortune and wrote also to his uncle instructing him to pay her £200 from his prize money. In June 1748, also, he wrote to her offering to pay all her debts, if she would tell him what they were. She did not, however, produce a list of them until his return to London the following December.

During the months of waiting for *Princessa* there were also visits to Portsmouth to galvanize the dockyard into action. As so often, Hervey soon bored of life in London, a process that was on this occasion hastened by an attack of pleurisy. Recovery was slow and little alleviated by the efforts of various doctors. Eventually, on 23 May, he went down to Portsmouth for the last weeks of fitting out. He was in time to see the prizes brought in from Anson's welcome victory over the French at the first battle of Cape Finisterre. There were joyous celebrations, for this was the first substantial naval victory of the war. Of the many visitors to the port a noble selection dined with Hervey on board *Princessa*, including Admiral Warren, Anson's second-in-command at First Finisterre, to whom Hervey in knocking Anson attributed much of the credit for the victory, and the Admiral of the Fleet, Sir John Norris, a friend of his grandfather, who was well into his eighties, and who had hauled down his flag as lately as 1744. His brother Frederick, then aged 17 and with whom he had not yet quarrelled, came over with the Rev. Edmund Morris, who was a former tutor to Frederick and the youngest brother, William, and was at this time rector of Nursling, near Southampton.

Hervey now got *Princessa* out into Spithead, the first time he had come to sail as captain of a ship of the line. Then on 10 June he took her down to St Helens, the move marred by a minor accident in sight of all the shipping in Spithead. The wind was moderate easterly and as *Princessa* went about she missed stays, according to her log[1] because the wind failed. Before he could get her under way again she was on the Dean sand. He quickly got out her stream anchor and was fortunate to be able to heave her off. Hervey had had much experience of handling ships of the line as a watch-keeping officer but had brought *Princessa* to sail only once before, when coming out of Portsmouth. Thus his knowledge of how she behaved was limited and with an inexperienced crew the mishap is excusable. Indeed it may be thought that he brought to it a cool head and a ready appreciation of the measures needed. He wrote to the Admiralty reporting the incident.[2]

The next day Hervey went ashore for the last time to put his business in order before sailing and dined with Captain Harry Norris, the Admiral's son, and Captain John Foulkes, Captain of Marines in *Princessa*. He had known Foulkes since their days in *Superbe* at Carthagena and it was a satisfaction to have him among *Princessa's* officers. Later that evening Hervey became involved in an unbecoming brawl outside the Kings's Arms, where they were having supper. A few days previously he had had words with a dockyard clerk of the name of Blankley, who 'had been very impertinent, and whom I had threatened to beat'. Presumably there had been some dispute or complaint on Hervey's part about the refitting of *Princessa*. Blankley arrived at the King's Arms, rather drunk, and asked Hervey for satisfaction. Hervey's account is that in view of Blankley's condition he refused to discuss the matter at that time of night, but offered to meet him in the morning. On this Blankley raised his stick at him and Hervey, who had himself undoubtedly also been consuming alcohol, gave him a good beating with it, causing quite a stir.

Early the following morning Hervey went to Blankley's house with Harry Norris and attempted to call him out. Blankley, however, refused to appear and eventually escaped by the back door. Two further attempts during the day were also unsuccessful, and as *Princessa* had gone down to St Helens and was under imminent orders for sea he had to content himself with ensuring that his side of the story was bruited about the town and port.

The incident clearly rankled more than the facts given in Hervey's *Journal* seem to warrant, and continued to do so. Five years later, in October 1752, when he was captain of the frigate *Phoenix*, there was a sequel. Blankley had by then become a naval officer and was stationed at Gibraltar. *Phoenix* arrived there on her first visit of the commission and Hervey immediately sent a Captain Morgan to Blankley and told him that they should meet with swords and pistols immediately, on the neutral territory below the Rock. Blankley, obviously a man of discretion, preferred to offer a public apology, which he duly made in the presence of Morgan and Lord Robert Manners, Hervey having to be persuaded that this was sufficient satisfaction. In retrospect Blankley, though he may initially have been at fault, appears to have been the man of judgement, while Hervey combined characteristic forthrightness with the long memory for insults of a haughty aristocrat.

Princessa sailed the next day, 13 June, as part of the escort of a Lisbon convoy of over fifty sail. The voyage was uneventful. Hervey had not entered the Tagus since his time in *Sutherland* in 1742 and had no opportunity to do so on this occasion, for his orders were to escort the victuallers and storeships onwards to Gibraltar and Minorca. At Mahon he found that Byng was blockading Toulon with a small squadron, while the C-in-C, Vice-Admiral Medley, was at Savona on the Ligurian coast, covering the siege of Genoa. The situation in northern Italy was in its usual state of complexity and confusion. In the previous year the forces of Austria and Piedmont, Britain's allies in the War of the Austrian Succession, had overrun Genoa and advanced along the coast westward into Provence. But the Genoese had rebelled against Austrian occupation and a strong French army had established itself in the city later that year. The allied armies had also been turned out of Provence. However, the Piedmontese littoral east of the Var river, including Nice and the port of Villefranche, was still in allied hands, as was much of the Ligurian coast as far east as Savona. The navy's prime responsibilities were to mask the French squadron in Toulon and to intercept the small craft which were making their way along the coast with men and supplies for the French in Genoa. Its bases on the coast were Villefranche, which had a deep and sheltered all-weather haven, and Vado Bay near Savona, equally sheltered except from the south.

Hervey found no specific orders at Mahon and after a few days there decided to escort the storeships to Medley at Vado, but on the way to make contact with Byng off Toulon. Since his arrival in the Mediterranean in April Byng had had a bad time, his lack of determination allowing the French to recover the strategically important Lerin Islands off the coast near Antibes. He was then sent to blockade Toulon. So when Hervey arrived on 27 July he found Byng piqued that he had been left off Toulon for two months, and giving out that he and the captains in his squadron had been got out of the way, and in particular had been deprived by Medley of the chance of profitable cruising.

Byng kept *Princessa* with him, and Hervey's account is of an unhappy squadron, of 'the neglect of everything under Mr Medley, no captures made but by some few favourite frigates'. The French in Toulon were inactive and there was no sign that they were preparing for sea. On 12 August, however, the mould was broken by the arrival of three ships of the line and a frigate from Vado with the news of Medley's death. Command in the Mediterranean thus devolved on Byng, who decided immediately to raise the blockade of Toulon and took the squadron into Vado, where it arrived the 16th of the month. Byng raised his flag in *Boyne*, not *Princessa*, telling Hervey that this would give him more freedom to go cruising. If this was the real reason Byng can be faulted on two counts. He had no business to favour Hervey in this respect, in doing so falling into the same partiality that he had complained of in Medley. Furthermore, if Hervey was the best choice for flag captain in January, nothing had happened in the meantime to alter that view in August. But all Hervey's officers except Captain Foulkes were transferred to *Boyne*, and *Boyne's* officers joined Hervey in *Princessa*. They included Peter Foulkes as first lieutenant, a position he was to hold in most of Hervey's subsequent commands.

Byng did, however, use Hervey's services more suitably in another way. Immediately the news of Medley's death had reached the Toulon squadron he had shown Hervey the correspondence that came with it from Vado. He now asked Hervey to help him with all the dead C-in-C's correspondence, which they found in much disarray, some of it unopened. Medley may be partially excused by the state of his health, but a further criticism of him is that he was living ashore with a Piedmontese mistress who was thought to be reporting on the movements of the British naval commander to Britain's allies in Turin. This was not the last time that Hervey was to be chosen by the admiral commanding to act as an unofficial chief-of-staff, something he was more fitted for in intelligence and ingenuity than most of his brother captains.

Hervey was familiar with the romantic Ligurian coastline but on this occasion it was not its beauty that he remarked on. As seamen he and colleagues found Vado an easy landfall but when they went ashore they saw the desolation that the armies of the two sides had created, the poverty, the damage resulting from war's passage and the destruction of the crops, olive trees and vineyards that were the only support of the rural population.

Hervey walked through Vado, noting that the people were 'as poor as rats', and a few days later went with Captain Foulkes up the road to Turin as far as Millesimo, twenty miles inland, finding every sign of misery. The women were ugly, though the children were generally pretty, a contrast which he attributed to the burdens that the former carried in the heat of the sun. But the landowners were still managing to keep up appearances and the Count and Countess of Millesimo welcomed them in, put them up for the night, and gave a musical entertainment in which the Countess sang to them. The Count escorted them back to Savona, which had been taken from the Genoese and was the principal allied stronghold on this part of the coast.

In the fleet and ashore there was the usual round of dinners and receptions, at one of which Byng 'offered' Hervey a cruise in company with *Essex*, Captain Hughes. Hervey subsequently gave a dinner on board *Princessa* to Byng, Count Millesimo, the Governor of Savona, the Scottish General Paterson who was in command of the Sardinian galleys and others, and in the last week of August *Princessa* and *Essex* sailed from Vado.

For the twelve months from August 1747 Hervey was to enjoy a period of intense activity, both at sea and in port. In this period Byng dispatched him on four lengthy cruises in the central and eastern Mediterranean, while in the intervals between them he enjoyed all the fruits and pleasures of the land. With more than sufficient funds coming in from the sale of prizes he was able to exercise his talents for conviviality and entertainment, and for the enjoyment of the companionship and other delights offered to him by the women of Italy.

The most promising source of rewarding prizes was the French merchant trade between Marseilles and the Levant. Since at this time there was no active French fleet in the Mediterranean these slow, defenceless vessels took their chance unescorted and the easiest place to intercept them was in the narrow waters between Sicily and the North African coast. So the two ships cruised off Cape Bon, the first incident of note coming on 8 September when they sighted a Maltese naval vessel, the *St Antonia* of 64 guns, bound for Toulon. Though the Malta of the Knights of St John was in theory neutral the organization was at this time dominated by the French interest and did what it could to support French activities at sea. Hervey suspected the *St Antonia* of carrying cannon destined for the French men-of-war at Toulon. He therefore demanded to be allowed to search her, a request for which there was no legal basis but to which her captain submitted when *Princessa* ran out her guns and made ready to fire. In the event no guns were found and Hervey had to content himself with the thought that the Maltese vessel's contact with him made her subject to forty days quarantine on arrival at Toulon. Quarantine was an irritating fact of life in the Mediterranean, for plague was endemic in the north African ports and the countries on the northern shore went to great lengths to prevent it reaching them. Twelve days later Hervey and Hughes were more successful, taking two Frenchmen from Marseilles with valuable cargoes for the Levant. *Essex* took them into Leghorn for disposal while *Princessa* returned to Byng at Vado.

Byng in his new position as Commander-in-Chief was having problems in liaison with Turin, where Charles Emmanuel III, King of Sardinia (in addition to which he was also ruler of Piedmont and Savoy) had his capital and power base. Admiral Medley had taken the easy way of agreeing to all the demands made by the British resident in Turin, Arthur Villettes, who had taken it upon himself to give detailed instructions on deployment of the fleet. At this time General Wentworth, who had been the cause of Admiral Vernon's failure to take Carthagena in 1741, was also in Turin, the purpose of his visit being to ensure that Piedmont and Austria were actually supplying the troops for which British subsidies were paying. Byng decided to send an envoy of his own to Turin and chose Hervey.

Hervey arrived at Turin on 9 October after a two-day journey and an overnight stay at a filthy inn at Cerasco. His *Journal* offers a picture of its author in the role of negotiator, one which he seems to have fulfilled completely to his own satisfaction. Officially Hervey was to present the compliments of the new C-in-C to the King. He had also to point out diplomatically to Villettes that the Resident did not have in his hands the disposal of the naval forces, but was only acting as a link between the King and the C-in-C; if necessary, the Admiral would appoint his own liaison officer to carry out these duties and not to go beyond them. On the 9th and 10th Hervey had business meetings with Villettes, at the second of which General Wentworth was present. Hervey describes Villettes as 'sensible and very artful'. His message to the Resident was that 'the Admiral only wished to know where and when he could serve the common cause', and that it was his responsibility as C-in-C to decide how his forces should be deployed. The Resident seems to have realized at once that Byng was determined on a different relationship to the kind that he had enjoyed with Medley and that the new Commander-in-Chief would not be his poodle.

With Wentworth Hervey had to discuss co-operation with the Austrian land forces, in particular Byng's suggestion for an attack on La Spezia, a useful port at the eastern extremity of Genoese territory. The Admiral considered that the capture of this fine harbour would give him full control of the sea along the whole of the Genoese coastline. Wentworth, however, was reluctant to ask Count Browne, the Austrian commander, to commit his forces in this way and no decision was taken.

Hervey was ten days at Turin and spent his time well. Villettes took him to Charles Emmanuel, who received him rather more graciously than George II had, rising to greet him and to receive a respectful message from the Admiral, delivered in excellent French. They spent an hour in conversation on matters pertaining to the British fleet, after which Hervey was taken to see the Duke of Savoy, the Kings's son and heir. He was shown round the palace, where he found the chapel, the opera house and the richness of the furniture especially impressive. He went to various assemblies and dinners and had two pictures of himself painted by the miniaturist Maria Clementi, one of which he gave to Byng. But his mind was on cruising again and on 14 October he wrote to Byng asking for permission to return to Vado. This being given he left Turin on the 18th and delivered letters from Villettes and Wentworth to Byng the next day.

Byng found Hervey a useful staff officer, yet by 28 October he had given him permission for another cruise. In this may be seen two of the great weaknesses of the British navy of the day – favouritism and the inordinate but understandable desire of the senior officers to make their fortunes. Byng seems to have encouraged this. In August he had 'offered' Hervey the chance of a cruise. Then in October he allowed Hervey to write his own orders for a second. Hervey himself was so besotted with it that he even offered Captain Horne of *Superbe* £400 to change ships with him, on the grounds that she was a smaller and more suitable ship and could more readily be spared. Prize money in itself was not necessarily wrong or unproductive. Certainly it was a way of providing extra remuneration to the service without additional demands on the national exchequer, but as practised at this time, with admirals weak enough to humour their favourites and to give high priority to their own financial advancement, it is doubtful whether it was, in the contemporary phrase, 'best for the King's service'.

Hervey, however, was one of those whom the system served very well. His four cruises in 1747–48 made him enough money to fund four years of expensive pleasure on half-pay after the cessation of hostilities. It has been estimated that by the end of the war his takings were of the order of £9000, a princely sum at the then value of money. Already, before he returned to Vado from his August cruise he had given instructions to his agent in Leghorn to pay his debts in London and to remit £200 to his wife. It is an intriguing reflection on the strange relationship that he had with her that one of the first things he did after the capture of the two French merchantmen in August was to write to her with the news of this success. At no other time does his *Journal* mention a letter to her while he was abroad.

So on 28 October he went to sea again and cruised in the central Mediterranean until 11 December. In this time *Princessa* took a French merchantman bound from Marseilles to Smyrna and sank a French pollacre. With the prize in company *Princessa* encountered the French frigate *Flora* of 26 guns and chased her in light winds for the best part of a week, losing her in the end because his prize was a slow sailer. On 9 December in company with *Antelope* he took another pollacre, and then being short of supplies set course for Leghorn, which he made on the 22nd, going on to Vado a few days later.

Princessa spent nine days at Vado refitting and provisioning. Byng then sent her off again, this time under orders first to look into Toulon, for which purpose she had the fireship *Conqueror* in company. Off Toulon Hervey transferred to *Conqueror* and went close in, getting a very clear view of the state of the French squadron from three separate view points; there were three men-of-war in the basin rigged for sea and five with lower masts up, and none in the roads. Sending *Conqueror* back with this information, Hervey sailed for Cape Bon and cruised for a month. He had some considerable success, taking three Frenchmen and returning to Leghorn on 20 February.

Princessa remained at Leghorn until 7 March, when she sailed for Vado. The previous day, a Sunday, Hervey had shown his mettle in one of those exploits that brought him to the attention of his peers and of English society in general as a man of bravery and action. *Princessa* lay in the roads and from the boat taking him ashore Hervey saw smoke and fire coming from the mass of shipping tied up alongside in the harbour. It was soon seen to be from the merchantman *Caledonia*, which was known to be carrying a considerable amount of powder. The reaction on the quayside and in the neighbouring ships was to abandon them without ceremony. Hervey in contrast made directly for the stricken ship and made to move her to a location where the likely explosion would not destroy quay, warehouses and shipping. With no assistance from *Caledonia's* crew, her endangered neighbours or the shore he went on board and himself cut her cables, having as he wrote in his *Journal* 'my coat burnt almost all the skirts off'. He towed her into open water, where almost immediately she blew up with a great explosion, fortunately with no casualties and no damage elsewhere.

In the town that day, where he was dining with Burington Goldsworthy, the British consul, he was cheered and feted, and the next day received formal visits of thanks from the foreign consuls for saving their shipping and from the Governor for saving the port. Back in England the incident produced a letter of praise from the old Earl his grandfather, writing from Ickworth.[3]

My Gallant Grandson

The love of my name and family has long gained so strong an ascendant over my affections that whatever happens to increase the reputation or credit of it is the most pleasing news I am capable of receiving. Nothing could more effectually gratify this passion than hearing what a noble part you voluntarily acted in saving the ships in the harbour at Leghorn by manning out your boats and cutting away the cables of the Caledonia and towing her out to sea, where tho' her powder room took fire, yet you nor no one of your crew were killed by it, a providence so signal I assure myself you will never no more forget it than I ever shall; and this fresh assistance of the divine favour, if gratefully remembered by us as it ought, will prove the surest protection that can attend you in all your future enterprises, which as long as I live shall be seconded by the prayers and best wishes of your most affectionate grandfather,

    Bristol.

Some of the gilt would have been skimmed from this gratifying encomium if Hervey had known that it had been prompted by his brother George, for Lord Bristol wrote to the latter the same day.[4]

'I have sent you, since you desired it of me, a letter to your brother Augustus, tho' I found it a little against the grain as a parent to be paying where I owed nothing, having never heard from him but when he wanted money; but his later behaviour on this last lucky occasion shall cancel all former prejudices . . .'

Old men – and Lord Bristol was 82 when he wrote the above – may be excused when they need reminding of family duties. But there appears to be more than a grain of truth in his comments, for Augustus had often been backward in keeping in touch with the head of the family and holder of the money bags, as is shown by a grumble to Augustus's father eight years earlier, when Lord Hervey had written telling him of his grandson's promotion to lieutenant. Grandfather's comments was: 'who methinks . . . might have given (himself) the trouble of a line or two to me also'. Lord Bristol was, however, proud especially of his title and it was his heirs, John Lord Hervey and after his death Augustus's elder brother George, who were the recipients of most of his attention and whose financial needs were almost automatically met whenever occasion demanded. For his other children and grandchildren an annual allowance of £50 or £100 was sufficient to keep the wolves from their doors while they made their way. These sums were not inconsiderable in value but need to be seen against the income from the family estates, which at that time amounted to well over £10,000 a year.

On reaching Vado Hervey was called by Byng to two councils of war with General Paterson at Savona. After the second he and Byng were walking through the town to go back to Vado in the Admiral's carriage when they saw a crowd of small craft on the sea to the east, off the village of Celle. The French, having brought 5000 men from Genoa to Celle by sea and marched along the shore road, were attacking Savona and in due course established themselves in a Capucin convent from which they kept up a strong fire into the town. Lord Roche, the Irish Governor, who had been in Piedmontese service for many years, retired into the citadel and resolved to defend it to the last. Byng and Hervey hastened back to the fleet at Vado where the Admiral ordered *Essex* and *Nassau* to Savona to provide defensive fire. After dining in comfort in Byng's flagship *Boyne* the Admiral and Hervey went along to *Essex* by barge. One of the main naval concerns was to prevent the Piedmontese galleys in Savona falling into enemy hands. Hervey therefore went by boat to the port, under heavy fire in which two of his men were killed, and ordered them out. The attack continued all day, but in the dark of the night the enemy melted away.

Later that month Byng sent Hervey to Leghorn to bring back some victuallers carrying supplies for Austrian forces. *Princessa* arrived on 27 March and Hervey made immediate contact with the authorities about the victuallers, but it was just on four weeks before *Princessa* got to sea again. His *Journal* gives the impression that he spent the next four weeks enjoying himself and had no other reason for staying. It was, however, a case of problems with the local merchant vessels. Good sailers as the local tartanes and settees were in fair weather they could not cope much better with stormy conditions than the grain vessels of Roman times, and Hervey was rather wiser on this count than he had been a few months earlier. On 15 April he wrote to Byng explaining the difficulties he was having in continuing alternations of storm and fair weather, that he had sailed once with his convoy but a change in the weather had forced the victuallers to turn back, and that even His Majesty's ships had been seriously damaged. So there is no evidence that on this occasion he delayed unnecessarily, though no doubt he found compensations on shore. Eventually the convoy got away on 23 April, making Vado on the 26th.

There he found to his surprise that Admiral Forbes had arrived from home with orders to raise his flag in *Princessa*. He should not in fact have felt surprise at this development, for *Princessa* had originally been sent to the Mediterranean to carry the flag of the second-in-command (then Byng), and after Medley's death the arrival of another flag officer was to be expected. The Admiral wanted a relation of the same name, Captain Forbes then in command of the frigate *Phoenix*, as his flag captain and taking the usual privilege of a flag officer on appointment desired Hervey to exchange with him.

Though Hervey might have objected on the grounds that it was he who had the Admiralty's commission to command *Princessa* he does not seem to have done so. Indeed, in spite of the reduction in status implicit in moving from a 74 to a 20 gun frigate he seems to have accepted the move gladly. Presumably he considered that as a flagship *Princessa* would no longer provide him with opportunities for cruising, so that he would lose in terms of prize money and would have little opportunity to spend time enjoying himself in the Italian ports. He took all his people with him, including his first lieutenant Peter Foulkes, while John Foulkes his Captain of Marines went home overland.

However, despite his apparently ready acceptance of the exchange Hervey was not completely satisfied with his new circumstances. On 2 May he wrote to Anson[5] asking for better things, because of his move to so much smaller a ship:

> I therefore entreat your Lordship's favour to get it considered that as I have had the honour to command such a line-of-battle ship for a year and a half . . . How happy I should be if I might be thought worthy of the command of some 50-gun ship whenever one is to be sent here . . .'

He also wrote to Lord Sandwich, recently appointed First Lord but still taken up with the peace negotiations in the low countries, and to others in London. It was, however, all to no avail, partly perhaps because of the approaching end of hostilities.

The approach of peace had an immediate effect on Byng and his captains. The smallness of his new command had not stopped Hervey entertaining the two admirals, the captains of the ships at Vado and General Paterson to dinner on board. But the same day, 4 May, news had arrived that a preliminary agreement for peace had been signed by Britain and France at the Hague, unwelcome news for the assembled company since it put a limit to their future prospects of prize money. All was not yet over, however, and Hervey took *Phoenix* on a six week cruise into the eastern Mediterranean, as far as the Aegean. The only ship he took was a deserted vessel with a cargo of grain that he came across. Neither crew or papers were to be found, so he sent her into Leghorn. There was an unfortunate financial sequel, for in 1753 he had to repay £375 in unspecified circumstances, but presumably because the vessel's owners had established title to her in such a way that she should not rightly have been taken as a prize. On 24 June he returned to Leghorn.

So much for Hervey's professional activities in the year that he spent in the Mediterranean. The spells at sea, at Vado and at Turin had, however, been punctuated by visits to the Italian ports of Leghorn and after the peace to Genoa. His *Journal* now begins to give for the first time a picture of him as the gay Lothario, flitting from one Italian enchantress to another and making the best he could of all of them. He was of course now in a much better position to indulge himself in this way. As a ship's captain, much of the time detached from the fleet, he had the opportunity to entertain on board and to spend time ashore; furthermore, he was often in a position to give himself considerable latitude by suiting the ships's movements to his own convenience. For the first time also abundant prize money furnished him with the where-withal to pay for a lavish lifestyle. His position as an English milord assured him of a welcome in society, both native and expatriate, in most European ports. And as Captain of one of His Britannic Majesty's ships, often the only one in port, he enjoyed a respected and influential position in the ports he visited. The social mores of the upper crust in the north Italian ports, and later in Lisbon, were such as to give him every opportunity for encounters and conquests, mostly of an essentially passing nature, encounters that can be used to justify his appellation as the English Casanova, or perhaps more aptly to support the old saw about sailors having a girl in every port; though in many ports he had several at one time.

Apart from these social advantages his successes suggest that he had some sexual charisma, though his portraits do not show it. He appears to have been a small man, considerably shorter than his sister Mary, with a round face and wide mouth, and if the caricature of him with his wife and the Duke of Kingston is to be believed with a sloping forehead and broken nose. Clearly from his record and from the desire that he attracted from a succession of women there was more to him than this.

His first visit to Leghorn at Christmas 1747 had lasted only six days. He lived at the house of John Birtles, in normal times the British consul at Genoa. Leghorn was then as now in Tuscany, a not very active member of the alliance. Hervey met the Governor, the Marquis de Ginori, who was 'particularly kind' to him, and the commander of the Austrian troops in the town. More to the point, he spent much time with the Signore Bonfiglio and Bonaini, two attractive and accommodating ladies, wives of important merchants in the town, of whom he was to see much more during subsequent visits.

He returned to Leghorn on 20 February, after his third cruise, and remained there until 7 March. This visit was marked by the fire on *Caledonia* at which he took such gallant preventive action and by an elaborate ball and musical enterprise that he gave on the canals of the town. In all, with his growing reputation for bravery and his penchant for spending large sums of prize money on lavish entertainment it is not surprising that he stood well with all the principal figures of the town. By this time he seems to have given preference to 'the Bonaini' over 'the Bonfiglio'. He passed the last evening of this visit to Leghorn with her, and on his return later in March the other lady snubbed him, refusing to attend a concert on board and a grand carnival through the streets and canals of Leghorn, all paid for with Hervey's prize money. As he says, and he was in a better position to know than most 'All that stuff (presumably jealousy or false jealousy) subsisted more among the Livornese women than anywhere'. This visit lasted from 27 March to 29

April. Its length is explained by delays in getting his convoy of seventeen supply vessels ready for return to Vado, and not at all as he is careful to say, by any thought that his pleasures should take preference over his duties.

By the time Hervey was next at Leghorn, on 24 June, the war was virtually over and he could legitimately relax. On arrival he was presented in the name of the Emperor, in recognition of his services, with a gold box set with diamonds and with pictures of the Emperor and Empress on the lid, a box that he left in his will to his son Augustus, though it subsequently disappeared from view. The next two months were for him a succession of social visits along the coast and to the Tuscan capital of Florence, where he spent several days in late June. He went up there from Leghorn with the two consuls, Birtles and Goldsworthy, and with Mrs Goldsworthy, staying in the city with Sir Horace Mann, the long-term British Resident with whom his mother's friend Horace Walpole corresponded for many years. There was much social life, and Hervey was especially taken by the goings on at the Trinita Bridge and in Mann's gardens, where the behaviour at last became so outrageous that their owner had to light up the dark corners to maintain a degree of respectability.

The visit to Florence lasted from 26 June to 1 July, but its shortness did not inhibit Hervey from the enjoyment of female company – 'During the whole time I was here the Marchesa de Pecori and the Marchesa Acciaioli was (sic) my intimates. I used now and then to go sup with the Parigi, who was the first opera woman kept by the Baron il Nero'. But he found time to be impressed by the Florence of 1748 with its museums and its magnificence just as much as today's city delights present-day tourists. Of the medieval bridges over the discoloured Arno it was the graceful Ponte Trinita, by then already 200 years old, which caught his fancy, as much as an architectural *tour de force* as for its convenience as a place of assignment. He noted the statues and fountains with which the city was adorned and the great art gallery in the Uffizi Palace, with its pictures and statues and valuables of every kind. The Pitti Palace was already, since the arrival of the Lorrainer Dukes, beginning to lose some its rich contents, whilst of the city's churches it is San Lorenzo with its Medici family associations on which he comments.

Back in Leghorn it was now Signora Bonfiglio with whom he had his way, though this did not stop him also trying it on with Bonaini, who rejected his advances. Nevertheless she gave a grand dinner in his honour, followed by a concert, ball and supper lasting until 8 am next day. On 9 July he sailed for Vado, having the previous day paid all his bills and remitted the balance of £5,800 to his agent in London.

From Vado Byng sent him to Genoa to open up relations with the Doge and the Genoese government on the cessation of hostilities. He received a most friendly welcome from the people in the streets and from the Doge,

Gian Francesco Brignole-Sale, the leader of the revolt against the Austrians in 1746. He went out of town to meet the Duc de Richelieu, commander of the French forces in the Republic. Richelieu had met his mother in France before the late war, and talked most kindly of her. There was also a link of a very different kind to be forged in future years; Hervey met Richelieu at a house belonging to Rodolpho Brignole-Sale, the Doge's brother, to whose wife Pellinetta the French general was currently *cicisbeo*,* though by all accounts this great lady's man never suceeded in making her his mistress. Hervey was to occupy the same position a few years later, and to receive from her a more adequate response to his attentions. But having at this time no acquaintances in Genoa, and wanting to get back to his amours at Leghorn, Hervey kept his time in the city as short as possible.

During the short voyage to Leghorn *Phoenix* ran into a sudden, fierce summer storm which split many of her sails and was close to driving her ashore. She only escaped by taking a narrow channel off Pisa, normally only used by the galleys of the Mediterranean fleets. There is a certain mystery about this visit, Hervey referring to the private business on which he had been sent to Leghorn, and which took him a fortnight or so to complete. It may be supposed that it was Byng who had sent him, but the secrecy in this matter contrasts with the usual openness of his *Journal*. Perhaps it was some private affair of the Admiral's that Hervey did not care to disclose or a matter of secret diplomacy or secret intelligence on which it is not productive to speculate.

Hervey used his time to enjoy the company of his lady friends, especially Bonfiglio, who gave him her picture in a gold and diamond ring before he left. Reaching Vado on 30 July he found that Byng had been ordered home with most of the fleet, including *Phoenix*. Hervey, who was enjoying the Mediterranean, was annoyed to find that Augustus Keppel, two years his junior in age but his senior on the Captain's list, was being sent out to command the small peacetime squadron. Byng sent Hervey to Nice in *Phoenix* to negotiate with Marshal Belle-Ile on exchange of prisoners. He was warmly received and dined with the Marshal in a church close to his house, an entertainment that lasted until 4 am, when he sailed for Mahon. *En route* he rejoined the Admiral and sailed in company to Gibraltar. At this stage Byng detached *Phoenix* and *Nonsuch* to Lisbon, a clear act of favouritism with the objective of helping their captains to remunerative freights home. When the two ships entered the Tagus on the night of 22/23 September it was Hervey's

---

* In Italy at this time a *cicisbeo* was the 'walking out' companion of a married lady, a man who had the acknowledged privilege of accompanying her at all times except in bed, though he might be present at her toilet and on other occasions of an intimate nature. It was permissible for her to be his mistress, but not blatantly so, and this was by no means always the case.

first visit since 1742, but he was soon in the company of friends. One, Theodore de Chavigny, the French ambassador, had know his father and mother well when he had been ambassador in London and made him very welcome. A second was Ellena Paghetti, the Italian singer who had welcomed him to her bed on a previous visit and who extended the same hospitality on this occasion. He spent many evenings and indeed nights at her house at Junqueira, on the Tagus a few miles from Lisbon.

It is a reflection on the naval procedures of the day that Hervey could keep *Phoenix* at Lisbon for two months for no reason of substance other than that he was awaiting a remunerative consignment of gold to take to London. He did not fail to amuse himself during these weeks, for in addition to his doings with his singer he went about the city with the Spanish Duke de Bagnos, visiting the well known nunnery of Odivellas, where he met the nuns, or more correctly the uncommitted ladies who lodged there, and conversed with them at the grates. He made up also to a good looking Portuguese singer, Francisca Brezio, following the local custom of parading below her window in a flowing cloak. In this way he claims to have been invited into the house, but makes no statement on what further transpired. His final comment on his doings in Lisbon makes the imagination run riot. One morning, with the Duke de Bagnos and the Comte de Vergennes (later French Foreign Minister under Louis XVI) he 'went in cloaks to upwards of, I verily believe, thirty ladys' houses – ladies of pleasure, I mean'.

But all good things come to an end and on 21 November *Phoenix* sailed with a freight of 80,000 gold moidores, worth about £110,000. At a peacetime rate of one per cent, Hervey would receive £1,100, of which one third would go to the Commander-in-Chief who had sent him to Lisbon. In contrast to the system operated for prize money, his officers and crew were not entitled to any share. *Phoenix* reached the Downs on 2 December and was paid off in the Thames on the 27th of the month. Byng took Hervey to Anson, who praised him for his conduct in the Mediterranean and told him that the Admiralty would always be glad to oblige him. It was, however, three years before the First Lord felt able to do so.

References

1. PRO, ADM51/731
2. Ibid., ADM1/1886
3. Hervey S H A, 1894, no 1287
4. Ibid., no 1288
5. British Library, Add MS 15956, f57

CHAPTER V

On the Beach

The pleasures of the land

Harry Hervey-Aston, Hervey's uncle, had died shortly before his nephew's arrival home from the Mediterranean. One of Lord Bristol's troublesome sons, he had passed from frivolity and licentiousness to a settled life of sobriety and respectability, taking Holy Orders and marrying a rich heiress whose name he adopted. He had been a good friend to his nephew, taking over from his Uncle William the management of his financial affairs in London. When in the dying days of 1748 *Phoenix* was paid off it was therefore natural that, with most of the family at Ickworth, Hervey should go to live at his aunt Mrs Hervey-Aston's London house.

There his wife arrived within a matter of hours, her behaviour contrasting sharply with that on Hervey's previous return from abroad – from the West Indies in 1746. On both occasions she had been and was being unfaithful to him. On the earlier occasion she had remained in Devon for several weeks after his arrival in London and when she did come up to Town there were recriminations from both sides about the delay; nevertheless, when these were put aside they covertly saw much of each other, though not living openly as man and wife. This time, however, it may be thought that her appreciation of her husband's potential was very different. In 1746 he had been a penniless lieutenant who had come home, if not in disgrace, at least with his tail between his legs; she might be persuaded to allow him his marital rights, and to enjoy them herself, but there did not appear to her to be any advantage in hurrying to his side or acknowledging her married state. Now, however, he was a post-captain with a reputation for courage and resolute action, and, more to the point, well-endowed with prize money. She brought with her the list of debts that he had asked for in the previous June and he gave her £500 immediately, followed by further payments of £200 and £100 before the end of the year.

Debts, however, were not all that Mrs Hervey had accumulated during her husband's absence. From the comments made to him, by her family as well as his friends, it was apparent that her lifestyle was a subject of common gossip, even in an age when scandalous behaviour and illicit sexual liaisons were within limits acceptable. This time – and perhaps his successes in Leghorn and Lisbon made him less susceptible to any allure that she still had for him – he distanced himself from her, going into the country to stay with his friend Byng for a few days. On his return he continued to keep aloof. When at the end of January she came again to Mrs Aston's he taxed her with her conduct, his aunt being present throughout, and refused to have any more to do with her. This decision in effect made an end to any pretence between them that their marriage might become a real one. Mrs Hervey continued in her free and easy ways and her husband ignored her. For his part he was now financially comfortable but had neither married life nor employment to keep him occupied.

In fact Hervey had early divined that there was no prospect of such employment. The end of hostilities meant that for officers in Hervey's position there was little prospect of a sea command. He was not and never would be one of Lord Anson's favourites and did nothing to improve his chances with the man who was now effectively in charge of the Admiralty. When on his return from the Mediterranean Anson had said that the Admiralty would always wish to oblige him Hervey's attitude had been that he had just had his request to stay on that station refused. In reality his comment is somewhat ingenuous; he had expressed annoyance that Keppel had been given the Mediterranean command – and salt had been rubbed into the sore when as *Phoenix* passed up the Thames he saw the new Commander-in-Chief's ship *Centurion* fitting out at Sheerness – but timing was such that any request that he might have made could not have reached London in time to be granted before his return. Furthermore, it was command of the squadron that he hankered after, though a ship might have been an acceptable consolation prize. More than this, however, within a few weeks he managed to do as much as necessary though legitimate opposition to the Government's policies to place himself well outside the pale.

As usual on his return from foreign service he was presented to the King, who as usual ignored him. His Majesty King George II was not the most affable of individuals, but at this time Hervey had offered little reason for such treatment. He was a member in good standing of a prominent Whig family who had given constant support to the House of Hanover, and his grandfather and brother were still solidly Whig in their sentiments and fully supportive of the Government. Granted that Hervey did not care for Lord Anson and may have been outspoken in private conversation, it may be thought that up to this time a certain degree of emollience would have kept him in the government camp. As it was, with no encouragement to support either monarch or government, he gravitated towards the opposition which in true Hanoverian style gathered round the standard of the heir to the throne, Frederick Prince of Wales. It is doubtful, however, if he would have become actively involved in politics at this time if the Government had not precipitated a political furore affecting the navy. The introduction into the Commons of the Navy Bill, with its harsh provisions on the treatment of half-pay officers, was just the spark that was needed to set off Hervey's zealous indignation for the rights of his colleagues.

The Navy Bill, introduced in February 1749 just as Hervey was settling into reluctant half-pay, was in essence an attempt to codify and simplify the law concerning discipline in the naval service. It followed a comparable bill on military discipline for which the impetus came from the Duke of Cumberland, who wanted to introduce into the British army the rigorous disciplinary control which was currently exercised in the armies of many German states. The military bill tightened discipline in several ways, one of which made half-pay officers subject to military discipline.

When in February 1749 Sandwich as First Lord and Anson as the most influential naval member of the Admiralty Board brought forward the Navy Bill of that year it was found that they also had been tempted into the introduction of more stringent discipline, including critically a new Article of War, the 34th, making half-pay naval officers subject to full naval discipline and to courts martial. This article immediately caused much disquiet. It meant that any sea-officer on half-pay who refused to take up an appointment would be liable to disciplinary action. The Admiralty took the view that half-pay was in effect a retainer, while the sea-officers considered it to be a reward for past services; perhaps in practice it was a bit of both. The sea-officers, however, found themselves threatened with a dangerous dilemma. In the navy of the day those with interest filled the most desirable posts, while those without, or who had shown themselves to be politically opposed to the government of the day, were liable to be offered posts in such unpleasant commands as the West Indies; if the Bill became law they would no longer have the option of refusing any post to which they were appointed, or of refusing to serve under any superior officer whom they found distasteful.

The Admiralty's timing was injudicious, for with the cessation of hostilities the number of officers affected, and who therefore objected strongly to the proposal, was very large. The new provision immediately came to the notice of the so called Sea Club of naval officers, which met at Will's Coffee House and later at the King's Arms in Palace Yard. Several meetings were held and a clear majority of the one hundred or so officers present, mostly captains and commanders, were in favour of presenting a petition to the Admiralty asking for its withdrawal. There were a substantial minority who did not wish to protest, including most of Anson's followers, and some such as Hawke and Rodney who sat on the fence. Fortunately for the protesters, however, they had obtained the support of the Admiral of the Fleet, the highly regarded Sir John Norris, by this time almost 90 years of age.

The petition was presented to the Board on 20 February by three captains.

They were told to go away and find what support they had among the flag officers and to come back next day.[1] Hervey, of course, had found this a cause to which he could dedicate his all. Not only was this something that he saw as a personal threat, it was also a stick which, if he could not use it to beat the hated Anson he could at least wave around the Admiral's head. So he readily signed the petition and regardless of any opprobrium or lack of favour that opposition would bring quickly became one of the steering group set up to take the campaign forward. He talked to the Prince of Wales who encouraged him in the course he was taking, as did many members of the parliamentary opposition. He wrote a number of pamphlets some of which verged on the abusive, even the mutinous. Even discounting the fact that he was himself a half-pay officer hoping for a command his actions seem injudicious in the extreme, for it was only a few years since Admiral Edward Vernon, one of the heroes of the early campaigns of the late war, had been struck from the list of flag officers for writing supposedly seditious pamphlets.

When the three captains appeared again before the Board on 21 February they were accompanied by a galaxy of senior officers and many captains, including Hervey. The Secretary made the official minutes of this meeting[2] a very incomplete, even one-sided, account of the proceedings, giving a full account of what the First Lord said and little prominence to the substance of the objections, and carefully omitting the names of those who spoke against the new Article. Hervey's *Journal* gives a different slant, naming several of the speakers and giving the text – which must have been written out beforehand – of his own quite lengthy contribution. Five admirals spoke against the clause and only one officer, Rear-Admiral Mostyn, in favour. It was surely no coincidence, given the standards of the age, that he was made Controller of the Navy only a month later. The meeting was then addressed by the First Lord in most threatening language, objecting to the officers joining together in such a petition and to their having advertised their meetings, describing these activities as seditious and mutinous.

Hervey's intrepidity, however, was proof against verbal threats as much as against physical dangers and he was not put off delivering his contribution. He tried to be emollient, pointing out that the petition had been addressed to the Admiralty Board as the sea-officers' natural protectors, when it might have been directed in much more public and antagonistic form to Parliament itself. He was on less certain ground when he tried to justify the officers' joint action and did not carry the Board with him. Lord Sandwich told him to stop and the meeting broke up. The group then met at the King's Arms Club and Hervey was deputed to draw up a petition to Parliament. Before it could be delivered, however, there was another less rumbustious meeting with the Board and by 23 February the word had been given that the Article would be withdrawn. Nevertheless the petition was presented to Parliament by a bevy of senior officers including Sir John Norris and the Government's resolution collapsed. However, the Bill as passed into law still included the provision that negligence in the face of the enemy was to be punishable by death and by no lesser sentence, a provision which eight years later brought Admiral Byng to his untimely and undeserved end.

Hervey was now at a loose end. He went down to West Wratting near Newmarket, the seat of Sir Robert Smyth who had married his aunt, Lord Bristol's daughter Louisa, and then on to Ickworth to see his mother and grandfather. He had had a letter from Mrs Artis, the young lady of Yarmouth whom he had encountered in 1743. She had recently lost her aged husband and having had little satisfaction from his will may have had in mind that some of Hervey's new wealth might be diverted in her direction. She was living in Norwich and seems to have threatened to make trouble by turning up at Ickworth to confront Lord Bristol with his grandson's youthful peccadilloes. Hervey met her by arrangement at Newmarket races and stayed with her for two nights at an inn. What transpired we do not know. It does not appear that he was at all enamoured of her, and it seems probable that he made at least a token move to satisfy her financial demands. But as far as is known he was to have no further contact with her.

Much as Hervey appreciated his family background Ickworth without any occupation held no joys for him, and nor after the few weeks that he had spent there did London. He therefore decided to travel on the continent, his first plan, (most of which was never carried through) being to visit Paris and then go through France to Italy, visiting on the way all the French naval ports that he could get permission to enter. It may of course be thought that his real objective was the ladies whose company he had so much enjoyed in Leghorn.

As a half-pay officer he had to obtain permission to go abroad from the Admiralty, permission which was granted without quibble, though it resulted under the current rules in the loss of his half-pay. When Lord Bristol heard that the Admiralty had allowed his grandson to go abroad rather than provide useful employment to such a promising young officer he was scandalized. Perhaps it was fortunate that he did not know about the loss of half-pay, for on 22 May he wrote from Ickworth to Hervey in London a long letter[3] in which he regretted the Admiralty's attitude:

I must begin by taking notice it is not only my opinion, but will undoubtedly be the judgement of the public, that your wise and able masters of the a——-y ought instead of giving you leave to travel have prevented that request by appointing you some beneficial station, as was so much your due, in ye Mediterranean, or some other post equal to the timely and voluntary service and honour you had done your country and our allies in saving all the ships from being destroyed by fire at the port of Leghorn . . .

His Lordship concluded that it was by that time too late to remedy the situation. Perhaps it was his age rather than naivety that led him to expect that Hervey, after his forthright stand on the Navy Bill, should be in good standing at the Admiralty, or that the incident at Leghorn – not strictly a naval matter – ought to count highly in his favour. Hervey had at this time established a reputation as a more competent officer than most, but had done nothing special to force a reluctant First Lord to bring him to the head of the list of captains to be employed in time of peace. His time was to come.

His wife had kept away since his rejection of her at the end of January. Her unseemly behaviour continued and at the Venetian Ambassador's Ball at Somerset House in early May, which formed part of the celebrations for the Peace of Aix-la-Chapelle, she excelled herself. She appeared in considerable *déshabillé*, described by the bluestocking Mrs Montagu in the following words:

> Miss Chudleigh's dress, or rather undress, was remarkable; she was Iphigenia for the sacrifice, but so naked the high priest might easily inspect the entrails of his victim.

Certainly the picture of her in this 'costume' that appeared after her death indicates an unusual degree of undress, even by the lax standards of the day. Perhaps she was almost naked; perhaps, alternatively, she was wearing one of the costumes advertised at the time, a costume which clung so closely and was so diaphanous that it gave the illusion that it had been left at home in the wearer's wardrobe. Whatever she was wearing she gave offence to the Princess of Wales, who threw her wrap over the errant Maid's shoulders, and even to the other Maids of Honour ('not of maids the strictest'), who may in reality have been offended that her daring exceeded theirs.

It is said that one person who was not offended was the King himself, who desired to place his hand on her breast (instead she placed it on his own forehead, declaring that this was a softer spot). Two years later he made her mother housekeeper at Windsor Castle. Whether the 70-year-old monarch got the reward that he desired for this promotion is not recorded. If so it was *sub rosa* and short lived, for it was normal for his mistresses to be acknowledged and elevated to a peerage. It is much more probable that his age or the 'protection' provided by his mistress, the Countess of Yarmouth, frustrated the king's intentions. It is unlikely that reluctance on the part of the young lady, wanton and promiscuous as she was, was a barrier.

But at the end of May, presumably hearing of Hervey's imminent departure for the continent, she arrived at Mrs Aston's as he was packing. This time, however, he was 'deaf to all the siren's voice' and she got no satisfaction, either personal or financial. The meeting was the last recorded occasion on which there was any pretence on either side that the marriage was or might be made a real one. Their legal status as husband and wife was to continue, with a number of vicissitudes, until Hervey's death. Though many rumours were current there was no public acceptance or belief that the marriage had taken place and as Miss Chudleigh she remained a Maid of Honour to the Princess of Wales, a position open only to unmarried women, until her 'marriage' to the Duke of Kingston in 1769. The rumours, however, allowed one of the wits (usually believed to be Lord Chesterfield) to pen the following:

> A wife, whom yet no husband dares to name,
> A Mother, whom no children dare to claim,
> All this is true, yet it may yet be said,
> This wife, this mother, still remains a Maid.

The legal twists and turns of Captain and Mrs Hervey's marital fortunes will become apparent later. It must, however, be said that the existence of the marriage, whether known to society or not, prevented the husband from producing an heir to the Bristol earldom and took the wife into the trammels of the law, under which she was eventually tried by the House of Lords and convicted of bigamy, on the grounds that she had gone though a form of marriage with the Duke of Kingston. It was as the husband of the bigamous 'Duchess of Kingston' that Hervey was best known for over 150 years, until the publication of his *Journal* in the middle of the twentieth century.

Hervey left for Paris on 3 June, travelling with William Skrine, a friend in whose company he spent the first few weeks in the city. There they lodged in the Rue des Petits Augustins, in accommodation found for them by M. de Chavigny, Hervey's old acquaintance from Lisbon days and a friend of his mother and father in the thirties when he was Ambassador in London. Chavigny and his nephew the Comte de Vergennes, also a Lisbon friend, came to see them that evening and Vergennes in particular was to see much of Hervey during the next twelve months. For once in Paris Hervey found its attractions and distractions such that he could not tear himself away. Apart from a short visit to England in the summer of 1750, he was to remain there for a year and a half, finally returning home in the first few days of 1751.

Indeed in Paris Hervey, to use a phrase with which he was undoubtedly unfamiliar but which he would readily have understood, 'had himself a ball'. He was just 25, a personable young man who had spent most of the previous fifteen years shut up in ships of war, and was now to find every opportunity for enjoyment that he could wish for. Since he also had the financial resources needed to make a social splash and keep up with the highest level of French society he was under few inhibitions. His family background, of course, lowered all the social barriers in Paris. Though hostilities between Britain and France had come to an end less than a year earlier, the British and French aristocracies immediately came together, picking up old friendships and making new ones, entertaining one another grandly, as if there had been no war, and almost in the belief that there would never be another one.

Hervey went almost immediately to Colonel Joseph Yorke, acting head of the British Embassy, who took him to Versailles for the weekly presentation of foreigners to Louis XV. The King spoke one word to him in passing, making His Most Christian Majesty just one word more gracious than King George. He was presented also to the Queen, to her daughter the Duchess of Parma (married to the Spanish Infante) and to Madame de Pompadour. Hervey's reputation, at least as a sailor, had preceded him and grown in the telling – the Duke of Luynes wrote in his memoirs of this young Englishman of 24 (he was actually 25) who had already fought in fourteen campaigns, had been captain of a ship of the line of 74 guns and had commanded a squadron of twelve ships. So it was only to him, of those presented, that the Duchess and the Pompadour spoke, asking him his views on Italy and Paris. The Court of France he found much grander than that of St James, an opinion that he retained even when he came in the next reign to spend much time at the latter.

It was not just at court that Hervey made his way. In the first few days in France he had various letters from his mother to deliver, including one to the Marquise de Monconseil, one of her friends from her pre-war visit. As well as seeing the sights at Versailles he visited the Tuileries Palace and the Palais Royal, at that time one of the principal residences of the Duke and Duchess of Chartres. It then contained the great collection of pictures, mainly Italian old masters, acquired by the Regent Duke of Orléans and now duly admired by Hervey.

At first it was the growing English community with whom he spent most of his time. Two Englishmen with time on their hands were Lord Cathcart and the Earl of Sussex, who were held in Paris as hostages for the return, under the terms of the Treaty of Aix-la-Chapelle, of Cape Breton in Nova Scotia. They lived in luxury as guests of the French government and with them Hervey went to see the royal palace at Meudon, Madam Pompadour's famous house of Bellevue nearby and to St Cloud, where they admired the elegant contents. Hervey was to see much more of St Cloud during his stay, for it was another of the Duke of Chartres' houses, and the Duke and Duchess made him very welcome throughout his stay. They went on to Versailles, where the fountains played in the two hostages' honour, and where they saw the Trianon and the menagerie.

In July he moved along the Rue des Petits Augustins to the Hotel Luxembourg, where he took apartments at 16 louis (about £14) per month. He entertained handsomely and frequently, and his *Journal* is studded with references to the dinners and suppers that he gave and those that he was invited to in return. Lord Cornbury, the Jacobite Member of Parliament for

Oxford University, and his nephew Lord Charles Douglas were frequent companions. The Earl of Albemarle arrived in July as Ambassador and in August dined with Hervey and an imposing company of expatriates and diplomats. Hervey was unimpressed by the professional and other activities of this great man, whose son was his naval contemporary and rival Augustus Keppel. The new ambassador kept a French mistress, Mlle Lolotte, renowned for the licentiousness of her behaviour throughout the French army, and whom Hervey suspected, probably rightly, of being in French government pay. Albemarle entertained grandly in Paris, but it was the English community who were the most frequent guests at his table.

The very best of names in French society flit across Hervey's pages. The Duke of Penthièvre, grandson of Louis XIV and Admiral of France, who had distinguished himself at Fontenoy, opened his Paris house to him and they went hunting together at Compiègne. Introducing a naval flavour for a brief moment the Duke in January 1750 was indiscreet enough to show this potential enemy of his country several French shipbuilding projects. One was a proposal by a junior officer for a submarine, propelled by oars, with an iron beak to ram ships at anchor. It was laughed out of the room, the usual naval or military reaction of the day to new ideas – though it was to be only twenty-five years later that one of the first submarines was used by the American colonists to attack, unsuccessfully, a British ship in New York harbour.

Illustrating the compactness of European society there were some whom Hervey had met before. The Marshal Duke of Belle-Isle was the commander in Provence to whom he had been sent to make arrangements for the release of prisoners a year previously; he figures little in the *Journal*, except for a ball that he gave for 700 guests of whom Hervey was one. The Duke of Richelieu, who had met Lady Hervey before the war and was to be the conqueror of Minorca, remembered Hervey from contacts at Genoa in July 1748, at the conclusion of hostilities in Italy. And among the visitors to Paris whom Hervey met was Annetta Marchioness of Brignole, sister-in-law of Pellinetta Brignole-Sale with whom he was to have a passionate affair at Genoa a few years later.

The closest friends that Hervey made in Paris were the Duke and Duchess of Chartres. The Duke, who shortly after succeeded to the Orléans dukedon, was a grandson of the Regent Orléans and enjoyed the patrimony granted to this branch of the Bourbons by Louis XIV, including the great palaces of St Cloud and the Palais-Royal. The Duke had done well at Dettingen but took little part in the public life of the peacetime years. The Duke and Duchess were parents of Philippe-Égalité and grandparents of the last Bourbon to reign in France, Louis-Philippe. In their position as the junior branch of the French Bourbons they maintained a semi-regal Court of considerable magnificence. They were of a similar age to Hervey and invited him to make use of their two great houses. He spent much time in their company and was at St Cloud when he fell ill of an unspecified and unidentifiable fever and pain in his side in early September. He was very ill for six weeks, which of necessity he spent at St Cloud, receiving all the medical treatment that was then available – treatment that consisted mainly of being blooded. In spite of the blooding he recovered and returned to Paris in the second half of October.

Throughout his time in Paris Hervey was much in the company of the Duchess of Chartres. Accounts suggest that she was notorious for the laxness of her sexual behaviour. He describes her as 'charmingly entertaining and droll, very pretty', though she had poor teeth and a skin condition on her face. He supped with her, he accosted her at a masked ball (at which she was much pleased) he went with her to many other balls, he played dice with her until four o'clock in the morning. Yet there is no suggestion that she should be included in the register of those with whom he scored his usual successes, or even that he made the attempt. Perhaps he was inhibited by her royal blood and the possible penalties of obtruding on it. More likely this failure to score – if failure it was – may be explained by the Duchess's circumstances at the time. In the second half of 1749 she was closely linked, to the point of scandal, with the Comte de Melfort, a general in the French army, of Scottish descent, who was subsequently banished from the French court for this conduct towards her. By early 1750 she was with child, a child that the Duke acknowledged, and was brought to bed in June of that year. It may be concluded that Hervey liked her company but had little chance of closer favours.

Between all this social activity and entertainment – and the sexual paper-chases described below – Hervey had not been neglecting his physical well being. He describes a typical routine in the early months of his stay; rising early, riding or fencing for an hour every morning, practising his dancing for half an hour (it may be assumed that His Majesty's service had allowed little opportunity for so unwarlike a pastime), and playing the harpsichord for two hours after dinner.

He naturally had a servant with him, not William Cradock, of whom we first hear when he married Elizabeth Chudleigh's maid Ann in 1752, but a man of the name of L'Allemand, who it is temptingly logical to suppose was a Frenchman of German extraction; whether this was so or not Hervey left him behind in Paris when he finally departed for England. For much of the time he kept a coach and horses, and indeed his style of life took little account of the need for financial care. He had a considerable sum in prize money to spend and was not loath to make use of it, though within a week or two of his arrival he comments that 'I found I was spending all my money too fast'. So when he came to settle with his Paris banker before leaving for England in July 1750 and again in December on his final departure the money passed reluctantly. But however reprehensible his grandfather might have found this rashness, if he had known of it, Hervey can be congratulated that when funds were drying up at the end of 1750 he made a clear decision to leave Paris, avoiding the easy option taken by so many of his contemporaries of running up debts regardless of foreseeable ability to pay.

One of the pleasures of Paris on which Hervey laid out much of his money was as always the fairer sex. Among his successes, as related in his *Journal*, we may count the dancers and singers, the wanton young women, the lewd baroness, the bored wife, the older woman, and as a grand climax the neglected young wife with whom he fell madly in love. He lost no time in starting his explorations. At first he looked for companionship and recreation in what would now be called the *demi-monde*. The first that he mentions is 'La Corrolina', an actress at the Comedie-Italienne whom he met at the theatre on 23 June, a fortnight after his arrival. She was being kept by the Prince of Monaco. The Corrolina is one of the very few failures that Hervey admits to. He made her an offer of 1000 louis (some £850); she may have thought that he was trying to buy her outright, or simply have been too surprised at this inflated valuation of her qualifications to be able to say yes. Whatever the reason she flatly refused him and he was flabbergasted.

Not discouraged, however, he soon took up with the elder of the two Bellno sisters, an opera dancer, beautiful but the mistress of the Great Chamberlain of the Polish court in exile. Almost contemporaneously he began to keep company with another dancer, known as the Lani, in approaching whom he was as maladroit as with the Corrolina, but more successful. She appears to have been 'chaperoned' by her mother and between them they convinced him she was a virgin; he paid the pair of them the consequent extravagant rate. How often he patronized the Lani in the following months he does not say but it may be deduced that when other avenues opened up she or her mother were difficult to shake off. Six months later he arranged with the Sardinian Ambassador, the Marquis de St Germain, for her to dance at the opera in Turin. Hervey paid her off with £200 to buy herself the necessary clothes. With the Bellno, in contrast, he was in more congenial hands. He saw her regularly throughout July and August, though with no pretence of fidelity. Though he obviously found her less than ravishing she was straightforward and amenable and readily available. From September onwards, however, there is little mention of her, though in October, after his illness at St Cloud, she came to dine with him. There is no indication that they went to bed on that occasion, possibly because he was not yet sufficiently recovered. He gave her a diamond ring costing 50 louis (about £42) and we hear no more of her.

Though during July Hervey was involved with these two dancers he was obviously on the lookout for other talent and was attracted to a lady who he saw at a house across the street. He got himself introduced to her through another neighbour, the Marquis de Ganis, but found that distance had given her an aura of prettiness that closer acquaintance could not sustain. But with de Ganis, who he describes as a 'strange fellow', he had uncovered a whole glittering seam, though again on closer examination it became a seam of fool's gold. The man was a pimp who introduced two more ladies, a Mme de Belleveau and a Mme de la Motte. Hervey, however says they 'would not do, I did not bite'. Nevertheless, de Ganis wanted, but did not receive, payment for his services.

On 6 August Hervey went to the Comedie-Francaise where Mlle Romainville, one of the principal actresses, made it plain that she 'had some mind for a slice of me'. She was the mistress, later the wife, of a *fermier-général* (general tax collector) named Maison-Rouge, which seems not to have inhibited her one whit, for Hervey found her entirely promiscuous. Nevertheless, though he found her looks less than satisfying she was 'very sweet and very fond' and he accommodated her once or twice, before her promiscuity discouraged him from further contact.

In the middle of the month he was accosted in the galleries of the Palais Royal, a favourite location for such activities, by yet another member of the opera company, Mme Coupé, who he found a 'most luscious jouissance'. He kept to her for a week or so but should not have been surprised, in view of the ease with which he had acquired her, that she also flitted from one man to another as the whim took her. In September he was approached after a performance at the Comedie-Francaise by a Mlle Blotin, with her mother. Whether there was a mercenary motive or it was simply that the mother was beyond shame he does not say. They went home with him to supper and the young lady spent the night in his bed while her mother slept in the anteroom.

After Hervey's illness in September these brief liaisons are mentioned less frequently. In December he had an experience that he appears not to have enjoyed. Introduced to Baronne Blanche, the next day she forced herself upon him – in his own words 'I could not avoid being more intimate with her that I had an inclination for'. She was a 'great, black, lewd woman, about 30' and 'amused herself in that style with whom she took a fancy to'. At the end of the month he had the last of these *ad hoc* relationships in Paris, or at least the last that he records. He met a very modest young married woman, a Mme de Mirancourt, at a masked ball and took her home. She stayed with him overnight, both of them returning to the ball in the morning to cover her tracks.

Among the rollcall of Hervey's partners during these months there is one surprising name. On arriving in Paris he had taken his mother's letter to her friend Mme de Monconseil. She was at the time a woman of 43, and appears to have been for many years a mistress of the exiled King of Poland. She coupled this with the most respectable contacts in England, being a correspondent and friend of Lord Chesterfield as well as Lady Hervey. Hervey saw her once or twice without any special comment and then, on 23 August, records that he went to Bagatelle, her house outside Paris, and found her there alone. He had supper with her, after which she showed him a remarkably fine boudoir. Nor, he comments, did he waste his time while in it. He does not say why he went to Bagatelle that evening, but whatever the reason their love-making certainly provides a remarkable example of his ability to take his opportunities as he found them; but the next night he was back with the Bellno.

Hervey continued to see Mme de Monconseil from time to time, but the intervals between visits lengthened and they were seldom alone together. In January 1750 matters came to a head, the lady upbraiding him with his lack of attention to her. He did not defend himself, for it was true, and in addition he sensed that she was no longer so keen on him; perhaps she had heard about the wide range of his activities. He saw little more of her, and it is interesting to note that accounts of his mother's stay in Paris in 1750/51 give no prominence to contacts with her.

Though Hervey does not say so it is clear that the promiscuous and extravagant lifestyle which he had adopted soon gave rise to comment, not all of it uncritical. As early as September, when he dined with the Duke of Richmond at Lord Albemarle's the Duke told him that he had spent enough time in Paris, that he should go back to London or continue his journeying: but the delights of the French capital had him tightly enmeshed. The Duke's advice appears to have been sensible and well meant, possibly that of a family friend, or even emanating specifically from Lady Hervey or her eldest son. In December the Duke of Hamilton and Lord March passed through Paris on their way to Toulouse and more southerly climes, and failed to persuade him to accompany them. Again in January 1750, Lord Doneraile wrote from London with the same advice. Doneraile was a member of the Tory King's Arms Club with which Hervey had become associated during the wrangling on the Navy Bill and Hervey makes it clear that the letter had the support of, indeed may have been instigated by, the Prince of Wales. Nevertheless, Hervey resisted, being 'engrossed with all these voluptuous pleasures'.

The fact was that by December Hervey had found a new and much more binding attraction to keep him in Paris. For once he had fallen in love. On 12 November, taken to the masquerade by the Duchess of Chartres he saw and immediately, so he says, fell in love with Madame Susanne-Felix de Caze, with whom he was to have over the next year one of the few truly passionate affairs of his life. The initial reason for this new attraction was clearly the lady's unparalleled beauty. Susanne-Felix Lescarmotier was the daughter of a government official and had been in line for installation as mistress to Louis XV, but was forestalled by the Pompadour. She became the second wife of a *fermier-général*, Anne-Nicolas-Robert de Caze.

On this first meeting Hervey was inhibited by the presence of the Duchess, to whom he was committed for the evening, but contrived to show Mme de Caze his interest in her by the somewhat childish procedure of tweaking her gown several times. From then on his thoughts were absorbed in how to get to see more of her and as their intimacy developed how to achieve the ultimate accolade of love. For some time he found difficulty in meeting her again. For example, five days later he went to another ball with the Duchess, and 'very well entertained I was except that Mme de Caze was not there'. It was in fact the second week of January 1750 before he actually spoke to her. He went to the masquerade again with the Duchess of Chartres and her ladies and there found and spoke to Mme de Caze. The response was encouraging, for she told him she would be at Mme Pleneuf's at supper two days later. Hervey had known of the friendship between Mme de Caze and this lady and had taken steps already to make the acquaintance of the latter. So on 16 January he duly went to supper there and, joy of joys, sat next to Mme de Caze.

From this moment the affair developed steadily, though less quickly than was Hervey's wont, and their lives for the rest of the year became inextricably bound up with one another. Having the green light, he called on her next day with M. Vergennes. There he met Monsieur for the first time and was unfavourably impressed. Some of the explanation of Mme de Caze's wanderings – for Hervey was not alone, though he had the field to himself during the course of their affair – may be found in the character of her husband. Hervey describes him as a coxcomb and a drip. His behaviour during the affair suggests that he alternated between an overweening confidence that his wife would not look elsewhere and the jealousy and doubts inevitably attaching to a small-minded and suspicious nature.

On this visit Hervey stayed for supper, meeting two of M. de Caze's sisters, and soon became a constant visitor to the house, also starting to escort Mme de Caze to balls and other entertainments. By early February he had been invited to accompany Monsieur and Madame to the villa which de Caze was building at Torcy, about fifteen miles east of Paris, where they stayed several days and Hervey found plenty of opportunities to press his case. So matters went on for two months, with more visits to Torcy, sometimes without the husband, though there were others in the party. About the middle of February 'At last we found an opportunity to open our minds to each other and found our inclination mutual, but that we were obliged to have much management'. They continued to meet most days, at her house or at those of Mme Pleneuf or Mme Chaumanette, two friends wholly in her confidence. They also met by going at the same time to the painter Liotard, who painted them again and again – though Hervey had no high opinion of him as a portraitist. So they continued to keep company, becoming less and less circumspect, though there is no indication at this stage that her husband had any suspicions. Hervey seems to have drawn him off by giving him an expensive horse.

In spite of his infatuation Hervey kept up many of his other friendships, especially with the Duke and Duchess of Chartres; though at first in this quarter there was disapproval of his new amour. But the singers and dancers were all dismissed, with one unnamed exception. His *Journal* for early March makes the following cryptic comment 'There was one which on every account I could not drop, and which I was obliged to have some consideration for'. But who it was remains a mystery. He certainly continued to see Mme de Monconseil from time to time, but she was hardly to be classified with the members of the *demi-monde* whom he had just discarded.

On 30 April he went to Mme de Caze after dinner and made a further step forward – 'I do believe I should have obtained all had her mother not come in'. But her mother arrived and broke up a promising tête-à-tête, much to his chagrin, though Madame intimated that the intention was mutual and the climax need not be much longer delayed. Four days later de Caze set out for his father's château at La Bôve, in north east France, and she lost no time in sending for Hervey. That day 'we remained together all afternoon and evening till midnight, giving and receiving the last charming proofs of an unbounded love'.

They met continually at Paris, at Torcy, and towards the end of June at Compiégne, where the Court had gone. Hervey followed her there and took lodgings opposite those occupied by the de Caze party. It was at Compiégne that she told him she was expecting a child, which she attributed to their night together before her birthday on 25 May. Shortly after, however, she left Compiégne for her father-in-law's estate near Reims, from where she went on to Dijon with her husband. Hervey was not to see her for nearly two months. He took steps to keep in touch, however, sending his servant L'Allemand to Reims with letters, with instructions to pass them to her secretly via her servant La Jeunesse. Later he sent letters to her at Dijon.

With Mme de Caze out of Paris Hervey decided to make a quick visit to England. Amongst his reasons for the journey was that he knew his mother wanted to visit Paris and might return with him. He left Paris on 17 July and on arrival in London went to her new house in St Jame's Place – a house built and furnished in the French taste which became notable as one of the most elegant in London. He spent much time with her but saw many other members of his family also. It as at this time that he first heard of the trouble developing between Lady Hervey and his brother George, on account of her Jacobite sympathies – of which more later. He went down to Ickworth to

The Herveys at Paris, 1750. From the picture at Ickworth by Hubert Gravelot and others, reproduced by courtesy of the National Trust. The sitters are (from left to right): Constantine Phipps (Later 1st Lord Mulgrave), Hon Mrs Lepel Phipps★, Hon Mrs Mary Fitzgerald★, Captain George Fitzgerald, Augustus Hervey, Mary Lady Hervey. ★Hervey's sisters.

see his ageing grandfather and later to Hampshire to see Mr and Mrs Ord, his friends from Jamaica days.

There now came about a veritable migration of Herveys from England to Paris. When Hervey left for that city on 13 August he was accompanied not only by his mother but also by his sister Lepel and her husband Constantine Phipps. His sister Mary and her husband George Fitzgerald were to follow later. When the first party arrived on 16 August they took rooms in the Rue de Condé, with a Mme le Blanc, at a rent that he notes was 500 livres a month for the first floor and 150 for the second. He took his mother and the Phipps to be presented at St Cloud and for a tour of Versailles, and spent time shopping with them. He was, however, impatient to see Mme de Caze and soon heard from her that an opportunity might be found. Accordingly he set out on 23 August for Dijon, taking L'Allemand with him and 'half a dozen shirts'. The journey took thirty-two hours by post-chaise, during which he did not once alight at any of the thirty-six posts.

Mme de Caze was staying at the house of the Marquis de Beau-Pré, whilst her husband had gone to Besançon on business. On instructions passed through her servant La Jeunesse Hervey, who had taken a room at a hotel in the town, went to the house at midnight and stayed in her bed all next day. She feigned illness and only La Jeunesse and her maid Fanny knew of his presence. He left her at 4 am the next day, leaving Dijon immediately for Paris, having as he says seen nothing of the town except by moonlight.

Back in Paris Hervey took his mother and sister about the town and to Versailles again, where they were present at a firework display and were presented to Mme Pompadour. His mother had of course many old friends in the city, so that there was no lack of social activity. Sister Mary and her husband arrived on 3 October and it must have been during this month that the intriguing picture of the family in Paris was painted, much of it by Gravelot but the portraits by Liotard, the painter who had provided Hervey and Mme de Caze with a safe cover. At least, this is the only period at which they were all in Paris together, though some of the portraiture in the picture may have been painted in later. It shows Augustus dominating a family group with as background a representation of his former command *Princessa*.

There was at this time one of the last recorded comments from old Lord Bristol on his naval grandson. Sadly it seems to miss the point, for writing to Lady Hervey in Paris in October 1750, less than three months before his death, he says, somewhat wanderingly:[4]

'I hope Augustus loses no ground by being better known, and that he will return so thoroughly well qualified in every part of merit as to make those ashamed of having sent him abroad to seek his fortune after so very gallant an action in the late warr as would and ought to have made it in any

country but his own, My blessing shall always attend him, wherever he
is . . .'

Mme de Caze returned to Paris on 4 October and the affair continued apace.
Her husband was becoming increasingly suspicious, and indeed jealous, so
that some circumspection was necessary; though he must have been preoc-
cupied, for instead of discouraging her contacts with Hervey he made a point
of lavishly entertaining the whole Hervey family. The lovers continued to
spend much time together at Liotard's, an interesting sidelight on the latitude
given to his clients by a successful society painter. Hervey took her to the
houses of her friends, to her social engagements and on occasion to her father's
house in the country. On one occasion it all came very near to ending in
tears. On a Sunday evening in early November he had taken his sisters to
visit Mme de Caze at home, and remained behind with her when they left.
Soon they were *in flagrante*, when her husband came in; though he saw their
embarrassment he fortunately did not perceive the extent of their disarray.
He went off in a huff, Hervey assuming that he thought they were only
kissing – a peculiar reflection on what was permissible and what was not.

Many evenings Hervey went to her while her husband was engaged with
his duties at Versailles, staying until two or three o'clock in the morning. But
by December de Caze was becoming increasingly jealous and making un-
pleasantness for his wife, who was by now seven months pregnant. What was
probably more decisive, Hervey's money was running low and he had little
prospect of continuing his extravagant lifestyle in Paris much longer. He
decided to return to London but continued to see her and on the night of
17 December (27 December by the Gregorian calender) stayed with her until
6 am.

He now began to make his farewells, apparently intending to leave Paris
on 25 December/4 January. That day he went to Versailles to take leave of
the Court and had supper at the Palais Royal with the Duke and Duchess.
After supper, at which he was reproached for his continuing passion for Mme
de Caze, he went to be let in as usual, when La Jeunesse came before he
could alight from his cab saying that though de Caze was supposed to be at
Versailles he had just come in and was searching the house for a lost briefcase,
though presumably actually expecting to find Hervey under the bed. So he
delayed his departure for a few days and it was the New Year of 1751 before
he finally said goodbye to Mme de Caze, with mutual vows of eternal
attachment. L'Allemand was left behind to act as a channel for letters between
them.

In spite of the vows little more is heard of the lady. In February 1751
Hervey received a letter from her servant Fanny giving news of the birth of
a son on 12th of the month. Given the consonance of the dates there can
be little doubt that he was Hervey's child, one of the three that he is known

to have fathered. The boy grew up to become a medium level civil servant and the father of three daughters – Hervey's only known grandchildren. They continued to correspond, but when he wrote to her after he was appointed to *Phoenix* at the end of 1751 he found that she had turned over a new leaf, had confessed her sins and decided not to be unfaithful again; that she would be happy to treat him as a friend, but no more. They must have continued to write, but not for long. In November 1752 while *Phoenix* was at Genoa he was surprised not to have had a letter from her and found that she had taken up with Count Kaunitz, the Imperial Ambassador. When Hervey had met the gentleman in Paris he had thought him nothing but a coxcomb. Of such is the stuff of professions of everlasting love, and of repentance of ill-doing.

The journey to London took four days. The first night, after taking leave of Mme Caze in the morning, was spent at Clermont, forty miles north of Paris, and the second at Boulogne – after a six-hour delay outside the gates of Amiens, caused by obstruction on the part of the guards. On the third day Hervey crossed to Dover and took a coach in execrable weather to Canterbury, arriving in London on Sunday 6 January 1751 and staying once again with his aunt, Mrs Hervey-Aston.

He was there a week, being presented to the King the day after he arrived, and being as usual ignored and hearing to his displeasure that Mrs Chudleigh, his mother-in-law, had been appointed Housekeeper at Windsor.

On 10 January he went down to Ickworth where his grandfather lay very ill with a strangury (which would now be ascribed to an enlarged prostate) and not expected to recover. Lady Hervey was there as was George Lord Hervey, making plans for his future as Earl of Bristol, while his sister Lepel and her husband were at Bury. On 29 January the old Earl died at the age of 85. He was buried a week later in Ickworth church between his two wives; but it was his first wife's letters which he had desired to be placed in the coffin with him, and the blue turkeystone ring that she had given him which was on his finger.

The death of the 'good old lord' soon brought into the open the deep divisions which had arisen in the Hervey family, differences that were partly personal and partly political. The 1st Earl had always been a firm if somewhat inactive Whig and a devoted supporter of both George I and George II. His grandchildren, however, were less consistent and perhaps less principled. George William the 2nd Earl remained a Whig, serving Newcastle's interest while the Duke retained office and influence. In the months after his accession to the title he attached himself to the Dukes of Grafton and Dorset, so firmly that is was said that the King would only speak to him at the behest of Dorset, then Lord Lieutenant of Ireland. Augustus, on the other hand, had little time for George II and his Whig supporters, and had early become disenchanted with Anson, who held the post of First Lord for almost the whole of the

1750s. In early 1751 Augustus was a follower of Frederick, Prince of Wales (as he had been in 1749 before his departure for Paris), and much in the company of the opposition group led by Lord Egmont, who hoped for power and interest when the old King passed from the scene. It was, however, Frederick who died first, in March 1751, leaving his supporters without royal patronage until the future George III came of age.

Lady Hervey was even more out of line. Hervey had first heard of the family dissent caused by her views from Sir Robert and Lady Louisa Smyth, though his reference to it in his *Journal* for July 1750 does not say when. Arriving home from France on 19 July he had gone to his mother at her new house in St James's Place, though there is no mention in his *Journal* that she said anything to him on the subject. On 26 July, however, he went to Rickmansworth to see his Uncle William, 'where several of my relations were, from whom I heard the whole state and situation of the shattered family' – an apparent reference to events related to him two days later by his brother George. Lord Hervey, as he then was, told him that their mother had allowed her Jacobite sympathies so much rein that she had made her two youngest daughters Caroline and Emily (then 14 and 16 years of age) 'rank Jacobites and taught them to reverence the Pretender'. and that he had been forced to remove them from her care. He had obviously worked himself into a state on her iniquities. Hervey, however, refused to take sides, a policy he was to follow throughout the years that followed.

For Lady Hervey sympathy for the lost cause of the Stuarts was nothing new. Perhaps it originated with her father, for when Nicholas Lepel first came to England he was closely associated with the court of the future James II, then Duke of York. Her francophile sentiments led her to visit France in the thirties and to make many French friends, at a time when the Pretender was still very much in favour in that country. She made a point of showing her Jacobitism by wearing a white rose, the Stuart colours, on 10 June, the Old Pretender's birthday.

Nevertheless, when in 1745 it came to the crunch, she, like so many English men and women who had raised their glasses to the king over the water, pulled back from her yearnings. With them she decided that keeping the little old man from Hanover on the throne was preferable to bringing the Pretender back from Rome. But her 'Jacobitical drift' continued and in 1749, she is to be found writing to the Rev Edmund Morris on the merits of the white rose:

> In the middle of it [her rose garden at Ickworth Lodge], raised above all the others, is one of the most beautiful kind, who, conscious of the right to possess that place, does not blush in doing so.

The old Earl was aware of her views but appears to have accepted them as harmless. Perhaps, however, he was unaware how much she tried to influence her younger children. By the summer of 1750, certainly, his heir saw things in a more serious light. George William was a Whig like his grandfather, but one who intended to take an active part in the Whig government of the day. He is generally regarded as a conceited man, conscious of the noble status of the head of the Hervey family and anxious to enhance it. At times he even fancied that his position and his capabilities could only be duly recognized by advancement to a dukedom. However, he never reached the highest office, neither was he a man of great influence in court or government circles. Becoming successively Minister in Turin and Ambassador in Madrid he developed considerable ability as a diplomat and later served for a short time in the Duke of Grafton's administration as Lord Lieutenant of Ireland and in his father's former office of Lord Privy Seal.

It was, one must suppose, the new Lord Brisol's political ambitions which aggravated the breach with Lady Hervey. For a prominent Whig to be seen to have a mother who was a convinced Jacobite was bad enough, for that man to do nothing about it would be intolerable, and might lose him his prospects of office. Taking his mother's younger daughters from her control led to a period of ill-feeling which was not to be wholly mended for several years. Worse still, Augustus's sister Lepel, by this time married for some years to Constantine Phipps, took Lord Bristol's side. This appears not to have happened until after the family visit to France in late 1750, when Lady Hervey, her daughters Lepel and Mary with their respective husbands and Augustus spent an amicable time together in Paris. By February 1752, however, the damage was done and Augustus reports a conversation with his mother on her return from France . . . 'she talked to me much about her situation with my brother and mentioned having had several letters from England acquainting her that my Sister Phipps had not played her fair there'.

Hervey affected not to give credence to such machinations on the part of a well-loved sister, an attitude that he may have adopted either to reassure his mother or as an attempt to evade the issue. There is, however, evidence from Lady Hervey's correspondence that Lepel Phipps had taken her brother George's part, if indeed she was not the leader of the coalition against her mother. A letter from Henry Fox to Lady Hervey in France dated July 1753 clearly shows, referring to ' . . . those who ought to be your greatest temptations to come here' (i.e. return to London), that more than one member of her family was making trouble for her. Lady Hervey's reply affirms that Lord Bristol was by then behaving in a more friendly way, possibly, she says, because of the absence of his sister (who was at her husband's family home in Yorkshire that summer). She also refers to 'the falsest, the basest, and the most artful woman alive' influencing him against her. Incredible as it may seem, who could fit the bill but her daughter Lepel? The case is further supported by the absence of Lepel's name from future correspondence and from Lady Hervey's will. Perhaps an ambition to become a peeress – her husband was later to be ennobled as Baron Mulgrave – was a factor in her attitude. Through all this, however, Augustus managed to retain good relations with both sides of the family divide.

After his grandfather's death Hervey return to London. He was now short of money and without employment. The two activities which he thirsted after were not open to him; Paris and Mme de Caze because of his shortage of funds, a sea command because the Admiralty had no suitable ship to offer him. He found that the pleasures of life in the capital and the country houses of his friends and relations sat uneasily with the frustrations of idleness. Such, however, was to be his life for nearly a year, a time that he spent for the most part in and around London, broken by several excursions to the provinces.

One set of friends, the members of the Tory opposition grouped round the Prince of Wales, had been thrown into disarray by the Prince's unlooked for death in March, an event which clouded the future for those who had hopes of his favour when he succeeded. Hervey was not, however, a born politician and soon shook off any disappointment he may have felt. For a time he associated with the famously beautiful Gunning sisters, though his marital imbroglio barred him from laying siege in earnest to either of them. In any event, both were in pursuit of more worthwhile quarry than the impecunious brother of an earl, both being married within little over a year, one to the Earl of Coventry and the other to the Duke of Hamilton.

His brother-in-law Constantine Phipps had a house in London and Hervey was frequently there and in his company and that of his sister Lepel. His younger sister Mary Fitzgerald and her husband stayed with the Phipps for a time. The Fitzgerald marriage was beginning to fall apart and Hervey was present at one of their quarrels, in which Fitzgerald's treatment of his wife was outrageous, leading Hervey to take his sister's part and for once come near to quarrelling with a member of his family. Many other names pass across the pages of his *Journal*: Mr and Mrs Ord, his friends from Jamaica days; Lord Sandwich, under whom Hervey was to serve twenty years later as a Lord of the Admiralty; Lord Coventry, who put him up for White's Club, to which he was duly elected in June; and many more.

In April he had been persuaded to go to Newmarket, though horse racing had never been one of his favoured recreations. He spent his time there hunting and gambling, the latter diversion one at which he lost more money than he could afford, and returned to London somewhat dissatisfied. Later he met and was attracted by the wife of the Imperial Ambassador, Mme de Richecourt, with whom together with the Russian Ambassador and his wife he went to Tunbridge Wells, where they spent a fortnight together. He is too discreet in describing this occasion to give any detail of his relations with the lady, but the affair, if it warrants such a description, suggests that his interest in Mme de Caze was beginning to fade.

A longer expedition, which combined what would now be called sightseeing with family relationships, was the visit he made that autumn to Constantine Phipps' Yorkshire home at Mulgrave Castle. He travelled much of the way with Lord Bristol, taking in the places of interest of the day, for the most part country houses of the aristocracy. At Stamford they visited Burleigh House, where he says the interior was unfinished and not well furnished, though there were some fine pictures. They went to Belvoir Castle and to Belton House, both near Grantham, and at the latter were pressed by Viscount Tyrconnell and his wife to stay there. The journey continued via Sleaford, where Hervey left his brother on the family's Lincolnshire estates. Hervey went on to Mulgrave on his own, through York and past Castle Howard, a journey not without inconveniences. South of Doncaster his post-chaise broke down in the forest at night and in stygian darkness, while north of Malton he failed to make the crossing of the Yorkshire Moors before nightfall and had to sleep in a 'wretched hut' at Slatersgate, in the middle of the moorland.

He reached Mulgrave Castle for breakfast, however, and there found his sister Lepel and her husband, his brother Frederick and his two youngest sisters, Emily and Caroline. Lord Bristol arrived about a fortnight later, at the beginning of October. His arrival brought together six of Lady Hervey's eight children, and did so in amity, perhaps the last time so many of them were gathered in one place. Hervey was at Mulgrave for about a month and enjoyed his stay – Mr and Mrs Phipps were the 'the most pleasing and obliging people to live with that were possible, and did everything for their company with an ease and exactness that left noone unwatched, whilst they appeared without the least care upon them'.

While Hervey and his brother Frederick were at Mulgrave together we may discern the first inklings of the quarrel between them which was to intensify and last until the death of Augustus twenty-eight years later. Hervey heard from his sister Lepel the first tidings that he had had of Frederick's intended marriage to Elizabeth Davers, daughter of their Ickworth neighbour Sir Jermyn Davers and niece of Hervey's Jamaican *bête noire* Vice-Admiral Thomas Davers. Hervey had at least two reasons to be less than enamoured by this alliance – his memories of the prospective bride's uncle, and the local rivalry between the two families; the Davers family were Tories, not in itself something of which Hervey would necessarily disapprove at this period of his life, but the political difference carried with it competition for the two parliamentary seats for Bury. There is, however, no mention in his *Journal* of dissatisfaction at the news. What he does comment on, in a matter of fact way, is some marks Frederick had made in a book in the Mulgrave library:

I had whilst here an opportunity of penetrating into my brother Frederick's disposition *au fond* and an accident which led me to look into a book he had been reading, called La Bruyér's *Caractéres, ou Moeurs de Siecle*, wherein he had marked [certain pages] fixed me with regard to him.

In what respect Hervey found his brother unsatisfactory he does not state, but the shadow cast by this incident was not that of a passing cloud.

Hervey and Lord Bristol left Mulgrave for London on 19 October, arriving the 24th. On the way they went over York Minster and the new Assembly Room with its forty windows. As they approached London they visited Lord Salisbury's Hatfield House, 'which was going to ruin'. The Earl, an eccentric whose main recreation appears to have been acquiring and driving stage coaches, was at dinner and did not receive them.

Hervey found little satisfaction or enjoyment in London, probably because by this time his funds were virtually exhausted. He went to stay with his Uncle William at Rickmansworth and visited his friend Admiral Byng at Wrotham Park in Hertfordshire. On 20 November he and Lord Bristol left London for Ickworth. Hervey was in Suffolk for a month, using Ickworth as a base to visit all the neighbouring gentry. On 21 December he received a letter from the Admiralty which brought him post haste back to London.

References

1. PRO, ADM3/60
2. Ibid.
3. Hervey SHA, 1894, no 1338
4. Ibid., no 1366

CHAPTER VI

The Mediterranean

A licence to philander

Ever since Hervey's return from France in January 1751 he had been angling for a ship. He does not say how active his brother was on his account. On one occasion, however, the new Lord Bristol refused Hervey's request that he might be presented to the Duke of Newcastle, in whose gift almost any appointment lay if he could be persuaded that it was in his interest to support it. Certainly in June 1751 Hervey tried Lord Anson for a command on the Newfoundland station. The timing of the request seems illogical, for he must have know that Captain George Rodney had already been appointed to command there for the third year running and his small squadron was already under orders. The most he could expect would be command of any extra ship the Admiralty might be thinking of sending; but whatever his motivation his application was unsuccessful. Applying then for a ship in the Mediterranean he was refused one of 40 guns but was offered a small frigate. This he disdained, partly so he says, because of his developing association at that time with Mme de Richecourt.

So perhaps he was lucky that Anson persisted and that the letter he received at Ickworth in December 1751 offered him a 20-gun frigate. In financial terms this was just in time, for the small fortune in prize money that he had accumulated in his previous command was by then exhausted, by what his grandfather would undoubtedly have called extravagant expenditure, on riotous living, on gambling, on women, and to an extent on generous giving to his estranged wife.

His instructions were to take command of his old ship, the frigate *Phoenix*, at the time refitting at Deptford, and to join the small peacetime Mediterranean squadron. He hastened to London, once more his first thoughts being that a small frigate was not the 40-gun command for which he had hoped. He therefore went to Lord Anson inclined to refuse what most officers of his age would in peacetime have given a fortune for, a potentially suicidal approach when so many captains senior to him and without his record as a trouble-maker were unemployed. But for once the First Lord had some influence on him, persuading him to take the offer, since no better was likely to become available. This it may be thought was Anson at his most positive and professional, going out of his way to employ one of the most competent of his younger captains and setting aside any resentment he may still have felt about Hervey's attitude to the Navy Bill. However, though the First Lord gained his point there was no change in the deep disfavour with which Hervey looked upon him.

On 3 January 1752 he took command of *Phoenix*, thus joining the select band of captains with a peacetime command, a command which he was to hold for four pleasant, pleasure-seeking, exhilarating and relatively carefree years, until in the aftermath of the battle of Mahon Byng promoted him once more into a ship of the line. He got Peter Foulkes as his first lieutenant and several of his other officers from his last commission – and very glad they must have been to find employment in the piping days of peace.

Three months elapsed between Hervey's first notification of his appointment to *Phoenix* and her departure from home waters. Between visits to the ship he had time to go down to Ickworth, where he tried unsuccessfully to make peace between his mother, who was still in France, and her eldest son. He went to Bury to take leave of the Corporation, a visit with apparent significance for his hopes of a parliamentary seat, for at Bury it was the Corporation who formed the electorate.

In February his mother returned from Paris and he was able to see her before he left – the last time for nearly five years, since he was not in London again until his return to England to give evidence at Byng's court martial in 1757.

By late February, however, Hervey was under pressure to get to sea, as he was under orders to carry with him Abraham Castres, the British minister in Lisbon, and Lord Tyrawley, who was being sent out as a special envoy. James O'Hara, Lord Tyrawley was by this time an old man, having served under Marlborough and been wounded at Malplaquet. He had later become a diplomat and had been British Minister in Lisbon from 1728 to 1741. He was a byword for sexual promiscuity and is reputed to have returned from Lisbon with three wives of varying status and fourteen illegitimate children. In spite of – or because of – this he was popular with the Portuguese authorities and was being sent out to mediate in a vexing dispute between them and the British merchants in Lisbon. He and Hervey must have had many common interests to mull over on the journey.

Hervey got *Phoenix* into the Thames on 2 March and made a remarkably quick passage to Spithead, which he made by evening on the 3rd. On 8 March his important passengers arrived at Portsmouth but the wind was unfavourable until the 20th. Sailing that day *Phoenix* arrived at Lisbon on the 29th.

Portugal at that time was in the throes of political change. Its rulers and its people had slowly been debilitated by the massive flow of gold and silver bullion into the country from Brazil, a process which had removed all incentive to effort and all care for the real economy of the home country. In the long reign of King Joao V, who died in 1750, all thought for the country's well being had been set aside. The King was a religious zealot who channelled the nation's wealth towards the Church, building lavishly and establishing in Lisbon a patriarchate and sacred college on the Roman model, with numerous monasteries and convents. He managed to combine this almost pathological attitude to sanctity with a free-ranging approach to sexual morality, using the 'nuns' in the great convent at Odivellas as a harem. The aristocracy became equally licentious. Hervey describes the sexual mores of the wealthy families in the following passage:

> the Portuguese ladies . . . are all very amorous and very intent at never losing an opportunity of amusing themselves, their husbands being very jealous and very watchful of them, which makes the strictest of them have their wives and daughters chiefly fall a sacrifice to their upper servants . . . [both men and women] partake of those joys which the rigidness of their parents and husbands refuses them, and which the climate and their constitutions induce them to, and their no education in general does not restrain them from.

This was a situation which Hervey found much to his advantage.

It has been calculated that one in ten of the population was a servant of the Church. Since the wealth of the country was devoted in this way to the Church and also to the maintenance of the great families the middle and lower classes suffered and the economy faltered. The country's trade had been allowed to fall into the hands of foreign merchants, principally the English, whose prosperous firms in Lisbon were organized in a Chamber of Commerce known as the Factory, which dominated trade in the city, as did the parallel body in Oporto. This virtual monopoly of trade was encouraged by a series of advantageous treaties made with the government of England's oldest ally; and because Portugal's productive capacity had been allowed to atrophy the country's imports (mainly from Britain) vastly exceeded her exports, the balance being made up by exporting bullion.

The commanding position held by the Factories and the ostentation with which their members lived had begun to irritate the Portuguese. When the new King, José I, appointed Sebastiao de Carvalho, later Marquis of Pombal, as his principal minister and virtual dictator there was an immediate move to restrict the Factories' privilege and to revive the reciprocal rights accorded by the treaties to the Portuguese. The Factories resisted and it was to support their resistance that Lord Tyrawley had been sent to Lisbon.

Many unaccustomed restrictions were place on the British merchants but the immediate problem was the attempt to uphold the Portuguese law forbidding the export of bullion, a law which had been honoured in the breach for many years. In accordance with Pombal's harder line bullion destined for export belonging to the English firm of Burrell was seized by the Portuguese customs. The Factory raised a cry and lobbied the British government for redress, and it was to negotiate a settlement that Lord Tyrawley had been sent to Lisbon. When he came to assess the situation he concluded that the Portuguese were within their rights and that the Factory had become accustomed to privileges far beyond those conferred by treaty. Nevertheless, he obtained satisfaction for its complaint. Such disputes were common and once Pombal had taken charge not all were settled in the Factory's favour.

The squadron that Hervey was to join consisted of no more than three or four weak ships of the line with a similar number of frigates. It had been commanded since 1749 by Augustus Keppel who was on the point of handing over to George Edgcumbe, under whom Hervey was to serve until war came in 1756.

Edgcumbe, though he later attained flag rank – in which his family connections and influence in the numerous Cornish boroughs doubtless had a hand – was not a forceful commander and it is perhaps fortunate that his peacetime command made few demands on him. The duties of the squadron were few and not onerous. The most demanding was to ensure that the Barbary corsairs, sailing out of Algiers, Tripoli and other north African ports, did not prey on British shipping. Apart from that its principal occupation was showing the flag, and Hervey's account of the three and a half years of peace that he enjoyed is structured around movement from port to port, in an area bounded by Lisbon on west and Naples in the east. The squadron enjoyed the facilities of two British bases, Gibraltar and the magnificent harbour at Mahon in Minorca, where all the essential dockyard services were available. The navy was also welcome in most of the ports on the northern shore, including Leghorn, Genoa, Villefranche and Marseilles, and its ships spent long periods in the Tagus. For much of the time the ships of the squadron, especially the smaller ones, operated independently and the squadron commander had little real influence on their movements and even less on the timing of them. Thus we have a picture of Hervey taking, for the most part, his own decisions on how long to stay in port and often on which ports to call at.

In peacetime there was one thing lacking. There were no prizes to be taken and therefore no prize money to be had. There remained, however, the other valuable perquisite, freight, which was restricted to ship's captains and the flag officer commanding. Trade was then financed by the physical movement of large quantities of bullion and coinage, much of it arriving at the Spanish ports and Lisbon from Spanish and Portuguese America. The navy was the only secure method of moving such valuable cargoes, especially in the corsair-infested Mediterranean, and payment for this service, usually, in peacetime at a rate of one per cent, was made to the ship's captain, who paid one-third to the admiral commanding. Thus virtually every captain tried to arrange his movements so as to be in the right place to pick up such rewarding cargo. Hervey's earnings from this source were sufficient to finance a lavish lifestyle in the Mediterranean until the outbreak of war in 1756 opened the floodgates of prize money once again.

Hervey had a second strong motivation in deciding his ship's movements. His desire for female company and his attractiveness to women had both grown greater, if that were possible, with the passage of time, and it was in this period beyond any other that he earned his soubriquet of the English Casanova. In his *Journal* there pass before us a succession of women, Portuguese, Italian, French and English, Duchesses and Dogessas, of high estate or picked up in the streets and taverns, young and not so young, well proportioned or well endowed, usually fair of face and all of easy virtue, which would do justice to the powers of several less energetic men. One only of them, the Genoese Pellinetta Brignole-Sale, was with any certainty the subject of a more than physical attraction, and Hervey's affair with her may be ranked with his passionate attraction for Madame de Caze a few years earlier.

Phoenix was at Lisbon for nearly six months. No operational reason for this is apparent, but when Hervey left it was with a substantial freight of specie – 30,000 Portuguese moidores, worth over £40,000 and therefore bringing Hervey over £400 in commission. The station was in fact virtually without a Commander-in-Chief, since Keppel's time was running out and Edgcumbe had not arrived. During July Keppel put in at Lisbon on his way home in *Centurion* and was there until 7 August. On only one point did he attempt to assert his authority over Hervey and that was to order him to take the money for the Gibraltar and Malta garrisons. If Hervey had accepted this as a legitimate order Keppel would have been entitled to one-third of the freight commission. However, Hervey challenged its validity on the grounds that by the time the freight was delivered Keppel would have been paid off. He made no payment to Keppel. They appear not to have met again until February 1757, when Hervey was in London after giving evidence at Byng's court martial. Keppel asked him about his share of the freight and the matter went to arbitration, the arbitrators being Admirals Norris and Forbes and Captain Moore. Presumably they looked at Hervey's orders from the Admiralty,[1] which were to take on board his diplomatic passengers 'and when you have landed them [at Lisbon] you are to proceed up the Mediterranean and put yourself under the command of the Senior Officer there'. Whether Keppel on his way home had surrendered that position was a nice point, considering that Lisbon was, in the practice of the day if not in geographical terms, very much part of the area in which the Commander-in-Chief Mediterranean held sway. However, the arbitrators seem to have had no doubts. They ruled unanimously in Hervey's favour.

When he arrived in Lisbon Hervey was very quick to pick up old friendships and to make himself at home. There is no mention this time of Ellena Paghetti, who had accommodated him on two previous visits, but he went immediately to Don Joao de Bemposto with whom he had been very friendly. Bemposto moved in the highest circles. He was an illegitimate son of Don Francisco, brother to the late King, by Donna Maria de Sousa but had been legitimated and was thus the King's cousin. Bemposto took him to be received by the King and Queen at court and went on to make much entertainment for him. He arranged a window overlooking the royal procession on the feast of Corpus Christi, one of the great festivities of the Lisbon year. He took Hervey to several of the nunneries around Lisbon, where many of the inmates were not members of religious orders but secular women who found it convenient to live there. Their grates were the venue for much sexual intrigue and enjoyment and of this Hervey took his full share.

In his *Journal* Hervey is unusually unspecific about his successes with women in this first protracted stay in Lisbon. Perhaps he took a little time to find his feet in these unfamiliar surroundings, where the pleasures of promiscuity were there for the taking, but in which society had stringent punishments for those, especially the women, who overstepped the mark – laxly as this was defined. Between entertainments, therefore, it is clear that he sought introductions to suitably receptive ladies. Quite shamelessly he relates one case of attempted procurement: 'I got an old woman that had been very useful to the late King, called Ellena, that Don Joao recommended to me. She promised to give me a letter to the Condessa d'Atougia, but tho' she told me she had, I met no success from it . . . '. another 'very beautiful' woman wrote to him and they met, presumably with the usual result, though he does not say so. He saw at a religious festival a 'very fine country-girl called Vincennes' whom he followed and got to know, and 'a most lovely piece she was'. One pleasure he put off until his next visit. At a bull-fight towards the end of August he met Marie-Anne-Leopoldine Princess of Holstein, married to a member of the Portuguese nobility and 'soon perceived she was game, which I thought would do when I returned'. In due course, it did.

On 2 September *Phoenix* sailed down-river, with Bemposto on board as a farewell gesture. Seeing that the royal castle was flying no colours Hervey turned to his guest saying that if it was was not for the latter's presence he would lower his own, to which Bemposto said 'Pray, do, it will be a good reproof to them'. *Phoenix'* colours were duly lowered, at which the castle fired a gun at her. Hervey anchored and went straight to the Secretary of State and had the officer in charge arrested, but obtaining an assurance that no Kings' ship would be fired on again he agreed to the officer's release. The whole incident underlines the corrupt state of Portuguese affairs, for the castle was not manned by its garrison but by others paid by them to do their duties.

It may be thought that in spending so long at Lisbon Hervey had laid himself open to a charge of dallying for his own convenience and pleasure; and indeed there was a sequel. In the summer of 1753 Hervey discovered that his Journal for the period had not been certified by the Admiralty, with the consequence that his pay was not authorized. It was not simply the length of stay at Lisbon that was the problem, but his apparent failure to carry out one part of his orders from the Admiralty – to carry with him from England and deliver to Gibraltar and Mahon two boxes of official documents. He had in fact passed these boxes to Captain Arbuthnot of *Nightingale*, which left Lisbon for Gibraltar in April 1752, only a fortnight or so after his arrival in the Tagus; and he notified the Admiralty of this. Nevertheless, the Admiralty was not satisfied that he had adequately fulfilled his commitments and would not approve his Journal for the period so that the Navy Board could not authorize his pay. A year later, on 25 July 1753, he wrote to John Clevland, the Admiralty Secretary in explanation:[2]

Sir

I am very sorry to find by a letter to my agent that their Lordships have thought proper to refuse the Certificate for my Journals on account of my stay in Lisbon River in my outward bound passage from England; I can assure your Lordships 'twas neither inclination nor pleasure that induced my stay there but finding his Majesty's ships *Garland* and *Nightingale* both bound up [ie into the Mediterranean] with remittances under Commdre Keppel's orders I remained for no other motive than that of not interfering with their sailing (and coming last there) to sail after them with the remittances for the troops in the garrisons, which I did as soon as ever they were shipped, besides Mr Keppel being then expected down [ie from the Mediterranean] every day after the *Garland* sailed I waited to see him that if he had any other orders to give me than those already received from the Admiralty I might put them in execution, as it was I pursued those given me by Captain Proby of his Majesty's ship *Lyme* dated the 5th of August 1752.

I hope these reasons in general will induce their Lordships to give me the necessary Certificate to my Journals for the receiving my pay, if not I shall beg leave to trouble them more particularly for I should be very sorry whilst I am endeavouring to merit their applause to have only proofs of their censure.

On consideration the writer would surely agree that it was not a well constructed letter, and the arguments in it can be better arranged as follows: By handing the documents over to Captain Arbuthnot I endeavoured to ensure their arrival at the earliest possible time. Subsequent events – the delay while I waited for remittances for the garrisons and for Commdre Keppel who was expected daily – surely show that I was right to have done so. His case, however, for staying so long (he was at Lisbon from 29 March to 15 September) was not a strong one, and in view of the alternative conclusion which might be drawn – that he had succumbed to the temptations of the land – he is perhaps right to present his case in a roundabout and confusing way.

His letter was considered by their Lordships on 27 November and his reasons were accepted. The Secretary wrote on the reverse: 'For the reasons given to pass the Journal. Let Cap Hervey know.'

There followed a circuit of the western Mediterranean, the first of several taking up the next three years. This one lasted six months, punctuated by calls at Cadiz, Gibraltar, Mahon, Villefranche, Genoa and Naples, and on the return leg at Gibraltar and Cadiz, reaching Lisbon again on 19 March 1753. At Cadiz he missed the freight from two Spanish vessels just arrived from the Indies but succeeded with $500,000 of the King of Spain's money for Naples, which won him a commission of about £1100. At Villefranche, which he was forced into by bad weather off Monaco, he was given immediate pratique, a more relaxed attitude by the King of Sardinia's officials there than was to be expected by British ships at most Mediterranean ports. The countries along the European shore had indeed a need for caution, since the British allowed North African trade into their ports at Gibraltar and Minorca, and North Africa was rife with plague, which had by this time almost disappeared from Europe.

At Villefranche he saw many old acquaintances including General Paterson, now governor for the King of Sardinia at Nice. The weather was stormy and *Phoenix* was held in Villefranche for several days. Hervey was at lunch with the officer in charge of the port and his daughters, old friends, when he became aware that a felucca carrying a number of passengers had been driven in and that the party was ashore in some distress. Going to them he found that it was the Marquis de Bernis and his wife, on their way to Venice where he was French ambassador. The lady he describes as 'very handsome indeed', though it would be uncharitable to assume that this was a factor in the assistance that he offered them. The ambassador and his wife accepted his offer of a passage to Genoa in *Phoenix*, coming aboard accompanied by a priest, a physician, a maid, an accompanying officer and four servants. They put to sea on 15 November, only to run into more bad weather from the eastward. In very violent conditions Hervey turned back for Villefranche. Most on board were sea sick, including Mme de Bernis, to whose needs *in extremis* Hervey attended personally, managing even in these circumstances to make up to her.

The ship now needed refitting and caulking, providing a week in which Hervey and his passengers enjoyed the hospitality of the shore, and in which he fell for the lady's charms and amiability. *Phoenix* was towed out of Villefranche by the boats of the Sardinian galleys on 23 November and this time made an easy passage to Genoa. Indeed, so good was the weather that he and his passengers dined on deck under an awning, to the strains of music provided by members of the crew.

At Genoa the passengers went ashore to lodge with the French minister, who invited Hervey to dinner the next day. By this time Mme de Bernis had fallen for him and welcomed all the attentions he paid to her as he sat next to her. Her husband, however, was more protective than many, leading Hervey to describe him as surly. But they soon departed for Venice, the lady crying at her parting from him. The incident provides a remarkable example of the charm and facility which enabled Hervey to make his way with women, and of his will to exert these qualities in the least favourable and least promising of circumstances.

Phoenix remained at Genoa for a month. It was for Hervey a round of dinners, balls, operas, suppers and musical entertainments among the upper strata of the nobility, allowing him the usual scope for affairs with married woman. He now became more familiar with the system of dalliance which may be described as *cicisbeatura*. This feature of Italian society in the mid eighteenth century is well described in relation to Horace Walpole,[3] who perhaps surprisingly was *cicisbeo* to one of the ladies of Florence in 1740, during his Grand Tour. Essentially, a *cicisbeo* was a married women's walking out companion, accompanying her in a devoted and dog-like way to social occasions as well as at home, though how intimate the relationship became varied from case to case. The *cicisbeo* was accepted as such by the husband (who was often engaged in similar activity elsewhere) and the existence of and frequent changes in these couplings was a matter of consuming interest in the fashionable society of the town.

Young Englishmen visiting Italy were much sought after as *cicisbeos*, and this formalization of infidelity provided Hervey with numerous opportunities during his visits to Italian ports – though his temperament did not always allow him to show the desired degree of subservience.

In fact, Hervey was not enthusiastic about any of the women with whom he associated on this visit to Genoa. Early in his visit he had met for the first time Pellinetta Brignole-Sale, then aged about 27, married to Rudolpho Brignole-Sale who was to be Doge of Genoa in 1762–64. He had met her sister-in-law in Paris and had been told something of Pellinetta herself by the Marquis de Bellegarde before he left England. Perhaps Hervey had expectations of her beauty, for he seems to have been immediately struck by her, describing her as 'very handsome and sensible for an Italian'. Nevertheless he did not improve his acquaintance with her during this visit, though thoughts of her may have dulled his appreciation of the other talent on offer.

He was introduced by M. Chauvelin, the French envoy, to many of the ladies of Genoa but in particular to Mme Doria and her daughter Mme Geronima Grimaldi de la Pietra, whose husband was in Rome. They attempted to establish him as the daughter's *cicisbeo*, but though Hervey was prepared to pay his attentions to her with considerable familiarity he would not be entrapped. A Mme Spinola, who already had a *cicisbeo*, was also desirous of acquiring him and he was in demand from the Brignoles. He seems to have enjoyed the competition.

On New Year's Day 1753 he left Genoa and coasted down towards Naples, where he had freight to deliver. He saw the dome of St Peter's in the distance, looked into Terracina, used the opportunity to familiarize himself with and record the sailing conditions in and on the onshore side of Ponza and the other islands in the Gulf of Gaeta and arrived in the Bay of Naples on the night of 4 January.

Naples at this time had been ruled since 1735 by the Spanish Bourbon Don Carlos who later became Carlos III of Spain. It was an uncomfortable rule, the native aristocracy disliking the Spanish and the people being poor and discontented. The Bourbon court was attached to the French interest, and though there was much good feeling towards the English among the Neapolitans themselves Britain had little influence and did little trade.

Phoenix was expected, indeed long expected, for she was carrying an immense cargo of specie from the King of Spain, and it may be thought that Hervey had dallied unprofessionally on the way – it was three months since he had taken it aboard at Cadiz. By way of welcome, or perhaps thanksgiving for its safe arrival, he was given immediate pratique and allowed into the quayside. The whole Neapolitan fleet was in port – four vessels, a 64, a 40 and two 30s.

Hervey immediately entered into an intense social life, meeting the British consul, the general commanding the fleet and the Princess of Franca-Villa, wife of a high court official, for whom he had letters of introduction, and many others. His visit coincided with the bankruptcy of the consul, Edward Allen, from which arose the need, or perhaps the opportunity would be a better description of how Hervey saw it, for him to take upon himself the interests of his fellow-citizens in the city. To this end he went to the chief minister, the Marquese di Fogliani and among the matters he raised was the case of John Vernon, an English visitor.

Vernon had for some time made a mistress of his washerwoman's daughter, and intending to move on to Sicily had decided to take her with him dressed as a man. The girl's parents had prevented this at the last minute, Hervey says for the money to be made from the case, and the girl had made a deposition accusing Vernon of rape. Hervey went to Fogliani a second time and remonstrated with him, to no avail because the case had by then become politically sensitive. Vernon was in due course arrested and held in the Castel Nuovo, adjoining the royal palace. The British in Naples wanted to make an official protest, but Hervey now counselled discretion, at the same time writing to Lord Holderness, Secretary of State, on this and other concerns. He had, however, a plan.

He gave orders that if Vernon came on board *Phoenix* he himself should not be told. He then arranged with his officers and an adventurer named Charles Lee that they should visit Vernon in the Castel Nuovo by night going in a coach, dress the prisoner in an officer's greatcoat, and bring him out with them. This simple plan defeated the guards and Vernon went secretly on board *Phoenix*. The result was uproar among the Neapolitans and delight in the British community. An officer was sent to Hervey next day to demand the prisoner back, to which he responded that he would have been told if he was in *Phoenix*, and that they must have murdered him in the castle. In any case, if he did come on board he (Hervey) would on no account give him up. A boat was hired and Vernon was sent away to Civita Vecchia, in the Papal States.

These happenings did not prejudice Hervey's standing in Naples society, indeed they may well have enhanced it. He dined, he danced, he supped, he went to the opera, he made love. Mrs Mahony, wife of an Irishman in the service of the King of Naples, brought him together with the Contessa di Palena and tried to establish him as her *cicisbeo*. Hervey was 'rather taken by a kind of surprise here than from any inclination of his own', for the good lady was not as young as she professed to be and only of moderate looks. However, she was willing and very passionate, and he made the most of his frequent opportunities.

The Contessa, however was not the only one. Hervey went to Caserta where the court was at the time, was received by the King and Queen, and visited Fogliani but refused to dine there, the suggestion being that he took this attitude to show his displeasure at the minister's equivocation over Vernon. He went on to dine, however, with the Princess of Franca-Villa and stayed all afternoon, performing miracles twice before he left. With the beautiful Princess of Alieno he was equally successful, but to have three mistresses at once in the same port was excessively – and surely unnecessarily – hazardous. The Contessa found out and made a public scene at a ball.

But all good things come to an end and on 22 February, after a stay of seven weeks *Phoenix* left Naples and calling at Gibraltar for orders reached Lisbon on 19 March. This time he stayed for little over a fortnight. The operas, the convents and all the life that he had enjoyed on his last visit were still there but he quickly picked up a freight of 65,000 moidores (£87,000) and left on 5 April. Before he did so, however, he had an argument with the merchants. Captain Howe had been there shortly before and had agreed to take a commission of one-half per cent only, half the going rate. Hervey refused to accept less than one per cent and when he came up with Howe in *Dolphin* at Gibraltar he continued to disagree with him.

Hervey now took *Phoenix* on a second circuit of the western Mediterranean, calling at much the same succession of ports as previously and not returning to Lisbon until September. His itinerary was dictated by the destinations of the freight he was carrying, which included Mahon, Marseilles and Genoa. At Mahon he met Edgcumbe for the first time since the latter had taken up the command. He also had the distinction there of being admitted a member of the local Lodge of Freemasons, though there is no evidence that the brotherhood played any important part in his subsequent life. At Genoa he was refused immediate pratique and therefore, after landing his freight and talking to many friends at the pratique office or in boats that came out to him, sailed on to Leghorn.

The Florentine authorities were more accommodating, the Governor sending to Florence for special pratique, which was granted two days later. After a few days he had a letter from Mme de la Pietra at Genoa regretting that he had not waited there for pratique, to which he was able to reply that they ordered these things much better at Leghorn. The entries in Hervey's *Journal* while he was there reflect a wide range of interests. He records that he sent as a present to the Duchess of Chartres in Paris, a 'very fine box of flowers . . . that had been bespoke a year . . . put in a box of blue velvet embroidered with silver, and the Orléans arms over it, that was put in a white satin case, embroidered with gold, and the direction to "To the Duchess of Chartres" in gold letters embroidered . . .' But what kind of flowers? They cannot have been fresh flowers, neither are dried flowers likely to have been a year in the making. It seems probable that they were of silk, and what the whole assembly cost cannot now be estimated. He found by reading the English periodicals that at Lord Bristol's request the King had given his sisters the status and title of an earl's daughters, as if their father had lived long enough to succeed to the title. By a peculiar quirk of the system he and his younger brothers could not be recognized in this way, since the style he enjoyed as the son of a Baron, the Honourable Augustus Hervey, was the same as that to which he would have been entitled as the younger son of an earl. Hervey's view of the matter was that his brother should have busied himself with obtaining something of more substance, though he had no doubt his sisters would enjoy being Ladies.

Another letter told him of the bankruptcy of M. de Caze in Paris, owing two million livres, and indeed the family were soon reduced to relative poverty. Lord Bath (the William Pulteney who had brought the young Elizabeth Chudleigh to London) wrote from England asking him to send him 400 yards of crimson damask. He went to Pisa for a festival with illuminations and there met Sir Horace Mann, the consul in Florence, who brought a party of English with him including Hervey's friend the Earl of Pembroke and Lord North, the future Prime Minister. Back at Leghorn he had nearly a month of entertainment and enjoyment. He dined with the Marquis de Silva, the Spanish consul, he gave a concert at which the famous violinist Pietro Nardini performed, he gave dinners on board for the Governor and others, he was dined by the Governor in return, he gave them all an illumination along the canal and its bridges with music and a cold collation. In all, he spent a great deal of money. Several of the ladies whom he met he describes as beautiful but he only became intimate with one, Signora Testori, wife of the commissary, with whom he spent 'many agreeable evenings'.

On 20 July he sailed for Naples and after a short stay on to Marseilles where with his usual facility, after being entertained for several days and going to the theatre, he met the mistress of a French colonel, a Mlle Sarrazin. The next day he decided to sail, whereupon the young lady insisted that she would come with him. She was entirely determined and came on board with one of her maids. There must be some reservations about the relationships of a ship's captain with his female passengers and Hervey says nothing more than that she was a 'delightful fine woman'. Nevertheless, on reaching Lisbon he set her up in a quinta that he rented and lived with her there between his other activities.

On his way he called at Mahon and then Gibraltar. There he heard the first rumbles of trouble with the Moors with which he had later to deal. The governor, General Braddock, wrote an account to him but as he appeared to be in negotiation with them Hervey sailed on, following the letter of the orders which he had received from Edgcumbe at Mahon, and doubtless following also his inclination to get to Lisbon as soon as possible. At Cadiz he found Howe in *Dolphin* and had another disagreement with him. Howe, who was his senior in the Navy list by two years, had also heard of the problem with the Moors. When Hervey sent him the orders he had received from Edgcumbe Howe made to change them, in the sense that Hervey should stay at Cadiz to be ready to go to Braddock's assistance. They quarrelled, but eventually Howe allowed the original orders to stand. *Phoenix* reached Lisbon on 12 September and Hervey immediately found Mlle Sarrazin accommodation at Bairro Alta which they could enjoy together.

The fact that Hervey had set himself up with a mistress in a private establishment did not prevent him from pursuing and enjoying others of the laxly promiscuous women of Lisbon. Indeed, while he was there he had one of the most intriguing – and sexually rewarding – experiences of his life, an experience that did not lack a due input of mystery and fear. His account of its inception cannot be bettered:

Saturday 23rd (of October) in the evening as I was coming from Odivellas convent and over Campo Pequeno, my chaise was stopped by a man on horseback, who very civilly pulled off his hat and said he must speak to me. I asked him what he wanted and if he knew me. I was extremely surprised and thought it was some design of assassinating me. He said my name was Hervey and he had something to speak to myself. I never went without pocket-pistols and therefore held one in my hand and told him to come and speak to me. He came up, and begged me not to be surprised, that on the other end of the *campo* in a by-land, there was a chaise which waited for me, and had orders to conduct me to a lady that would and must speak to me. I said I knew of none that I would risk such an adventure for, and that if he did not go off I would shoot him. He said that might be, but if I did, me and my family would repent it; that he was not surprised at my receiving him so, but that he would deposit himself in the hands of my servants and remain in my chaise until my return, providing I would give my word of honour not to be followed, and that he could assure me I should have a reason to thank him. Whilst he talked thus another came up, and told me I must go. So, in short, I found myself in a manner taken, and thought I might as well go by fair as foul means. I could make nothing of it, but began to find it was not to rob me however. I got out of my chaise and left orders for that to wait there till my return. I walked with these two across the *campo*, where I found a chaise called a pacquet boat, that is an Italian chaise, four wheels and six mules in it. The servants had brown liveries. I got in and they immediately drove like the devil. I then indeed began to fear I was nicked and going to be sent to some d—'d place for some work or other of the convents that I was discovered in, and knew I could not help myself.

'Twas now about two hours in the night when I arrived at a little quinta, after having been turned and turned about I know not where or how. We stopped at a wall, and I was conducted in at a small door at a garden, and conveyed in the dark to a house that seemed pretty large, up a small pair of stairs. I was quite struck with all this, as not a word passed, but one of the men led me by the hand without a syllable, and I knew all resistance would be vain, and if I was to be murdered there needed not this ceremony. At length I came into an apartment, small but very finely furnished, and with six large wax tapers in it. Here I began to take a little comfort. I was however left and told to wait here. I could not conceive what this was to end in, and a thousand ideas took possession of me by turns, and so quick that I had not possession of myself to form any conjectures. But soon after I was brought a pen, ink and paper and bid to write to my servants to wait for me till daylight in the same spot, or at least to be there at that time. This I complied with, and liked that very much. Soon after this a small hanging door opened, and I was called by a female voice into another room that was very finely hung, and a very rich bed in it, only one silver lamp on a table.

The lady was of a very fine stature, fine hair, fine teeth and eyes, much painted after the Portuguese manner. She caressed me very much, and told me if she had not seen me so, she should have been the most miserable wretch in the world, as she had been ever since the bull-feast last year that she saw me, and perceived I had taken notice of her. I could not recall anything about it, nor was I recovered of my surprise, it appeared all a dream to me. She perceived the amazement I was in, and caressed me the more. However, feeling myself in the arms of a very fine and a very luxurious woman, those sensations began to get the better of all others, as they were ever ready enough to do with me. A maid servant soon after brought some sweetmeats and water. I took only a dried apricot and ate it. She told me our time was short and we must go to bed, which I did not hesitate as she had fired me all over. I put my pocket-pistols under my head, and passed a most joyous night.

About 3 or 4 in the morning she told me I must dress and be gone. I asked if I was not worthy the repetition of this feast, and if I was not to be trusted with whom I was indebted for it. She told me 'twas impossible for me to undertake anything, that I might be sure whenever she could she would see me, for she had long had no other happiness, and much to the effect that all this preparation had been long bringing about to have me here. She cried very much, and said she would rather die that moment than not hope to see me again soon. In short, she gave me every proof that she was very much in love with me, and I had reason to believe it. She told me she would send the same person to me that first came to my chaise, and who should now conduct me back, and that I must always do as he directed me and never attempt to alter the time or even an hour of her appointment, as hers did not solely depend on herself. She then slipped a very fine diamond ring on my finger and told me to keep it, but I refused it and gave it her again and asked her for a lock of hair, which she gave me, and a little bawbling ring she had on her finger. I told her I would keep that and no other. She kissed me and pressed me to take the other, but I would not, and threw it on the bed, and told her I should be very much affronted if she insisted any more. I took my leave of her, intreating I might soon see her again, for I was very much in love with her.

The man drove him back, refusing to be bribed into telling Hervey anything about the lady. When he got back to his own quinta he had the suspicions of Mlle Sarrazin to cope with, she refusing to believe that he had been at cards all night.

It was 7 November before he heard from the mysterious lady again, when she made an appointment by letter for him to be brought to her the next evening. Pretending to go to Odivellas he was again picked up and taken to another quinta, nearer at hand than on the previous occasion, where he spent another glorious time, though it was curtailed to only four hours.

Shortly after this second meeting Hervey left Lisbon and was away for three months. The story continues in March 1754, when he returned. It was not many days before a letter was delivered to *Phoenix* in which the lady gave him directions for another meeting at the same quinta. He followed the instructions and was entertained as before, until 3 am. A further summons came later in the month and he spent the night at the quinta, returning on board the next morning and spending the day in bed.

He found the lady more attractive than ever but still determined not to reveal her identity. The style in which she lived and the deference shown her by her servants showed that she was a person of some account and he determined to find out who. It was three weeks before he heard from her again, and this time he arranged for one of his servants to follow the chaise in which he was carried on his way. In this way he found out where the quinta was and who owned it, but the trail did not follow through to the occupant. Four days later he was summoned again, and again took measures to trace her. The servant waited after he had left the quina and when a chaise drawn by six mules left followed it into Lisbon. His report showed that Hervey's admirer was the Duchess of Cadaval.

Hervey was amazed, more because the Duchess had concealed her French origin and facility in French than because of her exalted status. She was formerly Henrietta-Julia-Gabriela, a Princess of the House of Lorraine, and had married the Duke in 1739. At the time of her liaison with Hervey she had been a widow for two years and was suffering from the intrigues and dangers of life at the Portuguese court. Unwisely, it may be thought, Hervey now determined to show the Duchess that he had discovered her and went to her house on the pretence of having a petition to present. She was surprised and disturbed to see him and told him how dangerous their association could be if it became known. He saw her once more, when in early June she sent for him to her house in Lisbon. He records simply that he did not stay long because of the danger of spies.

References

1. PRO, ADM2/74
2. PRO, ADM1/1888
3. Ketton-Cremer, 1964, p65

CHAPTER VII

Sorties into Africa

A natural diplomat

Returning to November 1753, we find Howe at Lisbon in *Dolphin* and again putting pressure on Hervey to return to Gibraltar to be at hand to deal with the Moorish problem. Reluctant as he was to go without identifying his so secretive lady friend, on 17 November he dropped down the Tagus in preparation for departure, and had the honour of being escorted by the King and Queen in their yacht. The next day he sailed and on 23rd of the month reached Gibraltar, where he intended only to victual ship and proceed to Mahon, where the dockyard would be able to give *Phoenix* a much needed overhaul. General Braddock, however, requested him to go over to Tetuan, forty miles away on the African shore, and settle matters with the Moors.

The relationship between Britain and the inhabitants of the North African littoral was an equivocal one. On the one hand North Africa, Barbary, was a viper's nest of corsairs who preyed on European shipping in the Mediterranean, especially the rich cargoes passing to and fro between Europe and the Levant, and Britain was as concerned as any other nation to hold such attacks in check. This was one of the remits of the squadron kept there in time of peace. The most pernicious sources of trouble were to the eastward, at Algiers and Tripoli. In the western Mediterranean, however, Britain had an opposing interest, because of her bases at Gibraltar and Minorca. Since both footholds were on territory regarded by Spain as entirely Spanish the amount of co-operation and trade to be expected from Spain was minimal; and in time of war of course lack of co-operation was replaced by hostility. Britain therefore had treaty arrangements with the Moors under which they provided Gibraltar in particular with supplies and in return Moorish ships were allowed access to the two British ports, virtually the only places of trade or succour open to them away from the North African coast.

Morocco was ruled by the Sultan, but remoteness from the towns such as Tetuan on the Mediterranean shore rendered his control weak and often ineffective. In 1753 the Alcaide (Governor) of Tetuan, a gentleman whose arabic name Hervey transliterates as Mahomett Lucas, was asserting his independence from the Sultan and attempting to blackmail the British into providing presents and better terms in return for an undertaking to continue the town's trade with Gibraltar. The Alcaide in fact held some strong cards, for Gibraltar was dependent on provisions from the Moroccan towns, of which Tetuan was one of the nearest, while if they abandoned trade with the British the Moroccans could expect it to be replaced by other northern European traders.

Hervey arrived at Tetuan on 28 November. The anchorage in the bay he describes as nicely sheltered with a westerly wind but dangerously exposed with the wind in the east, a factor destined to play an important part in his negotiations. The beach was defended by a small fort and the river on which the town stood, several miles inland, had a dangerous bar at its entrance but no other means of defence.

He began with letters to William Petticrew, the British consul, and to the Alcaide, the latter combining sorrow that British interests were being treated so brusquely with a statement that he would not leave until matters were righted. Petticrew replied that he had been ordered to leave, on which Hervey told him to show some backbone or risk losing face. Hervey's intention was to divide the principal merchants of the town, who were dependent on the British trade, from the Alcaide, who appeared to want status and presents. He was fortuitously assisted in this by the arrival of a tartane carrying the chief imam of the town, Ahmed Barracha, on his return from a four-year pilgrimage to Mecca, together with his wives and servants. He now kept Barracha on board *Phoenix*, a move which disturbed the townspeople, with whom their chief imam was popular, and who blamed his detention on the Alcaide's attitudinizing. He increased the pressure further by preventing an incoming Swedish merchantman from trading with them.

A reconnaissance of the countryside between the beach and Tetuan itself showed that boats could row upriver without any difficulty to within two miles of so of the town, and that the remaining distance was open and did not allow any prospect of ambush. Nevertheless, he preferred the diplomatic approach to any show of force and sent Barracha ashore under parole to return, to enable him to muster opposition to the Alcaide. Petticrew then wrote to him that the Alcaide would not negotiate with him, only with Hervey, and he should come ashore and meet him. Hervey, however, had little faith in the consul's judgement and feared a trap. He agreed to come ashore, but only if Barracha and two of the leading men of the town came on board *Phoenix* as hostages.

This plan was put in hand, but as Barracha came into sight on shore on the morning of 4 December the wind came strong from the east and Hervey was forced to cut his cable and run for Gibraltar. He was back the next afternoon and determined on the morning of the 6th to go to the Alcaide with Barracha, trusting that the imam's presence would avert any false play.

At nine o'clock he was on shore with Barracha and an escort of forty horsemen provided by the Alcaide to take him to town. As they were about to move off *Phoenix* got under way and made a signal. The wind had gone easterly again, forcing Hervey to abandon the enterprise for a second time and to return to the ship. This time it was nearly a week before *Phoenix* could get back from Gibraltar.

On 13 December, then, Hervey went ashore once more and was escorted with Barracha up to the town, a walled place on a hill, with narrow Moorish streets and surrounded by groves of oranges and lemons. They went to the Alcaide, who received them in state sitting on a cushion surrounded by his retainers, while Hervey was provided with a chair close in front of him. The Moors were mainly old men, Barracha with a long white beard, contrasting sharply with the 29-year-old British naval officer, a difference that the Alcaide was not slow to comment on. The negotiations that followed were wordy but, it being a Friday the Moslem holy day, soon completed. Hervey combined much soft soap about the Alcaide's character and the cordiality between the two countries with harder arguments about the strength of the British position and the benefits that Tetuan gained from trade with them. The Alcaide's complaints, in so far as he voiced them, were that they were unsatisfactory partners, and that the British were opening up trade with Arzila, a town to the westward ruled by an uncle of the Sultan who was said to be in rebellion against him.

By one o'clock the Alcaide and Hervey had signed an agreement, essentially a repeat of the existing treaty, more compliments had been exchanged and presents given. The Alcaide offered to entertain Hervey with some shooting ashore and a boar-hunt, Hervey gave him six barrels of gunpowder and distributed $100 as presents to his retinue. The powder was a troublesome gift. The Alcaide complained that he should have received six full barrels, not the small casks of Admiralty issue, while Hervey had much difficulty in obtaining approval of this outlay from the British authorities. Indeed for the monetary presents given he failed to obtain any recompense at all.

Hervey, Barracha and the other principal men of the town then returned to the consul's house for dinner, which he describes as 'indifferent . . . from the damn bad cooks'. The next day was windless so Hervey went shooting and had much sport. The boar-hunt was scheduled for the following day, but the wind coming favourable he excused himself and set sail for Mahon, where he arrived on Christmas Eve.

Hervey was at Mahon for seven weeks. He took the opportunity to have *Phoenix* careened in the dockyard and found most of her sheathing gone. It was before the days of copper sheathing and no seasoned wood was at hand to re-sheathe her, so she went unsheathed. All this took time. During January 1754 he records that he had his first attack of gout, causing much pain in his left foot, so that he could not use it for ten days or so. By the end of the month he was bored with Mahon and wanted only to get to sea.

He had brought Mlle Sarrazin with him from Lisbon, indeed she had been on board throughout the negotiations at Tetuan, and found her 'the best tempered creature that ever breathed, always in good humour, cheerful and ready to oblige; she made time pass away very agreeably'. She was, however, very much affected by seasickness and while at Mahon was much concerned about her mother, whom she had heard was ill at Aix-en-Provence.

Hervey determined to land her at Marseilles. He left Mahon on 11 February but off the French coast was hit by a very hard westerly and forced to run to the east, taking shelter in the bay of Hyéres. When the wind eased he made for La Ciotat, where he landed Mlle Sarrazin, hiring a chaise for her and giving her two hundred half-skinner pieces – about £350. No doubt she got to Aix. Hervey tried to meet her at Marseilles in the following August but was unable to obtain pratique.

Lisbon now beckoned and after calling at Gibraltar and Cadiz, where no freight seemed likely, he arrived in the Tagus on 11 March. *Phoenix* remained at Lisbon until 21 June and during these three months Hervey entertained himself in his usual way. It was during this stay that he had the second series of assignations with the Duchess of Cadaval, referred to earlier. Her Grace's favours did not, however discourage him from seeking other female company. As usual he spent much time and had much satisfaction at the grates of various convents. He now became intimate with the Princess of Holstein, the lady who he had marked down as 'game' on an earlier visit. She wrote to him to visit her and they duly had their way with each other. She may have been almost too much for him; he comments 'She was a very fine woman but very fat. I went and supped at the French Ambassador's to recuperate'.

One day, coming back from Odivellas he went by appointment to meet a young lady called Donna Felliciana de Sylvera, a beautiful girl of about 15 to whom he had made up many times below her window. This time he persuaded her, after two or three hours together, to (using one of his favourite phrases) 'let me make the best use of our remaining time'; to his delight they met again many times. There were several others.

All was not pleasure, however. In April of 1754 Hervey stood for St Edmundsbury at the general election, *in absentia*. In contrast, however, to the usual situation there was a four-cornered fight for the two seats. Bury normally returned two Whig members, and it was to be expected that the candidates nominated by the heads of the two prominent Whig families in West Suffolk (Lord Bristol at Ickworth and the Duke of Grafton at Euston) would be returned. If there was any doubt the small electorate, consisting of the twenty-eight members of the Corporation, could readily be persuaded by suitable financial inducement, which ran as high as four figures per head, that the candidates put up in the Bristol and Grafton interests were the best. On this occasion Lord Bristol nominated his brother Augustus while the Duke put forward his son-in-law, Lord Petersham. The Herveys, however, failed to present an unbroken front; Augustus's uncle Felton Hervey, one of the 1st Earl's younger sons who had already held the seat for some years, also put himself forward and was supported by the Tory interest, headed by the Davers family at Rushbrooke. In addition to the embarrassment implicit in Hervey fighting Hervey there was the position of Frederick Hervey (later the Earl-Bishop), who had married the daughter of Lady Davers and the late Sir Jermyn — the latter never a favourite of the 1st Earl of Bristol and brother of Augustus's bête noire in the West Indies, Admiral Thomas Davers. Lady Davers headed the Felton Hervey interest, while her daughter and son-in-law lived at Ickworth and attempted to forward the affairs of the absent Augustus. A Mr Crofts stood as the second Tory.

At first there was no concern among the Whig Herveys, but Felton began to make his mark — perhaps Lord Bristol, who combined pride with obstinacy, did not dig deep enough into his money bags — and on the day Lord Petersham received 16 votes, while the two Herveys each polled 15. Augustus was still at Lisbon when he heard from Lord Bristol of the tie. The news arrived on 12 May, seven days before his thirtieth birthday. Following accepted procedure the tie was referred to the House of Commons, who later in the year declared Felton Hervey elected. His nephew had to wait for a by-election in 1757 to win a seat.

Hervey had now made three leisurely circuits of the western Mediterranean and was to make two and half more before the threat of war again loomed over Europe. Though the next fourteen months, from June 1754 to August 1755, were mostly, for *Phoenix'* captain if not for her crew, a time of dining out and dalliance they were punctuated by two short spells during which the King's business took precedence.

When he left Lisbon he was again in poor health with gout-like symptoms but had recovered by the time he reached Gibraltar on 13 July, where he found Edgcumbe in port. Two days later the sloop *Raven* arrived from England, carrying the British consul at Algiers and the customary presents from the King to the Dey, presents whose principal objective was to keep the Dey to his treaty obligations, including not preying on British shipping. Edgcumbe sent Hervey to Algiers to deliver both the presents and the Consul. After a slow passage with light winds *Phoenix* arrived at the end of July and was duly saluted with twenty-one guns.

Hervey found the bay open and dangerous in rough weather, full of shoals and with a strong swell setting in, all of this a serious barrier to any attack or bombardment from the sea.

Algiers was nominally part of the Turkish empire but the Dey was in practice an independent ruler. The next day Hervey went ashore, receiving a salute of nine guns, and after meeting the commanding Admiral and dining with one of the principal English merchants was received in audience by the Dey. This luminary sat in an alcove in a long gallery, where the newly arrived Consul and the English merchants kissed his hand, though Hervey shook hands and kissed his cheek. The Dey was very taken by one of the presents, a high quality fowling piece, but took little notice of the cloth, the watches and the furniture that the King had sent him. The Dey gave Hervey ten bullocks and a large amount of fruit and vegetables for his crew.

Algiers was by no means a closed city at this time. As well as a number of English merchants Hervey saw a group of Spanish friars running a charitable hospital and had dinner with the Swedish consul and his two pretty daughters. The women of Algiers all veiled themselves on his approach, though he noted that the better looking of them took a little time to do so, allowing the foreigners to see something of their beauty. Noting also the numerous family burial places he was told that these were the favoured places for widows to meet their lovers. He found the countryside around Algiers pleasant but little cultivated, and noted an abundance of shells and other fossils at quite high elevation.

The next day Hervey took leave of the Dey, whose Treasurer gave him two tigers. These he intended for the Emperor, but gives no reason why. An English lady, a Miss Douglas, gave him an antelope which he also took with him when he sailed next day. Faced with an unusual proposition Hervey was seldom at a loss and the tigers were on board until *Phoenix* arrived at Leghorn later in August. There he handed them over to the Governor of the city to give to the Emperor. Whether they eventually reached Vienna is not recorded.

After a circuit of the French and Italian ports *Phoenix* arrived at Gibraltar in October and was called upon for a second time to settle the affairs of the Moroccan towns. At Tetuan the Alcaide was again making difficulties because of British trade with Arzila. This time Hervey decided on a show of force and called in *Raven* from Malaga to join. Meeting *Dolphin* as he left Gibraltar he took her also and on 16 October the squadron anchored off Tetuan. Hervey exchanged letters with the Alcaide, in which the latter affirmed that he did not care who traded with Arzila. However, before further negotiations could take place the wind went into the east and the squadron had to run for Tangier. There Hervey corresponded with the Governor and obtained an assurance of friendship from him, but did not go ashore because of the weather.

He sailed at once for Arzila on the Atlantic coast, was saluted in due form and went ashore. The town was controlled by Mullah Mustadee, an uncle of the Sultan, who had asserted his independence, bolstered by a force estimated by Hervey to be of 10,000 men. He had started to trade with Gibraltar, a trade which led to concern among the merchants at Tetuan that they would lose out. Hervey went ashore to the rather wretched town and was escorted through streets lined with armed men to the Mullah, an old man who received him sitting in a mahogany chair of English manufacture. The usual expressions of desire for friendship with the British and for trade with Gibraltar were given and presents were exchanged; Hervey gave a gun, a pair of pistols and six half-barrels of powder, receiving in return a fine horse from the Mullah's stable. British naval power had been displayed once again, expressions of friendship would have at least a temporary calming effect, and Hervey had concealed how dependent Gibraltar was on the trade about which the Moors were squabbling.

After this North African expedition Hervey spent Christmas at Lisbon, arriving on 18 November and leaving on 4 January 1755. He passed much of his time with Don Joao Bemposto, visiting convents and generally enjoying himself. Bemposto took him often to court, including a private concert of the Queen's at which her daughters sang. He describes a visit to the palace at Belem at which the King had a good-humoured conversation with him and the Queen showed off a Maltese dog that Hervey had given her.

On 23 April after visiting Gibraltar, Mahon and Genoa, he returned to Lisbon for a stay of two months. Bemposto took him almost immediately to Court and he received a ticket for the King's new Opera House, a magnificent and correspondingly expensive baroque building by the architect Joao Carlos Bibliena, destined to be destroyed with most of the city in the great Lisbon earthquake later that year. The work performed was Alexandre nell' Indie. On the King of Portugal's birthday he dressed ship and fired a salute, later in the day going to the opera again, this time to see a performance of a pre-Mozartian version of La Clemenza di Tito.

He mentions few women on these two visits, probably because his mind was taken up with Mme Brignole-Sale away in Genoa. The Princess of Holstein's name is mentioned, Hervey spending a long evening with her while her husband was away. In December he took on board and kept a local woman of the name of Joanna, perhaps the only time that he admits to deliverately taking a mistress into one of his ships. A preliminary whiff of the great Tavora conspiracy of three years later comes from his pages at one point. He noticed at the opera that the King had eyes for no one but the young Marchioness of Tavora. Later at the theatre Hervey flirted gently with her, not daring to venture very far onto what might be considered royal territory. In avoiding involvement he did right. The conspiracy, in which an attack was made on the King and the origins of which were complex but included His Majesty's love affairs with members of the Tavora family, was used by the minister Pombal to rid himself of political enemies, and most of the family were executed.

On 18 June Hervey gave a farewell dinner on board *Phoenix* to his

Portuguese friends and took her down the Tagus. At the same time he heard that nine French men-of-war were off Cascais and found that Castres, the British minister, knew nothing of them. He went with Bemposto to the King, who was displeased at their presence. Later Bemposto took him in a Portuguese yacht to Cascais and they identified each ship. The Portuguese were most displeased at this unwelcome visit and would let only six of the Frenchmen come up the Tagus, this being the limit allowed by treaty. *Phoenix* was the only British man-of-war at Lisbon and Hervey was quick to send a full account of the Frenchmen to the Admiralty,[1] an admirable example of his sense of the importance of good intelligence gathering. On 24 June he left the Tagus carrying much wanted stores for the fleet and intent on letting Edgcumbe know of the French position. After calling at Mahon and meeting Edgcumbe at sea he reached Genoa on 27 July, where he soon found that the shadows of impending war were beginning to darken the European scene.

But for Hervey, in spite of all these diversions, pleasant or as duty called, the years 1754 and 1755 were taken up, as often as visits to Genoa permitted, with one of the few affairs in which his heart seems to have been touched as well as his passions aroused. Hervey had first heard of Pellinetta Brignole-Sale in January 1752, when on a journey down to Deptford the Marquis de Bellegarde had given him a long account of her. He met her in person for the first time at Genoa on 30 November 1752, and again several times during the following month, when he was *cicisbeo* to Mme Grimaldi de la Pietra. She was then about 27 and he was immediately attracted. Their relationship does not, however, appear to have made any progress at that time, in contrast to the usual momentum with which his affairs developed.

Apart from a fleeting call in June 1753, during which *Phoenix* was not given pratique, Hervey's next visit to Genoa was not until August 1754. Within a day of two of his arrival he was invited to a conversazione at Pellinetta's and it was on this occasion that their association really began. It ripened quickly and by September he was escorting her about and had in fact become her *cicisbeo*. He gave a party on board for her and thirty guests at which they danced nearly all night. She now made many professions of love, of which her relations appear to have approved, though others in the town, including the Grimaldi family to which Mme de la Pietra belonged, thought less highly of the new arrangement. Hervey describes Pellinetta as very beautiful, a fine musician, religiously minded and not happily married. Her husband Rodolpho Brignole-Sale, the future Doge, he thought a 'sour, niggardly, ill-looking man', whose main preoccupation was his money.

After a fortnight of enjoyment Hervey took *Phoenix* off to Leghorn, where he landed the tigers from Algiers. With him went his close friend the Earl of Pembroke accompanied by his current mistress, known as the Rena. At Leghorn there was much entertainment but Hervey kept away from his lady friends there on account of Pellinetta. After a week it was time to return to Genoa and Hervey determined to make fools of the health authorities there. Sending *Phoenix* under his first lieutenant he went with Goldsworthy the consul and servants overland along the coast to Lerici, where they took a felucca and landed at Genoa the next morning. In absenting himself from the ship without good reason he was overtly breaking the rules and would have been liable to court martial and to severe penalties had anything gone amiss. *Phoenix* had, however, arrived safely and was still in quarantine, a matter for considerable amusement at the authorities' expense. Pellinetta was at her country home at Torazzo, about six miles from the city. He lodged with her sisters and walked out most days to her house, the road being bad for horses. Thus he saw much of her, but only for a short time, *Phoenix* sailing for Mahon on 29 September.

Hervey did not return to Genoa until 2 February 1755. His arrival was marked by another campaign against the Genoese health office, who at first insisted that *Phoenix* would have to undergo routine quarantine, having come from Gibraltar, a port in direct contact with North Africa. Hervey protested that she had been three weeks at sea and had no illness aboard. He was told, perhaps grudgingly, that he could have pratique the next day, on which he went immediately to the Brignole house. It was carnival time in Genoa.

M. Kinsky, nephew of the French minister, had been trying without success to gain acceptance as Pellinetta's *cicisbeo*. Though egged on by those about her he had so far not succeeded and with Hervey's return had no chance of doing so. But in spite of Pellinetta's attentions and declarations to him Hervey was annoyed at Kinsky's aspirations and asked for a public sign from her. She therefore gave a great dinner for Hervey and his officers to which the Frenchman was not invited thus bringing his visits to an end.

Hervey was in demand also from other women of his acquaintance, including Momima de la Pietra, but at Pellinetta's insistence kept away from such entanglements. In return he got her to let him stay with her all night, a dangerous enterprise fraught with difficulties and needing much pretence to keep his presence from her husband and her servants. Three weeks after his arrival their plan was put into effect. She feigned an eye infection and darkened her room for day or two. In the evening he made as if to leave as usual, on which she asked everyone present to leave the room for a time. Hervey then slipped into the bedroom by a side door and got into the large curtained bed, covering himself with a very thick quilt which in the gloom concealed him well enough. The company came back, including her husband, and were there for an hour. The husband came in again after supper and showed her some Indian handkerchiefs, for which he wanted to bring up a light, also offering what Hervey calls 'his d——d *douceurs*', all this giving the aspirant lover something of a fright as he lay concealed beside her. But shortly he went away, leaving as Hervey says 'me in the arms of one of the loveliest women that ever was. I lay till near daylight and performed wonders.' In the morning he escaped from the house without difficulty.

A repetition of this escapade a few days later encountered greater difficulties. The night was as enjoyable as ever but when Hervey tried to leave he found all the doors locked. He hid behind a curtain, in considerable trepidation, and when Pellinetta and her servants all went to mass managed to find a way out. The fright made her forbid a further attempt. However, by this time an all night stay was a work of supererogation, for he was in her bed every morning before company arrived and again in the evening after they had gone.

Hervey had a poor opinion of the education and general thoughtlessness of Italian women in general. In an earlier letter to Lady Townsend he describes their inadequacies at some length, including this damning passage on their intellectual capabilities:

> The Italian women are such fools that if three of them are got together; 'tis possible that one may say that 2 and 2 makes 4, another that 2 and 2 makes 5, and whilst the dispute grows warm the third shall be embarrassed which to decide for.

Hyperbole, perhaps, but a reflection with much truth in it of the general state of female education even among the best of Italian society at that time. He gives the impression that Pellinetta was several classes above such witless inanity, an impression that is supported by his usual preference for company of reasonable intelligence. Nevertheless, she had taken a vow, consequent upon her child's illness, not to go to the opera all that carnival season. And now she swore on the cross which she wore round her neck that she would never admit any other to her bed. Hervey was not sufficiently naive to believe her.

Phoenix left Genoa on 11 March, after a five-week stay. When Hervey reached Mahon, he says, his love for her made him cross and annoyed at everything around him; one can sympathize with his crew. He wrote frequently to Pellinetta while he was away and the fact that he was enamoured with her became widely known, certainly reaching Lisbon. At a concert there the King came up to him and lightheartedly reproached him with wanting to return to his love in Italy. But he was soon away again, making Genoa on 27 July and this time receiving immediate pratique. Hervey went at once to Pellinetta and was much in her company and that of members of her family during the next few weeks. On this visit, however, he could not devote his time exclusively to her because of preoccupation with the worsening international situation and the naval precautions that became necessary. He left on 7 September.

Before they met again Hervey had news, received off Mahon, where he was serving in Hawke's fleet after the loss of Minorca, that she had given birth to a daughter on 13 April 1756. Hervey had been with her from 27 July to 7 September of the previous year, so the dates would narrowly fit a suggestion that he was the father. There is no evidence in the *Journal*, however, that this was so, neither is there any further mention of the infant.

They met again in July 1757 when Osborne ordered Hervey, by this time captain of *Hampton Court*, into Genoa to discover whether the Genoese, who were neutral at the time, were building ships for the French. He went to Pellinetta's and to the theatre with her, where he caught cold and in the night developed gout in his left foot. The scope for amorous activity seems thus to have been rather limited. He returned on board and the next day received a visit from a Signor Lilla, 'one of those flattering sycophants that . . . is ever well with the ladies'. Lilla was begging ostensibly on behalf of Pellinetta, who he said had had large gambling losses. Hervey sent him away with a flea in his ear. The following day, however, when Pellinetta and other ladies of Genoa came aboard he slipped her a box containing 200 pistoles. He saw much of her during the few days that *Hampton Court* was at Genoa but whether the intimacy of previous visits was renewed he does not say.

He saw her again in the late summer of 1758 when he was in Genoa in *Monmouth*. The purpose of the visit was to convey his brother to Spain, where he was to take up his appointment as ambassador in Madrid; Hervey was at Genoa for about a fortnight, much of which was taken up with the new ambassador's business. There was the usual round of dinners and entertainments but the critical passages of his *Journal* have been removed – usually an indication of the nineteenth-century censor's disgust at what he considered an obscenity. The only clear indication is that on one occasion Hervey went to the theatre as Pellinetta's *cicisbeo*. How intimate they were it is impossible to decide.

Reference

1. PRO, ADM1/1890

CHAPTER VIII

The Approach of War

Too little too late

In July 1755 when Hervey arrived at Genoa the few short years of peace were numbered. The prospect of war between Britain and France increasingly held the attention of all and drew Hervey's thoughts from scenes of pleasure towards the iron disciplines of war. Very shortly, indeed, news reached the city that Admiral Boscawen had taken *Alcide* and *Lys*, two French men-of-war, in the North Atlantic. This use of force (which had been authorized by instructions from the Admiralty) raised the temperature of European diplomacy and increased tension in the Mediterranean as well as in the rest of Europe – though in an area of potential conflict stretching from the forests of the Ohio valley to the north German plain the Mediterranean and the activities of Edgcumbe's small squadron were at first perceived as something of a sideshow. This perception, however, was soon to be altered, and not to British advantage.

Britain and France had at this time conflicting interests in India, in the West Indies and more particularly in North America. In principle there was no conflict in Europe, but for Britain the problem was Hanover, George II's electoral domain. If any colonial war between the two countries became general the defence of Hanover was a prime British commitment, but a commitment that was very difficult to fulfil without suitable alliances, and alliances depended on painstaking diplomacy.

It was in North America that the crisis came to a head. The French were well established in Canada and at New Orleans and in 1754/55 set out to complete a chain of forts along the Ohio and Mississippi rivers, linking these northern and southern settlements. If it had been successful such a move would have confined the British colonies to the eastern littoral and the Appalachians, isolating them from the vast territories in the west which formed their potential hinterland. Both countries sent reinforcements from Europe and in the force under General Braddock went Hervey's brother William, serving in the 44th Regiment. In an attempt to block French reinforcements Boscawen was sent with a strong squadron to North American waters, with orders to stop any French vessel carrying troops or supplies. The worst of both worlds came about, however, when most of the French ships eluded him while he captured only two, *Alcide* and *Lys*, off Nova Scotia. Their capture was considered a warlike act in many countries and lost Britain much diplomatic support, while during the summer the French reinforcements that had slipped through played a considerable part in the defeat of Braddock's forces before Fort Duquesne, on the site of what is now Pittsburg.

To discourage France from sending more troops the British government deployed a strong squadron in France's western approaches, with orders to take all French ships and escort them into British ports. The ships taken were not classified as prizes, but held in port with sealed hatches until the legal situation became clearer; the undoubted intention was that on the outbreak of war they would be declared to be prizes. In the Atlantic the navy had at first little success but between August and November a powerful squadron under Admiral John Byng captured much French shipping. These activities, however, strained the resources of the navy and the dockyards to their limits, and were an important contributory reason for the Admiralty's inability to reinforce the Mediterranean in the early months of the following year.

Though the French government was incensed at this warlike attitude neither side was yet ready for open war in Europe. The autumn and winter were spent in diplomatic quadrilles and in reluctant and dilatory preparations for war. For France there were two maritime options in European waters. One was the recurrent theme of an invasion of Britain or Ireland and for this the French government hankered as they had at the start of the previous war in 1744. That this was their intention was suggested in the second half of 1755 by the massing of troops along their northern coastline and the making ready of ships at Brest and Rochefort. The other was the capture of the British Mediterranean bases at Minorca and Gibraltar, with all the advantages that would accrue from the elimination of Britain's power to intervene east of the straits. Consular reports as early as August of that year warned that a descent on Minorca from Toulon was being planned, though chatter from French court circles on this subject was so blatant that it was suspected of being a blind.

For the British government the defence of the home country was paramount. Only ten years had gone by since the Forty-Five had ended at Culloden, and the Bourbon monarchy still dreamed of the return of the francophile Stuarts to St James's Palace in place of the grumpy old Protestant from Hanover. It is a recurrent theme of British history that the Islands were protected from conquest not by land forces but by the protective shield of the navy, a theme that had been confirmed again and again since the defeat of the Spanish attempt a century and a half previously. Certainly in 1756 British soldiers were thin on British soil. The government and the House of Hanover would have found it difficult to survive a successful landing by 20,000 men in southeast England, provided their communications with France remained unbroken. The safety of the country therefore depended on the presence in the Channel or off Ushant of a strong fleet that could keep the French in harbour, or in the event that they came out could defeat them in battle or at worst survive to harry the invasion routes.

Thus it was not just the invasion scare which ran through London society that autumn but strategic necessity that led Anson at the Admiralty to keep the great majority of the available ships in home water throughout the winter of 1755–56, though it is fair comment that he deployed too many ships in trade protection and cruising for prizes. The corollary of all this was an apparent neglect of legitimate interests and concerns in the Mediterranean. In January 1756 Commodore Edgcumbe had three weak ships (one of sixty guns and two of fifty), four small frigates and a sloop with which to guard Minorca and Gibraltar, to protect British trade against the French and the Barbary pirates, to keep a watch on the French and Spanish navies and – forlorn hope – to counter any move by the considerable French squadron at Toulon, which was slowly but purposefully being prepared for sea.

At the end of July 1755, therefore, Hervey as the senior captain at Genoa was alert to the possibility of hostilities and did his best to keep the Admiralty informed of developments. This he was well placed to do because the overland route for mail to England was considerably faster that the packets from Mahon or Gibraltar. In early August, therefore, he is to be found[1] writing to the Admiralty with information on shipping movements, English and French, and on the warnings which the French Consul was giving to merchantmen. On 14 August he received a letter from the Secretary of State, Sir Thomas Robinson, warning all British ships of the dangers. He summoned the masters of all the merchant ships in port and read it to them. In early September this warning was reinforced by a further letter from London, brought by the bomb sketch *Speedwell*, and which was dated 24 July – forty days from London. He wrote direct to London the next day[2] 'certain information' on the preparations being made at Toulon. He does not name his source, presumably for reasons of security, as the letter went overland, reaching London in twenty days. He does, however, give much detail on the numbers of ships and circumstantial background – for example the French had gathered in 'all the carpenters, shipwrights and caulkers that were to be found among the shipping at Marseilles and La Ciotat' – providing information that should have been sufficient to persuade the Admiralty that the French were deadly serious in getting their Toulon ships ready for sea. The same day Hervey left Genoa for Villefranche, where he wrote again[3] confirming the intelligence that he had sent from Genoa and adding that the Genoese seemed fully willing to supply the French with both ships and men. He also wrote to the consul at Genoa asking him to make a strong protest to the Genoese authorities at their attitude. In all this can be seen Hervey's clear view of how important it was that the Admiralty should have all relevant information without delay.

Arriving at Mahon on 12 September he had his ship careened and cleaned down ready for war. There were several merchantmen in harbour, home-bound from the Levant, and Hervey took them towards Gibraltar in convoy. On the way he fell in with an east-bound convoy escorted by *Bedford* and *Portland*. Captain Douglas of *Bedford* was carrying orders for all ships in the Mediterranean to take any French vessels that they came across and send them into a British port, to be sealed and held until such time as the uncertainties resolved themselves. He also brought Hervey orders to take the east-bound convoy as far as the Aegean with *Portland* under him, while *Bedford* took the west-bound convoy on to Gibraltar.

The next day *Portland* took a large French ship bound from Marseilles to Martinique and by the 16th of the month they were back at Mahon, where the Frenchman was sealed and held. *Portland* then took on a convoy for Italy while Hervey remained at Mahon and on 22nd had one of his infrequent contacts with Commodore Edgcumbe, who arrived that day. Edgcumbe confirmed his orders and the next day *Phoenix* took the Turkey convoy on towards the Levant.

On passage *Phoenix* took two French pollacres and on leaving the danger zone, there being no French ships of war in the Aegean, he parted from the convoy and went cruising. On 5 November he took a large and rich French merchantman out of Smyrna for Marseilles and then, the wind coming strong westerly, made for Argentiera (Kimolos) in the Cyclades. Though the port of Milos on the adjoining island of that name was the larger harbour Kimolos provided the better anchorage, and could be got out of in any wind.

The Cyclades were nominally Turkish territory but Kimolos lacked any government presence or fortifications. Accordingly, Hervey considered himself free to take in charge a number of French vessels he found at anchor, though little good it did him in the longer term. The French consul came out to him and denied his right to take ships under Turkish protection, not to say in time of peace. Hervey rejected these protests, but accepted the request of some local Turks that their property on board should be left to them. He put prize crews aboard but being short of men decided to ransom some of them. This he did for goods transferred to those vessels that he retained, which eventually he took into Mahon.

In taking French vessels in a Turkish port, even one where the Turkish writ was so uncertain, and in ransoming some of them without authority to do so Hervey had allowed his zeal to outrun his discretion. He must have realized this, for he wrote to the British ambassador at Constantinople, Sir James Porter, warning him that the French would no doubt make strong representations to the Porte about his actions. This the French ambassador

H.M. Ship Phœnix Capt Hervey taking 14 French Ships at Argentiera, Nov.r the 9th 1756.

Augustus Hervey in Phoenix taking 14 French ships at Argentiera*, November 1755. From the picture at Ickworth by Dominic Serres, reproduced by courtesy of the National Trust. *Kimolos in the Cyclades

(Hervey's old friend from Lisbon days the Comte de Vegennes) duly did and the Turkish government duly took up the matter with Sir James. By February of 1756, when the 'prizes' were secure in Mahon harbour, the complaint had passed through the hands of the Secretary of State and had reached the ears of the King. Indeed it was not just the French and the Porte who complained. The Turks reacted against British trade in the Levant and the British merchants then brought their fear and alarm at possible loss of profits to His Majesty's attention. Whatever the Admiralty's private thoughts on harassing the French may have been their Lordships had no alternative but to issue an order limiting the actions which the navy had been authorized to take against French ships trading in Turkish waters.[4]

> 'In pursuance of the King's Order-in-Council upon a petition to his Majesty from the Governor's Company of the merchants in England trading into the Levant seas you are hereby required and directed not to take any French vessels out of any port belonging to the Ottoman Empire, on any pretence, nor to molest, detain or imprison the persons of any of the subjects of the Ottoman Empire, and also not to detain any French ship or vessel whatsoever which you shall meet with in the Levant Seas, bound from one port to another in those seas, or to and from any port in Egypt, having any effects of Turks on board'.

This letter was sent to all the consuls and captains of King's ships in the Mediterranean. But to Hervey, who had kept the Admiralty informed of his doings in the usual way, they uttered in addition though their Secretary perhaps the most unequivocal rebuke that he was at any time to receive at their hands.[5]

> 'Sir
>
> I have received and read to my Lords Commissioners of the Admiralty your several letters of 11 November, 9 December and 6 January last, and in return thereto am commanded by their Lordships to acquaint you that they are very much surprised at your conduct in taking any of the ships out of the Turkish roads, at which the Grand Signor and his Ministries are greatly dissatisfied and therefore in pursuance of His Majesty's pleasure signified by Mr Fox one of his Principal Secretaries of State it is their Lordships' strict direction that you immediately release all the French ships you have taken under these circumstances or in any other manner not agreeable to the enclosed order for your future conduct.
>
> With respect to your ransoming some of those ships their Lordships look upon it as still more extraordinary, being done without any kind of authority, your former orders only directing you to seize French ships and vessels and carry them into port, to be preserved 'till further order'. Their Lordships therefore direct you to send the ransom notes as soon as possible to Mr

Porter at Constantinople to be by him delivered to the Ottoman Ministry and at the same time to let him know what ships you release.

Hervey received this letter at Mahon on 17 March but did not reply until 11 April when he was Leghorn. He had no option but to apologize to their Lordships[6] and make restitution. He was £97 out of pocket. To add to his discomfiture, the ships whose capture did not transgress either his orders or Turkish neutrality were left in Mahon when the French took Minorca in April 1756, so that he made not a penny from any of them.

It was now mid November and bad weather with unfavourable winds frustrated Hervey's first two attempts to get away from Kimolos with his prizes. He could readily get out of harbour in *Phoenix* but gales made it impossible for his prizes to hold their course. However, on 25th of the month with the wind northerly he succeeded and headed westwards. *En route Phoenix* took two more French prizes but was inhibited from taking more by shortage of men. So much had his prize crews denuded *Phoenix* of officers that Hervey himself had to take watch and watch with the Master. Bad weather constrained him to go into Malta with his prizes, except for two which had parted company, and to endure the hostile attitudes of the French, who though the Grand Master was Portuguese had a controlling influence on the ruling Knights of St John.

Probably for diplomatic rather than health reasons he was not allowed pratique and the French in the island let it be known that the Grand Master had detained *Phoenix* for piracy in taking French ships without a declaration of war. To show that he was a free agent Hervey took her to sea and captured yet another French merchantman. When he had the gall to take this latest prize back into Valletta the French interest was naturally incensed and the French envoy demanded the ship be released. Hervey received a note in the name of the Grand Master notifying him of this demand, but not supporting it, and replied in diplomatic French as follows:

Messieurs, je suis très obligé de l'attention de son éminence; je serai très fâché de donner aucune juste occasion aux religions de Malte de regretter la reception que le vaisseau du roy mon maître trouvoit ici; mais je suis très supris de la réclame qui a fait le ministre de France. Je suis bien aisé que ce n'est pas de la part du Grand Maître. Je regard le prise légallement fait, un bâtiment si eloigné de votre port. Ainsi, Messieurs, le Ministre de France peut être assuré que je ne la rendrai pas'.

In the matter of distance, according to the customs of the day, he had a valid point. It was, however, a temptation to fortune to take such a vessel into a potentially hostile port.

Shortage of men forced him to sell more of the small prizes and after a fortnight he left Malta with a small flotilla of captured ships. Putting in at

Cagliari on the way *Phoenix* and her flock reached Mahon on 1 January 1756. The two missing prizes, under her first lieutenant, Peter Foulkes and Andrew Purdy, master's mate, had already arrived. All the captured vessels were laid up in Mahon harbour.

In his *Journal* for this period Hervey makes many comments on the inadequacies of British naval strategy. The British naval position in the Mediterranean, as elsewhere, was indeed an unhappy one. The stringencies of peacetime finance had everywhere reduced the navy to a shadow of its wartime self, in numbers of ships, in their state of readiness, in crews to man them, in the state of the dockyards and in the adequacy of munitions of war and other supplies. Hervey, however, was a sea-going officer with little contact with London, having been in the Mediterranean since 1752. He therefore had little knowledge of the difficulties that Government and Admiralty had in matching scanty resources with the multifarious demands that preparations for war put upon them and his comments show how little he understood the consequent constraints on government action. Before and after the loss of Minorca the *Journal* is full of diatribes against the Ministers; as usual Anson came in for the greatest opprobrium, but Newcastle and Henry Fox, respectively Prime Minister and Secretary of State, were not denied their share.

Hervey found Edgcumbe at Mahon in *Deptford* with *Princess Louisa* and *Portland*, but three days later the squadron sailed for Leghorn leaving *Phoenix* to refit. Dockyard facilities were excellent and he had her hove down, her bottom cleaned and all made ready for sea. As usual, this was something that could be left to his officers and her captain made himself free of the pleasures of the land. The officers of the garrison, especially those of Colonel Cornwallis's Regiment made congenial company. Hervey lived ashore at an inn kept by an Englishman name Smallbridge, whose daughter was 'very pretty' and amenable to his advances. His *Journal* shows how satisfactory his arrangements were: 'As I lay at the house we had no interruption'.

Minorca had been taken from Spain by Sir John Leake and General Stanhope in 1708 and retained by Britain at the peace of Utrecht. Its great asset was Mahon harbour, a narrow inlet over three miles long with deep water for almost all it length and strongly defended by St Philip's Castle at its entrance. Properly supplied and garrisoned, it had all that was needed to shelter and maintain a large fleet. It was well situated as a base for surveillance and aggressive action along the Mediterranean coasts of France and Spain, and particularly for the blockade of Toulon.

Though Mahon harbour was virtually impregnable the long island coastline was difficult to defend against determined attackers. There was a garrison nominally of four regiments of infantry but in January 1756 it was not at a high state of readiness. The Governor, Lord Tyrawley, the commander of the troops, Major General Stuart, and most of the field officers had been

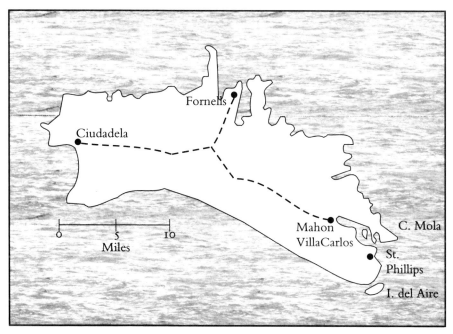

Map of Minorca

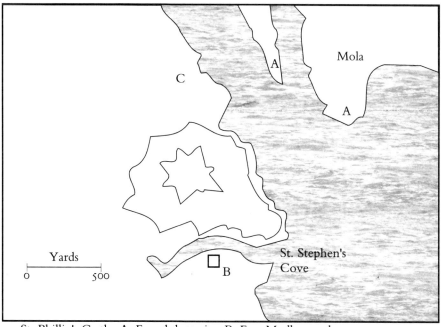

St. Phillip's Castle: A. French batteries; B. Fort Marlborough
C. Site of St. Phillip's town.

MAP 3 Minorca

absent for several months and overall command was in the hands of the Lieutenant-Governor, Lieutenant-General Blakeney. Blakeney was man of parts, having served in Marlborough's wars, fifty years previously. He had a powerful reputation as a soldier, but lacked 'interest' and had not reached general rank until he was 69. In 1756 he was 84, competent and capable for his age but often bedridden with gout.

Though warnings of impending invasion had been current since August it was well into the New Year before Blakeney and his officers set out to prepare for it. The government at home was equally at fault. They did not insist on the absent senior officers returning to their posts; they did not send drafts to bring the regiments of the garrison up to strength; they did not take any steps to ensure that supplies of food and munitions were adequate; and it was March before they decided that substantial naval reinforcements were necessary. Edgcumbe had done what he could, providing intelligence of French activity at Toulon and begging a small contingent of troops from the Governor of Gibraltar to be embarked in his ships.

It was not until 5 February that Blakeney summoned a council of war, which Hervey attended as senior naval officer then in the island. Hervey was careful to ensure that the navy and he as its representative should receive due respect at this primarily military meeting, arranging beforehand that he should be saluted by the guards, should sit next to the Lieutenant-Governor and have precedence over the acting regimental commanders.

The council met almost daily for the next fortnight. It was generally agreed that the island could not be defended by the forces available against a full scale French attack, neither could the town or port of Mahon. There was, however, a reasonable prospect that St Philip's Castle could be held for a time, thus preventing the French from using Mahon harbour. The council passed many resolutions for putting the island in a proper state of defence, for example on bringing the guns of the prizes in the harbour into St Philip's, on securing the many prisoners on the Isla del Rey in Mahon harbour and on the provision of 30,000 fascines to bolster the defences of the castle. Hervey was among the foremost in proposing what should be done. He was concerned about the prisoners, watchful of the fate of all the naval stores at Mahon and wanted to set up a reliable channel for intelligence from the mainland.

Some of his proposals suggest that his touch in terrestrial matters was not as fine as it might have been. There were many Jews on the island, a few of whom were leaving the sinking ship. He had their departure forbidden, on the grounds that it would indicate that morale on the island was poor and thus encourage the French to attack; an unnecessary, or at least marginal, concern when the French were already decided, and when they were already in touch with the disaffected islanders.

One of the few decisions of the council that were promptly acted on was to retain *Phoenix* at Mahon, against Hervey's orders from Edgcumbe which were to meet him at a sealed rendezvous on the Italian coast. On 7 February he wrote to Edgecumbe and to the Admiralty[7] explaining the reasons for this decision and reporting to the Admiralty that the French had 25,000 men assembling at Toulon, where twelve of the line would be ready by the end of the month, and were widely believed to be preparing an attack on Minorca. This letter was received in London on 6 March and the information was immediately passed to Henry Fox and the King. It provided some of the most up-to-date intelligence available when the Government came to its decision a few days later to reinforce the Mediterranean by sending out a squadron under Admiral Byng.

He reports also in this letter the action he had taken to suspend the captain of the packet ordered to take dispatches from Blakeney to Edgcumbe, dispatches which would certainly have urged the Commander-in-Chief to return to Minorca forthwith. Twenty-four hours after receiving these dispatches and a letter from Hervey to Edgcumbe the packet was still in Mahon harbour. When Hervey spoke to her master the reply was 'that by God he would not, damned the service of the island and he wished he was turned out, though he would not quit'. So Hervey suspended him and replaced him with one of his own officers.

On 16 February the council resolved at Hervey's instigation that he should sail for Villefranche to gather information. There he found orders from Edgcumbe who was still at Leghorn to join him there, orders which he decided to ignore 'as knowing it best for His Majesty's service' that he should continue his mission on behalf of the council in Minorca. Going over to Nice he saw his old acquaintance General Paterson, who gave him a full account of French preparations at Toulon and of their intentions, information which he sent overland to the Secretary of State and the Admiralty. He also arranged, as requested by the council in Minorca, for the consul at Nice to send any further information about the French without delay. What was equally vital, he guaranteed that the expense of doing so – always a bone of contention since the Admiralty would not pay and the consul had no funds for the purpose – would be met by Blakeney. No record survives of whether he had Blakeney's blessing for such a guarantee, and with the loss of Minorca a few weeks later it seems unlikely that the Lieutenant-Governor actually paid out.

Arriving back at Mahon on 10 March Hervey attended meetings of the council that day and the next, together with Captain Noel who was now back in port. He was much concerned – perhaps indignant is a better word, since the navy had fulfilled all it commitments while the army had done little – that no action had been taken to enforce the previous resolutions to put the island in a state of defence. Orders had been given but Blakeney was loath to press the Minorcans for levies or forced supplies of foodstuffs and warlike stores. Perhaps Blakeny harked back to the most noteworthy incident in his career, when he had successfully defended Stirling Castle against the Young Pretender's Highlanders. He had taken no obvious defensive measures, encouraging them to attack and opening fire with devastating effect at the last minute. The castle was held and its defender promoted to Lieutenant-General. But the case at Minorca was very different, with much to be done to put St Philips's Castle in order and to minimize the losses of men, materials and ships that might result from the capture of Mahon itself.

By the next meeting of the council, on 12 March, Hervey had convinced himself that the military had to be shaken from their complacency. His main concern was to force the islanders to assume some of the burden and he harangued the council at length. His principal theme was the lack of support from the islanders for their rulers. The Minorcans had in fact prospered under British rule and the civil administration had been left in their hands. They were, however, much influenced by their Catholic clergy, who were fundamentally opposed to Protestant overlordship, while the British in the island did little to foster good relationships. Hervey must have been aware of their misgivings. His remarks should perhaps be seen as carefully avoiding direct criticism of Blakeney while indicating that much more needed doing to bring the island into a high state of readiness. He was supported by two of the lieutenant-colonels and a motion was carried for a 'voluntary' levy of $30,000 (£6,750) on the Minorcans to set up a war chest. However, when in the next few days the leading inhabitants were summoned before the council they produced only $11,000, and the Church $400.

Several councils were held during the next twelve days and from 17 March were attended by Commodore Edgecumbe, who had returned from Leghorn. Hervey continued to urge more drastic action; that the island should be put under martial law; that the town of St Philip's close to the castle and hindering its defence, should be demolished; that all cattle should be driven in from the outlying parts of the island to deny them to the French; that the levy should be made compulsory; that a boom be prepared to block the harbour mouth and two fireships provided; and finally on 22 March that 'all the previous resolutions should be put into immediate execution, and that every measure should be pursued for the defence of the island as if the enemy were to be landed tomorrow'. Little of this received any support from the army officers and with the exception of the defence of Mahon harbour none was agreed to.

Eventually on 22 March Blakeney showed his mettle in the face of this irrepressible and no doubt irritating sailor, proposing that a ship be sent to cruise off the north of the island to give warning of the enemy's approach. Edgcumbe could see little purpose in this but did not oppose it, and *Phoenix* was ordered to sea for seven days. Blakeney's motives in setting up this little coup are obvious while Edgcumbe may well be excused for falling in with it, in the hope that he could himself command more influence in the council in the absence of such an outspoken subordinate. Hervey, knowing well that he was being banished, sailed on the 22nd, endured five days of storm, saw nothing and returned on the 28th.

Ordered immediately to Leghorn and Villefranche to gather intelligence and to pick up any overland letters *Phoenix* was detained in Mahon by the weather until 5 April. At Leghorn on 11 April Hervey heard that Admiral Byng had sailed for the Mediterranean five days earlier with ten ships of the line and on the next day news reached him that the French fleet had sailed from Toulon on 10 April. The expedition was under the overall command of the Marshal Duke of Richelieu, with the fleet commanded by the Marquis de la Galissonière. If Byng's squadron had been sent a month earlier the knowledge of their coming would surely have deterred the French from invading. As it was there was nothing to stop a successful landing and the question was whether Byng would be strong enough to drive the French away from the island leaving their troops to wither on the branch.

Phoenix sailed for Villefranche on 12 April and waited there several days for incoming letters. By 17 April Hervey was in a position to write to the Admiralty[8] with copious up-to-date intelligence of the state of the combatants, if two nations between whom war has not been declared can realistically be described as such. The letter casts an interesting light on his state of mind and his intentions. This was the first time that he had come near to a major operation of war since his time at Carthagena in 1741, and he found himself separated from the rest of the squadron and without any orders to cover the new situation. For Hervey, however, the case for standing towards the enemy was incontrovertible, and he declared his intention to do just that:

> Though I have no orders for proceeding if I find the French sailed, yet I intend to endeavour to get into the harbour of Mahon, as I know the men of the ship will be much wanted, though the ship may not be of much use . . . if I find [Mahon harbour] so blocked up or their scouts too numerous to attempt further . . . [I] shall just drop into some bay of Majorca while I despatch one of the island boats over to Mr Edgcumbe . . . to let him and the general know that a fleet is actually sailed from England . . .

Clearly his information on Edgcumbe's plans as they stood before *Phoenix* had sailed from Mahon led him to believe that the Commander-in-Chief and his squadron intended to stand there and fight in defence of the port. However, defending Mahon from attack by sea was pointless if it was defenceless from the landward side, and rather than allow his ships to be bottled up in the harbour and captured Edgcumbe had in fact retired to Gibraltar to await Byng

– and it was surely the right decision to strengthen the British relieving squadron in this way.

Villefranche was an ideal place at which to garner intelligence of French activities, for shipping moved freely along the coast and French officials passed through on their way to and from Genoa. Furthermore, General Paterson went far out of his way (though a Scot he had long been in the service of the King of Sardinia) to convey it to the British. Thus the letter gives much detail of the French expedition, though Hervey understates the strength of their battle fleet by two ships, listing ten of the line instead of twelve. When the letter reached London on 7 May it found the Government in a state of distraction that the squadron which they had sent under Byng was not strong enough; but Hervey's understatement allowed the Duke of Newcastle and others to comfort themselves that Byng would be the stronger, a state of mind that probably contributed to their furious reaction when they heard that he had been defeated.

There is much in the letter about the military's plans for the defence of St Philip's Castle and Hervey shows no hesitation in making apparent his lack of confidence in the army's sense of urgency. Nor does Edgcumbe escape the same implications; he describes the steps that he had a particular hand in to make ready for the evacuation of the naval stores, the French ships held in the harbour and the prisoners. But in the event all the stores and shipping were left behind to fall into the hands of the French.

Though he draws attention to the possible effects of bad weather on the French expedition his views on French prospects are prescient, though he rather naturally fails to forecast the failure of the British fleet – 'I think it will be impossible for the enemy to make such progress as will prove effectual before our fleet arrives which must either destroy that of the enemy or oblige them to forsake their troops ashore and desert their transports'. He may be excused for failing to anticipate his patron Byng's lack of fortitude.

Phoenix sailed for Minorca on 17 April with in company a settee that had been sent for intelligence under Captain Ourry of the fireship *Proserpine*. Edgcumbe having retired to Gibraltar *Phoenix* had for the next month the distinction of being the only British man-of-war in contact with the enemy. Unfortunately Hervey suffered badly from rheumatism on the voyage, which turned to gout in the left toe and then to pleurisy. On 24 April when he thought he was close to the north coast of the island he ran into fog. In clearer weather at dawn on the 25th he made out the island about fifteen miles ahead but at the same time saw the French fleet about nine miles ahead, off Fornells.[9] Five ships were sent to chase him and it took him several hours to throw them off. On the morning of the 27th, however, he had another encounter, coming close in the haze to a two-decker which imme-diately gave chase and at first came up with him. But the wind freshened, forcing her to reef while *Phoenix* was able to spread her topgallants and by midday had shaken off her pursuer. All this time Hervey continued to keep his bed, except for the two episodes of pursuit, when he had himself carried on deck.

Deciding that Minorcan waters were unsafe, Hervey made for Majorca to seek intelligence. Pausing only to take a French tartane loaded with bullocks, which were a welcome addition to the ship's store, he took *Phoenix* into Palma on the afternoon of 29 April. Whatever the sympathies of the Spanish government Spain and Britain were in principle friendly nations and on arrival *Phoenix* gave and received in return the prescribed gun salutes. The reality, however, was rather different. At all levels the Spanish had no liking for the British, and were unfavourably impressed at the British government's failure adequately to defend Minorca. The French had landed at Ciudadela on the 18th, had been welcomed by the Minorcans and by the 24th had occupied Mahon and all the island except for St Philip's Castle. Edgcumbe had left Captain Scrope with a force of sailors and marines, ten guns and a quantity of stores for the garrison. Byng was still on passage to Gibraltar.

All this Hervey heard from shore contacts at Palma, the most helpful of whom was Don Juan Troyola, one of the few British supporters in the island. His illness prevented him going ashore until 3 May, when he visited the Viceroy, the Marquis del Cayro, who received him in great state and with much civility. Hervey's purpose was to register complaints about the partiality shown to the French; that the Majorcans were supplying the French in Minorca with all they needed; that quarantine regulations were being set aside for French arrivals from Minorca; that he was being prevented from talking to English merchantmen in the harbour; that information about events in Minorca was being kept from him. The Viceroy was polite but gave no ground and Hervey showed his dissatisfaction by refusing an offer of dinner.

Early on 5 May two French warships, *Hippopotame* of 50 guns and *Gracieuse* of 26, arrived in Palma Bay, and the latter anchored close by *Phoenix*. They were in effect blockading her in Palma, a neutral port, and by 7 May Hervey felt justified in making further representations to the Viceroy. Again the response was noncommittal; the Viceroy expected the French not to attack *Phoenix* at anchor, but could not hold himself responsible for their actions if she attempted to leave. Spanish sentiments were with the French, but in any case the Viceroy had no force with which to control their actions. They were present in Majorcan waters in considerable strength and could defy Spanish complaints, should they be made, with impunity. This time, to retain what little influence he had with the Spanish authorities Hervey accepted an invitation to dinner the next day, which he describes as a poor meal, poorly served, and at which he met the Vicereine, aged about 50 and very ugly.

Hervey also comments on the fare in *Phoenix* while he was in Palma Bay,[10] a matter which gave him particular trouble as he had left his purser behind in Minorca. The bullocks taken from the French off Minorca provided a welcome respite from salt fare, enabling fresh beef to be served every meat day, but he was short of bread and of pease and oatmeal. The Spanish authorities, however, made no difficulties and Hervey bought 'soft bread' ashore, which 'as it comes infinitely cheaper than the King's price I hope the Victualling Office . . . will approve'. Pease and oatmeal, evidently not Mediterranean fare, he had to reduce to two-thirds allowance and wine he bought ashore as needed.

The French men-of-war continued to make free of Palma and its bay, anchoring where they wished and on 12 May actually taking an English merchantman within full sight of the port and town, later bringing her into port under a prize crew. Hervey, still suffering, went to the Viceroy yet again where to his indignation but not surprise he again got little satisfaction. The Viceroy said[11] that he had complained to the French captain, who had replied 'that he had only to obey his Admiral and no other'. But to preserve appearances two Spanish officials were placed on the prize, while orders were awaited from Madrid.

On 16 May a tartane that Hervey had sent with letters to Barcelona came back into Palma with the information that Byng had arrived at Gibraltar a fortnight earlier. Sensing that he must by now be close at hand Hervey determined to break out of Palma the next day. He went to the Viceroy to make this plain – 'if the *Gracieuse* came near me I was determined to engage her, which I hoped to do in sight of his town tomorrow'. Returning to his ship with Don Juan Troyola he gave orders for her to be cleared for action. As they were about to sit down to dinner *Gracieuse* was seen to be signalling busily; almost immediately she weighed anchor and left port in a flurry. A lookout sent to *Phoenix'* masthead reported two sail making for Palma and by 1700 hours Hervey could see seventeen sail from his quarterdeck. Byng had arrived.

References

1. PRO, ADM1/1890
2. Ibid.
3. Ibid.
4. PRO, ADM2/76
5. PRO, ADM2/703
6. PRO, ADM1/1891
7. Ibid.
8. Ibid.
9. Ibid.
10. Ibid
11. Ibid

CHAPTER IX

The Battle of Mahon

Discouraging the others

Byng's fleet of ten of the line had got away from Spithead on 7 April, just under four weeks after he had been ordered to the Mediterranean. Considering the unready state of his ships and the difficulties in filling up their complements, this was a creditable performance. It could not, however, disguise the face that many of the ships were in poor condition and that the drafts were of poor quality. Byng was under orders to proceed to Minorca, taking on board one of the regiments at Gibraltar and throwing it into the island. However, after a remarkably pessimistic council of war when he reached the Rock the Governor, General Fowke, refused to release the troops and Byng sailed on without significant military aid for the island. He had on board Lord Robert Bertie's regiment and the missing officers of the Minorca garrison. This regiment, however, was not intended as a reinforcement for Minorca but as a replacement for his ships' marines, who had been redistributed to other ships at Portsmouth.

Byng sent the sloop *Experiment* into Palma for the latest news and Hervey went by boat to meet her. The next day he sailed from Palma and went on board *Ramillies*, Byng's flagship, to impart what little intelligence he had. He was now under a Commander-in-Chief with whom he enjoyed a mutual liking and respect and they evidently commiserated with each other that Byng's squadron was so few and so ill founded, and predictably that Lord Anson kept all the best ships cruising in home waters.

The fleet proceeded on its way towards Minorca and on 18 May Byng detached the frigates *Phoenix*, *Chesterfield*, and *Dolphin* under Hervey and sent them ahead to land letters to General Blakeney. Early on the 19th the small squadron approached Mahon from the south in a light breeze, past what in the parlance of the day Hervey refers to as the Laire of Mahon (the Isla del Aire). *Phoenix* was close to the shore about three miles from St Philip's when the wind failed and he had to tow off with his boats. He made the pre-arranged signals to St Philip's but was not seen by the garrison until about 1000 hours. Blakeney then found it necessary to hold a council of war and it was not until 1500 hours that Robert Boyd, the quartermaster, was sent off in a boat to make contact with *Phoenix*.

In the meantime Byng with the main squadron had come up to the Isla del Aire, within a mile or so of *Phoenix*, and could hear the gunfire between St Philip's and its besiegers. At this critical moment, with the British squadron virtually becalmed under the lee of the land, Galissonière's ships were seen to the south east, approaching under a fresh breeze. Byng immediately recalled his frigates and transferred men from them to make up the complements of his line ships. Boyd rowed for an hour and a half but could not reach the British squadron as it manoeuvred to meet the French.

So Hervey returned to the fleet, went on board *Ramillies* and offered *Phoenix* as a fireship for the coming battle. She was prepared for this service but not in the event called upon to perform it. The next day (20 May) the French were in sight and the two fleets manoeuvred to close. Much has been written about the Battle of Mahon and its aftermath. It was the greatest sea action at which Hervey was to be present, and present in such a way that, placed by Byng behind the flagship to repeat her signals, he had a panoramic view of events, which he recorded in detail and which later made him a prime defence witness at Byng's court martial.

Though Byng had a numerical advantage of one, his ships were less powerful and certainly much slower than his opponents, who in Galissonière had as their commander one of France's most outstanding admirals. Byng may have lacked resolution but he did not lack courage, and there is no doubt that he did his best to engage the French. His tactics, however, were not of the best and poor handling of their ships by some of his captains added to the problems. The British ships came into action seriatim, several ships taking severe punishment as they did so, and indeed *Ramillies* and the British rear were never closely engaged before the French, using their superior speed, drew off as night approached. There was in fact never a close or total engagement and when the French withdrew neither side had gained a victory.

That evening Hervey went on board the flagship again and spoke to Byng and his second-in-command, Rear-Admiral West. Byng was at this time intent on continuing the action in the morning, telling Hervey that 'Lord Anson had sold him, but by God he would fight till every ship sunk before he would give this up.' Hervey's view was different. He appears from his *Journal* to have advised the Admiral the previous day that first priority should be to land the officers and troops at St Philip's. The position of the two fleets on the morning of the 20th – Galissonière appears never to have been within twelve miles of Minorca, with the British fleet interposed – made an attempt at that time quite feasible, risking only the absence of a single frigate from the battle, but by next morning visibility was very poor and by this time the French fleet was between Byng and Minorca. Unfortunately, also, there is no evidence that the land officers were zealous to take up their posts or that they encouraged Byng to enable them to do so.

The failure to make contact with the garrison was a fundamental disaster whose ill-effects have been overshadowed by the events of the next few days. The attempt was marred by failures both of planning and of execution. Why were the officers of the garrison not sent on board *Phoenix* to be landed immediately if circumstances permitted? Why did Hervey, once he was becalmed, not send a boat to attempt a landing at the fort? The topography was entirely familiar to him from his service at Mahon and there is no doubt that the fort was approachable by sea. Boyd got out, so a boat could have got in. Why did Byng recall *Phoenix* with the rest of the frigates when he saw Galissonière on the distant horizon? One frigate more or less would have made little difference to his strength in battle and the British fleet would have been between *Phoenix* and the French. A determined approach would have enabled the officers to be landed, would have provided the garrison with a boost to their morale and would have shown Byng that the fort was good for a long defence. Hervey seems to have been uncharacteristacally hesitant in his handling of the tactical situation. We do not know what verbal orders Byng gave him, but the whole incident seems to be underlain by Byng's pessimism and fears for the worst, the sort of fears that in the next day's battle and more particularly in the decisions taken after it brought him to his untimely end.

When the French drew off the battle had been neither won nor lost, but several of Byng's ships had been badly mauled and five were reported unfit for action. Captain Andrews of *Defiance* (60) had been killed early in the battle and two days later Byng appointed Hervey to command her in his place. Apart from Byng's high opinion of Hervey, this promotion was well deserved. Hervey's spell in command of *Princessa* in the previous war gave him every expectation of a ship of the line in this one and he doubtless considered that he had languished far too long in the tiny *Phoenix*. *Defiance* was in these circumstances something of a mixed blessing. She was ill-found and badly damaged, with her foretopmast down, and when Hervey went aboard he was able to muster only 226 men against a complement of 400. In his *Journal* he states that he had her in order by the same evening, though the minutes of the forthcoming council of war show that her foretopmast was not up until two days later.

Byng called a council for 0700 hrs on the 24th, a council that has become a byword for pusillanimity and did more to hasten the Commander-in-Chief's end than the botched battle of the 20th. It was attended by Admirals Byng and West, twelve ship's captains including Hervey and four senior army officers including Major-General Stuart. At this council the Admiral showed to the full his habit of magnifying his own problems while ignoring those of his opponents. Several of his ships were damaged and at least one, *Intrepid*, had to be escorted to Gibraltar. He had a number of casualties and much sickness on board, and no hospital ship. The French fleet was stronger than his and might attack at any time with every prospect of victory, thus, as he conceived, laying Gibraltar itself open to attack – regardless of the fact that the French military were tied up in Minorca. Byng had in effect decided that his fleet could not maintain itself before Minorca and that he must retire to Gibraltar. He did not consider himself strong enough to harry the French supply lines from Toulon or to make landings on the island. He gave no credence to the possibility that reinforcements might be sent from England. And fundamentally, he felt in his bones that the French were in an impregnable position, while in fact their troops were short of supplies and suffering from sickness and their fleet was under orders not to risk an action.

So the Admiral put a series of leading questions to the council, all designed to give him advice that would justify retirement to Gibraltar:

1 Whether an attack on the French fleet gives any prospect of relieving Minorca?

2 Whether, if there were no French fleet cruising off Minorca, the English fleet could raise the siege?

3 Whether Gibraltar would not be in danger by any accident that might befall the fleet?

4 Whether an attack with our fleet in the present state of it, upon that of the French, will not endanger the safety of Gibraltar?

5 Whether it is not best for His Majesty's service that the fleet should immediately proceed for Gibraltar?

There was relatively little discussion. Hervey argued that the fleet should remain in Minorcan waters, should seek an opportunity to throw men into St Philip's and await reinforcements before attacking the French fleet. With the benefit of hindsight there is much to commend this view. Commodore Broderick was sent out with five of the line, arriving at Gibraltar on 15 June, and could with favourable winds have joined Byng off Minorca before the end of the month. Unreinforced, St Philip's held out until 27 June. But Rear-Admiral West, Byng's second-in-command, in particular seems to have been strong for retreat. Hervey convinced none of his colleagues and in the end he did not dissent from the unanimous recommendation to sail for Gibraltar. Some of the comments in his *Journal* – 'Had the French come down upon us (in the three or four days after the battle) we must have been undone, so shattered were we, with our masts and yards all down repairing . . .' – actually suggest that he thought Byng was right to retire, and that he, like Byng, had failed to take into account the reciprocal damage done to Galissonières fleet.

The fleet's passage to Gibraltar, shepherding the crippled ships, was slow and debilitating. Winds were light and at one stage in calm weather with a strong swell the fleet nearly went ashore on the coast of Africa. Progress was so slow that there were many opportunities for traffic between ships. On most days Hervey went on board *Ramillies* and had much talk with the two admirals.

There was much dissatisfaction with the way the battle had gone and West in particular considered that three of the captains had behaved ingloriously during the action. At first there was no feeling in the fleet that Byng had not done his duty, but this sense of satisfaction was not to last.

Hervey was sent ahead to Gibraltar to prepare the dockyard for the tasks ahead of it. Arriving on 16 June he found that Broderick had arrived from England the previous day with his five ships, one of which, the 64-gun *Hampton Court*, was intended for him. The decision to send her out for him pre-dated his advancement into *Defiance* after Mahon, and was the result of a campaign by Mary Lady Hervey to get him a ship of the line. There is no doubt that his record made him highly eligible for a larger ship than *Phoenix*, but for the Admiralty to send one out for him under another captain was exceptional. It appears[1] that his mother had been active on his behalf, importuning Henry Fox (Lord Holland), one of the Secretaries of State. Fox had been one of Lord Hervey's closest associates and had continued as a friend and frequent correspondent with his widow. Fox used his influence with Anson, who in spite of Hervey's dislike for him had a high opinion of his professional capabilities and took little persuasion.

However, none of this stopped Hervey's comments. His reaction to Broderick's arrival was, rightly, that sent earlier his ships would have saved Minorca, but he goes on 'Such was the inexcusable error of our wicked minister, that detested wretch Lord Holland, and that poor contemptible one Lord Anson'. Written not in the heat of the moment but ten years or so later, with Anson dead for several years, these words show continuing ill-feeling comparable at a different level with that shown earlier to the poor naval clerk Blankley. Nevertheless in July he wrote to Fox[2] to thank him for his efforts. He had already realized that there would be an enquiry of some kind on Mahon, and that he was one of those who would be wanted as a witness in London, and was concerned about his command, writing 'for it would be a cruel thing for one who by being in a frigate could only be a spectator to be taken out of my ship to be an evidence'. In the event he need not have worried.

The fleet came in to Gibraltar on 20 June. When Byng found that Broderick's reinforcements had arrived, giving him superiority over Galissonière, he immediately determined to return to Minorca. However, having come to Gibraltar to repair and recuperate, he judged it necessary to do so, though the dockyard was, as usual, unbelievably slow. It was during the next ten days that the dissensions among Byng's officers that had begun during the passage to Gibraltar emerged into the open. His captains would have been obtuse not to have realized that the Commander-In-Chief was about to incur the Admiralty's severe displeasure, and Hervey and Gardiner (Byng's flag captain) excepted − began to distance themselves from him. Rear-Admiral

West had begun this process off Minorca, refusing at first to sit in council of war with the captains of those ships at the rear of the line who had not got their ships into battle. Captain Cornwall of *Revenge* took particular exception to these remarks and at Gibraltar asked for a court martial, with the intention of scotching this slur on his name. West denied that he had said anything to justify such a request, at which Hervey, who was not one of the captains affected, argued that if he had been West's target he should certainly have objected to the Rear-Admirals's attitude. Hervey perceived that West was busy distancing himself from Byng and seems to have had quite a row with him. There were, his *Journal* says 'two or three sharp replies between Mr West and me; but I cared not, I saw what he was at.' After much ingenuous argument, West, who was named by Byng as President of the Court, backed down, and when the Court assembled on 28 June no evidence was offered. By this time the coolness between the Admirals was common knowledge, for the same day the Governor, General Fowke, asked Hervey to effect a reconciliation, a task that he refused.

Broderick's small squadron had been despatched to reinforce Byng as a response to the information of French strength at Toulon which Hervey had sent from Villefranche on 17 April and to the news of the French landing in Minorca. At the same time, because of this overt aggression war was declared on France. However, no further action to strengthen the British hand in the Mediterranean was taken until the end of May, when London received Byng's pessimistic despatch from Gibraltar giving an account of the council of war held there at the beginning of the month. By 1 June Newcastle had received from Paris the triumphalist accounts of the Battle of Mahon that the French were putting about, and Byng's goose was cooked. Byng's dispatch received a few days later put a better gloss on his doings but could not disguise his inadequacy.

However, before receiving it Newcastle had made his decisions. The Government was furious at Byng's pusillanimity, and at that of General Fowke in refusing to supply troops. It acted immediately to divert the blame from its own shoulders to Byng's. By 8 June Vice-Admiral Sir Edward Hawke was under orders to proceed to Gibraltar to supersede Byng, with Rear-Admiral Charles Saunders specially promoted to replace West as second-in-command and Lord Tyrawley, the absent Governor of Minorca, to take over as Governor of Gibraltar. These gentlemen with officers to replace those of the two flagships were sent out in the frigate *Antelope*, in what the London wits were pleased to call 'the little cargo of courage'. *Antelope* was to bring back those who had been displaced, Byng to face a court martial which had already been determined upon.

When *Antelope* arrived on the morning on 2 July after a thirteen-day passage Byng was still at Gibraltar. Hawke lost no time in raising his flag in *Ramillies*,

Byng transferring for the night to Hervey's *Hampton Court*, the next day going ashore. Hervey had been acting as something between a secretary and a chief of staff to Byng and continued to do so, helping him write a further dispatch and attending him ashore. Though nearly all the other captains had by this time distanced themselves from Byng there was considerable indignation at Gibraltar that Newcastle and Anson should have taken such precipitate action solely on the reports from Spain and France and before Byng's first Mahon dispatch had even arrived in London. The fleet had not yet appreciated the lengths that Newcastle in particular would go to at Byng's expense in an effort to save the Government from blame for the disaster. Even Hawke was somewhat abashed at what he had to do, having come to realize the motives underlying the speed with which he had been appointed and the harshness with which Byng was being treated.

There was more to Hervey's sense of dissatisfaction than Byng's disgrace. His relations with Hawke were amicable but not as close as those with Byng. Hawke and Byng were very different in courage and resolution but had a certain similarity in lack of organizational ability. Byng appears to have relied on Hervey for advice and staff work, but Hawke gave much responsibility into the hands of his secretary, a Scot of the name of John Hay. Hervey says that Hawke was 'totally governed by a damned interested Scottish secretary, a fellow without a grain of understanding who had been bred up to business in a shop and had the impudence to show his ascendancy over the Admiral to the whole fleet.' Hay had been Hawke's secretary for nearly ten years and was to continue in that office for another five. The secretary's true colours showed, however, many years later when he made an attempt to extract money from Hawke by writing a libellous travesty of the Admiral's behaviour in the attack on the Basque Roads in 1758.

It was not long before the captains of the fleet began to suffer from the secretary's officiousness. Hervey says that Hay was responsible for taking eighty of his best seamen to make up the complements of other ships. Piqued as he may have been he made his story good, for Hawke's order book gives a figure of thirty good foremastmen, to be exchanged for less experienced seamen. Hervey was also smarting at the loss of all the prizes that he had made before the outbreak of war and which he had taken into Mahon. When Edgcumbe left them there in April in the face of the French invading fleet a small fortune slipped from his hands.

Hawke had arrived at Gibraltar on 2 July and it was 10th of the month before the fleet sailed for Minorca. They made slow progress in light winds and five days later met a group of French transports bringing the captured British garrison of St Philip's Castle to Gibraltar. This was Hawke's first intimation that the castle had been surrendered, an event which took place on 27 June after a final assault by Richelieu's forces. When the fleet reached

Minorca on 19 July Hervey was anxious (in his *Journal*, but there is no record of his contemporary attitude) 'to know what would become of all our blustering, and what this mighty fleet was to perform which, had it been sent earlier, would have given the finishing stroke to France'. It was indeed a fine example of trying to shut the stable door after the horse was gone. Once it was known that St Philip's had fallen the fleet's objective was difficult to define. There was little chance of starving out the small French garrison in Minorca, and Hawke had no soldiers for a land attack. Galissonière's fleet was in Toulon, performing rightly and to perfection the function of a 'fleet in being', but with no intention of coming out to face Hawke. The British fleet therefore cruised around the island aimlessly, hoping in vain that the French would come out to meet them.

Courageous and tenacious as Hawke could be, there was nothing in Minorcan waters with which he could get to grips. Neither was he a commander of imagination or intuition, and he therefore appears to have floundered, torn between unimaginative orders from the Admiralty and the absence of any palpable enemy. Hervey was in Rear-Admiral Saunder's division and spent much time with him. Saunders, the naval commander whose tactical insight was an essential prerequisite for Wolfe's capture of Quebec three years later, was a commander of considerable ability and it is not surprising that his opinion of Hawke's actions at this time was unfavourable. Hervey's *Journal* gives a very critical view of Hawke's performance during the three months of this cruise, in great things and in small. The Commander-in-Chief was loath to send a frigate to Toulon for intelligence, relying instead on the reports of neutrals. Hervey's description of the fleet's attempts to water make a sorry tale. On one occasion Hawke took them into landlocked Pollensa Bay in Majorca at night, only in the morning discovering what Hervey says he knew all the time - that there was no water there to be had. The Admiral declined to go to Alcudia Bay or to Palma and chose instead, at Hervey's suggestion, to go to Barcelona for water. At this stage it was necessary to send word to *Experiment* at Palma to join the fleet, and according to Hervey Hawke, or John Hay, one takes one's choice, changed his mind five times as to how and when this should be done. In the event it was ten days before the fleet watered on the Spanish coast, though by this time Hawke had changed his mind once again, and they went to Altea Bay, two hundred miles south west of Barcelona. While watering there a French merchantman bound for Martinique was driven into the arms of the fleet right under the Spanish coast and taken prize. The flagship herself fired on her. The breach of Spanish neutrality was seen by Hervey and Saunders from the shore, and it was only at their instigation that Hawke released the vessel and made amends.

Such is the distressing tenor of Hervey's *Journal* for these wasted weeks. When he wrote it, some ten years later, he had served under Hawke with distinction in the western squadron in 1759 and it is difficult to believe that his comments represent a considered view of the great Admiral's capabilities. At the time of writing (probably between 1767 and 1770) Hawke was the First Lord and Hervey retired from sea service, but hopeful of a position on the Admiralty Board. It is one of the few pointers in the *Journal* to his purpose in writing it, and supports the view that it was for the eyes of Lord Sandwich, then out of office, but potentially a First Lord who might give Hervey the appointment that he wanted.

All this time the numbers of sick in the fleet continued to increase and the supplies of food and other stores continued to diminish. In late September Hawke decided to call it a day and set course for Gibraltar, which they reached on 2 October. Orders had already reached the fleet at sea for the witnesses required for Byng's court martial to be sent home. They included Hervey and nine other captains, depleting the fleet of many of its senior officers for several months. On 15 October Hawke sent for Hervey and gave him his letters and dispatches for England, at the same time saying that he had written to Anson asking for Hervey's return to *Hampton Court* after the trial. Hervey says that the Admiral chose him for this task to distinguish him from the other captains, and to allow him to go to London immediately on arrival in England. That Hawke awarded him this privilege certainly suggests that he had formed a favourable view of his capabilities.

The considerable group of officers required for the court martial took passage in *Colchester*, leaving Gibraltar on 27 October and coming into Spithead on 15 November. Hervey went straight up to London with Hawke's dispatches. On 17 November he saw Anson, who assured him that no other captain was to be appointed to *Hampton Court* while he was away from her. He had arrived, however, just as the Newcastle government was being replaced by that under the nominal control of the Duke of Devonshire; Anson went out of the Admiralty, to be replaced by Lord Temple. So he went to Temple also and was given a further assurance. Vice-Admiral Boscawen, who had remained a Lord of the Admiralty at the change of government, told him that the new Board had appointed a new captain for *Hampton Court*, on which Hervey went to Temple again and had the appointment cancelled.

Hervey was determined to defend Byng to the end and set out to do so. His campaign had, however, started much earlier. Before the fleet left Minorcan waters in May he had taken up the cudgels in a letter to Henry Fox, a letter which was for the most part fair comment on the battle and indeed provided an early and relatively unbiased account of its course; but Hervey went on to expatiate on the shortcomings of the home authorities, the key sentence in this section being:

Everyone here calls out loudly on the manner this fleet was sent and how late, how equipped, no storeships, no stores, no hospital ship, no fireship, nor no tender.

Fox as one of the ministers responsible for the actions criticized could not be expected to agree with the sentiments expressed. Displeased with Hervey's drift he was careful not to publicize the letter. Instead he sent it to Lady Hervey, presumably in the hope that she could persuade her son to adopt a less astringent line. There followed a bout of letter-writing between the three of them. All were perturbed; Hervey about the injustice which he feared would be done to his friend Byng; his mother that his forthrightness in a cause of which she herself was unconvinced would harm his professional prospects; and Fox that unless the blame were firmly fixed on Byng he and the Ministry would be driven from office.

Hervey now threw himself into pamphlet-writing in Byng's defence and helping him in other ways. The previous government had given much publicity to Byng's shortcomings – and it would be difficult to deny that his behaviour at Mahon had lacked assertiveness and aggression in the face of the enemy – and Hervey now tried to rectify the balance. Newcastle and Fox, however, still commanded much support, including that of the King, and were determined to obtained a conviction in order to shift the blame for strategic mismanagement off their shoulders, turning the issue into one of tactical negligence by the Admiral who they had appointed. Hervey even asserts that Anson, while still at the Admiralty, had arranged that the officers available at Portsmouth to be members of the Court should be ones who would favour the government view.

The Court assembled on board *St George* at Portsmouth on 27 December. Its membership is of interest, if only because it provides a list of names for which Hervey had in future years hardly a good word to say:

President:

    Thomas Smith, Vice-Admiral of the Red

Members:

    Francis Holbourn, Rear-Admiral of the White
    Henry Norris, Rear-Admiral of the White
    Thomas Broderick, Rear-Admiral of the Blue
    Charles Holmes
    Francis Geary
    John Simcoe
    John Moore
    James Douglas
    Augustus Keppel
    William Boyce

John Bentley
Peter Denis

Of these, only Keppel and to some extent Holmes managed to work their passage back into Hervey's good books.

Byng was accused under the 12th Article of War of negligence in the face of the enemy. The Navy Act of 1749 to which so many officers had taken exception had amended this article to make a sentence of death the only punishment for those found guilty. While the Government were for a conviction Byng believed, until late on in the case, that he would be found not guilty, or that the sentence would be commuted. He was to be grossly disabused.

Much has been written about the trial. It is sufficient here to say that little evidence was given that even suggested negligence; misjudgment, perhaps, particularly in the tactics employed, and excessive caution in not seeking to renew an indeterminate engagement. Hervey gave evidence at length, and though hardly impartial was the only witness who had been well placed to observe the course of the battle without being immersed himself in its smoke and thunder.

His evidence is generally reported to have been clear, concise and accurate, the latter so much so that one bystander (Mrs Montagu to Mrs Boscawen) gave him an involuntary compliment for factual precision:

'I admire Captain Hervey's method of watching the battle; I have known people boil an egg with a watch in their hand, counting the minutes, but I never heard that we were to do so when we basted the French. If I had been in court, considering the delicacy and effeminacy of the family, I should have asked him if he had not his tweezer-case on his left side'.

A more generous comment was made by Henry Fox, as reported by Lady Hervey in writing to Augustus on 13 January

. . . there is however one thing in which all agree which is that Mr Hervey's evidence was as fine and as masterly a thing as ever was heard – clearness and a perspicuity ran though the whole, not an improper or unnecessary word . . .

But inevitably, in view of the political dimension, the court on 26 January found the prisoner guilty of negligence, and having no alternative sentenced him to death. He was, however, acquitted of any suggestion of cowardice. By this time Hervey had returned to London and Lawrence, Byng's secretary, posted up to town overnight, arriving at Hervey's lodgings with the news at 3 am. He immediately went to the First Lord and to many others to object to the sentence and seek a review. There were indeed many who thought it excessive and the King was constrained to refer its legality to the judges. In spite of the anomaly that the court had convicted him of negligence but added to their judgement a rider that they thought him guilty only of misjudgment the sentence was upheld.

There was of course no established appeal procedure at that time but feelings ran high. At the King's insistence the order for the prisoner's execution was given on 17 February, but only three of the Board signed it. Admiral Forbes refused on the ground that he was uncertain about the propriety of the sentence. For his part Admiral West who was at Portsmouth refused to take a squadron to sea under such a legal framework and had to be persuaded to do so by the First Lord. Fox, showing a different face now Byng had been convicted, told Hervey at Whites that 'he was surprised the court martial could show their faces, that he would much rather be Mr Byng than one of the thirteen members of the court'.

Byng's case was debated on more than one occasion in Parliament, in which Hervey had no seat at this period. Members of the opposition initiated a debate on the 12th Article of War, in which inevitably the burden of the speeches were on Byng's situation. Both the First Lord and Pitt, one of the Secretaries of State, went to the King and are thought to have recommended mercy.

There was much disquiet among the members of the court martial about what they had done and some wanted to explain why they had made the recommendation for mercy. To enable them to do this, however, it would be necessary for them to be released from their oath of secrecy on the proceedings. Hervey and Rodney, then a captain and a Tory, went to Moore and Norris and persuaded them to ask for this release and Keppel was persuaded to say as much in the House of Commons. With opinion moving towards Byng a Bill to release the oath was carried through the Commons, with the support of Pitt but after a bitter debate in which Fox continued to oppose such a procedure. In the Lords, however, matters went differently. The members of the court were called before the House and all except Keppel, Moore and Norris denied, contrary to previous assertions, that they wanted to be free to speak. The Lords therefore rejected the Bill and Byng's fate was sealed. The tergiversations that went on and the pressures to which these senior naval officers were exposed – and to which most of them succumbed – make this effectively the last case in which judicial murder was carried out in Britain for political ends. Voltaire's *bon mot* about encouraging the others was in reality much off target. The execution was carried through for the much baser motive of saving political skins.

Hervey now saw that the legal process had been exhausted and moved off into a flight of illegal fancy – and he was not the only one, for a similar suggestion had been discussed already among senior politicians out of office.

On 5 March he went down to Portsmouth. On his way he left a set of horses at Ripley and ordered another to be ready night and day at Petersfield. He instructed his servant William Cradock to have horses saddled night and day in London and to hire a Dutch fishing boat for the journey to France. When he reached Portsmouth, however, he found Byng heavily guarded on board *Monarch*. When Hervey went off to the Admiral he found him resigned to his fate, though he agreed to a final petition to the King for commutation to banishment. Byng refused Hervey's several suggested plans for escape. Eventually, Hervey says, he felt too upset to take leave of his friend and crept off back to London.

Byng was shot on the quarterdeck of *Monarch* on 14 March and Hervey was back in Portsmouth on the 16th. He retired to Petersfield, however, refusing to sleep in Portsmouth while his friend and patron's body lay there. In his will Byng left Hervey a French clock ornamented with Dresden flowers, with the wish 'May time serve you better than he has served me'. It was seen many years later in the house of Mrs Nesbitt, Hervey's last mistress, to whom he left all his personal effects.

References

1. The Fox papers, (5), 1006, 1010
2. Ibid.

CHAPTER X

The Moonlight Battle

The chief of staff

After giving his evidence at Byng's court martial, and in full confidence that the Admiral would be acquitted, Hervey had quickly taken steps to get back to *Hampton Court*, still under her temporary captain in the Mediterranean. On 22 January, four days before the verdict was given, he wrote to the Admiralty[1] asking very firmly for orders to return to his command. Clevland wrote on the letter 'Ordered to his duty on board *Hampton Court*'. It seems likely, however, that when after the verdict he took up the case for a reprieve he regretted his impulsiveness, for there is no further mention of the subject until 12 March, two days before Byng's execution. On that day he asked for and was given an order for himself and three dependents to go out in *Monmouth*, commanded by his friend Arthur Gardiner.[2] *Monmouth*, however, was delayed and later in the month Hervey heard that Vice-Admiral Henry Osborne had been appointed to the Mediterranean command.

Osborne was a relation of the dead Byng and was one of those few admirals who ranked well in Hervey's hagiography. The new Commander-In-Chief offered to take Hervey out in his flagship *Prince*, of 90 guns. Nothing was ready, however, and Hervey continued to chafe at the bit in London and at Portsmouth. He tried without success for a transfer to *Invincible*, which was under orders for North America with Rear-Admiral Holbourn, and made himself useful to his new Commander-In-Chief in preparing signals and instructions.

He was still very bitter about the witnesses at and members of Byng's court martial and the apparently favourable treatment they subsequently received. About Captain Cornwall, who had been in command of *Revenge* at Mahon and to whom he ascribed (perhaps wrongly) much of the blame for the confusion into which Byng's line of battle had fallen, he wrote a pamphlet 'Queries to Captain Cornwall'. Cornwall's pension of £220 a year, awarded rather late in the day for the loss of his arm at the battle of Toulon in 1744, he describes as payment for the evidence that he gave to the court. Later he describes the appointment of Captain John Moore to be Commodore in the Windward Islands as reward for his services as a member of the court.

It was not until 8 May that Osborne sailed from St Helens escorting convoys for North America and Portugal. This long delay – it was over three months since Hervey had been ordered to return – did not go unnoticed at the Navy Board, that bureaucratic and semi-independent dependency of the Admiralty. In the usual way he wrote[3] to the Admiralty on his arrival at Gibraltar asking for an order to the Navy Board to make payment of his and his servants' pay for the period he had been away from *Hampton Court*, 27 October 1756 to 30 May 1757. The Secretary, John Clevland, wrote on the letter 'Usual order for him to be paid'. But eighteen months later the Navy Board had paid only part of the money, refusing to approve that for the period after his order to return. He wrote in February 1759[4] asking Their Lordships to authorize the remainder. Clevland wrote on the letter 'Refer to the Navy Board for precedents' and there the matter disappears from the surviving correspondence. Presumably in the end persistence paid off.

Difficulties with authorizations of this nature were, however, commonplace. The gift of powder to the Alcaide of Tetuan in 1753 provides a particularly long-running example, with which Hervey was still struggling at the time of Byng's court martial. In May 1754 he had discovered[5] that the Board of Ordnance 'hesitates giving a certificate' for the powder and had asked the Admiralty 'to give some directions therein'. On Hervey's letter asking for authorization Clevland indicated that the Board of Ordnance would be directed to allow the powder on his Gunners account. The Board, however, felt unable to do so, presumably taking the view that this was not a naval matter but an unauthorized gift to the Alcaide, as if from the King.

In February 1757, over three years after the gift, we find him writing to the Admiralty[6] once more asking for reimbursement and pointing out that Their Lordships had approved this in principle as long ago as February 1754. By now a second item was troubling him – failure to authorize payment for powder expended in saluting the King of Portugal on a festival day, something that the British Minister in Lisbon had asked him to do as matter of custom.

Clevland replied[7] that authorization awaited agreement from the King, to whom application had been made, in the case of the Alcaide's powder as long ago as June 1754. In April he asked again[8] and was told[9] that he should apply to the Council office . . .

Hervey had many other niggling difficulties, and it seems unlikely that his experience was out of the ordinary. The problem arose from the complex bureaucracy operated by the Navy Board and the strict rules that applied to expenditure of government funds, not assisted by the creative tension that existed between that Board and its nominal masters at the Admiralty.

Osborne made Gibraltar in under a fortnight, parting with the American convoy off Finisterre and dropping off the trade for Lisbon and Cadiz on the way. On arrival he found Rear-Admiral Saunders with five of the line, concentrated there to prevent the French Toulon squadron leaving the

Mediterranean and joining La Motte in Canadian waters. Saunders had had a setback, though not a defeat, in April when with an easterly wind five Frenchmen bound for Louisbourg had crept past in the night; when they were seen at daylight it was too late, for the British ships were foul and slow and the French easily outsailed them.

At Gibraltar Hervey took over *Hampton Court* from Captain Swanton, who had been in temporary command in his absence. By 2 June he was cruising in the Gut (to the west of Gibraltar) with *Revenge* under him and two days later they were joined by the whole fleet, consisting of eleven of the line and several frigates.

The Mediterranean theatre of war was now very much a backwater. Osborne's primary duty was to prevent the rest of the French fleet in Toulon from breaking out of the Mediterranean to reinforce their squadron at Louisbourg, at that time the first objective of Pitt's campaign to conquer Canada. In addition the rich French trade with Italy, the Levant and North Africa was there to be harassed and interrupted.

Osborne exercised the fleet for several days, during which Hervey spent much time on board *Prince* acting in effect as chief of staff. The Commander-in-Chief was 72 and while possessing all his powers had never, perhaps, had the best of grasps of strategy and organization. Hervey was adept at both and throughout the next few months, whenever *Hampton Court* was with the fleet, it was he who suggested the strategy to adopt and the allocation of ships to specific duties and stations. Of the two admirals Hervey writes: 'In short, these gentlemen would never give themselves the trouble to weigh and consider the intelligence they received and the different objects which a fleet such as ours were (*sic*) able to fulfil, but if ever they trusted their instructions and intelligence to others, I never found but in general they were glad to have all that work done for them'. Osborne's age and the good opinion he had of Hervey are a sufficient basis for this delegation of thought, but that Saunders should abrogate responsibility for such matters is surprising – Saunders who two years later carried the British fleet up the St Lawrence to Quebec, whose tactics were the foundation for Wolfe's brilliant campaign against that city and who later became First Lord under Pitt. Hervey's relations with Saunders are in fact something of an enigma. The impression that Hervey gives is that Saunders always fell in with his advice to Osborne but this may well have been because Hervey, who did not lack knowledge of men, went out of his way to ensure that his proposals did not run contrary to the second-in-command's ideas and interest. But it may also have been the case that Saunders, in a situation where he did not bear the final responsibility and in which he was hoping for better things elsewhere, felt it simpler to accept the younger man's plans, which if not perfect were a great improvement on Osborne's unaided performance, rather than to argue with or antagonize his Commander-In-Chief.

For the next three months the fleet cruised around the western Mediterranean. On 17 June Hervey was sent with *Revenge* to look into Toulon. *En route* they saw a man-of-war off the coast of Majorca and chased her in very light winds. At 2 pm on the 20th she hoisted French colours and was later identified as the frigate *Nymphe* of 32 guns. In a flat calm she began to row and tow towards the coast and at 4 pm Hervey ordered out all his own boats and those of *Revenge* as well to tow *Hampton Court* in pursuit. By dusk *Nymphe* was at anchor in a small bay to the south of Alcudia. Hervey kept *Hampton Court* close by overnight and in the morning found that the French had landed with their arms and that the French flag was flying ashore. Majorca was neutral territory but the shore was uninhabited and the French landing had already violated its neutrality. Hervey therefore took the view, in the then indeterminate state of international law, that he was free to take her. He sent a lieutenant in a boat under a flag of truce to demand her surrender, but while the boat was alongside the French set their ship on fire. Her guns, which were trained on *Hampton Court*, began to go off, distributing shot all round her, and worse still so close were the two ships that Hervey feared the effects of an explosion. So he fired several broadsides into her, on which she turned on one side and sank. Hervey and his crew received no prize money, but head-money was paid for the 220 members of her crew.

The same evening he got close to Mahon and the next morning in a flat calm 'had the mortification to see a French frigate towed into the harbour without being able to get at her'. However, during the onward passage to Toulon he took several small merchant vessels, including one bound from Toulon to Mahon with timber and dockyard supplies for two French ships immobilized there, and also had the satisfaction of recapturing the *Eagle* sloop, which had been taken a few days earlier by a French privateer. The captain of a French snow bound for Mahon told him that there were four sail of the line at Toulon nearly ready for sea and five more much undercrewed. When they reached Toulon both *Hampton Court* and *Revenge* hoisted Dutch colours. Hervey went aboard *Revenge*, the smaller of the two, and closed to within four miles of the harbour. Confirming what he had been told he could clearly see four ships of the line in the roads and five or six in the basin. The sea was alive with French shipping but lack of wind prevented the British ships getting at them. They took only a snow which was being brought in as prize by a privateer.

The same day *Monmouth* and *Princess Louisa* arrived with news that the fleet was within forty miles. Hervey sent *Revenge* to the Admiral with his intelligence and proceeded with his orders to gather intelligence at Villefranche. Savoy and Sardinia were neutral but General Paterson was still there as Governor. Paterson was anxious to avoid trouble with the French and sent to Turin for permission for the fleet to come in, though saying that up to five sail would be welcome and that supplies would be no problem.

Paterson showed Hervey an English newspaper which gave the news that he had been elected member for St Edmundsbury. His majority was one, 11 votes to 10 for Sir Robert Davers. With this small majority it seems possible that the members of Bury Corporation who formed the electorate were still not being looked after in the Bristol and Whig interest as well as they expected to be. The 1st Earl had been dead six years and his successor was abroad, serving as British envoy to the King of Sardinia at Turin. Perhaps also they were lukewarm in support of an absentee candidate who was likely to remain so as long as the war lasted.

Hervey was in contact with his brother, who does not seem to have expected him to have any political view or allegiance other than that of the head of the family – which was still unswerving, indeed sycophantic, support for the Duke of Newcastle. In June Lord Bristol wrote from Turin, to assure his patron that he had another certain vote in the Commons.[10]

> I have acquainted my brother Augustus with his being chosen for Bury, and I have reminded him at the same time of the many professions he has made of adhering steadily to me and my friends, of which list I have placed your Grace at the head; I hope I may congratulate you upon your having an additional friend in the House of Commons . . .

On 19 October he made a further commitment on Augustus' behalf.[11]

> My brother Augustus has not long since confirmed to me his former assurances of having no other connections than mine, and has particularly mentioned his resolution to serve your Grace. I hope the zeal of our part of the family for you will in some measure compensate our want of abilities, I am one that will adhere to you till you drop me, I really value your character, and neglect alone can alter me . . .

Augustus' letter of assurance has not survived, so it is not possible to assess which of the brothers had his tongue furthest into his cheek in concealing the younger's lack of affection, personal or political, for the Prime Minister. Having made these assurances Bristol went on in the second letter to ask for two favours for the Hervey family – that Brother Frederick should receive ecclesiastical preferment by appointment to a Canon's stall at Windsor or Westminster, or by appointment as Dean of Norwich on the expected death of the incumbent; and that he himself should be promoted from Turin to the important Embassy in Madrid.

Hampton Court was held in Villefranche for several days by southerly winds, allowing her captain time for social recreation. He dined with Paterson and with the commander of the King's galleys; he went to the Nice opera twice, once with the wife of Baron Tonda, a lady on whom he, unusually, makes no comment and who does not appear elsewhere as one of his amours. Eventually *Hampton Court* was towed out with the assistance of the Sardinian galleys. This was a paid service and it was a quirk of the penny-pinching Admiralty system that no funds were available to ships' captains for such extras. So Hervey had to pay out of his own pocket, though this was something he could well afford to do bearing in mind the cornucopia of prize money that he was accumulating.

The fleet was not at the rendezvous off Toulon, so *Hampton Court* cruised eastward along the coast. An encounter with three pollacres showed Hervey in a dashing but eventually somewhat ludicrous light. A Catalan vessel had told him they were French and in a dead calm he sent *Hampton Court's* boats under the second and third lieutenants, Shenery and Holmes, to board them. When at nightfall the boats came close they found the pollacres lashed together for defence and one of them of some strength; the boats returned. When Hervey heard the lieutenants' report he rebuked them for not at least finding out who they were. To show them he could do better he went himself next morning in the boats, taking from early morning until 2 pm to cover the ten miles or more that separated them. Their drooping colours showed white and were to all appearances French. Determining to take them by assault he fired at them from the pinnace with swivel guns and approached to board. On this their crews cried out and spread their colours, which then showed arms on a white background, readily identifiable as those of Naples, not France. Hervey was as he says 'all damped down' when he found he had attacked ships of a neutral country and went aboard to speak to the masters. In the end he persuaded the Neapolitans to feed his boats' crews (for which he paid) and one of them to tow the boats back to *Hampton Court* in the breeze which had sprung up.

Hampton Court rejoined the fleet off the French coast on 12 July. Many of the crews were sickening fast, having been over five weeks at sea, and he found Osborne intent on going to Leghorn for water and supplies. In Hervey's view this was a false step and he said so. In addition to the French ships of the line in Toulon there were a number of cruisers in Malta (still a friendly base for France) or operating thence in the Levant, and he suggested a disposition which would prevent them linking up with their main fleet. Saunders with five ships should go to Cagliari to water in turn, a movement which would enable him to cover the passage between Sardinia and the North African coast, while the remainder should go to Leghorn, where they could control the northern exit from the Tyrrhenian Sea. This strategy was more effective than Osborne's original intention, but is surprisingly deficient in one vital respect – it made no provision for the ships at Toulon, four of which

Hervey had found to be almost ready for sea a fortnight earlier. Perhaps there was an assumption that none would attempt to break out of the Mediterranean until all were ready.

Osborne's squadron was at Leghorn until 4 August and then sailed to cruise off the French coast and down to Sardinia, where on the 21st they found Saunders. His intelligence was that the French cruisers operating from Malta were all at sea, two in the Sicily channel, three south of Malta and two to the eastward off Cape Matapan. Nevertheless, the Rear-Admiral wanted to keep the fleet together. Hervey, asked for advice by Osborne on how to meet the fleet's multiple objectives, suggested that better use of the twelve ships of the line would be made by splitting them up. He recommended sending three or four around Malta against the cruisers, two to watch Marseilles and Toulon, five to remain to guard the channel south of Sardinia and two sickly ships to go into Cagliari to recuperate. Though an improvement on Saunders' stated preference the low priority given to Toulon is again surprising; it is unclear why Osborne, Saunders and Hervey all accepted that the French fleet would make no attempt to break out.

In this disposition of Osborne's fleet *Hampton Court* was sent towards Malta in company with *Monmouth* and *Princess Louisa*, Gardiner in *Monmouth* being in command. They cruised for three weeks, seeing nothing of the French cruisers but taking a number of prizes. One, surprisingly, carried forty tons of West India coffee destined from Marseilles for Turkey, showing how much the trade had altered from its traditional sources of supply in the east.

Back in Cagliari Bay on 14 September Hervey had yet another difference with the admirals on strategy. Osborne at first wanted to retire to Gibraltar but Hervey thought it unproductive to leave the Mediterranean to the French so early in the autumn and persuaded the Commander-in-Chief to change his mind. The Admiral then found himself in a cleft stick, having with Saunders' encouragement just written home stating his intention. However, Hervey says that he then suggested a slower and more complex retirement, which would be sufficiently close to Osborne's announced intentions to save face. Before making detailed proposals he spoke to Saunders, and found that he had a special reason for wanting to go to Gibraltar. He was expecting a recall to better things and anxious to be off. Hervey therefore devised a solution which allowed both admirals to take the principal ships direct to Gibraltar, while the smaller ships of the line went to show themselves off Toulon. In the event, these ships remained cruising off Sardinia for some time and *Hampton Court* then proceeded direct to Gibraltar, arriving on 27 October.

Hervey's plans for the fleet, as described in his *Journal*, always seem more purposeful than the relatively simple approach that Osborne favoured. It seems that Osborne was content with a quiet and uncomplicated life and Saunders' eyes were elsewhere. For his part, Hervey was always for the most forward and active policy, but managed as a rule to produce a situation that allowed *Hampton Court* a goodly share of profitable cruising.

Mediterranean cruising and staff work had not prevented Hervey from enjoying an active social life whenever opportunity arose. Sent to Genoa on 18 July to enquire whether this neutral state was actively building ships for the French navy, he went to the theatre with his old friend Pellinetta Brignole-Sale, catching cold there and bringing on an attack of gout. Pleasure was mixed with business, however, for he also collected the information he needed from the well informed Sardinian envoy and next day sent it off to Osborne at Leghorn. Incapacitated on board for twenty-four hours, he was not inhibited from having a number of notables from the city to dine with him, and the following day went to see the Doge. He managed to see Pellinetta twice more before he left Genoa, but does not say whether the previous intimacy was re-established.

A few days later *Hampton Court* joined the fleet at Leghorn. In the intervals of his services to the Commander-in-Chief Hervey went about the town with several of his former friends, including Signora Ricci, whose *cicisbeo* he had once been. She seemed no less attracted to him, and fearing his attention would wander to some of the other wayward wives of the company she took him away in her carriage and allowed him the usual liberties. But as so often he is reticent on how far the familiarity was allowed to develop.

The fleet had returned to Gibraltar essentially because of the need to refit after the long summer cruise. When *Hampton Court* returned on 27 October Hervey dined the same day with Osborne, the Earl of Home who was then Governor and Lord Robert Bertie, commanding the troops. The next day Osborne sent for him and had him prepare a plan for the fleet. Hervey's proposals were heavily biassed towards cruising in search of enemy trade, and *Hampton Court* in particular was to go along the Spanish and French coasts seeking intelligence, and thence to Malta and then Leghorn; they again took little cognizance of the possibility that the French ships at Toulon might attempt to break out into the Atlantic. In his defence it has to be realized that though Hervey may have seen this as a remote possibility his long service in the Mediterranean did not make for awareness of the dictates of global strategy – and he probably knew little of Pitt's great plan for North America and the importance the French attached to getting naval reinforcements to that theatre.

In any case the plan was not put into effect. The limitations of the dockyard meant that refitting was a lengthy process. Also, undoubtedly, Osborne himself was aware at this stage of the increasing probability that the Toulon squadron might appear in the Straits. The frigate *Ambuscade* was sent along the Spanish coast for intelligence but apart from her the fleet remained at Gibraltar. Hervey found inactivity unrewarding. The Rock was not a lively social milieu and the limited scope for entertainment there was all within the bounds of the military and naval fraternity. Social excitements were in a correspondingly low key. During November there was considerable and undoubtedly ribald gossip about a close friend of Lord Home, a Captain Leviston or Livingston, who eloped with the daughter of the Genoese consul, described as a 'good handsome girl'. Later, Captain Cary, son and heir of Viscount Falkland, married Anne Leith, daughter of Captain Leith of the Artillery. This romance must also have given rise to much comment, since the bride's mother had been a kitchen maid.

So bored was Hervey, or so desirous of prize money, that eventually, on 19 November, he cajoled Osborne into sending him cruising west of Gibraltar. Westerly winds kept him in, however, and on the 22nd there came a change in the whole strategic situation. Captain Gwyn of *Ambuscade* brought in news that a French squadron of nine ships under La Clue was off Cartagena, i.e. about 250 miles or two good sailing days away, and presumably intending to pass through the Straits with the first favourable wind. There was a scrummage of activity in the fleet, getting every available ship ready to go out with all dispatch, though with the westerly wind those within the mole were not got out until the 26th. The wind was now critical to Osborne's tactics. While it remained in the west there was little chance that the French would be able to approach the Straits but whenever it went easterly they had a chance to slip through. With a westerly wind Osborne therefore remained in port but every time it went easterly he scrambled to sea; Saunders' experience when the French had slipped past while the British waited for them in harbour was still fresh in everyone's mind. On 7 December came news that the French, making little progress against continuing westerlies, were off Cape de Gata, between Cartagena and the Straits; though in fact by the 6th La Clue had taken his squadron into Cartagena, news that did not reach Osborne until 22nd of the month.

Osborne remained at Gibraltar following this policy until the middle of December, when an easterly turn sent him to sea. By the next day, however, the westerlies had returned and the fleet was driven east as far as Malaga before it could make harbour again. For the next two months westerlies prevailed but the weather was changeable and the fleet was continually making sail and returning to port, seven times, Hervey says, within a few weeks.

Since Spain was officially neutral there was no dearth of reports on the situation of the French, from the British Consul and from neutral ships as well as from the British cruisers. La Clue was said to have brought with him six ships of the line and two frigates, which were reinforced in January by two further capital ships. The reports reaching Gibraltar suggested that four more under the Marquis Duquesne were expected from Toulon any day.

Thus if the French drew their squadrons together they would have a strength of twelve ships of the line, much the same as Osborne's. Nevertheless, La Clue's objective was to escape into the Atlantic, not to fight a battle in which at best he could expect damage that would put in doubt his capacity to make the long ocean voyage to Canadian waters.

Throughout this wait at Gibraltar it had been Hervey's contention, not accepted by the two admirals, that the fleet should attempt a close blockade of Cartagena, preventing La Clue coming out or Duquesne going in to him. On 26 February Osborne and Saunders, having heard that Duquesne was near at hand and with the wind in the west to southwest decided that they must prevent such a junction. The fleet therefore stood along the Spanish coast towards Cartagena in extended order, searching a wide stretch of sea as they went.

By 4 pm on the 27th they were able to look into Almeria Bay, which was empty. Osborne continued eastward through the night with *Hampton Court* next to the flagship as his second, and in the first glimmerings of dawn two large ships were seen ahead. The Admiral almost immediately gave the signal for general chase and daylight showed four French men-of-war scattering in flight ahead of the British squadron. Hervey at first went after the 64-gun *Orphée*, which was also pursued by *Berwick* and *Revenge*. *Hampton Court* was not, however, a good sailer and since the other two ships were outsailing her Hervey switched his attention to the largest of the Frenchmen, which was already the target of *Monmouth* and *Swiftsure*, though the latter was some way behind. He soon identified her as the 80-gun *Foudroyant*, wearing Duquesne's flag. The wind had fallen light, still westerly, and progress was slow. Osborne signalled for *Hampton Court* to return, but Hervey ignored him, taking the view, wrongly as it turned out, that *Monmouth* would be no match for the larger ship.

Such disregard of orders was not uncommon at that time (and a generation later Nelson did it on two famous occasions to general advantage) but in this case cannot easily be condoned. Osborne had more than Duquesne's squadron to concern himself with and needed every spare ship to interpose between the fighting and Cartagena, in case La Clue should come out. For the French commander, however, discretion was the better part and he remained in port under the protection of the Spanish defences. The pursuit of *Foudroyant* went on all day, in light winds in which *Monmouth* as one of the fastest ships in the fleet gained slowly on the enemy and engaged her some time before dark. Her Captain, Gardiner, who had been Byng's flag captain at Minorca, was wounded in the arm early in the action but continued to fight a sharp single-ship action. At about 9 pm Gardiner was killed by a bullet in the head and the battle continued until after midnight under his first lieutenant, Robert Carkett. Both ships were dismasted and suffered much damage and many casualties.

Hampton Court and *Swiftsure* had been left behind in the chase and in the light winds had come up slowly, seeing the battle begin and after dark steering towards the sound of the guns. When Hervey came on the scene, just before *Swiftsure*, all firing had ceased and *Foudroyant* had struck her flag to Lieutenant Carkett. Running *Hampton Court* under her stern Hervey refrained from firing, as the Frenchman had clearly surrendered. In *Swiftsure*, however, Captain Stanhope was less observant and fired a broadside into her, much of which went into *Hampton Court*. Hervey went on board *Foudroyant*, dismasted and disabled, and saw Duquesne, a *chef d'escadre* (equivalent to Rear-Admiral) and his officers. Stanhope, however, asserted his seniority over Hervey to take them into *Swiftsure*. They would have done better in *Hampton Court*, which was what Hervey had wanted, for he kept a good table and spoke their language both literally and figuratively, as Sir Horace Mann made clear from first hand experience.[12]

Captain Hervey, whose politeness is of their own sort [i.e. the French prisoners'] and whose magnificence probably exceeds any they have on board a ship.

There was, however, no doubt in anyone's mind that the honours of the day belonged entirely to the dead Captain Gardiner and his crew. Hervey for his part can only have been sad at Gardiner's death, for he was another of Byng's protégés. The three of them had served together in *Sutherland* and *Captain* over fifteen years previously, and Hervey regarded him as one of his oldest naval friends.

The fight, know as the Moonlight Battle, ranks among the fiercest of the single-ship actions of the times. That *Foudroyant*, the pride of the French fleet and Galissonière's flagship at Mahon, should have been defeated by a much smaller ship put heart into London and was a blow to morale in Paris. The tenacity with which *Monmouth* was fought is underlined by the difference in firepower – *Monmouth* of 64 guns and a broadside weighing 504 lb against *Foudroyant's* 80 guns and 1,222-lb broadside. But Duquesne was at a tactical disadvantage. He dare not sheer to put a full broadside into the nimbler and faster *Monmouth*, since to do so would have enabled *Hampton Court* and *Swiftsure* to come up with him. There was also a later report that part of *Foudroyant's* crew deserted their guns early in the engagement and took shelter below.

During the day, while *Monmouth* was in pursuit of *Foudroyant*, *Berwick* and *Revenge* had engaged and taken *Orphée* after a fight lasting under an hour, while a third large ship, *Oriflamme*, was driven ashore. A fourth, the frigate *Pleiade*, escaped. In strategic terms Osborne was lucky that his sortie from Gibraltar coincided so well with Duquesne's arrival in the neighbourhood of Cartagena. Events might, however, have been different if La Clue had had the sense to come out of Cartagena to join forces with Duquesne's weak squadron, making a total of eleven ships of the line to Osborne's thirteen. That La Clue did not appears to have been due to his false sense of the proprieties – as senior officer he refused to come out of Cartagena, insisting that Duquesne come in to him. The strategic effect of the destruction of Duquesne's squadron was to leave the French squadron in Cartagena too weak to run the gauntlet of the Straits with Osborne standing guard at Gibraltar. Within a month La Clue was back at Toulon and his squadron was being taken out of service. As a consequence no reinforcements from the Mediterranean reached Louisburg at this critical time for French interests in North America. But strategically useful as it was the destruction of Duquesne's squadron cannot readily be ranked as a major naval victory. It came, however, at a time when British naval performance had sunk into mediocrity and was sufficient to bring Osborne a vote of thanks from a grateful and relieved House of Commons.

The long chase had taken the four ships away from the fleet, which Osborne had kept near to Cartagena. At daybreak, therefore, the dismasted *Foudroyant* and her captors were on their own. Hervey went on board *Foudroyant* again and saw her officers, with two of whom he found he had previous connections. Indeed, one of them, the First Captain, De Lisle Callian, had been captain of the frigate *Nymphe* which he had driven ashore on the coast of Majorca. The crew was in a state of near mutiny and her officers had to take dire steps to get them to work on making her seaworthy. *Monmouth* was equally badly damaged and Hervey put eighty of his own crew into her to help with repairs. They then began the passage back to Gibraltar, *Swiftsure* towing *Foudroyant* and *Hampton Court* towing *Monmouth*. It was a slow business, in light westerly winds. After a few days *Monmouth* was able to get herself under sail and Stanhope took himself off to join the fleet whilst *Hampton Court* took over *Foudroyant*.

When eventually *Hampton Court* and *Foudroyant* joined the fleet off Almeria Osborne sent the prizes and the damaged *Monmouth* on towards Gibraltar and retained *Hampton Court* with him, keeping station to windward of Cartagena. Hervey was promised *Monmouth*, since she was so much faster that *Hampton Court*, while Lieutenant Carkett was promoted into *Foudroyant* in recognition of the fight he had made to capture her. Hervey was kept busy helping Osborne with the disposition of the fleet, with arrangements for the exchange of prisoners and with letters home and to British envoys in Spain and Italy. He had a long talk over dinner with Saunders and was pleased to conclude that he stood as well with the Rear-Admiral as with the Commander-in-Chief.

The fleet now made slowly towards Gibraltar. About midday on 25 March, when they were off Malaga, there was a signal for Hervey to go on board the flagship where he found that Osborne had had a stroke during the night.

His speech was impaired and he was partly paralysed, but he was still in command of his senses and remained in at least nominal command. On the afternoon of the 26th, off Fuengirola, Hervey was sent for again and found that the Admiral was somewhat worse. He was well enough to order the flagship to take him into Gibraltar while – the wind being easterly, with the possibility that La Clue might try for the Straits – the fleet stayed out under Saunders. The next day Saunders sent Hervey into Gibraltar where he was sworn into *Monmouth*. Osborne had been taken ashore to the Commissioner's house as soon as weather conditions allowed but had no intention of giving up his command. Nobody considered his flag captain, Gayton, a satisfactory deputy for the sick man. It was Hervey who took over, in effect carrying out the duties of Captain of the Fleet, and probably taking many of the decisions himself for several weeks, the flag of a Vice-Admiral of the Blue flying from *Monmouth's* mainmast. Though Osborne was improving he was desirous of going home to recuperate and wrote to the Admiralty to that effect. In the meantime Hervey dealt with the logistic and administrative affairs of the command at Gibraltar and passed Osborne's orders out to Saunders, who continued at sea whenever the wind was easterly.

Hervey continued his usual entertainment of himself and others, giving dinners for the Governor, other officials and their ladies. He also kept open table for the French officers who were being held at Gibraltar. On 21 April he went to San Roque, the nearest Spanish town of any size, to dine with General Buccarelli, the Commandant, who was an old acquaintance. Later in the day he was taken by an English merchant named Crutchett to see a very beautiful Spanish woman called Rosa. It is not clear from his account whether or not she was a prostitute. What is clear, however, is that Hervey thought so, for he offered her (and her mother) a large sum, which was refused. She did, however, allow him to 'toy' with her, though only in her mother's presence. Altogether he seems to have had a frustrating and dispiriting time with her.

There was during April and May a 'general post' of admirals, Osborne relinquishing the command because of his state of health and Saunders also asking to go home. On 24 April Rear-Admiral Broderick arrived from England after an eventful voyage. *Prince George* of 90 guns in which he was travelling caught fire and was lost in the Bay of Biscay. Broderick was an hour or more in the water before he was picked up. He was to take over the command; Hervey found the prospect unwelcome, probably because of the new Commander-in-Chief's membership of Byng's court martial. The change decided him that he should go home at the first opportunity.

Such thoughts must have been expressed in Hervey's letters to his mother, who wrote to Mr Morris on 4 May:

When I shall see my other son God knows; for I find he has changed from the *Hampton Court* to the *Monmouth*; they are the same rate but as the former is very foul, and the latter one of the best sailers in the whole fleet he hopes to be always in action when there is any. Poor dear boy, he is very unlucky; one admiral who was his particular friend, was cruelly and scandalously murdered, and another who is also a great friend is unfortunately struck with a palsy, to blast his laurels and damp the happiness of his friends and family in the midst of his glory

It was mid-May before *Monmouth* was ready for sea and before he relinquished the command Osborne ordered him (or rather Hervey 'prevailed' upon him and made out his own orders) to cruise in the Mediterranean with four frigates under him. The little squadron sailed on 29 May but soon separated and *Monmouth* looked into Toulon on 6 June. Hervey had taken a French tartane off Mahon and he now manned her as a decoy, so taking four more off Toulon. At Villefranche he met Baron Tonda, whose wife he had taken to the Nice opera not long before, and his old friend General Paterson. He was told that there were no ships ready for sea at Toulon and after selling his small prizes sailed for Leghorn.

Paterson had persuaded him, if he needed persuading, to take on board a Madame St Sebastian, newly married to an officer serving at Cagliari and desirous of joining her husband. His argument for the somewhat unusual course in time of war was that it would be well thought of at Turin and could help Lord Bristol in his duties as envoy there. Hervey describes her as an agreeable lady though not beautiful. With any contact that Hervey had with a woman it is natural to speculate how far the relationship developed. There is, however, no indication in his *Journal* that Hervey made any attempt on Madame St Sebastian's virtue during the fortnight that she was on board. Perhaps he did so and was refused. Alternatively, he did so and succeeded but thought it unwise to refer to such a matter in print, even ten years later. A third possibility is that for disciplinary reasons he judged it wise to keep relations on a proper footing, and a fourth, though unlikely given his extremely catholic taste in women, is that he did not care for her. On balance, he and the lady should be given the benefit of the doubt.

Outside Villefranche *Monmouth* sighted two French two-deckers who were thought to be going east to act as escorts for their homeward convoys. He outsailed them and lost them overnight and made a fast passage to Leghorn. There he confirmed earlier information that the French *Triton* of 64 guns had sailed from Toulon with three frigates to harass British trade in the Levant. This decided him to collect all the force he could and go in pursuit. The frigate *Lyme* was already at Leghorn and he sent for *Ambuscade* from Genoa. Pausing only to visit Signora Ricci he found her pregnant. He had last been with her on 3 August 1757, over ten months previously, so the tears that she had shed on that occasion had soon been forgotten.

Madame St Sebastian was still on board *Monmouth*, and according to Hervey quite satisfied with her position. Hervey, however, was in a hurry and meeting two Sardinian galleys off their coast put her with every courtesy aboard one of them to take into Cagliari. On 30 June they sighted three ships near Pantelleria in the Sicily Channel and assuming them to be the French cruisers chased them all day before finding that they were Dutch merchantmen out of Smyrna for Amsterdam. He now had *Lyme* and *Ambuscade* in company and made for Malta, intending to send *Lyme* into harbour for necessary repairs to her mainmast. On the evening of 1 July, however, off Malta, they came across a French frigate and in very light winds chased her all night.[13] The next morning she was towing with her boats very close in to the north coast, making for the Grand Harbour. *Monmouth*, however, was between her and the harbour mouth. Hervey had no intention of concerning himself about Maltese neutrality, as the Maltese were nothing but covert allies of France and even then fitting out a captured Bristol privateer of 26 guns, the *Tyger*, to serve as a French Frigate. He therefore moved to cut her off, right in front of the batteries. Fortunately for diplomatic niceties the Frenchman opened fire on *Monmouth*, which Hervey immediately returned. The Maltese showed their partiality by firing on *Monmouth*, with little effect. The frigate, however, ran herself ashore and before Hervey's boats could reach her caught fire and blew up. She was the *Rose* of 36 guns.

The Maltese authorities sent a boat out to protest at the breach of neutrality, and with it came the British consul who said they were in a mood to fire on him. Not put out by threats, but perhaps thriving on them, Hervey answered in French:

> *Qu'ayant eu l'honneur de voir son éminence le Grand Maitre sur son Balcon, je ne pouvait faire autrement que lui donner un feu de joie.*

He continued his defiance by telling the deputation that the next morning he would test the dominance of the French interest in the island and if they fired a single shot he would punish them by destroying their merchant galleys which were at that time in Sicilian ports loading with corn. The next morning he stood along the front of Valletta within musket shot, with his guns run out and followed by his two frigates. The Maltese made no move.

It was now Hervey's intention to take his squadron east to find and destroy the French cruisers in the Aegean. He was frustrated, however, by contrary winds and a shortage of water in *Monmouth* and sending *Ambuscade* off to Alexandretta for convoy duties he returned westward with *Lyme* in company. As he passed Malta the consul came off to *Monmouth*. Hervey sent back a belligerent message to the Grand Master about his partiality for the French. He was tempted to go in and burn *Tyger* where she lay in the Grand Harbour but held back because of the likely diplomatic rumpus. Instead he dared her

Augustus Hervey in Monmouth burning the Rose, French frigate, off Valetta. From the picture by Dominic Serres, by courtesy of the Trustees of the National Maritime Museum

to come out and fight the 28-gun *Lyme*, which he intended to leave off the entrance. *Lyme* spent most of the next day waiting but the challenge was not taken up. The two ships then made for Leghorn for water and orders, not arriving until 21 July.

After a few days of the usual wining and dining and a visit to Pisa, where he admired the baptistry and the magnificent bronze doors of the cathedral, he received a letter from his brother at Turin. Lord Bristol was on the point of leaving his post as envoy there to become Ambassador at Madrid. He enclosed a letter from the Admiralty instructing any captain at Leghorn to convey the new ambassador to a suitable Spanish port. Hervey was delighted to take the job for himself and wrote back accordingly, arranging to meet his brother at Genoa.

Monmouth arrived at Genoa on 1 August and there then began a succession of dinners and entertainments which in the three weeks that Hervey was there cost him the enormous and painful sum of £450. The meeting between the brothers, the first time they had met for over six years, took place outside the city at Campo Morano and was an emotional occasion. They returned to Genoa together and continued the round of receptions, dinners and visits to the theatre, where Hervey took Lord Bristol to Pellinetta's box.

Preparing to leave Hervey found that the transportation of an eighteenth-century ambassador was no simple matter. A Dutch ship was hired to carry his baggage and fifteen of his servants. Bristol himself with two liveried servants and four unliveried went on board *Monmouth*. They sailed on 20 August. The voyage was mendelsohnian, the brothers able to dine on deck most days and Bristol little troubled by sea sickness. Off Minorca they encountered two large men-of-war of French appearance, alarming Hervey because of the presence on board of a British ambassador with all his secret papers. He wanted to avoid the problem by putting his brother on board the baggage ship. Fortunately, however, the ships turned out to be Venetian and the crisis passed. *Monmouth* arrived at Alicante after a ten-day passage and the ambassador landed with all due ceremony; salutes of 19 guns from *Monmouth* and two of 15 guns from the town, one on landing and the second on departure into the interior. The guard was turned out and Lord Bristol gave the gifts required by etiquette – silver gilt boxes to the officers of the guard, money to the adjutant and money to the guard.

Hervey's next port of call was Barcelona, where he found orders from Broderick to proceed to Gibraltar. Arriving there on 12 September after a fast passage he was ordered home with a convoy. The wind was foul until the 24th, when he sailed with thirty merchantmen. He had a slow and stormy passage, with southerly gales in the Channel. In the severe weather most of the merchantmen failed to round the Isle of Wight and went in through the

Needles channel. *Monmouth* with only four merchantmen rounded Dunnose and arrived at Spithead on 29 October.

References

1. PRO, ADM1/1892
2. PRO, ADM1/1892, ADM2/707
3. PRO, ADM1/1892
4. PRO, ADM1/1894
5. PRO, ADM1/1889
6. PRO, ADM1/1892
7. PRO, ADM2/706
8. PRO, ADM1/1892
9. PRO, ADM2/707
10. British Library, Add. MSS 32871
11. Ibid., 32875
12. Lewis, 1937-83, (21), p193
13. PRO, ADM1/1893

CHAPTER XI

The Inshore Squadron

'Never did officer show greater courage and resolution'

When Hervey returned from the Mediterranean in October 1758 he was 34. His name had been in the captain's list for almost twelve years, for only four of which had Britain been at war. That he had held a sea command for nine years of the twelve thus made him more fortunate than most of his contemporaries. In peace and in war he had shown himself a man of resource and initiative, and one of those individuals to whom, at least in the heat of the moment, personal danger was of no account. Of his courage the aplomb with which he dealt with the burning ship at Leghorn in 1748 is a simple example; and he was never of the class of captain whose attitude in battle attracted the signal 'Engage the enemy more closely'. Resource he had shown within weeks of taking up his first command, when he took the French privateer *Bacquencourt* off the Isle of Purbeck, and this he had built on in several small but dashing actions in the Mediterranean.

In seamanship Hervey cannot easily be faulted and he used his skill to good advantage in the face of the enemy, for example when running from a stronger ship off Minorca in 1756. In diplomacy he was a forceful exponent of British interests, as when he negotiated successfully with the Moors in 1753/4. On occasion, however, he pushed diplomatic tact to its limits. His attitude and actions at Argentiera in 1755 had brought him a severe reprimand and when he destroyed the French frigate *Rose* under the guns of Malta he was fortunate in that the Frenchman unwisely opened fire first, providing a reasonable excuse for the action that he already intended to take. But later he rightly resisted the temptation to go into the Grand Harbour and destroy a second Frenchman.

In Hervey's day and indeed for many decades thereafter no provision was made for the training of naval officers in tactics, in fleet organization or in staff work. Hervey, however, had a better appreciation than most of his contemporaries of how a fleet's objectives could best be met and was used as an informal chief-of-staff and secretary by both Byng and Osborne. It is unfortunate that his long periods on foreign stations caused him to be out of touch with the wider considerations of worldwide strategy, so that he was always crying out against the blindness of the Admiralty to the needs of his own particular theatre of operations.

But fortune and advancement in the eighteen-century navy depended much on an officer's standing with influential senior figures, either naval or civilian. Hervey had made a most favourable impression on Byng and it was to him more than anyone that he owed his promotion to post rank. After Byng's death he was fortunate to serve under Osborne and to enjoy again much of the same combination of staff work interspersed with cruising that he had enjoyed under Byng. However, as Byng's misfortunes resulted in the loss of one patron so Osborne's illness took away another.

On the other side of the coin, Hervey had at no time gone out of his way to avoid making enemies. Since Byng's execution he had had no good word to say about any member of the court martial, so that he was very glad not to be required to continue serving in the Mediterranean under Broderick. Anson he had criticized both verbally and in writing ever since the Navy Bill of 1749 and he continued to do so regardless of the great Admiral's position as the fount of most naval patronage. Anson, however, was a far greater man than Hervey gave him credit for and there is no indication that he punished Hervey for his opposition and criticisms, which cannot have escaped the First Lord's cognizance. When in 1752 Hervey was given the frigate *Phoenix* it was Anson, at a time of severe cutbacks in naval activity, who made the choice from among many deserving and clamouring captains on half-pay; and when the outbreak of war in 1756 provided the opportunity it was Anson at the head of the Admiralty who had the ultimate say in giving him a ship of the line.

So on his return to Portsmouth that autumn Hervey had no need to feel that he would not be given the opportunity for further honourable and if possible lucrative service, though first *Monmouth* was in need of a complete overhaul. For over three weeks after his arrival, however, the Admiralty took no cognizance of him or his ship and Hervey fumed at the delay, at the same time passing the hours ashore in the company of companiable fellow officers and congenial women. He lodged for much of the time, without any suggestion of impropriety, with Lady Burnaby, second wife of Captain Sir William Burnaby. Awaiting orders, he was not in a position to leave Portsmouth, much to the frustration of his mother, who wrote to Mr. Morris as follows:

> It is true we are in the same climate, breathe the same damp, foggy air, but for any other use it is to us, he might as well be still at Gibraltar and I in Kent. He has been three weeks at Portsmouth, without receiving any orders from the Admiralty, though both himself and the ship stand in need of reparation. I wish they would order the one to dock, and the other to London.

Orders eventually arrived for *Monmouth* to proceed to Chatham for refit. On this Hervey had one of his spats with the Admiralty. As so often he was suffering from gout and asked leave to send her round under his first lieutenant. In his *Journal* he says he had no answer, in fact the Admiralty agreed to give him leave, but proposed appointing another captain to take the ship round. He took this badly, writing back that he could 'bear a great deal before I consent to any other gentleman being sent to do my duty'.[1] Easterly winds delayed his departure and it was 17 December before *Monmouth* reached Chatham dockyard. Hervey had asked[2] for leave for the ship's company, but this was refused as they were needed to prepare other ships for sea. He himself, however, was given leave to go to London. He reached town that afternoon and spent the evening with his mother at her house in Park Place, on the edge of Green Park, leaving her only for a brief visit to his sister Lepel Phipps' house nearby.

Pleased as he must have been to see his family again Hervey had no particular incentive to remain in London and was keen to be back at sea. *Monmouth's* refit was likely to take several months and much as he liked her he had already while at Portsmouth asked through Admiral Forbes, one of the Lords of the Admiralty, for *Resolution*, which was much nearer readiness. Anson, however, had already promised her elsewhere. In January he wrote to Anson again, asking for *Fame* (74) and later, probably through Saunders' influence, saw the First Lord. Anson, however, equivocated and Hervey felt unable to press for privileged treatment from his long term *bête noire*.

An early honour, indeed the day after his arrival in London, was for Hervey to be presented as usual to George II at St James's Palace. The King, however, looked as displeased with Hervey as he had on previous occasions and did not say a word. A more congenial monarch might have remembered the sinking of *Nymphe*, which the Admiralty had specifically drawn to his attention, and made some congratulatory remark on the subject. A day or so later he had a much better reception from George's grandson the Prince of Wales at Savile House and from his mother Augusta Princess of Wales. The young prince talked to him for some time.

This was Hervey's first opportunity to take his seat as member for St Edmundsbury, which he had held since 1757. He went straight from St James's to do so. In this, however, he failed for want of the necessary papers and had to wait until the next day. His sponsors were Sir William Rowley, a member of an old Suffolk family, and John Perceval, Lord Egmont. It was also his duty to look after his constituents in Bury by suitable entertainment. Accordingly he went down to Ickworth, arriving on 27 December and meeting his brother Frederick who was living nearby, an unbeneficed clergyman with a young family, as yet without any of his subsequent reputation as an ecclesiastic and as one of the great collectors of works of art. Frederick gave him some necessary background on the members of the Corporation, the twenty-odd members of which then constitued the electorate of the borough.

The next day he went early to Bury accompanied by the ringing of the church bells at Chevington and Horringer, and in Bury itself. His arrival was something of a carnival with morris dancers, flags and music, though his estimate of a crowd of three or four thousand to greet him may be thought to be an exaggeration. He made the required round of visits to the members of the Corporation. The celebrations lasted five days. He made visits to many of the local gentry and on the 28th dined with the Corporation, the Justices and others, sixty strong, dinner lasting until 1 am, by which time most of the diners were very drunk. The populace was not forgotten, Hervey giving six hogsheads of beer to the crowds on Angel Hill. The next day he dined out again, the festivities not dying down until 3 am on New Year's Day. On that day he was sworn in as Member by the Corporation and as was the custom renounced the salary once paid to members. That day he dined at the Angel with a large company and later gave a Ball to the Corporation and county gentry, attended by about 360 people. A good time appears to have been had by all and Hervey did not get back to Ickworth until 6 am. In the circumstances it is not surprising that he excused himself from dining with General Lord Cornwallis, who came over from Culford the next day to call on him. After the rejoicing came the settlement. He found that he had spent £358 on entertainment, in addition to £40 given to the town and £100 which he could not avoid lending to Mr. Wright, the Mayor, on his note of hand.

Hervey spent only a week at Bury before returning to London. He describes his life there as 'dissipated', to such a degree that when the House of Commons met in the New Year he was not in a condition to take much interest. He appears, however, to have attended fairly regularly, being present when over £12,0000,000 was voted for Supply, an enormous figure for the time but necessary to sustain the expenditure on Pitt's war endeavours.

His attention, however, was caught by a Bill introduced in early February by Alexander Hume 'for the more efficient manning of His Majesty's Navy'. Hume was an advanced social thinker for the time and the motivation for the Bill was the elimination of uncontrolled pressing as a means of finding crews for the navy's ships. It was of course one of the severest blots on the conscience of the age that men were arbitrarily dragged by the press-gangs from their families and their employment. Its only justification was the dire necessity that knew no other solution. Hume's Bill set out a most complicated and bureaucratic scheme for registering the crews of all merchant shipping, which provided the only pool of experienced seamen, and for ballots to be held for naval service whenever a merchant ship came into port. So complex were the arrangements that they appeared entirely impracticable and would surely have completely disorganized the country's trade without improving the lot of the pressed seamen or providing any better for the navy's need. Hervey's copy of the draft Bill is covered with adverse comments and so strongly did he feel about it that he was constrained to make it the subject of his maiden speech. According to the draft that remains among his papers at Bury[3] he began as follows:

Sir,

It may appear great presumption in me so early after my having had the honour of a seat in this House to intrude in its deliberations and I fear still more so, as I must be conscious how unacquainted I am with the forms of debate; if therefore on this occasion I do not continue to listen to the sentiments of others with silent reverance I hope I shall not be thought to have forfeited that indulgence or to have wearied that patience that I am certain they will ever meet with from this House, who mean well, however deficient they may be in knowledge or in eloquence.

Sir, I shall not trouble the House with all the objections I could make to every particular clause of this Bill, I hope to hear on this occasion Gentlemen whose abilities and experience better entitle them to your attention. I shall content myself at present with declaring that I have read this Bill with all the attention I am master of, have considered it in every light, and have conversed with many of my own profession on every different clause, and the oftener I read it, and the more I consider it, the more I am confirmed in my opinion that it is not only absurd and useless, but that if it could be put in execution would prove both prejudicial and dangerous, very prejudicial to His Majesty's Fleet in particular, and consequently very dangerous to the Nation in general. In a less critical situation I do not imagine that they by whom this Bill was drawn up could fail of producing some expedient on this head that might deserve your consideration. But at present, Sir, I think there cannot be a stronger motive for its being unanimously rejected than that of its being so generally opposed by the only people it was intended to gratify . . .

The Bill was in fact read a first time and sent to Committee, mainly because the members of the Board of Admiralty in the Commons did not oppose that course. When the amended Bill returned to the floor of the House Hervey made another impassioned speech against it, but ended on a more compromising note:

. . . a Bill which could only tend to the . . . impairing of [the country's] Naval force, and yet more sensibly, by diminishing the reputation of its legislature; at a less critical time I do not doubt but the Honourable Gentleman will hereafter be able to produce some scheme on this head to which I could venture to act as Godfather, for upon my word, Sir, I would with as much pleasure attend the christening of another as I hope to do the funeral of this.

The Bill was rejected by the House, rightly so, not because pressing was a fair and satisfactory system but because of the faults in Hume's proposals. The timing of such a far-reaching and problematical measure at the height of a war with France in which so far British forces had had little success was inept; and the measures in the Bill were likely to make it more difficult to man His Majesty's ships, while at the same time discouraging merchant seamen from coming forward to man merchant ships in British ports.

Hervey had taken a house in Scotland Yard, near Parliament and reasonably close to his clubs, to provide a *pied-à-terre* while he enjoyed London life. He saw his mother often, dining with her at home or on one occasion at Bubb Dodington's house at Hammersmith. He dined with Admiral Boscawen and met there the commander of the French squadron taken at Louisburg. Once he went to a *levée* given by the Duke of Newcastle, never his favourite politician, and asked him for a post for his brother Frederick, who was having difficulties in supporting his wife and several children down in Suffolk; the Duke made him one of his worthless promises and nothing came of the matter. This attempt is but one indication that the breach between Hervey and his brother Frederick was at this time by no means complete. There seems, however, to have been little good feeling on Frederick's part. In an undated letter from Frederick to his sister Lepel Phipps in Childe Pemberton, which may refer to this incident, Frederick says ' . . . Augustus amazes me by a letter I have just received from him – it differs totally from that I received from my brother [Lord Bristol], so that I hope he will be so good as to press his Grace [Newcastle] once more upon the subject of the Deanery of Norwich.' Frederick tried hard for this appointment, but when the incumbent finally died was unsuccessful, as Newcastle had promised it to one of his relatives.

Women continued to occupy much of Hervey's time and thoughts, and he took what he could as it was offered. He saw much of a young dowager, almost certainly the recently widowed Countess of Carlisle, who raised his passions without satisfying the resulting desires. He affects not to understand her attitude, since she attached herself to him in this way knowing he was married, that he had little time for a virtuous woman and that she was not herself prepared to be a trollop. Perhaps in spite of his long and wide experience of the sex he did not realize that a recently widowed young woman may well not know herself what she is about. Soon, however, he moved on and gained the acceptance of Kitty Fisher, one of the well know courtesans of the day, who was painted several times by Sir Joshua Reynolds. He was at Reynolds' studio in Bedford Row on 21 February and it may be that the future President of the Royal Academy was painting her as Cleopatra at that time. He was with her on and off until he returned to his ship in April.

For good measure he seized, or tried to seize, any opportunity that arose, for example sitting by chance next to a Miss D——ks, as he describes her, at Covent Garden. She allowed or perhaps encouraged considerable familiarity, not to say impropriety, throughout the play and then, having waited for the crowd to disperse and with no chairs to be had, he took her out into the Piazza and 'there passed our time until a coach could be found'. On a wet February night a less favourable venue for attempted seduction is difficult to imagine. The picture he paints is indeed more reminiscent of adolescents in the one-and-ninepennies at a 1950s cinema than that of a naval captain of 35 years of age.

But between times he kept more respectable company. One evening he spent at the home of his sister Lepel Phipps, where she entertained three ladies, the Countess of Carlisle, Lady Burnaby and Lady Caroline Seymour, with all of whom he was prepared to flirt, if nothing more. On another occasion he was surprised and most pleased to meet in the street Mrs Ord, his great friend from Jamaica days, and dined in Bedford Row with her and her husband.

In spite of all these delights Hervey chafed at the time *Monmouth* was spending in dock. His duties during this time were light. In December he had to go down to Chatham to pacify his crew, 150 of whom were being lent to *Temple*. At the end of February he went down again and saw the great progress that had been made with *Monmouth's* refit. The expedition was a rather special one, for he was accompanied by Prince Edward, Duke of York. The young prince took him down in his carriage accompanied by two young ladies and they all spent the night at Rochester. One of the women was Kitty Fisher, though so complex were her alliances at that time that it is not clear which beau she favoured on this occasion. This is the first mention of the Duke of York in Hervey's *Journal*. He was the younger brother of the future George III and at the time serving in the navy, in which at the age of 20 he held the rank of captain – and was to be promoted to flag rank at 22. He was, regrettably, a louche and insipid young man whose naval career was short and ineffective.

On 24 March *Monmouth* came out of dock and at the end of the month Hervey was ordered to lay in three months supplies for service in the Channel. The prospect of service so near home and Admiralty did not appeal to him, and in addition he was eager for greater things. He therefore wrote in the usual obsequious way to Newcastle, relying on one of the Duke's insincerities, asking for an alternative posting:[4]

Whitehall, March 27 1759

My Lord Duke

As your Grace has been so good to promise me your favor and protection I take the liberty of explaining my request & to remind your Grace of it, least (*sic*) it should be too late, as the ship I comand will very soon now be going to Sea, which is, that instead of returning to the Mediterranean again, I may be sent with the Comand of what Ships may go this Year to the Coast of Guinea, or with any other Comand of three or four Ships detached on any service; and if not, that I may be sent as one of the Ships to the Jamaica station for a year; I have little reason to hope for obtaining anything but for your Grace's Goodness to me, nor shall I seek it through any other Channel, as that is the most acceptable to my Brother Bristol, & will always be the preferable one to myself. I have been now twelve Years a Captain and have seen many favor'd with Comands that have given opportunities to distinguish themselves, who were much junior officers to me, tho' from my being kept so long a Lieutenant, have some little Seniority to me as Captain; I asked for one of the New Ships when I came home that I might be the sooner on Service, but Lord Anson told me they were engaged. Your Grace's time is of too much Importance for me to intrude on any longer; I will only beg leave to assure your Grace that I shall never be forgetful of, or ungrateful for any favor you may please to confer on, My Lord

Your Grace's Most Faithful
& most Obed^t humble Ser^t
A Hervey

He is ingenuous enough not to mention this letter in his *Journal*, though he does refer to requests he made to Admiral Forbes, a member of the Admiralty Board. But none of his importunity had any success and there is no indication that the Duke even replied to him.

In early April, therefore, Hervey went down to Chatham, under orders for service in the Channel. He took Kitty Fisher with him and they dined aboard *Monmouth*. However, the wind being unfavourable for the move down the Medway to Sheerness Hervey took her back to London. The lady's affairs were still confused. In spite of her contemporaneous affair with John, Earl Poulett, and Hervey's knowledge of it, he continued to dally with her for several days before rejoining his ship, spending a last night with her at Egham in Surrey before putting her on her way to his Lordship's house in Somerset.

When he returned he found his ship had gone down to the Nore without him and the next day he went to Chatham, watched the launch of the 90-gun *Sandwich*, and then joined *Monmouth*. There he found a letter from the Admiralty adjuring him to repair to his duty, for in spite of orders to proceed from Chatham to the Nore he appears to have been away from her making up to Kitty Fisher for the best part of twelve days. He apologized in his usual reproachful way – '. . . the very instant I found the ship was at the Nore I lost no time to get to her . . .'⁵ He also found orders to proceed immediately to Spithead but the almost inevitable bad weather delayed his departure until 18 April.

While in London Hervey had found time to worry about his crew, much of which had been sent off by the Admiralty into *Temple* and *Edgar*. On 26 February he had written to the Admiralty[6] asking for their return, and had been assured that this was intended. Now at the Nore he found that 150 men from *Edgar* were by Admiralty orders being brought round to the Nore in *Escort*, while *Monmouth* was under orders to sail at the first opportunity for Spithead. Concerned that the two ships would not meet he wrote[7] asking to delay *Monmouth's* departure but was refused – 'The Lords are of the opinion that he should not lose the advantage of a fair wind'.

When he reached the Downs he found that he had in fact missed *Escort* and sent a cutter in pursuit. She duly returned with the 150 men and he was glad to take them on board, making up his numbers with men whom he had already moulded into his ways.

Monmouth was four days at Spithead awaiting orders, allowing Hervey latitude to enjoy himself with the company available there, including Captain and Lady Burnaby and her Ottley relations, and to go on short expeditions out into the Hampshire countryside and onto the downs. On the third day, however, who should arrive but Kitty Fisher, who stayed overnight. Unfortunately, in this respect, the next day Hervey received immediate orders to sail for Plymouth, which he duly put into execution, having great difficulty in dissuading her from making the journey with him.

At Plymouth he found a small squadron under Vice-Admiral Sir Charles Hardy. There was another wait without orders until 14 May, when Hardy was ordered to take them all round to Torbay and place himself under Sir Edward Hawke, who was bringing fourteen of the line from Portsmouth. Hawke, however, had received no further orders and there was even uncertainty as to whether Anson himself might come down to take command, as he had in the previous year. The fleet spent several days completing its readiness for sea and one day Hervey, ever hospitable, entertained Hawke, Hardy, Edgcumbe (his Commodore in the Mediterranean before Mahon), Geary, about to be promoted Rear-Admiral under Hawke, and others to dinner.

On 20 May, however, Hawke received orders to take the fleet to sea. London was in one of its periodical bouts of alarm about invasion, and on this occasion rightly so. The French had assembled armies at various points on their Channel and Biscay coasts and were preparing a fleet at Brest. The first stage of their plan was for Conflans to break out from Brest and make his way to Quiberon Bay, a hundred miles to the south, pick up the troops assembled there and set out for Scotland, landing them near Glasgow. Then he would sail round the north of Scotland and pick up a second army 20,000 strong from Flanders and convey them to the Essex coast, whence they would march on London. Such a series of operations is peculiarly subject to inter-ruption and delay and Hawke's place in frustrating the French plan was to prevent Conflans leaving Brest. If this could be achieved there was nothing to fear. The Admiralty therefore ordered him in the first place to go off Brest and remain there for a fortnight, then to return with the main fleet to Torbay, at the same time taking steps to watch the French ports and to interrupt their coastwise traffic.

By 24 May the fleet was off Ushant. Hawke's information was that four of the line at L'Orient were ready to sail for Brest and might well get past him by taking the inshore Passage du Raz. He therefore detached into Audierne Bay a squadron made up of *Torbay*, *Magnanime*, *Fame* and *Monmouth*, com-manded respectively by Keppel, Howe, Byron and Hervey – four of his best captains, and as Hervey points out all members of the aristocracy. He was delighted to find that *Monmouth* was the fastest sailer and that 'if we met the enemy I should at least have had the satisfaction of leading these noble companions into action'. They cruised there until 3 June when orders reached them to rejoin the fleet, Hawke having learned that the four Frenchmen had slipped into Brest before he arrived off the port.

The first days of June saw the wind increasing and by the 5th the south westerly gales were so strong that Hawke had to run for Torbay, leaving Conflans penned in Brest until such time as the wind should go easterly. The fleet watered and sailed for Brest without delay but the wind coming very strong and westerly again several ships suffered storm damage, one indeed was dismasted, and they returned to Torbay. Hawke had become disenchanted with the open blockade which had until this time been the normal, indeed the only practicable, approach, and which allowed considerable scope for the French to slip out while he was away watering or because of the weather. If he went into Torbay because of westerly gales he could not get back to Ushant quickly enough to stop them if they seized their chance as soon as the wind went into the east.

Accordingly he developed, with Admiralty encouragement, a system of continuous blockade in which the fleet remained continuously off Brest and was watered and victualled from Plymouth, two ships at a time being sent in to clean. In terms of the health of the fleet he was fully up to date with the most recent advances in knowledge. The importance of citrus fruits in pre-venting scurvy was not as yet understood but the first inkling of understanding of the role of fresh fruit and vegetables was influencing the nature of the supplies sent to the fleet. So scurvy was kept at bay and Hawke's advanced ideas on hygiene reduced the incidence of typhus and other diseases. But the logistical aspects of supplying a fleet at sea gave rise at first to great difficulties, which were gradually overcome as the summer advanced.

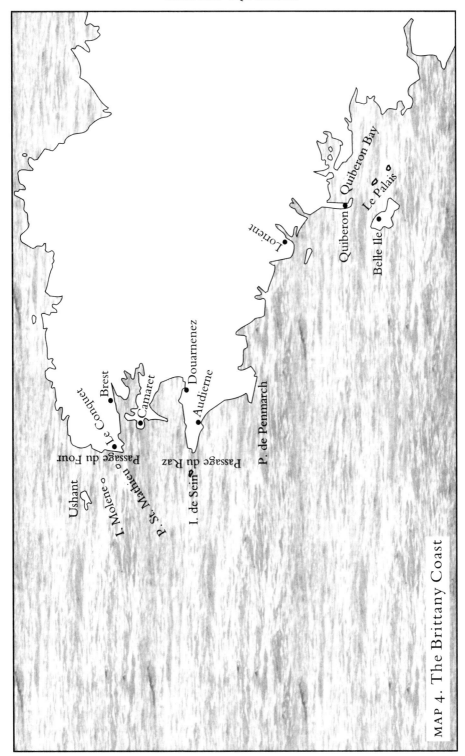

MAP 4. The Brittany Coast

Hawke estimated that in spite of the difficulties he could keep the fleet at sea, at least in summer. The stations that he took up depended on the wind. When it was easterly the fleet held a position off Point St Mathieu, almost in the entrance to the Goulet, while with a westerly, onshore wind, it rendezvoused forty-five miles west of Ushant. The fleet as a whole, however, was too ponderous to seal the port and keep watch on the shipping in it at all times, and Hawke saw the need for an inshore squadron to carry out these duties.

On 16 June, therefore, he sent for Hervey to breakfast with him on board *Ramillies* in Torbay. Hervey had served under Hawke before, when the Admiral had superseded Byng in 1756 after the Battle of Mahon, but two factors had inhibited the development of any close relationship. Hawke's awareness that Hervey was an out-and-out protagonist of the previous Commander-in-Chief must have made him cautious of allowing a relationship to develop, while Hervey had felt himself distanced by Hawke because of the way the Admiral appeared to devolve so much of the management of the fleet to John Hay, his unsatisfactory secretary. Nevertheless, Hawke was a fine judge of the qualities of his captains and knew Hervey's capabilities for the job he had in mind. He was also a competent communicator of his intentions to his subordinates. At breakfast that morning, therefore, he told Hervey that he was appointing him to command the inshore squadron, whose duties, irrespective of the where-abouts of the fleet, would be to keep close observation of the ships in Brest and to prevent any coastwise traffic entering or leaving the port. Hervey was to be taken up with these duties for the next four months.

The wind coming northwesterly the fleet sailed on 19 June and two days later was off Ushant. Captain Duff in the 50-gun *Rochester* was still off Brest and reported no movement on the part of the French. For the next ten days Hawke exercised the fleet in manoeuvres. Victuallers arrived on 2 July and Hawke took the opportunity to fill up *Monmouth* in particular in preparation for her inshore work. Up to then he had not sent her in, apparently not wishing to risk one of his 64s so close in until the heavier French ships showed some sign of activity. But on the 3rd of the month Hawke withdrew Duff and sent for Hervey, ordering him to go close in with the frigate *Pallas* in company and to watch the French fleet and harass all movements in and out.

At this critical and exciting moment Hervey's *Journal* comes to an abrupt end, on the words 'I made sail away, and at 4 in the afternoon . . .' Why he abandoned his account is not known. He broke off in mid page and mid sentence, just as he began his most noteworthy period of service. It would not have been in character for him to have been averse to describing his exploits. Perhaps he broke off for some trifling reason and before he put pen to paper again the motivation for and purpose of this the longest of his known literary works fell by the wayside. If, as Erskine suggests, it was written between

1767 and 1770 it is possible that its completion was overtaken by his appointment in early 1771 to the Board of Admiralty. When he was so elevated he may have had, or felt he had, insufficient time for pen and paper. If he was writing it for particular eyes – and his comment 'and as I write this over purely for my own satisfaction of recalling to my memory most of the events of all kinds of my life . . .' would if true contradict this hypothesis – then the eyes may have failed, or circumstances may have changed so as to make the enterprise no longer necessary; for example, if the eyes were those of Lord Sandwich and the purpose was to persuade him of the writer's suitability as a Lord of the Admiralty.

Whatever the reason it is a pity that he did not leave us his own description of those glorious and fateful four months in which he was the spearhead of Hawke's blockade. He started as he meant to continue. On 3 and 5 July he took *Monmouth* and *Pallas* to within four miles of the French fleet in the port of Brest and made detailed observations on them. He reported twenty two-deckers with colours flying and many people on shore and in boats watching these impudent British intruders. He observed, however, that there were few people to be seen on deck, deducing correctly that Conflans had not been able to man his ships at all adequately. In very light winds on the night of the 5th he anchored close in and sent his cutter to take a small fishing boat and its crew of five. Her skipper confirmed what he had seen, that the Breton peasantry was being pressed to crew the ships and also that they could not all be armed until guns arrived from Rochefort and Bordeaux.

The news pleased Hawke, though he warned Hervey not to rely too much on word of mouth from the enemy. In early July he sent Hervey a second ship of the line, *Montague* of 60 guns, and later in the summer his strength was to be increased to five heavy ships and several frigates and light vessels. The French need for guns from the south prompted Hawke to double the guard on the Passage du Raz, Hervey watching it from the Brest side and Duff being posted with two ships in Audierne Bay. Light vessels from Hervey's squadron were posted to close the approach from the north through the Passage du Four, whose rocks and reefs made its waters difficult for the larger British ships to work in.

A few days later Hervey showed that he was prepared to be one of the hard men who are to be found in the records of warfare throughout the ages. By the skipper of the captured fishing vessel he had sent a message to the commander of the batteries at Point St Mathieu, that if they fired on him again he would level their church. The reference was to the prominent church of the convent of St Mathieu, and it was so obviously within Hervey's power to carry out his threat and more besides that the Frenchman complied, allowing Hervey's boats to intercept, unmolested, a Dutch merchantman coming through the Passage du Four.

Weather conditions in these summer months were generally congenial enough for Hervey not to be inconvenienced, though in mid July the swell in the approaches to Brest was too great for him to look in properly. However, on the 20th he was able to land a party on the island of Benequet, off Conquet, for intelligence from the islanders. As a welcome extra the landing party found twenty-one head of cattle on the island, which they rounded up and brought back with them. 'I take the liberty of sending you one, Sir' Hervey wrote to Hawke 'as well as the other admirals, and have divided the others to the *Montague*'s people and our own for a day's fresh meat for them tomorrow'.

When a group of storeships tried to come through the Passage du Four Hervey's squadron blockaded them in Conquet. Conflans sent four of the line to drive him off, but without success. Judging rightly that the Frenchmen were far from ready for a fight Hervey, who was off St Mathieu's Point, formed his three ships, *Monmouth, Montague* and the frigate *Pallas*, into line, ordered *Colchester* of 50 guns and a frigate which were in the offing to close on him, hoisted the broad pendant of a commodore and stood towards the enemy. The French, who comprised a 74, a 70 and two 64s, retired precipitately, clearly believing that a strong squadron was within call, while their main fleet began to make some preparatory moves to support them. Hervey fired on the four Frenchmen at a distance and scored several hits but there was no real battle. Seeing all this activity Hawke had moved in and during the French retreat was as near as Point St Mathieu. His report strongly commended his inshore commanders; 'Never did officer show greater conduct and resolution than did Captain Hervey, and was bravely seconded by Captain Lendrick [of *Montague*].'

But in spite of these excitements most of their time was spent in watch and ward and in routine activities. Ships of the inshore squadron took detailed soundings in Douarnenez Bay, against future need. It was a particularly hot summer and even at sea this caused victualling problems. Bread and fresh meat went off more quickly and there was trouble with the Plymouth beer. Continually, it was bad before it reached the fleet, reducing the crews to drinking stinking water.

By the end of July the news that Hawke had the principal French naval force in his grip was widely known and a subject for geat exultation in London. On 1 August Lady Hervey wrote from Chevening to her son, who received her letter off Brest on the 13th of the month. The letter gives a good impression not only of how proud she was of her poor Augustus (a favourite form that she used in writing about him) but also of the delight that London society was taking in this turn in British naval affairs:

Indeed my dear Augustus, if you go on at this rate you will quite blind me. I have been forced to read and write so many answers to letters of congratulations on your behaviour and success that I can hardly see; and

this moment I have received your letter of 22 July with the pleasing account
of farther and greater intrepidity, and, thank God, with safety still on your
part. Four seventy four gun ships to be made to retire by only two of sixty
four is indeed nobly done and must gain you immortal honour, though
the account in the newspapers mentions it as slightly as possible "that part
of the Brest fleet was under sail Monday sennight to come out of the
harbour, that the headmost ship had exchanged a few shot with the
Monmouth and *Montague*, but that on Sir Edward Hawke appearing and
forming a line of battle they all returned and went to anchor again". Lady
Stanhope and Miss Hamilton, to whom I had told the contents of your
letter, were so angry that they called the newspaper writers and Admiralty
(whose business they thought it was to have had the whole given with due
commendations of you to the public) many harsh names, and they were
very pressing with me to draw up an article in a proper manner, which
they would have sent away immediately to be inserted in the first newspapers,
but as your letter was so short, so little explicit, and by some omissions of
words from hurry, so unclear, I could not do it; otherwise indeed I believe
I should. Your first action was very well and properly related in the *Evening
Post*, perhaps the next newspapers may bring a better and fuller account,
at least I hope so, when they may perhaps have a better and a more particular
information. I have this day reeived a very pretty letter from Ld Chesterfield
on this occasion, and last post brought me one from Mrs Osborne with
congratulations both in her own and the Admiral's name. Also one from
Mr Bateman very obliging. I also had one from Lord Lyttelton, who never
wrote to me before, to congratulate me on the *glory you have gained by your
brave and spirited action at Brest*. Mr. Walpole, who is always the first and
most obliging on all such occasions, said they were all in joy and full of
praises at Holland House. This good family who, no more than myself,
have not wore a smile for many weeks before, expressed the greatest pleasure
and joy on this occasion, and Ld Stanhope, who returned this day from
London where he has been for some days, drank your health and wished
this country produced many such gallant men as Mr Hervey. He is just
come into my room with Lady Stanhope and all of them with the newspapers
of this morning which he has just got, in which there is a full and most
delightful account of the action and of *Commodore* Hervey and at the end
of it some verses of which these are the last two lines.

> "Britons exult! all Gallia trembling stands,
> While Hervey executes and Hawke commands,"

They all beg I would make their compliments to you and assure you how
great a share they take in your glory and my joy. Ld Stanhope came back
after he had gone four steps to say very kindly and very prettily "Pray give
my congratulations to Mr. Hervey as your friend, as his humble servant,

and as an Englishman." God bless you my dear Augustus, and keep you safe; now you have had an opportunity of showing yourself would to God we had a peace and my dear boy was safe at home. I will write to your brother, and make him as happy as I am with all this good news.

Lord Stanhope tells me Mr Elliot of the Admiralty cried you and this brave action up to the skies; and that Mr Pitt said your conduct had been equal to your courage which was as great as possible. Thank God for all this good news. Oh that that dear good friend[*] I have lost could have lived to have shared and increased my joy, which she would have done.'

The letter sheds a brilliant light on the conditions of the day, in society as a whole as well as in the families of the fighting men: Lady Hervey rejoicing at her son's achievement and at the recognition he had achieved, while at the same time fearful for his well being while the war continued; the relief of London society that after a period of concern about invasion the navy had taken a grip on affairs; and – a complaint with modern parallels – her annoyance that the press had at first given an inaccurate, or at least incomplete, account of her son's gallant action.

On 27 August Hawke brought the whole fleet close in and off St Mathieu's Point its guns fired off a *feu de joie*. Conflans and his crews knew well what their enemies were celebrating – the great victory earlier in the month at Minden, where Prince Ferdinand with a large British contingent in his army had forced the French into pell mell retreat and for the time being saved Hanover from occupation. Hawke could indeed congratulate himself that the navy's actions had done much to draw French troops away from Germany to defend their own shores, and so had a share in the triumph.

A few days later Hervey's fellow philanderer the Duke of York, who was serving with Hawke, came in to him, dining and sleeping in *Monmouth* before returning to the fleet, though Hervey's intention to take him close in to view the French fleet was frustrated by a strong onshore wind.

In mid September Hervey, who now had five of the line in his squadron, landed on the two Molines islands between St Mathieu's Point and Ushant, taking all the cattle from the smaller island and levying a contribution from the larger. Two beasts were sent to the flagship. A few days later Conflans tried to get three ships of the line from Brest into the Morbiham. Their method for several nights running was to come forward into Camaret bay on the south side of the approach to Brest and try to slip through at night. Each time Hervey came forward and they retreated into Brest. Eventually Conflans supported them by sending six ships into the Goulet but Hervey continued to advance and they turned tail.

On the 29th Hervey initiated, and himself led, one of those intrepid

* Lady Murray, a close friend of Lady Hervey of forty years standing. who had recently died

endeavours which characterized his style of leadership. Finding that a schooner anchored under the guns of Camaret was reporting on his movements he mounted a night attack with five boats and took her with her crew of two officers and thirty-six men. There was considerable resistance and much fire from the shore. The attackers suffered no casualties, though Hervey had a shot through his coat. He gave up his share of the prize money to the seamen who had accompanied him.

By October the perils and difficulties of the winter weather in the Bay of Biscay were beginning to loom large. Hervey, troubled by fog, wrote to Hawke that though he expected the inshore squadron to be able to keep its station it was almost inevitable that eventually Conflans would get some of his ships out. The fleet had now been off Brest for over three months but on 11 October a strong and worsening westerly gale came up and on the 13th Hawke and most of the main fleet were fored to run for Plymouth, which they reached the same day. Hervey and his inshore squadron rode it out and six of Hawke's ships also stayed at sea. On the 19th Hawke returned to his station and was relieved to find Hervey still there and that nothing had moved out of Brest in his absence.

By this time, however, Hervey was suffering from gout in both feet and was having to be carried about the ship as his duties demanded. *Monmouth* had been at sea, indeed had hardly been out of sight of the rocks and cliffs of the Brest coastline, since 19 June and was beginning to leak badly. She was by no means a new ship and the wonder is that she had stood the buffeting of wind and waves for so long without respite. Even more remarkable was that her crew continued in good shape, having withstood the crowded conditions below decks and the restricted diet provided by the victuallers, supplemented by their own efforts on the offshore islands, tolerably well. The trickles of fresh foods that came aboard had been sufficient to ward off scurvy and hygiene had done the rest.

But by 3 November *Monmouth's* condition was deteriorating fast and her captain's gout was also worse. Hawke ordered her back to Plymouth, writing to Hervey;

> I heartily regret your being obliged to go in, and sincerely wish you the re-establishment of your health. Believe me, Sir, I shall cheerfully embrace every opportunity of acknowledging the sense I have of the officerlike manner in which you have performed the duties of your station.

Monmouth made Plymouth on 5 November. How bad her condition was is shown by Hervey's letter[8] to the Admiralty reporting his arrival there, which was in response to Hawke's order:

> . . . sent in return to an account I had sent to him of my ship's making
> 21 inches of water an hour, even laying to in smooth water; which I found

myself at last obliged to transit to him, tho' neither my health (which has been long bad and being still confined) nor the ship's making 15 inches an hour for three weeks before at anchor, could induce me to represent my situation . . .

Hervey found waiting for him another of those letters from his mother which show how proud she was of him and how concerned about his safety. She had written from London on 27 October:

Tis an age since I heard from my dear Augustus and ten days since I wrote to him. I have been extremely hurried since I came to town and, for some hours, again alarmed by those vile newspapers, they have put in an article to say the *Monmouth* was by a storm drove on the coast of Brittany. I immediately wrote both to Mr. Forbes and to Mr. Stanley [both Lords of the Admiralty] lest one should not be to be found, but as it happened, it being Saturday, neither were in town; in the anxiety I was under I wrote a note to Mr Clevland at ten o'clock at night he was not at home, but in half an hour returned and immediately wrote me a very obliging note to dissipate my fears, by assuring me there was no news of any kind come from those parts to the Admiralty, and 'twas very sure that a ship and a commander of that importance could not have had a misfortune of that kind without the Admiralty being first informed of it, there being so many ships in company; therefore he did not doubt that Captain Hervey was safe and would continue to render further services to his country. On Monday I received a letter to the same purpose from Mr Forbes, and a visit from Mr Stanley to confirm it. I called at Lady Mary Forbes' door on Monday and left my compliments with thanks to the Admiral for his letter, on which he very politely made me a visit on Tuesday and stayed here alone an hour. He said he had taken the liberty to chide you about the affair of the boats and really said all the things I had wrote to you about it; he said it was not an occasion worth risking an officer of such consequence as you was of, that your character wanted nothing extraordinary to be done; but when it was for some distinguished service, then, and then only, extraordinary risks were to be run. He spoke kindly of you, he seems to be a sensible serious reserved man. On Wednesday night between ten and eleven Mr Clevland sent me a letter to say he had that moment received an express from Sir Ed. Hawke with an account that you was well on your station on the 20th, which he hoped would make me quite easy on your account, that he thought himself happy to be so soon able to remove all my fears. In short, my dear, he has been most extremely civil and indeed obliging to me on this occasion, and I know that both he and Lord A——- [Anson?] have spoke most handsomely about you to different people. Why therefore perpetuate enmity and be perpetually blowing those embers that are near extinguished?

The letter shows her pride at the name that her favourite son was making for himself and exults at Britain's successes in this year of victories, unaware that for the navy the best was yet to come.

While *Monmouth* lay at Plymouth refitting and Hervey did his best to recuperate gales again drove Hawke off his station and this time the inshore squadron, now under Captain Digby, came with him. Before they could return Conflans, bolstered by many experienced seamen from a squadron that had recently slipped in from the West Indies, got his fleet to sea. He was making for the Morbihan but before he could get there Hawke was back and on 20 November caught up with him in a full gale as he made for Quiberon Bay. In spite of the weather Hawke hoisted the signal for general chase. In the confused battle that followed the French fleet was destroyed as a fighting force and for the rest of the war was unable to play any worthwhile part in events.

Hervey must have been desolated when he heard that he had missed by a fortnight such a glorious climax to so doughty an endeavour. If *Monmouth* had been there, fit and clean, there is little doubt that she would have been one of the leaders in the chase and would have added much to her honours and those of her captain. He clearly intended to return to sea, for in mid November he wrote to his brother Frederick at Ickworth 'in great spirits', intending not even to go to London if he could soon get *Monmouth* seaworthy. In the event, however, his health let him down again, and on 28 November he wrote from *Monmouth* at Plymouth to John Clevland as follows:

Sir,
  You'll please to acquaint their Lordships that notwithstanding my earnest inclinations of proceeding to sea with His Majesty's Ship under my command yet I find myself under the necessity of desiring their leave to remain onshore 'till the recovery of my health.
  Their Lordships will give me leave to have the honour of congratulating them on the success of His Majesty's fleet, tho' I shall ever condole with myself for the misfortune of not having had it in my power to contribute towards it.

I am Sir,
Your most Obed^t, Ser^t,
A. Hervey

He had more than earned the compliment paid to him by Corbett:[9]

  . . . Augustus Hervey, who in the course of this command was to clinch the reputation he had already established as one of the most brilliant officers in the service.

References

1. PRO, ADM1/1893
2. Ibid.
3. SRO(B), 940/50/5, p277
4. British Library, Add. MSS 32889, p270
5. PRO, ADM1/1894
6. Ibid.
7. Ibid
8. Ibid.
9. Corbett, 1907

CHAPTER XII

Dragon

A brave and deserving officer

As the war with France entered its fifth winter Hervey's record was a good one, certainly good enough to please his masters at the Admiralty. He had had more than his share of action, both in the Medeterranean and off the French Atlantic coast, and was beginning to feel that promotion to flag rank should surely be his due, though his lack of seniority on the captains' list was to deny him this recognition for many years to come.

His health, however, continued to trouble him and at the end of January 1760, nearly three months after he had left *Monmouth*, his mother was still despondent on the subject. She wrote to Mr. Morris:

> . . . but my son Aug^s, who has not been well, and has been forced to keep his house, as I have been forced to keep mine, came in, and has stayed with me 'till I have barely time to bid you adieu.

Gout and the strain of continuous contact with the enemy are sufficient to explain Hervey's condition. In the event he did not return to *Monmouth* but at the turn of the year was appointed to *Dragon*, a new 74 approaching completion at Deptford. Completion, manning and getting ready for sea was as usual a protracted process and he did not join Boscawen's fleet blockading the French coast until June. He spent much of the winter of 1760 in London, where Parliament was sitting, but took no prominent part in its business. His *Journal* had by this time come to an end, so that the almost daily comment on his social life and amatory affairs that it provided for earlier years is no longer available; but there is no reason to believe that either had significantly abated, at least whenever his state of health allowed.

He had in fact found that manning *Dragon* was far from easy. A series of letters to the Admiralty,[1] the first dated 13 March 1760, shows why. The difficulties were in part due to the fact that *Monmouth* remained in commission and her crew and most of his followers were still in her and not readily available. In addition the Admiralty had sent into *Dragon* a considerable contingent of men from *Revenge* who were far from satisfied with this turn in their fortunes; as well as a forced move into a strange ship, always calculated to have an adverse effect on morale, they had been denied leave when *Revenge* paid off, as the Admiralty needed them to get *Dragon* rigged and ready for sea. The course of events does, however, suggest that Hervey was less popular with his crew than with the superior officers who found him such a dashing commander.

In early March he asked for *Monmouth's* boatswain and gunner to be transferred to *Dragon*, a course of action with which Their Lordships were pleased to concur.

Their order could not, however, be put into immediate effect since *Monmouth* was far away in the Bay of Biscay. *Revenge's* boatswain and gunner were therefore appointed as stopgaps, but a month later the boatswain had not appeared on board. Worse still, the temporary gunner was ill, so that there was no authorized person in *Dragon* to whom the Ordnance Board could deliver powder and shot. The Admiralty again appointed a replacement but by 6 May he had still not arrived.

This reluctance on the part of the warrant officers from *Revenge* was matched by problems with the lower deck, arising from their forced transfer into *Dragon*. In early April, the ship being rigged, they petitioned for leave, which was granted for fourteen days. While Hervey supported their petition he was concerned that many of them would not return. His fear was justified, for twenty-five went absent and to these must be added thirty-five who had never reported from *Revenge* and never been borne on *Dragon's* books. Short as he was of seamen Hervey did in contrast receive *two* Masters-at-Arms. The MAA of *Revenge* had come with that contingent and on 17 May another arrived with an Admiralty warrant appointing him to *Dragon*. Hervey sent the second back to the Admiralty saying he would have either but not both.

When in June *Dragon* reached Admiral Boscawen's fleet in Quiberon Bay she brought with her an Admiralty order instructing him to exchange her officers and crew with those of *Monmouth*. However, Hervey at whose request the order had been given, was fonder of his former crew than many of them were of him. Most of them objected and petitions were presented to Boscawen by groups of officers, petty officers and seamen. The most succinct is that by the petty officers:

> As the Hon. Captain Hervey is appointed for the *Dragon* and we are informed has made application to Their Lordships for all the officers and ship's company of the *Monmouth* to be turned over on board of her, we the undersigned beg leave to acquaint your Honour that such a change will be quite contrary to our inclinations, and humbly crave your Honour's interest to continue in our present ship . . .

Boscawen took the hint, rightly judging that a wholesale change would cause much dissatisfaction. Instead, every individual serving in *Monmouth* was given the option of transferring; it was taken by Peter Foulkes, Hervey's long-time first lieutenant, by the gunner and boatswain, the marine officers and all the marines, and sixty-two members of the crew. Though the incident provides no vote of confidence in Hervey as a loved and respected ship's captain his men's rejection of him should not be taken too harshly. *Monmouth's* crew had served in her as a body for many years before he had come to them on Captain Gardiner's death in the Moonlight Battle, and there is no doubt that sailors readily developed an affection for their ship, an affection that was strengthened by apprehension at the prospect of change. Furthermore, they had not had an easy time under Hervey, who was not a captain to evade hardship and danger when the King's service required it, and who had kept them at sea in considerable discomfort in the latter part of his command of Hawke's inshore squadron. And of course the iron test is not whether he was loved but whether he was an effective captain.

Dragon was soon in action. In early July she chased a French merchantman into a river near Port Louis, where the vessel took refuge under the guns of a shore battery. Hervey ran *Dragon* in close and her fire drove the artillerymen from their guns. Then he himself led a party by night in the ship's boats and at daybreak surprised the guard on shore, destroying the guardhouse, throwing the guns into the sea and bringing off the ammunition. But by the time the boats got to the vessel she was hard aground; so they burned her, returning with thirty prisoners.

Later that month Boscawen sent Hervey with a squadron of four ships to make a descent on the Ile de Groix (in the English spelling of the day 'Groua') off Lorient. The island commands the entrance to Lorient and Port Louis; it is about five miles long and at that time was heavily defended, especially the small port and town. Its capture would have made the two ports virtually unusable and it has been suggested that it was Hervey who proposed the attempt to Boscawen, in the same way that he was to propose the naval attack on the Moro fort at Havana two years later. He was told to proceed, but not to risk any but minor losses in doing so.

Hervey bombarded the defences and attempted a surprise landing at night. He found, however, that the island was better garrisoned than he had been led to expect and lacking sufficient troops decided to discontinue the attack. But before giving up entirely he brought up some victuallers to look like troop transports and called upon the Governor to surrender. His opponent, however, was a man of spirit and refused, saying he would fight to the end. Hervey remained before the island for several days firing into the defences as opportunity offered, but a strong gale coming up he was forced to retire.

In August 1760 Hawke took over the command from Boscawen and remained in Quiberon Bay all winter, blockading and controlling the whole French Biscay coast. But in October *Dragon* returned to Portsmouth and saw no further action until after a winter refit. While she was in port Hervey was given quite extensive leave and at the same time many of his crew made their own leisure arrangements. Late in October Their Lordships asked him why in his absence sixty-six men had run. He replied[2] that all normal precautions had been taken – the doubtful characters placed in the guardship, sentries posted in *Dragon* and petty officers sent ashore to pick up deserters; there was no reason to think his officers had been negligent; very few of those gone would be of loss to the service and he could 'only impute it to the natural levity in seamen and the mixture which a new ship's company is mostly composed of'.

By the time *Dragon* was ready Keppel had taken over from Hawke with orders to implement Pitt's long planned descent on Belleisle. He sailed on 29 March, taking with him ten of the line, several frigates, fireships and bomb vessels, and over one hundred transports carrying 9000 men and three companies of artillery; in the fleet was *Dragon* presaging for Hervey another long summer off the French Atlantic coast. The first attempt to land on Belleisle was heralded by a bombardment of Locmaria on the east coast of the island by *Dragon* and two other ships, effectively silencing the guns. French resistance to the landing was, however, very fierce and the troops had to be taken off with substantial losses.

At this critical point in affairs Hervey had a stroke of luck. There had been few blockade runners during the operations off the French coast, and correspondingly few prizes. *Dragon,* however, was now ordered to chase and duly took a French brig inward bound from San Domingo with a rich cargo of sugar and indigo. Meanwhile Keppel and the land commander made a more extensive reconnaissance of Belleisle and, identifying a less strongly held stretch of coast made a lodgement and soon overran all the island except the fortress of Le Palais. It was not until 7 June that the Governor surrendered after a desperate resistance. *Dragon* was in at the finish, her boats helping to evacuate the French garrison

After another two months with the fleet *Dragon* returned to Plymouth for a further refit and was there until November. During October Lady Hervey wrote to Mr. Morris.

My son Aug[s] is now at Plymouth, preparing his ship for foreign service, according to his orders; but where he is to go, with whom or to whom, he knows not. He will be ready to sail the 25th, if the wind will permit. God send him success and safety wherever he goes . . .

If in October Lady Hervey did not know what these duties were the world was soon to find out. On 26th of the month Hervey was under sealed orders, requiring him to sail from Plymouth as soon as the wind allowed and to open them when he reached a position thirty leagues west of the Lizard. It was 30 Otober before the wind served and that morning he prepared to sail. Before he could do so, however, there came out to him orders from the Port Admiral to take under his command the bomb vessel *Granado*, which was under open orders to join Rear-Admiral George Brydges Rodney's squadron in the Leeward Islands. He wrote to the Admiralty.[3]

> Rear-Admiral Durrell has instructed me to wait for the bomb *Granado* destined for Rodney . . . I have acquainted the Admiral that this [an order to proceed in company] was the only direction I could give Captain Botterell as I knew not nor had the least intimation whether I was to join Ad Rodney, nor was I authorized to suppose it.

Clearly the Admiralty's left hand did not appreciate that its right hand believed that the operation in which both were engaged was secret.

In spite of Hervey's apparent mystification Durrell's gaffe surely told him that he was bound for the Caribbean, a destination which was confirmed when a few days later he opened his orders. The substantial squadron on the Leeward Islands station under Commodore Sir James Douglas was that autumn reinforced by more ships from home waters and to the West Indies also went Rodney to take overall naval command. *Dragon* was only one of many ships that were withdrawn from Keppel's squadron off Belleisle and got ready for this expedition. Hervey duly read his orders and arrived in Barbados on 12 December. There he found Rodney with a large fleet, accompanied by a considerable military force under General Moncton.

The objective of this concentration of forces was the capture of Martinique, the principal remaining French stronghold in the West Indies. Its reduction was a main plank of Pitt's programme for the winter of 1761/62. The British forces rendezvoused at Barbados and the attack on Martinique was set in motion in the first days of the New Year. Rodney arrived at St Pierre in the north of the island on 8 January to find that Douglas had already silenced the batteries, allowing him to take the town. The primary objective, however, was Fort Royal on the west coast, a strongly defended naval harbour whose entrance was commanded by the virtually impregnable fortress of the Ile des Ramiers (Pigeon Island). Since a frontal assault was almost impossible the plan was to land on the south coast at St Anne and march across country to take Fort Royal in the rear. Simultaneous diversions were arranged on the east coast at La Trinité and in the south west, where Commodore Swanton's squadron was sent with two brigades to Petite Anse. Swanton sent Hervey off to Grande Anse, further north and closer to Fort Royal, where he promptly silenced the battery and landed his marines to occupy it. Reinforced from Petite Anse, these forces marched north to Gros Point, opposite Pigeon Island, where they successfully drove off an attack from Fort Royal.

In the meantime the main attack from St Anne had been called off because of topographical difficulties – the British commanders had not realized how broken the countryside was – and Rodney settled for a flank attack from a landing point at Cas Navires, north of Fort Royal. The batteries were soon dealt with and the troops were landed without loss in three divisions, one of which was led by Hervey. Using the impeccable combined-operations techniques that had been developed in North America, and with much assistance from the sailors of the fleet in handling the guns, Fort Royal and the Ile des Ramiers were taken by early February. Immediately the town had surrendered Hervey with a small squadron was sent round to La Trinité where he found the frigates that had been sent as a diversion. Landing 500 seamen and marines he took the town, whereupon the whole district submitted.

As soon as Martinique had been subdued Rodney started on the other French islands, sending Hervey with four ships in company to take, if he could, St Lucia and then St Vincent. Hervey duly hoisted the broad pennant of a commodore, but when he arrived off St Lucia the narrow entrance to the harbour prevented him making any assessment of the defences. He therefore used his customary ingenuity, sending in a summons to surrender under a flag of truce and accompanying it himself dressed as a midshipman. In this way he was able to reconnoitre the defences, finding only a single fort, so situated that his ships could range alongside and destroy it. However, when the next day he stood in to the attack the Governor capitulated. Such is the account given by Corbett. *Dragon's* log, however, is content with a much simpler statement.[5]

> PM sent on shore a Flagg of Truce to summon the Island. At 5 (am) they capitulated.

Corbett does not, however, seem to be excessively adulatory when he writes 'as it were single-handed this intrepid officer had the honour of adding to British possessions that famous naval base which in the future was destined to be the key of our position in the Caribbean Sea'. Before he could do more, however, Hervey's little career of conquest was brought to a premature conclusion by an urgent recall to Martinique.

For the reason it is necessary to look at the wider developments of which Rodney had gradually become aware. On 15 December Spain had at last declared war, bringing into the reckoning against him her considerable naval forces and extensive colonial possessions in the Caribbean. This news reached him at the end of January 1762. In the meantime Keppel's blockading squadron had been driven from Brest by severe gales and the French Brest squadron of eight of the line and five frigates under Blénac had slipped out and was making for the Caribbean. Rodney heard this in early March, by which time Blénac was close at hand. He therefore took urgent steps to concentrate the British forces, including Hervey's small group, at Martinique.

When, however, Blénac arrived and found that the island had been taken he sailed straight on to Cap Francois, the naval base in the French half of Hispaniola (now Haiti). At this stage Rodney heard from Jamaica of the death there of the Commander-in-Chief, Rear-Admiral Charles Holmes, and at the same time was asked for assistance against the double threat that the Jamaican authorities perceived from the Spanish and from Blénac. He decided to blockade the French squadron in Cap Francois. However, before he could get further than St Kitts fresh orders reached him from home, including the news that he was to be superseded by Vice-Admiral Sir George Pocock, who was to conduct a major but unspecified operation against the Spanish colonies in the Caribbean. Rodney was ordered to have all available ships and transports concentrated in the Leeward Islands in readiness for the new Commander-in-Chief's arrival.

The receipt of these orders (and comparable ones to the dead Holmes at Jamaica) placed all the commanders in the West Indies in a quandary.[6&7] The Admiralty orders were dated 5 February and arrived at Martinique on 22 March – not an unusual lapse of time for the passage from England. Inevitably, however, they took no account of recent developments and in particular, if obeyed to the letter, ignored the presence of Blénac at Cap Francois and the risk of a combined Franco-Spanish attack on Jamaica. Of course, the uncertainties inherent in naval warfare in the days of sail arising from distance, the passage of time, the various options open to the enemy and the unpredictability of the weather made this a common problem. Rodney and his second-in-command, Douglas, dealt with them in impeccable form by means of a series of deployments in which Hervey played no inconsiderable part. Their dispositions, though different from those specified by the Admiralty, countered the threats that they perceived from the enemy without prejudicing Pocock's unspecified operations against Spain; in all probability they both rightly calculated that there were few objectives which would justify an expedition of the magnitude of that planned, and that the capture of Havana in Cuba ranked high among them.

Rodney found himself constrained to remain in the Leeward Islands but immediately sent Douglas to Jamaica with ten of the line including Hervey in *Dragon*. However, by the time Douglas arrived there on 12 April he had concuded from intelligence received *en route* that the risk of attack on the island was very small; as so often happened the Governor and those around him had cried wolf. He read the Admiralty instructions to his predecessor[8] and heard from Captain Forrest, the senior officer in temporary command, of a troop convoy coming down from North America under weak escort. This provided what Douglas wanted, a plausible reason for putting his squadron between the French at Cap Francois and the Spanish at Havana, thus preventing them joining forces. Compelled by his orders to stay himself at Port Royal he sent Hervey with eleven ships to cruise off the island of Tortuga, just west of Cap Francois and therefore between Blénac and the Spanish squadron and also close to the Windward Passage through which the convoy from the north must come if it was to reach Jamaica. Hervey hoisted his broad pennant again and cruised alertly but uneventfully with his squadron off Tortuga until early May.

Hervey's original orders had been to remain on station until the convoy arrived and then escort it past the French. On 22 April, however, Douglas decided that Hervey's ships must be completed with water and stores in accordance with the Admiralty orders to Rodney and Holmes, and sent orders recalling them to Port Royal for this purpose.[9] When, however, Hervey with part of his squadron arrived off Port Royal on 13 May he met Douglas coming out with every ship that was fit for sea. Events had moved on, Pocock had arrived at Martinique on 25 April and had ordered Douglas to rendezvous with him off Cape St Nicholas (close to Hervey's cruising station) without delay. Douglas turned Hervey's ships round and they returned through the Windward Passage with him. There was no opportunity to take on much needed food and water and consequently *Dragon* in particular was short for much of the coming campaign.

Douglas had been delayed by contrary winds and now ordered each ship to make the best possible progress. The first group of them, including *Dragon* and the flagship, reached the rendezvous on 23 May, where they found Pocock already arrived with the ships and transports from the Leeward Islands; when all were assembled they totalled over 200 sail. The objective of this vast armada was indeed to take Havana, the principal Spanish city in the Caribbean and the port at which the annual plate fleets assembled before their voyage to Spain. The plan was Anson's made in his last months as First Lord, and for it Pocock was to work in double harness with the Earl of Albemarle, who was provided with a force of 12,000 troops. The fleet was to approach Havana from the east, along the north coast of Cuba by the little used and difficult Old Bahama Channel.

No knowledgeable pilots had been found and it had been necessary for the channel, which was treacherous and in places only a few miles wide, to be surveyed and marked with beacons before the fleet could pass through. Pocock divided the fleet into seven divisions, of which *Dragon* was in the first, led by the flagship, *Namur*.[10] They passed through the narrows with great care, continually sounding and often sending the ships' boats ahead and to the flanks to feel the way. By magnificent navigation the fleet got through with no significant loss and was off Havana by 6 June.

The layout of the city and its defences had been studied by Admiral Knowles during the course of an official peacetime visit. Havana itself lay on the west side of the harbour, which was overlooked from the east by the Cabana ridge, at the seaward end of which was a precipitate, detached eminence surmounted

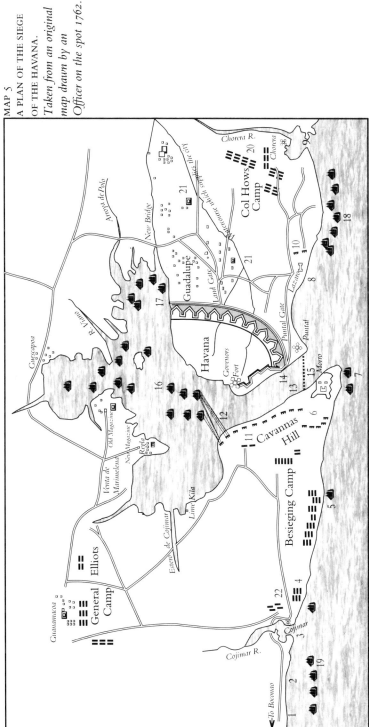

MAP 5
A PLAN OF THE SIEGE
OF THE HAVANA.
Taken from an original
map drawn by an
Officer on the spot 1762.

1. Place where the troops landed June 7. 2. March of the army after landing. 3. The *Dragon* against *Coximar* 4. Where the army first encamped. 5. Where the cannon &c. were landed. 6. Batteries against the *Moro*. 7. The *Dragon, Cambridge* and *Marlborough* against the *Moro*. 8. The bombs against the *Punta*. 9. *Belleiste* against Chorea fort. 10. Batteries against the *Punta*. 11. Batteries on the Cavanois hills. 12. Howitzers against the shipping. 13. Three Spanish men of war sunk. 14. One company's ship overset. 15. The chain and boom. 16. Spanish admiral and fleet. 17. Two ships on the stocks. 18. Admiral Pococke, with the men of war and transports. 19. Comodore Keppel, with ditto. 20. Camp at the watermills. 21. Fortified houses. 22. Head-quaters.

by the Moro fortress, whose guns dominated the harbour entrance and the town. The harbour was defended by the Spanish fleet and the coast to the west of it was thought – wrongly as it turned out – not to offer scope for a landing. Accepting the general view that the Moro was the key to the city Lord Albemarle made the fortress his first objective; his unimaginative plan was to land nearby, establish his batteries on the end of the ridge and lay siege to the fortress, for all the world as if he was confronted with a fortified town in the Low Countries. The fortifications may have been similar, but the climate was very different, as Vernon and Wentworth had found at Carthagena in 1741. Land warfare in the West Indies was a race, not against time or the enemy, but against the onset of tropical diseases which could very quickly render an army in the field powerless to attack.

As Pocock approached he detached a squadron under Keppel, his second-in-command and coincidentally Albemarle's brother, to land the main body of troops at the mouth of the Coximar river, about fifteen miles east of the Moro. The first troops were landed successfully to the east of the river mouth, Hervey commanding one of the divisions of boats. The river crossing, however, was found to be defended by Spanish troops in a breastwork and a stone fort. Rather than risk a land attack across the estuary Albemarle asked for naval assistance and Hervey was sent in with a second ship and two bomb vessels to destroy the fort by gunfire. The Spanish quickly abandoned their positions, whereupon Hervey landed his marines and occupied the site. During the next four days the army advanced and occupied substantial areas to the east and south of the Moro, including the Cabana ridge overlooking the fortress. Albemarle then began the construction of batteries on the ridge for the attack on the fortress itself.

A Spanish naval squadron of twelve of the line was in the harbour, where they quickly barricaded themselves from attack by sinking three of their number in the narrow entrance. With no naval opposition, therefore, the navy's main task was to land artillery and stores, to provide men to assist the army, to set up diversionary operations west of the harbour and generally to harass the other fortifications and the town. Pocock's officers, however, as soon as they saw the Moro began to consider how it might be attacked from the northern, seaward side. As early as 9 June, two days after the first landing, Hervey went close in to the fort in a sloop and made a favourable report on the possibilities,[11] finding that ships could get in close to the northern face without being exposed to fire from other forts. He tried to take soundings to ascertain whether ships could anchor close in but was driven off by fire from the Moro. He clearly thought an attack was practicable and asked Pocock to let him command it, or indeed to lead any other landing that might be made to the westward. Further surveys were made from ships' boats by night and it was established that it should be possible to anchor close in to the

Moro. However, the darkness prevented any assessment of the height of the fortifications in relation to the maximum elevation at which ships' guns could fire. Hervey offered[12] to take *Dragon* in close in good sailing conditions, running the gauntlet of the fort's guns while taking more soundings and assessing the height of the fortifications but nothing appears to have come of this suggestion and for the moment Albemarle considered that a bombardment from the sea would not be helpful.

It took until 1 July for Albemarle's batteries to be ready and as the day approached opinion veered towards a naval bombardment, to be synchronised with that from the land. Hervey was given the command, under Keppel, of what would now be called a task force of four of the line, to go in early on the morning of the 1st. He weighed anchor the evening before and stood off and on overnight, intending to get into position at daybreak. In the morning, however, the wind fell light and to make matters worse his leading ship, *Stirling Castle*, made little sail. He hailed her from his quarterdeck and sent an officer in a boat to her captain, James Campbell, who said that he had sent ashore most of her sails and booms – a measure sometimes taken to avoid unnecessary damage when it was expected a ship was likely to come under fire; but Hervey could see her mainsail and sprit sails in place but furled. So *Stirling Castle*, which was intended to provide a diversion while the others anchored close to the fort, fell behind and *Cambridge, Dragon* and *Marlborough* did not get into position until between 9 and 10 am. The three ships immediately opened fire on the fort, which replied vigorously. It soon became apparent, even in the blinding clouds of smoke which enveloped both sides, that the fort was too high for the ships' fire to reach the gun emplacements and that they were firing at the rocky cliff face and the lower masonry. The guns of the fort, for their part, could be not depressed far enough to fire directly on the hulls or decks of the ships, but began to do considerable damage to the masts and rigging.

Though *Dragon* had anchored in four and a half fathoms of water the tide was falling and before 10 am she went aground, fortunately with her broadside bearing. At 11.20 am Hervey sent a graphic note to Keppel describing his situation.[13]

Sir,

I have just got time to send the lieutenant of the *Cambridge* to you with this report and to desire your orders about it. I am unluckily aground but my guns bear. I cannot perceive their fire to slacken . . . I am afraid they are too high to do the execution we wished. I have many men out of combat now, and officers wounded; my masts and rigging much cut about, and only one anchor. I shall stay here as long as I can and wait your orders.

Augustus Hervey in Dragon attacking the Moro Fort, Havana, July 1762. From the picture by Richard Paton, by courtesy of the Trustees of the National Maritime Museum.

And somewhat later, asking for assistance to get off and scribbling on the back of his private signals:

Sir

I have the misfortune to be aground. Pray send a frigate to drop a bower [anchor] off, and send the end of the cable on board here. We are luckily on a good line for our fire on the fort; but the smoke makes it impossible to see the effect we have had or likely to have, nor can we tell when the army will advance.

Often duller, and ever yours, A Hervey.

No frigate was sent but shortly after midday orders arrived from Keppel to disengage. In the meantime Hervey had ordered Captain Campbell to drop one of *Stirling Castle's* anchors to seaward of *Dragon* and bring the cable on board, an order which he failed to obey. Eventually one of *Dragon's* own boats carried out her one remaining anchor and his crew 'hove a great strain'[14] on her capstan and she came off the ground. But to get her off he had had to stave her water barrels and lighten the ship by unloading stores into her boats. *Dragon* suffered considerable damage above and below and lost sixteen men killed and thirty-seven wounded, among the latter being Hervey's nephew Constantine Phipps (later 2nd Lord Mulgrave) who was her fifth lieutenant. In *Cambridge* the casualties were much more numerous and her captain, William Goostrey, was among the dead.

Thus when Hervey's squadron withdrew it had done little damage and had itself suffered disproportionately. Hervey had not misjudged the capability of ships to attack and neutralize land defences – his three ships had between them concentrated over 200 guns against the north wall of the Moro, which was defended by a fraction of that number – but it had been a serious omission not to clarify the angle of elevation needed before going in. Nevertheless the naval attack provided an important diversion in support of the bombardment by the land-based artillery.

Hervey's conduct in this affair has marked the attack on the Moro as one of the high points of his naval career. A hundred years later he might well have been thought eligible for the award of the Victoria Cross. Not only did he, when ordered, take his ship without qualm or hesitation into a maelstrom of enemy fire but in a much more deliberate way he had for the previous three weeks been asking his not-over-enthusiastic superiors to be allowed to do so. It takes an unusual degree of resolution, as well as courage, to maintain such an attitude, knowing that the operation would take him into a veritable killing field – the open quarterdeck of *Dragon* on which he would be obliged to stand exposed, with no protection from a withering enemy fire, for the duration of the engagement. The whole episode may be thought to be one which ranks him with Marshal Ney – 'the bravest of the brave'.

Not all post-captains in the navy were of the same calibre. The behaviour of Captain Campbell of *Stirling Castle* had not gone unnoticed. 'Shyness' – the naval equivocation for cowardice in the shape of failing to engage the enemy as closely as the situation or orders demanded – was not unknown and this seemed a clear case; Campbell had not made sufficient sail in bearing down towards the Moro, he had failed to provide succour for the grounded *Dragon* during the morning and he had delayed in towing the crippled *Cambridge* out of action when ordered to at the end of the action. Hervey's letter to Keppel, who appears to have been inclined to turn a blind eye, shows his view.

My Dear Sir

. . . I am very happy to find that we have given satisfaction, and that we were of such use to the General, as Lord Albemarle's letter flatters me with. As to the *Stirling Castle*, I think the Admiral seems to have seen enough to be a judge how far it is right to trust *such* a ship to *such* a commander; and I would not write a complaint, since you seemed so merciful to him; but I believe his officers will represent his conduct . . .

Your faithful and obedient servant

A Hervey

Campbell was duly tried by court martial and dismissed the service.

The Moro was not captured until the end of July and Havana itself held out until 14 August. When the city fell Pocock chose Hervey to take his dispatch home, a duty which was generally regarded as a reward for gallant and meritorious service during the campaign. During the voyage home he was fortunate to encounter and take a large French frigate carrying military supplies to Newfoundland where in a desperate attempt to blunt the British hold on their North American affairs the French had mounted a short-lived attack.

Dragon reached Spithead on 29 September and Hervey immediately set out for London, spreading the good tidings as he travelled the Portsmouth road. One early recipient of the news was the Duke of Newcastle, who was at his country house, Claremont Park in Surrey; soon after Hervey passed through Cobham it reached him and he exulted. Hervey arrived at the Admiralty between 7 and 8 pm and went straight in with Pocock's dispatch. He went on to see Lord Bute, by this time Prime Minister, who was dining with the Duke of Nivernois.[16] The Frenchman was taken aback but managed to say that he could not but be glad of the news since it would certainly contribute to facilitate a peace. Having performed his official duties Hervey went to White's to sup with his fellow members and regale them with the splendour of the takings. The news was the subject of great rejoicing, so much so that the guns of the Tower were fired in celebration as soon as orders could be given; they woke the city at 1 am the next day.

Pocock's dispatch[17] ended with fulsome praise for Hervey:

> I shall now beg leave to refer their Lordships to Capt. Hervey for all further particulars, whom I send with this letter and who has approved himself a brave and deserving officer in this expedition, and therefore think myself obliged to recommend him to His Majesty.

Amongst all the rejoicing and the plaudits Walpole wrote to Lady Hervey to congratulate her on such a son and on his safe return.[18]

> I hope you are free from any complaint, as I am sure you are full of joy. Nobody partakes more of your satisfaction for Mr. Hervey's safe return; and now he is safe, I trust you enjoy his glory; for this is a wicked age; you are one of those un-Lacedaemonian mothers, that are not content unless your children come off with all their limbs . . . '.

It was, however, the last occasion on which she would need to worry that her Augustus would not return from war. In December *Dragon* was paid off and her captain went ashore. Effectively, this was the end of his sparkling sea career. But his yearnings for the sea remained as great as ever and his hopes were to be raised, and dashed, more than once. He had one further command which lasted only a few weeks. Twice as a captain he was ordered to raise a commodore's pennant, and on both occasions the orders were rescinded before he could put them into effect. And once, as a Vice-Admiral, he was offered, but felt it necessary to refuse, the prospect of raising his flag as second-in-command of Britain's principal fleet in time of war. Although he never held another sea command his behaviour in the years remaining to him demonstrate how closely he continued to concern himself with the well-being of the navy and how much he strove to foster its strength and its capacity to maintain Britain's greatness – not least during his time in the seventies as a Lord Commissioner of the Admiralty.

References

1. PRO, ADM1/1895
2. Ibid.
3. PRO, ADM1/1897
4. Corbett, 1907, p226
5. PRO, ADM51/270
6. Syrett, 1970, *passim*
7. Corbett, 1907, *passim*
8. Syrett, 1970, p xvii
9. Ibid., p96
10. Ibid, p138
11. Ibid., p176–178
12. Ibid., p200
13. Keppel, 1842, p353
14. PRO, ADM51/270
15. Keppel, 1842, p353
16. British Library, Add. MSS, 32942, f418
17. PRO, ADM1/237
18. Lewis, 1937–83,(31), p27–28

CHAPTER XIII

Peace and Politics

The reluctant politician

In spite of his achievements Hervey had left *Dragon* in a state of uncomfortable awareness that his future as a sea officer was an uncertain one. Though the capture of Havana had given a further lease of life to the Seven Years War (by preventing Lord Bute, who was then leading the Government, from agreeing to a premature and unsatisfactory peace) there was little doubt that its prolongation was a matter of months, not of years. He must have remembered his experience at the end of the previous war when in spite of impeccable service the Admiralty had not found him a ship in the small peacetime navy, and for three years he had joined so many of his fellow captains on half-pay.

While doubtless keeping his hopes of sea service alive, and applying as occasion demanded for a suitable command (as he had always done, regardless of his opinion of the First Lord to whom he was obliged to apply) Hervey now began to consider how he could best make himself a political career. Since 1757 he had been one of the members for St Edmundsbury, a seat which he of course owed to the influence that Lord Bristol exercised over the small number of electors in the borough. He therefore felt himself to be under an obligation to his brother – less because he would need his support at the next election (which was not due until 1768) than from considerations of family accord and brotherly affection; and Bristol for his part expected Augustus to be a faithful political follower as well as a loved and loving brother to him.

In this expectation lies the nub of the dilemma which dogged Hervey's political footsteps throughout the decade, for Augustus had a high regard for Lord Bristol, but disliked his political friends. The result was a series of quarrels, fortunately always followed sooner or later by reconciliation. The dichotomy was not new, for when Augustus was first elected Bristol had pledged his brother's support to Newcastle and his allies in no uncertain terms; and it would have been difficult at that time to assess which out of Newcastle and his associates Henry Fox and Lord Anson Hervey disliked most.

While Hervey was a serving sea-officer this had mattered little, for he had not spent much time in London and when he was there had not been interested in politics. His only serious intervention in the Commons had been on a naval

Augustus Hervey *c.* 1763. From the picture by Sir Joshua Reynolds, courtesy of St Edmundsbury Borough Council (Manor House Museum).

matter, Hume's bill to abolish pressing. Even so, however, whenever he had looked for political friends in the fifties it was to groups other than his brother's friends that he had turned. He was then more at home with the dissident Whigs who had clustered round successive heirs to the throne than he was with Newcastle and his ministers, or indeed with the unfriendly King himself.

By the autumn of 1762, however, two things had changed. One was Hervey's reinforced interest in making his way in politics. The other was the nature of British political life. George II had been dead nearly two years and his successor was bent on managing the nation's affairs in a very different fashion. It soon became clear that the untrammelled ascendancy of the old Whig oligarchy was over. Pitt, the great war-leader and Newcastle the political fixer and nominal Prime Minister were forced from office, to be succeeded by the new King's former tutor and favourite the Earl of Bute, and then in April 1763 by Hervey's old friend George Grenville. A sea-change had come over British politics as the young George III determined to wrest back from his ministers many of the powers that had slipped from the grip of his three predecessors. He conceived that ministers were to be truly the servants of the Crown, and not the nominee of Parliament chosen solely because they had the support of a majority in both houses; though in the event George obtained parliamentary support for the royal appointees by the judicious use of patronage and bribery. The difference was that patronage was no longer the tool of a Walpole or a Duke of Newcastle but was in principle taken back into the royal hands from which it had sprung, though in effect it passed from the hands of a fixer in the Treasury to a favourite 'behind the curtain'. The King's attempt was a brave though injudicious one and it took twenty years for the Commons to reassert their independence.

It was the King's assertion of what he regarded as his hereditary powers, including the right to be served by ministers of his choice, ministers who only coincidentally enjoyed the support of Parliament, that was at the heart of the convoluted politics of the day. The Whigs, though much divided, were still dominant in Parliament so that in practice the King's choice in the early years of his reign (apart from Bute's short term in office) had to be made from among their ranks; though Bute, at the King's instigation, was a principal channel through which patronage and money were brought to bear on the many members of the Commons who were susceptible to such pressures. Furthermore, governments were not made more stable by the presence in the background of the greatest statesman of the day. William Pitt, later Earl of Chatham, combined his oratorical power to influence the Commons with the energy and clear sightedness which had brought victory over France and Spain. He was, however, an increasingly sick man and the temptation of successive administrations to seek his support and active participation was frustrated by his gout and at times by his mental instability.

So throughout the decade none of the politicians who were appointed to the Treasury were of the highest ability or achievement. Grenville, who soon became Hervey's patron and the man whom he eulogizes again and again, was more positive but no more successful than the rest. When in power he brought trouble on both Government and Parliament by the arrest and prosecution of the turbulent and radical John Wilkes, while his attempts to tax the American colonists sowed the seeds of the American revolution. He made no effort to humour the King, or even make himself agreeable to him, and it was the Monarch's dislike of him perhaps more than any failure in policy that led to his dismissal from office. He appears, however, to have been an upright and honourable man, ambitious but no servile self-seeker, and Hervey would have found it difficult to identify among the jostling crowd who moved back and forth between the government and opposition benches a more suitable and creditable political patron.

When Hervey returned from Havana in the autumn of 1762 all this was in the future. He had been away from London and political life for a considerable time and it was natural that he should gravitate to the group around the new King, who were to all appearances the successors of those opposition figures with whom he had consorted when George III was still heir to the throne. He was therefore an obvious candidate for the receipt of favours from the new fount of patronage. Only six weeks after his arrival home he was appointed Colonel of Marines, Plymouth Division, a well paid near-sinecure post used by the Crown to provide for well-thought-of officers. The appointment with its salary of £800 per annum provided a firm baseline for his finances, always precarious when his naval activities were not bringing in prize money. It is not necessary to take up an exaggeratedly cynical viewpoint to be able to see in this a step towards ensuring that the Government would receive his continuing support in the Commons.

Though Hervey's flirtation with Bute seems to have been a short one its existence is confirmed in a later letter – one of those anonymous letters to the press described below – which contains the telling sentence 'I was once weak enough to be deceived in your Lordship and entertained a favourable opinion of your integrity and uprightness'.[1] He is also known to have been writing on easy terms to his Lordship in January 1763.[2]

It is not surprising that Hervey's change of political allegiance soon became obvious to his brother; it quickly brought trouble. Lord Bristol was deeply offended at what he conceived to be a perverse betrayal and wrote him two intemperate letters[3] precipitating one of those crises between them that were to be features of the next ten years. Hervey found himself in an intolerable situation and in January wrote to Lord Bute intimating that he wished to resign his seat, asking for:[4]

any little stewardship that will vacate my present seat in Parliament, that according to my first and determined resolution I may make use of it, unless my Lord Bristol on my acquainting him again therewith, and finding it in my power, should then leave me at liberty to take that part which he before prevented me, and which from every principle and motive I am inclined to.

Neither Hervey nor his brother changed their minds and in February Hervey was appointed Steward of the Manor of Old Sarum, one of those offices of profit under the Crown which require the holder to vacate his seat in the Commons. In thus resigning the seat which he owed to his brother he shows a sense of propriety that exceeds that of many of his contemporaries. There is, however, little doubt that he had in mind, as soon as a vacancy occurred, exchanging St Edmundsbury for one of those seats that were effectively in the gift of the Administration.

In April Bute resigned and Hervey's friend George Grenville became First Lord of the Treasury, while Lord Sandwich went to the Admiralty. With both of them he had much closer links than with the court party round Lord Bute, and accordingly his prospects of naval employment became more rosy. He did not have long to wait. In early May he was appointed captain of the 50-gun ship *Centurion* (the ship in which Anson had gone round the world twenty years previously) and was nominated Commander-in-Chief of the small Mediterranean squadron with the rank of Commodore. The Mediterranean command was a sensitive one, for in addition to his purely naval duties the C-in-C was a kind of roving ambassador and might at any time have to cope with delicate diplomatic problems without reference to London. It was a position for which Hervey was ideally suited, by his considerable experience of the area and the robust approach to diplomacy which he had practised in the fifties as well as on strictly professional grounds.

It is not difficult to imagine the eagerness with which he looked forward to these new responsibilities as well as to a return to the delights that he had enjoyed during previous commissions. There were, however, the usual delays before he could get *Centurion* to sea. She was refitting at Woolwich and because of her age needed much attention. She was not a good sailer and not expecting to have need of her main armament he asked[5] for the heavy 24-pounders on her lower deck to be replaced by 18-pounders to improve her behaviour in a seaway. Their Lordships agreed but the Navy Board brought forward a string of objections, which in fact appear to have been well founded; there would be delay in supplying 18-pounders since they had none in stock; *Centurion's* gun ports necessitated the provision of special gun carriages for them, for which there would be no use when *Centurion* had finished with them; and so on. So Hervey had to be content with what he had.

It was late July before he got the ship into the Thames and mid August before she was ready for sea. From this stage onwards politics began to take over from purely maritime considerations. On 17th of the month, with a pilot already arranged to take her round to the Downs, Lord Egremont, one of the Secretaries of State, called him to London to charge him with a message from the King which was to be delivered to the Knights of Malta.[6] Their

Lordships gave permission for the ship to go round to Spithead under her first lieutenant and his business in London completed Hervey joined her there at the end of the month.

Before he left the Thames, however, the complexion of his journey to the Mediterranean underwent a radical change. He was to be accompanied as a passenger by none other than that paladin among naval personalities the 22-year-old Vice-Admiral of the Blue, His Royal Highness Edward Duke of York, the King's brother. The Duke and Hervey were not unknown to each other, having joined in a number of amatory excursions in the months before Hervey took *Monmouth* to sea in 1759. In these activities they had a mutual interest and no doubt the Duke looked forward to guidance from Hervey from his wide experience of such matters in the Mediterranean. On 9 August Hervey wrote to the Admiralty:[7]

> . . . I am to desire you will please give orders that his Royal Highness's proper standard [may be supplied] and what convenience may be necessary for his retinue.

On the 23rd of the month the Admiralty sent him his formal order to take on board his august passenger.[8]

> 'You are hereby required and directed in pursuance of the King's Pleasure signified to us by the Earl of Sandwich to receive on board His Majesty's Ship under your command His Royal Highness the Duke of York and retinue, servants and baggage, and give them a passage to the Mediterranean, victualling His Royal Highness his retinue and servants whilst on board as the ship's company.'

In spite of the wording it seems unlikely that Their Lordships actually meant His Royal Highness to eat ship's biscuit and drink from her water barrels.

At about the same time it becomes obvious that Hervey had political irons of his own in the fire. He had been without a seat in the Commons for six months and had no doubt been urging his need on Sandwich and his other friends in government. A vacancy had arisen at Saltash, a Cornish borough effectively controlled by the Admiralty, and Hervey was brought forward by Sandwich as the government candidate; all that was needed was suitable massaging of the electors' interests in the meantime. So on 9 September with *Centurion* under orders to make her way with all despatch to Plymouth, but held at Spithead by contrary winds he was constrained again to ask permission to leave her to his first lieutenant and make his way overland to Plymouth because 'business of great importance to me requires my being at Plymouth by 15th inst.'[9]

During these days also all the routine and special orders relevant to his forthcoming command began to reach him;[10] details of the ships in his squadron

– the 50-gun 4th rate *Centurion*, two 32-gun frigates, three frigates of 20 guns and two sloops; the frigate *Deal Castle* and the *Vulture* sloop were in home waters and he was to take them under his command immediately; that he should hoist a broad pennant at his maintopmasthead 'when you get out of the Channel', the usual orders about the squadron's duties, their priorities and how it was to be deployed; orders to proceed to Malta as soon as convenient to convey the Government's dispatch to the Knights; and details such as the seconding of surgeon's mates to the hospital at Minorca.

The last of these orders was dated 31 August. In parallel with these naval preparations, however, changes were occurring on the political front. The urgent business that Hervey had at Plymouth was of course connected with the forthcoming election at Saltash, which would make Hervey one of the Government's supporters at Westminster. Unfortunately Grenville was at this time under pressure from both the King and his political opponents. On 21 August Lord Egremont died and in the following few days His Majesty tried unsuccessfully to get Pitt to form a government. Under these pressures Grenville felt it necessary to call in all hands to support him at Westminster. At some time in late August or early September – the letters concerned between Plymouth and London have not survived – Hervey as presumptive Member for Saltash was therefore asked to withdraw from the Mediterranean appointment, and it can readily be accepted that it was with the utmost regret that he agreed to do so. On 7 September, only a week after the last order from the Admiralty about the Mediterranean, Sandwich wrote to him both informally and formally setting out the new position and on the same day sent him a formal order to stand down from his command.[11] The First Lord's first letter[12] casts an uncertain but fascinating light on the political manoeuvring that took place and on several aspects of their joint interests; it is of sufficient substance to be given in full:

Admiralty, September 7 1763

Dear Hervey,

I did not receive yours till this morning and could not dispatch the answer till after I had seen the King today; I will write you an ostensible letter about your coming back, as I have other things to say to you which had better not be shown to all your present company. You will be happy to learn that everything goes on with flying colours, the vacant offices are all to be filled on Friday, the Duke of Bedford joins us heart and hand, and agrees to accept the Presidency [of the Council] , he will therefore kiss hands with the rest on Friday; this I believe you will allow to be a material point gained. I believe Lord Egmont will succeed me in this office [Sandwich was in the process of being appointed Secretary of State], which I think considering all things is tolerably well, Winchelsea declined it.

I have seen both Lord Halifax [one of the Secretaries of State] and Mr. Grenville and they both think your request about the Bedchamber thoroughly reasonable, and they desire me to assure you that they will join with me with all their strength to get it done; I rather think there may be some difficulty about the present vacancy, but they are both of them so explicit and so pleased with your behaviour that I consider the matter certain.

I wrote to you last night by the Post to Plymouth enclosing a letter from Lady Mary, and desiring you to inform your friends at Saltash that on your recommendation I had appointed Lieutenants Trehearne and Field to a guardship at Plymouth.

A packet will go today with all the necessary papers and commissions for Captain Harrison, they will be sent to Commissioner Rogers to be delivered to you, who will give them to Harrison or return them as things shall turn out; tho' I have no idea how it is possible for the Duke of York or anyone to persuade him to decline the command after what has already passed.

I hope all your negotiations at and near Plymouth and everywhere else will succeed to the utmost of your wishes, I believe I need not add with how great a warmth of heart I am most faithfully yours

Sandwich

Sandwich was not, in the groupings that had taken shape among the Whig politicians, a supporter of Grenville but of the Duke of Bedford and is thus reporting that his chief had been persuaded to join the Government. His reference to 'Lady Mary' is to Hervey's sister Mary Fitzgerald, by this time separated from her difficult husband and with whom Sandwich was to be very friendly for many years.

There are in the letter references to three matters of immediate concern to its recipient. The first is the Mediterranean command, on which the First Lord wrote a separate 'ostensible' letter[13] of the same date and enclosed orders for Captain Harrison to take Hervey's place. The 'ostensible' letter reads as follows:

Dear Sir

The violent attempts that have lately been made by the opposition make it necessary for those who wish well to government to strengthen their hands as much as possible, and a person of your parts and activity is not to be spared in the critical times. I have mentioned you today in this light to His Majesty, and am ordered by him to tell you that he is very desirous you should remain on shore to attend your duty in Parliament. I know how disagreeable it will be for you to quit your attendance on His Royal Highness, but I hope this alteration will be the less unpleasing to you, as

I think we have found a person to supply your place who has the honour of His Royal Highness's protection; I mean Captain Tho. Harrison who is now at Plymouth, and who I dare say will be happy to be put in your place in this very desirable and pleasant expedition.

If His Royal Highness will allow us to make the proposed change, I hope to see you in town as soon as the business you have in the West will admit of . . .

So Hervey was eased out of his circuit of pleasure and Harrison took his place. There is a hint in both letters that the new Commander-in-Chief might not welcome the opportunity, a surprising attitude in this time of retrenchment. On the other hand it requires no effort to accept that Hervey would regret the change, indeed the problem at first sight is to understand how he came to acquiesce. It was a matter of priorities. Was it right for him to try to continue with his naval career, in a command which must have been his heart's desire, but at the probable cost of loss of favour with Sandwich and Grenville? Or should he gravitate towards the parliamentary life, in which he was just beginning to enjoy the thrills of political intrigue and manoeuvre, and which might well lead to more influential offers at home? There are two probable and not mutually exclusive explanations for his decision, one defensive, the other more positive. The first revolves around his parliamentary position. He had set his mind on a seat and there is no doubt that his candidature at Saltash now depended on his staying at home; certainly he was doing his best to win Saltash and Sandwich was doing his best to help him, as shown by his willingness to appoint Lieutenants Trehearne and Field to positions which the electors of Saltash had asked for through Hervey's agency. There is, however, no doubt that continuance of government support now depended on his relinquishing the Mediterranean. More positively Hervey may have had in mind that if he was available in London some greater prize was in prospect, perhaps a Lordship of the Admiralty, a position to which he undoubtedly aspired. Certainly Newcastle, out of office, wrote.[14]

'They talk with great confidence that . . . Commodore Hervey . . . is kept at home to shine in the Admiralty'.

But Sandwich left the Admiralty later in September on appointment as Secretary of State and Egmont, his successor, was not one of Hervey's close associates.

In retrospect it is easy to see that this was a cardinal decision, a turning point in Hervey's career. It is tempting to conclude that he got it wrong. Three years or so in the peacetime Mediterranean would have enabled him to show his merits as a squadron commander and a diplomat, and would have been a feather in his professional cap. The climate might well have eased his gout and he could have returned to London with an enhanced reputation and enhanced prospects of further naval employment; and a seat in the Commons could easily have come his way, for example by reconciliation with Lord Bristol. It could have provided a more productive and more rewarding scenario than the life on the fringes of politics which was actually his lot for the next few years.

At some time during these negotiations Hervey had sought appointment as a Groom of the Bedchamber, an appointment which would compensate to an extent for the loss of his naval command and its financial perquisites, and would be in the family tradition of service at Court, his grandmother, mother and father having all held such positions during the previous two reigns. He was duly appointed and held the post until he succeeded to the Bristol earldom in 1775. In addition he was in October given the command of one of the royal yachts, potentially a sea appointment but one with limited duties and responsibilities.

Hervey won the Saltash seat and at the end of this political foray into the west returned to London to participate fully in the hurly-burly of political life. Few changes in eighteenth-century lifestyle can have been more far-reaching than that which he was now to experience, retirement from the sea. But in Hervey's case there is no doubt that when in October 1762 he went ashore from *Dragon* and again when he agreed to surrender the Mediterranean appointment eleven months later, he did not regard his naval career as over; of that, and of his continuing passionate interest in naval affairs there is much evidence to be brought forward later. In the meantime his shore appointments brought him a modest income, £800 a year from his Colonelcy of Marines and £500 as Groom of the Bedchamber, sufficient for the life in the higher strata of English society to which he had been born. There is little doubt, also, that some portion of his prize monies remained unspent, for during the last five years of war, in the Mediterranean, off the Atlantic coast of France and in the West Indies, there had been little time or opportunity for lavish expenditure. Whatever the details, his philosophical approach to financial affairs and the adequacy of his financial state are well summarized in the letter, quoted later, that he wrote to George Grenville after his mother's death in 1768.[15]

For the next eight years Hervey seems to have lived a somewhat peripatetic life. Letter headings show that when in London he spent much of his time at his mother's house in Park Place. Earlier he had had a succession of small *pieds-à-terre* in London but there is no mention of any from this time on. He made many visits to Ickworth and to the country houses of his friends, including Wotton and Stowe in Buckinghamshire, the country seats respectively of George Grenville and Lord Temple, and Lord Sandwich's house at Hinchingbroke.

Hervey was frequently at Bath, chiefly on acount of the chronic ill health from which he continued to suffer for the rest of his life. Gout had been a problem to him on and off since 1756 when he was approaching his thirty-second birthday. This early onset should cause no surprise, for the condition ran in the family, his mother being a particularly severe case; and his lifestyle – an unbalanced diet, a superfluity of meat, often at sea accompanied by little in the way of fresh foods of any kind, an even greater superfluity of alcohol and an unavoidable lack of exercise, though no different from that of many of his contemporaries, cannot have helped. A further consideration is that the West Indies were notorious as a hotbed of malaria, yellow fever and other tropical diseases. Apart from whatever illness drove him ashore from *Cornwall* in 1746 we do not hear that Hervey was ill during his service there, nor is there specific mention of any other complaint after his return. Gout, however, continued to worry him, and seems to have been considerably worse after his time in the West Indies than beforehand. Thus in a letter to Mr. Morris in September 1767, five years after his return, Lady Hervey writes:[16]

> . . . poor Augustus, who is gone to the Bath with the gout in his stomach, where the best he can hope is to have it transferred to his limbs. He has never had tolerable health since he was at the Havana.

The extent of the problem is shown in one of Hervey's letters to George Grenville, written from Bath on 17 October in the same year, and seemingly referring to the same attack:[17]

> . . . this has been as tedious in the convalescence as it was dangerous in the attack; but I flatter myself that a few days more of these waters will entirely set me up, and that the half-year's tax that my detestable constitution (as it has become) pays every spring and fall for its continuance in this delightful world is over for this time. . .

Nevertheless, between times he managed a full and active life, as his reference to 'this delightful world' suggests. He had by no means lost his taste for female companionship, though few specific names are mentioned. The last reference in his *Journal* is to Kitty Fisher, who was still in attendance in April 1759, just before his long stint in command of the inshore squadron off Brest. From then until his return from the West Indies in 1762 he had few opportunities for dalliance; the first name mentioned after his return is that of Kitty Hunter, a flighty young lady who had lost no time in acquiring a notorious past. She was the errant daughter of Mr. Thomas Orby Hunter, a Lord of the Admiralty, and was unwise enough to have eloped with Hervey's friend the Earl of Pembroke. Attempting to reach the continent they were intercepted and brought back, whereon the young lady's father disowned her. The liaison with his Lordship continued and a child was born. But Pembroke was married already and the affair shortly came to an end, the father doing his duty financially by mother and child.

Soon after this, probably in 1763 or 1764, Miss Hunter took up with Hervey and in due time bore a son of whom he was the undoubted and acknowledged father. Hervey was of course in no position to marry, even if he had wanted to, and this affair quickly ran its course. Kitty Hunter went on to marry an army officer who later became Field Marshal Sir Alured Clarke. She appears not to have had any desire to be encumbered with Hervey's child, who was christened Augustus, was known by the name of Hervey and was brought up by his father as a well-loved son; of him more later. Only two other names emerge from the shadows – Miss Moysey of Bath, his attraction for whom set in process a complex series of legal proceedings in 1768–69, and Mrs Mary Nesbitt, with whom he spent in unmarried comfort the last nine years or so of his life.

Since Hervey's relationships with women justify calling him a 'Casanova' some mention should be made of his reported meeting with the original of that name. Giacomo Casanova was in England from June 1763 to March 1764 and reports in his memoirs[18] a conversation he had with 'Lord Augustus Hervey' while walking in St James's Park. Bleackley as editor comments that the meeting surely took place, since Casanova describes Hervey's charmingly cynical approach to life so precisely. If they discussed women he does not say so, but confines his account to a discussion of honour, wrong-doing, crime and expiation.

As the sixties lengthened and prospects of a sea appointment faded Hervey was fortunate to have a strong political base from which to foster the causes in which he was interested. Apart from the best interests of Augustus Hervey himself his principal concerns were the navy and the well being and position of Britain in the world. His membership of the Commons was to continue until he became a peer in 1775. His attendance at its sessions was frequent if not remittingly regular, but he made few speeches in the House. Several of the draft speeches among his papers are marked with notes such as 'Was ill and did not go down [to the House]'. He was also a Groom of the Bedchamber and took his due share of court duties. The combination of parliamentary and court positions was a strong one, and one that he used to advantage.

That Hervey had quickly attached himself to George Grenville, who became Prime Minister in April 1763, is shown by an anonymous letter in the *Gentleman's Magazine* for July of that year. Though no manuscript exists among Hervey's papers it is so much in his style – rotund verbosity combined with a flowing line of argument and bolstered by a wide but apposite vocabulary – and its defence of Grenville is so similar to that in his later writings for the press that there can be little doubt that it is from his pen. As an answer to an earlier letter attacking Grenville the letter begins:[19]

> If I thought that there was the least probability that the Rt. Hon. Gentleman whose name appears prefixed to your letter, would condescend to give you

a reply to it, I should by no means think of taking up the pen to engage in your correspondence; but as I hope his time is much more usefully employed, I am tempted to give way to the indignation I feel, upon reading a *performance as void of truth, as it is full of impudent malignity.*'

The principal thrust of the previous letter had been an attack on Grenville and his government for their attempts to silence Wilkes, the publisher of the *North Briton*, and Hervey's rebuttal shows an establishment-orientated view. For example 'In effect, what is the *North Briton* labouring with so much pious zeal for the benefit of his country. To destroy that union of the two kingdoms, so mutually advantageous to both nations, to revive faction and the odious distinctions of party, to depreciate in the opinions of mankind not only ministers but even Majesty itself, together with both Houses of Parliament . . .' Again, 'When a man is charged with being a sower of sedition [as Wilkes was] can it be called a hardship that he is barred the means of diffusing its influence?' And so on.

The letter is not a good example of political philosphy but indicates how soon and how closely Hervey had tied himself to one among the crowd of politicians who sought the King's mandate to govern. He continued to support Grenville for the rest of the decade. One of his services to his patron was that he was able to relay Court gossip to him, gossip obtained by virtue of his office as Groom of the Bedchamber. A letter from him dated 21 October 1768 shows this very well:[20]

> . . . I hear the Chancellor continues, but that Sir Edward Hawke [then First Lord of the Admiralty] must soon give way to the earl of Sandwich. That is the talk at St James; and that Barré is to be turned out of the Vice-Treasurership, so that it will be a fine mixture at last. There is a meeting tonight to think of the Speech.
>
> Lord Harcourt and Lord Holdernesse are competitors for the Embassy to France, but 'tis thought the first will have it. Poor Colonel Brudenell died last night. There seem more candidates for his Regiment than for his place at Court today [he had been Vice-Chamberlain to the Queen and Lieu-tenant-Governor of Windsor Castle]. . .

It may appear only tittle-tattle, but one may suppose that it was the sort of information that was commonplace among ministers and courtiers, though not so readily available to politicians out of office. It need hardly be said that all this support for Grenville and the supply of information to him was intended as a staging post in Hervey's own ambitions for office; though Grenville was never again to be in a position to offer him any satisfaction.

He also kept himself active in the field of political advocacy by participation in the work of the Commons and by continuous campaigns of letter and pamphlet writing. The letter in defence of Grenville referred to above was soon followed by others on related subjects. In general publishers of the political journals of the day, the *Public Advertiser* and *Gazetteer* in particular, needed no persuasion to accept his letters, which were all fine swashbuckling stuff, good for circulation. Indeed, when one on naval half-pay did not appear within a week or so Hervey assumed, rightly, that it had gone astray and sent a second copy.

His letters were usually datelined from rural England, typically 'Somersetshire', and were signed with various *noms de plume*. The most common was 'A True Englishman', while others were adapted to circumstances or subject-matter. They included 'An English Country Gentleman', 'A Briton', 'An Officer', and 'A Friend to the Navy of England'. They were forthright and usually made a point in the controversial and rumbustious politics of the day.

Some of the earliest for which manuscripts exist were not on overtly politically subjects at all. Published in the *Gazetteer* and *Scrutator* in the spring of 1764 they described the gerrymandering attached to the election of a new High Steward of Cambridge University. The candidates were Lord Hardwicke, son of the great lawyer and former Lord Chancellor, and Hervey's friend Lord Sandwich. The electorate consisted of all Masters of Arts of the University, of whom few were resident. The Vice-Chancellor had managed to assist the chances of Lord Hardwicke, the candidate favoured by resident dons, by changing the date of the election at a very late stage, making it difficult for non-residents to reach Cambridge to vote. Many were country parsons and had timed their visit to Cambridge to coincide with the original date of the election. When others tried to book a place on the stage coaches to Cambridge for the new date they found that the Vice-Chancellor's party, forewarned of the change, had already taken them all. In the event, the candidates polled the same number of votes and recourse was had to the courts before Hardwicke was declared the winner. Predictably Hervey was most incensed, and expressed his dissatisfaction with his customary frankness.

Politically Hervey was fairly quiet during the twenty-seven months of Grenville's administration, from April 1763 to July 1765. In the spring of 1765, however, the prospect of active service came his way again. Relations between Britain and Spain became strained, with problems in the financial settlements agreed in the peace of 1763 in relation to the two principal colonial cities captured by Britain during the war – Havana and Manila. In addition there was continuing Spanish interference in the affairs of the British log-cutters in Honduras on the central American mainland, a cause of friction which the treaty was intended to bring to an end. In this situation the neutrality of France, smarting from her defeats in the Seven Years War, could not be counted upon. Britain began to prepare for the possibility of war and a fleet was got ready under the overall command of Sir Charles Saunders. Hervey, whose friends in office included Egmont as First Lord of the Admiralty and

Sandwich as Secretary of State as well as Grenville, was nominated to the command of one of the divisions of the fleet with the rank of commodore.

There were however, mutterings and intrigues about the chief commands. Augustus Keppel, by this time an admiral, wrote from Bath to Lord Rockingham (then in opposition, and of whom Keppel was a supporter) on 29 April.[21]

> . . . Sir Charles Saunders. . . surely. . . plunged head over heels [in accepting the command] without considering – I don't mean that the King and public were to be deprived of his services, but his health was a good and real pretence to beg time to consider, and at no rate to have undertaken the command without naming his assistants. Instead of which he finds himself saddled with Captain Hervey for one of his divisions. He [Hervey] writes me word he had asked Lord Sandwich to have me with him, which was answered in the negative. . . . . .
>
> Would you believe it? I had one of the most civil epistles from Captain Hervey, upon the very first of the equipment, telling me how much he was paying court to the public voice, in saying civil things of me to the Board of Admiralty, as the properest person to command this fleet; (not then knowing it was to be commanded by Sir Charles Saunders). I must confess this letter puzzled me much for an answer. I don't know whether you will agree with me in the answer I at last determined upon and sent. I gave him joy on being employed on the present occasion, and said "For myself, I am no child or favourite of ministers, and own I am particular enough not to wish any advocate's good words with them; though I say this, I am not the less obliged to you for your good meaning;" and so I concluded I shall have no more of his formidable interest, if he understands my letter as I would have him.

The interchange shows some interesting facets of the relationship between Hervey and Keppel. They had had brushes in the past, for example the disagreement on entitlement to freight charges at Lisbon in 1752, and as a member of Byng's court martial Keppel had been out of Hervey's favour. On the brighter side Hervey had served without rancour under Keppel during the Belleisle expedition in 1761 and at Havana in 1762. For Hervey's part, therefore, his wish to see Keppel in command of the fleet in 1765, and to serve under him, suggests no lasting ill will. Keppel, on the other hand, was probably annoyed that an officer junior to him in rank should be asking political favours on his behalf. He reacted harshly to Hervey's approach, in effect telling Rockingham that Saunders ought to consider Hervey a tiresome subordinate. The matter was not, however, put to the test, for the crisis shortly abated and the naval preparations were aborted.

In May of the same year Hervey was instrumental in providing a particular service to Grenville, personal as well as political. Grenville had for some time been at loggerheads with his brother the quick-tempered Lord Temple, who had taken offence because Grenville appeared to have become closer to Bute than to himself and had allied himself with Pitt. Hervey now attempted a reconciliation writing on 20th of the month to Grenville[22] – presumably there had been some previous talk on the subject – announcing his intention to talk to Temple carefully and tactfully, and begging him to:

> Trust to a younger man than yourself for once [Grenville was twelve years older than Hervey], whose head may not be as good as his heart, but who will never risk your name, or even a word you have ever said to me; but I think I see a prospect of what I wish, and every friend to you and your country must, and wish I may soon be an instrument of bringing it about.

He spoke to Temple and then again to Grenville at 10 am on the 21st, persuading him to meet Temple at midday. They duly met but at this first meeting failed to compose their differences. The next day Temple wrote to Grenville for another meeting, at which they successfully agreed to forget the quarrel and resumed fraternal relationships.

Drawing Temple away from Pitt in this way propped up the Grenville government for a little longer but it was moving inexorably into rougher and rougher water. It became less and less acceptable to the King and in June lost the support of the Duke of Bedford and his party. In July the King, influenced still by Bute 'behind the curtain' dismissed his First Lord of the Treasury and appointed the Whig Marquess of Rockingham in his place. Hervey could not be expected to approve of the change and shortly began a campaign of letters and pamphlets against the new Administration. An early contribution was a pamphlet[23] published as 'A Letter to Lord Bute' on 1 August 1765. On the back of the manuscript Hervey subsequently wrote that it was first written at Sleaford on 9 July, while he was waiting for his brother, who was dealing with estate matters with his steward; it was not at that time meant for publication. He read it, however, to his brother in their chaise on the way south and on reaching London found that, as he puts it, Bute had forced from office and 'disgraced' all their political friends. So he revised it somewhat and showed it to Grenville and then to Sandwich, who had it published after removing a few of the extravaganzae in it.

Rather long, it may be summarized as follows. The writer – it is signed 'No flatterer but your best friend and truest counsellor, A Plain Dealer' – has a duty to King and country to make representations to Bute because of the latter's powerful position behind the scenes. He compliments Bute on his acceptability to the King but chides him for bringing down troubles on His Majesty when he was head of the government (in 1762/63). He refers to Bute's 'selfish and sinister purposes' and to 'the very many intimate connections you have formed and then wantonly broken, through revenge, caprice and jealousy'. Bute had found the country united under a young patriot King and a capable minister (the Pitt/Newcastle administration of 1757–61) but had had a baleful influence ever since. After Bute's own short-lived administration broke up he had continued to meddle with and obstruct Grenville's government. For Grenville the pamphlet has nothing but praise, for restoring public credit and starting to reduce the national debt, referring to his 'cool head and honest heart'. Bute's efforts to put together a government acceptable to himself and the King he describes as desperate and he holds him responsible for the existence of Rockingham's administration, which he forecasts will be a disaster. The final shaft is to recommend Bute to flee the country for his own good. In this he seems to be drawing a parallel with the fate of the favourite of an earlier king – Strafford, whom Charles I could not save from impeachment and execution.

In all this Hervey was writing as a faithful supporter of Grenville's ousted government and there is no reason to expect him to maintain an academic, unbiased view of events. Bute did become a negative influence on the political life of the country for a number of years after the young King's accession. He acted, however, as the adviser, agent and mouthpiece of a king who in those years was intent on re-establishing the rightful power of the throne as he conceived it.

There followed from Hervey's pen several months of letters on the iniquities and inadequacies of the new government, letters in which he continued to extol the virtues of the Grenvilles. On 7 August[24] he inveighed against the shortcomings of the 'triumvirate' – presumably Rockingham, Grafton and Newcastle – and on 25 August[25], commenting on their apparent lack of purpose, wrote that '. . . though they may have the best of reasons for not communicating to us what they intend doing (as not knowing themselves). The First Lord [of the Admiralty – Egmont, Grenville's appointee, still in office]. . . was able and well-informed'. He states that Rockingham and his colleagues were having difficulty in filling posts, an assertion that sits ill with a remark on 4 September that they were selling government offices to those prepared to pay for them.

On 9 September[26] Grenville and his government were again praised to the skies and Lords S and H were defended against 'dark and false insinuations' made against them . . . I could never find any particular charge except an excess in their passion for women.' S is undoubtedly the promiscuous Sandwich, of whom the remark is certainly true, and H is probably Halifax. Later in the month 'A True Englishman' wrote from Somersetshire[27] deploring the inexperience and giddiness of the new government and pointing to the dissatisfaction with it that the City had expressed. About Hervey's longstanding *bête noire,* Newcastle, the writer said that he was 'made to believe he has some influence in the A————n'. The army is described as 'drooping back to that Germanized discipline which was the bane of it for many years'. Further letters from the same *nom de plume* drew attention to inexperience and corruption, and this time overtly compared Bute with Strafford.

In December[28] Hervey appears in another guise, that of 'An Independent but Loyal Country Squire' from Cornwall and comments on various recent letters, including those from his own pen:

> The True Englishman, with a zeal becoming the character he assumes, has maintained his cause with more decency and energy, tho I acknowledge he has sometimes in his warmth exceeded the strict bounds of decorum, but in general has made a strong impression on his readers and left a sting in those he has attacked which they will not easily get rid of.

In the early months of 1766 Rockingham's Government determined to repeal Grenville's Stamp Act, which had imposed taxes on the American colonies to provide finance for their defence. Hervey opposed the repeal, and since this conflicted so directly with the government's policies asked the King for permission to resign his place at Court,[29] permission that the King refused. In the Commons he declared that he had supported the measure when it was introduced and still supported it, in spite of the unrest that it had caused. He had indeed expected it to cause a degree of unrest in the colonies, but that this should ripen into near rebellion was surely due to those now in power who had failed to control it and to those on the European side of the Atlantic who had encouraged seditious thoughts in the colonies. The constitutional position as he saw it was that Parliament had authority in all the British Dominions, and he could see no other satisfactory arrangement. And why should the colonists not pay their share of the financial burden of their defence? In this he was of course following closely the attitude taken up by the King, by Grenville's government when the tax was introduced, and by subsequent governments, especially that of Lord North. But in spite of opposition from Grenville's supporters Rockingham was successful in getting the Act repealed though little effect the repeal had in moderating the attitude of the colonists in America.

Hervey had again shown a regard for the established way of conducting affairs and for the rights of the King and of Parliament, as he had when Wilkes was arrested in 1765, with no thought that either the changes which were occurring in society or the increased size and complexity of King George's dominions warranted a fresh look at the way in which these dominions were administered. It was an attitude taken by many of his contemporaries and was in a few years to bring the country almost to its knees.

References

1. SRO(B), 941/50/5, p317
2. Bute MSS, quoted in Namier & Brooke, 1964
3. Namier & Brooke, 1964, p617
4. Bute MSS, quoted in Namier & Brooke, 1964
5. PRO, ADM1/1898
6. Ibid
7. Ibid
8. PRO, ADM2/90
9. ADM1/1898
10. PRO, ADM2/90 & 91
11. ADM2/91
12. NMML, the Sandwich Papers, F41/10
13. NMML, the Sandwich Papers, F41/11
14. British Library, ADD. MSS 3251, f69
15. Smith, 1852, p356
16. Hervey, 1821, p327
17. Smith, 1852, (4), p175
18. Bleackley, 1923, p53 et seq.
19. *Gentleman's Magazine*, July 1763, p325
20. Smith, 1852, (4), p383
21. Keppel, 1842, p377
22. Smith, 1852, (3) p39
23. SRO(B), 941/50/5, p317
24. Ibid., p337
25. Ibid., p347
26. Ibid., p361
27. Ibid., p369
28. Ibid., p405
29. Walpole, 1894, (2), p183

CHAPTER XIV

The Private Member

A wife, no wife

In July 1766 Rockingham's administration fell and after complex negotiations the Duke of Grafton became First Lord of the Treasury and nominal head of the government. In reality the new government was intended as a vehicle for William Pitt, shortly to be made Earl of Chatham, who had been persuaded to return to office as Lord Privy Seal. It had been thought that Grenville would return to office and on 19 July Hervey wrote to him reminding him gently of his wish for a seat at the Admiralty Board.[1] In the event the Grenvilles remained in opposition and nothing came his way. Very soon, however, another prospect opened up. Pitt offered Lord Bristol a place in Government, and Bristol (whose quarrel with Hervey had by then been composed) in turn offered his brother just what he had wanted from Grenville – a place at the Admiralty. Hervey, however, refused the offer,[2] on the grounds that he would not take office without his political allies, at the same time saying that with Bristol in office he would not openly oppose the Government.

Bristol was appointed Lord Lieutenant of Ireland and immediately asked Hervey to be his Secretary – the office later known as Chief Secretary for Ireland. Hervey again refused but his brother was so insistent that in the end he grudgingly accepted, writing to Grenville on 29 August in the following terms:[3]

> Ill health, inabilities and *other things* had made me determined not to go, and to remain quiet as I was, I told him this and declined it, but had you seen the effect of it and how impossible it was for me to persist after what he said, you would both applaud and pity the determination. So there I am embarked in what I know nothing of, nor like.

Pitt is thought to have intended Bristol to introduce a policy of amelioration for the downtrodden Irish Catholics. In the event, however, the Lord Privy Seal's continuing poor health prevented him from taking any real part in the Administration and Bristol achieved little in the ten months for which he held the office. Hervey assumed the Secretary's duties almost immediately and on 16 October was sworn of the Privy Council for Ireland. Remarkably, though not inconsistently with English attitudes to Irish affairs at the time, neither of the brothers visited Ireland during their period in office, the Irish Parliament did not meet and no new policies were introduced.

If Lord Bristol did little to improve the lot of the Irish he did fulfil, indeed more than fulfil, his duty towards his family, enabling Walpole to quip to Lady George Lennox:[4]

. . . all the Herveys in the world are going to Ireland.

In addition to Bristol's brother Augustus two other relations benefited from his bounty. He immediately appointed his brother Frederick, who was still languishing as a clergyman with a large family and little income, to be his First Chaplain. Much more important, Bristol obtained from the King an understanding that his new First Chaplain should be appointed to the first episcopal vacancy in Ireland. This was expected to be at Derry, where the revenues of the diocese were the largest in the country, and where the Bishop was in poor health and not expected to live many months. He lived on, however, and it was in the event the Bishop of Cloyne, a much less prosperous diocese in the south of the country, whose death created the first opportunity. In early 1767, therefore, Frederick Hervey was nominated to the vacancy and in May was consecrated Bishop of Cloyne in Dublin Cathedral.

This was not, however, the last honour that came Frederick's way at Lord Bristol's hands. In July the Irish Lord Chancellor died and the office was not filled. Instead Commissioners for the Custody of the Great Seal of Ireland were appointed, and amongst those named was the new Bishop of Cloyne; and in August the Bishop was appointed to the Privy Council for Ireland, an unusual honour for a holder of one of the minor bishoprics. The Bishop of Derry outlived Lord Bristol's tenure of the Lord Lieutenancy, but when he eventually died in January 1768 the King held to the understanding and Frederick succeeded him. The third family recipient of an Irish honour was Constantine Phipps, husband of Hervey's sister Lepel, who during Bristol's last days in office was raised to an Irish peerage as Baron Mulgrave of New Ross.

Hervey's duties as Secretary to the Lord Lieutenant, while not onerous, were by no means a sinecure. His notebook for the period shows that in the course of a little under a year some 450 items of correspondence passed through his hands. While the Lord Lieutenant and his Secretary remained in England the government of Ireland was carried out by appointed Lords Justices in Dublin. They were obliged to refer many administrative and financial matters to Departments of State in London and most of these were channelled through Hervey. The record shows that a very high proportion, about three-quarters, of the correspondence concerned military matters; appointment and transfer of officers, placing officers on half-pay, approval for officer's leave of absence, expenditure on establishments and equipment; but apart from correspondence arising from the exchange of several regiments in Ireland with others serving in North America the correspondence hardly mentions operational matters at all.

The Lord Lieutenant also concerned himself with appointments and promotions in other spheres. In addition to the new Lord Mulgrave, Bristol was responsible for four advancements of existing Irish peers and one new creation. Dublin Castle had to be put in order for His Excellency's projected but never consummated visit to his satrapy, and accommodation had to be found for his train. A request for £600 was granted for the maintenance of the Royal Hospital. At the King's command pensions of £3000 per annum were to be paid from Irish revenues to two of his royal but unruly brothers, the Dukes of Gloucester and Cumberland – to be paid 'during pleasure', i.e. until the King changed his mind; a convenient source of funds for a monarch with so many demanding if not deserving relatives to support.

With all this, what of the Irish? There is little indication that the ordinary Irishman or woman and their problems figured largely in the concerns of their rulers in London. In response to poor harvests exports of wheat and potatoes were prohibited in the autumn of 1766, but this action was taken in Dublin and only subsequently referred to London for approval. The problems of Irish society, the poverty of the country people, the alienation of the Catholic population from the Government and from the Protestant ascendancy, all seem to pass unnoticed by the Lord Lieutenant and his Chief Secretary. As far as the Hervey family is concerned, it was left to Frederick, in his long incumbency as Bishop of Derry, to take up the cudgels on behalf not only of the members of his own Protestant Church of Ireland but also on behalf of the Catholic majority.

At the opening of Parliament in the autumn of 1766 Hervey was drawn into overt support at Westminster of the Administration of which he was a reluctant member. It happened in this way. He was asked by Secretary of State Conway, who lead for the Government in the Commons, to second the address in reply to the King's Speech; and when the proposed mover of the address, Horace Walpole, dropped out Hervey was asked to move the address himself. He seems to have been deliberately picked out for this task to highlight his position in the Government and his separation from his friends (political friends as well as personal) the Grenvilles; according to Grenville[5] he was in fact most unwilling to commit himself so fully, and only did so at Lord Bristol's insistence.

The Speech was very run-of-the-mill; it drew attention to the embargo which had been placed on the exports of wheat and flour from Britain as well as Ireland; it regretted the civil disturbances which had occurred in response to rising prices and drew attention to the steps taken to control them; the Monarch congratulated himself on a new trade treaty with Russia and on the marriage of his sister Princess Caroline with the King of Denmark; and it asked the Commons to consider the financial estimates for the coming year.

Hervey's reply[6] can best be described as anodyne, doing his duty to the Government without showing any deep commitment. He agrees with the embargo on exports and with the measures to curb unrest, though blaming the disturbances on the indulgence shown by the previous Administration to 'those subjects of a more distant part of His Majesty's Dominions'. On the financial estimates he managed in the following words to combine respect for the Commons' privileges with subservience to the King:

> It would also, Sir, very ill beome me to recommend to this House the giving of any assurances to His Majesty of our cheerful determination to grant the supplies that shall be found necessary for the service of the year.

This may be interpreted to mean that he thought that the Commons should cheerfully accede to the Government's demands, but that it was not his place to tell the King he thought so.

During the next few months he appears to have taken to heart the plight of the poor and the need for a considered economic policy. A letter to the *Public Advertiser* later in November[7] signed 'Justice' – not one of Hervey's normal signatures – makes an appeal for less waste by the moneyed classes on gambling and luxuries, so that the money saved should cirulate back to the tradesman and the worker. In March 1767 another letter[8] in the same journal signed 'A True Englishman' deplores the reduction of one shilling in the pound on land tax voted by the Commons (whose members of course represented in an overbearing way the landed interest), against the advice of the Government. In this he is seen to disagree, anonymously, with Grenville, for it was at the latter's instigation that the reduction was proposed. But Hervey's view of the difficulties and straits which the poor were in and the affluence enjoyed by the landowning class was a true one, and he writes:

> Would it not be better to have continued this shilling one year more, and have taken off the tax on leather, coals, candles, soap, beer and whatever would relieve the Poor? And have doubled the tax on plate and coaches, and effectively levied them? . . . Would it not have been better to have lowered the price of provisions of every kind – and taxed horses, servants and every species of luxury? Would it not be better to find some method of easing the poor and employing them at home, not let the country be depopulated as it is for want of employment, for want of shelter and nourishment to the poor labouring Cottagers, those real supporters for so many centuries of the landed gentlemen, not only for cultivation and encouraging stock of every kind, but also the true riches (which are people) to the Country?

So far he seems to have been supporting the Government but in the same month he introduced what may be regarded as a private member's motion with strong cross-bench support. It was on a naval subject close to his heart. There had now been four years of peace and, with no indication that serious hostilities were at hand the navy had been reduced to its usual peacetime rump. Most of the seamen had been discharged, and most of the officers placed on half-pay. That of a lieutenant was two shillings a day, entirely insufficient for the upkeep of the family of a professional man. Some idea of the severity of their problems is shown by the presence in debtors' prisons, by 1764, of nearly five hundred half-pay officers from the two services.

Hervey had for some time been disturbed by the predicament of these half-pay officers and at the serious implications that any depletion of this officer corps had for the future manning of the navy. In November 1765 he had written a letter to the *Public Advertiser* setting out their grievances, datelining it Portsmouth and signing it 'A Poor Half-Pay Sea Lieutenant'.[9] Senior officers including those in Parliament, he wrote, had taken little notice of their problems – 'Can it be thought that because five or six gentlemen of the services are justly distinguished and rewarded for their great services, that the rest of the officers in their different ranks should be abandoned to a perishing existence?' The only politicians to have had their interests in mind were Pitt, the Duke of Bedford and Grenville, the last-named as usual receiving the greatest praise.' He drew attention to the effect on the Admiralty that representations by senior officers had had during the debates on the Navy Act of 1749.

Within a month he had followed this with another letter,[10] this time as from Plymouth, signed 'Another Poor Half-Pay Sea Officer'. This time he attacked the Admiralty for opposing the candidacy of senior naval officers for seats in the Commons, specifically the borough of Rochester, where a by-election was pending to replace Admiral Townshend: 'What, of all that great list of sea officers . . . was there not one, either Admiral or Captain, that was thought worthy of being recommended by the A————y to that ancient naval city . . .'. Thus, not only does he accuse the Admiralty of neglecting the interests of the service, but he suggests not for the only time, that their Lordships were happiest when naval representation in the Commons was minimized and informed criticism therefore muted.

By March of 1767 a petition had been organized on behalf of the half-pay officers and Hervey presented it to the House. His speech musters the humanitarian case for additional help for this very necessary but ill-rewarded body of men, and points to the inexpediency of letting their expertise and experience be lost to the country as they sought other means of supporting themselves or went abroad.

The motion and its proposer were well received by the House, which approved a petition to the King that he should increase the rate by up to a shilling a day, fifty per cent, and affirmed that the necessary funds would be voted by the House when it was asked to do so. In due course this incease was put into effect and Hervey could justifiably feel satisfaction at a campaign well carried through.

By June, however, Hervey, still in office, was becoming much more critical of the Government. Early in the month the *Public Advertiser* published a letter[11] from him signed 'A True Briton' lamenting the failure of Pitt and the Government to achieve any of their policies, exemplifying the land tax fiasco, failure to relieve the condition of the poor, failure to control the colonies, failure to stand up for the interests of the British merchants in Portugal. Pitt, he said, had sold himself to Bute for a peerage, and it was Bute's sinister influence that was at the root of the problem – probably an overestimate of the Favourite's influence with the King, which by this time was waning rapidly. He followed this in July by a letter[12] to the *Gazetteer* in which he again complains at the ineffectiveness of the Grafton/Pitt administration. There is no doubt that it was in the doldrums, and that this was Pitt's doing. His illness and his peerage, which deprived him of his ability to influence the Commons even when he was in good health, are jointly to blame.

Hervey's colleages in government must have been tolerably certain who had written these letters. It is therefore not surprising that by the end of June there should have been a serious deterioration in the relations between Hervey and Lord Bristol. As early as April, as he reports in a letter to Grenville,[13] he had been summoned from Bath to London by his brother, who had read the riot act to him about the need to act with 'more circumspection and more vigour than the rest' because his attachment to the Grenvilles was so well known. Hervey's response had been to say that even Grenville knew of his determination to support his brother above everyone, and Grenville above everyone except his brother. However, Bristol continued to make difficulties and to upbraid Hervey with his friendship for the Grenvilles, apparently taking the view that the world in general suspected him (Bristol) of carrying on through his brother an intrigue with the Government's opponents. By 30 June, therefore, Hervey had decided to resign as Secretary for Ireland. He wrote to George Grenville to explain his action:[14]

> I am now to tell you that I have this moment wrote (in the civilest manner) to desire to resign my employment, a brother's conduct and coolness to me making it impossible for me to keep it, as I would have done to have dropped with his change, if there is to be any . . . though I find it insinuated everywhere that it is [due to] my constant attachment to you and your brother . . .

His resignation was accepted on 1 July, but he was required to continue in office until a successor was appointed and able to take up his duties.

In the meantime Hervey, using his position as Groom of the Bedchamber to gain easy access to the King, had taken to the royal presence the grievance he felt at his brother's attitude. He saw the King twice, showing him three letters which had passed between his brother and himself, in which Lord Bristol gave reasons for his coolness. He reported the outcome to Grenville on 4 July:[15]

> The King was as much surprised at my brother's reasons as I was, as the world is, and as I believe you will be. However, yesterday at the *Levée* I went up to him [Lord Bristol] and insisted on some *éclaircissement* when all he had to say was, that he was told by people that he met, Lord Temple and yourself [were] several times at my house to transact business. I asked if that was a crime in me . . . desired that he would never think more of me, but as a brother.

Hervey was extremely annoyed at Lord Bristol's small-mindedness, which was presumably a result of his Lordship's lack of confidence that his qualities and reputation matched his high ambitions. But as with all their transactions, the stand-off turned out to be a temporary one and by September Bristol had given his brother total freedom in Parliament.[16]

To complete the story of the Irish involvement, Pitt resigned his office later in the summer, and in consequence Lord Bristol, as Pitt's appointee, resigned as well, leaving office in August.

The fact that Hervey had left office did not mean that he had lost all desire for its continuation. After Pitt's resignation Grafton also resigned but was faced with the task of forming another administration. During July Hervey had a long conversation with Lord Charles Fitzroy, Grafton's brother, in which he was informed, for Grenville's ears, of Grafton's views on the form of the next government – Grenville of course not being among Grafton's 'friends' but having considerable influence and being a potential candidate for high office. Hervey duly reported the details to Grenville and went on to write:[17]

> . . . that I, for one, made no secret of declaring that I wanted nothing but the Admiralty, which I thought I had a right to after those I had seen there, but that I never desired it 'till you came in, or supported the Administration; that he knew I might otherwise have been there at the opening of this present Administration . . .'

However, neither Grenville nor Hervey's other friend the Bedfordite Lord Sandwich were destined to serve in Grafton's reconstituted government, and Hervey had to wait another three years before he received any degree of satisfaction.

Sometime in the late summer of 1767 Hervey went down with one of his severe attacks of gout but by October had recovered sufficiently to fire off from Bath a salvo of letters to the press. By this time he had passed from indifference to the new government to outright dissatisfaction, fuelled by the failure of his friend Grenville to regain the reins of power, and by the need to prepare for the general election due to be held in the spring of 1768. On 9 October the *Gazetteer* published a letter from him[18] signed 'A Briton' attacking the power of 'The Favourite Thane' (Bute), and his behind-the-scenes ability to control which ministers continued to enjoy the King's favour. He also attacked another letter from 'Agrippa', the writer of which had made a fulsome argument for the return of arbitrary power.

A further letter from Hervey, this one signed 'A True Englishman' which appeared on 19 October is worth quoting in full, not only because of the language and the case he puts, but also because of the way he again comments on his own previous correspondence – this time recommending as a True Englishman the letter he had earlier written as a Briton:[19]

Mr Printer

It must give great pleasure to all lovers of liberty, to find the dareing, designing and insulting letters of Agrippa in your paper, were no sooner offered to the public but they were attacked by A Briton some days ago, and since by Capius in your paper today; 'Tis happy that there are as yet some left amongst us, who still retain a love for liberty, and shudder at the very thoughts of arbitrary power – which Agrippa has recommended. 'Capius' has bravely taken fire at this infernal attempt of Agrippa's. Yet 'tis to A Briton's nervous pen we owe the salutary alarm – that true British writer (whoever he is) has proved himself worthy of the cause he supports, he has proved himself well-informed throughout his correspondence, and has nobly and generously employed that information to warn his countrymen of their approaching fate under the influence and secret designs of The Thane and those most destructive minions of his power (i.e. the ministers). He has set in a true light the characters of the present Junto who compose the Favourite's Council, and who are held out as M———-rs; he has represented their conduct so clearly, and so masterly, that it must be our own degeneracy, our own profligacy, and our own pusillanity if we do not take the warning he has kindly given us, and be upon our guard against all the snares which that Scotch Favourite has long been laying for us, and all those evils which his Hired Crew are ready to execute upon this country.

This wretch Agrippa who preaches up despotic power has dared to justify his doctine and has proved himself to be some Hungry Minion of the Thane, some remaining, unprovided-for Dreg of that set that was ever famous for being equal in enmity to the liberty of these Kingdoms, and to the family who was happily brought to the G———t of them, to restore and protect our liberty.

Now is the time, my countrymen, now at the eve of your elections; banish Scotch-men and all the adherents of the Thane from representing you; show yourselves to be Englishmen, and therefore be represented by Englishmen – 'Tis the earnest and disinterested prayer of your friend.

A True Englishman.

The letter may be weak on argument, but it does not lack vigour, it is full of concealed self-praise, and it is a rousing clarion-call for the coming elections, in anticipation of which Hervey had concerns about his own parliamentary position as well as for that of the anti-government forces in general. It may be wondered how widely the authorship of such letters was known at the time. Certainly it is a remarkable tirade for one courtier, a Groom of the Bedchamber, to bring forth about another who was the King's favourite, and Hervey is careful in the penultimate paragraph, to assert that Bute's 'minion' (and by implication Bute himself) are both 'in enmity' with the House of Hanover, thus dissociating the author from any criticism of the Monarch himself.

Certainly Hervey was concerned about the coming election. In the run-up to it the Government took what steps it could to prevent eminent naval officers from standing for the new Parliament. Grafton's administration was embarrassed by their independence and the Admiralty in particular tried to prevent a number of senior officers from standing in those boroughs where Government had considerable influence. Hervey himself appears to have decided not to stand again for Saltash for on 3 November he wrote to Grenville as follows:[20]

> . . . I go to Saltash tomorrow, where I think things are in a very good way; and they have assured me that nothing shall hurt me there, so that I hope (between ourselves) to get young Phipps [his sister Lepel's son, later the 2nd Lord Mulgrave] chose there *malgré Monsier le Duc de G——*.

In December the *Public Advertiser* and the *Gazetteer* published a letter from him datelined Rochester and signed 'A Half Pay Sea Lieutenant'. In it he drew attention to the Admiralty's withdrawal of support from Sir George Pocock at Plymouth, Keppel at Winchester, Rodney and others. He draws attention also to his own position and his own merits:[21]

> Another brave and meritorious officer (Captain H—v—y) who to the latest ages will have the blessing of this Profession, for his distinguished and singular perseverance in the behalf of our poor Corps whom he has saved from starving, we hear is threatened to be turned out of that Sea Borough he now represents but whose constituents have had judgement to distinguish

his great merit, and spirit to determine to support his interest against all attacks.

To do him justice, he refers only to his efforts on behalf of the half-pay officers, and the eulogy is much less abandoned than those to Pocock, Keppel and Rodney; but the comment on his position at Saltash may be thought somewhat disingenuous when considered together with his earlier letter to Grenville. He did not in fact stand for the Cornish borough but having regained Lord Bristol's support returned to the family seat at St Edmundsbury, where he was duly re-elected in the spring of 1768.

In June of that year Lady Hervey reported, in the last of her long series of letters to the Rector of Nursling, that Hervey was at Bath: 'My son Augustus who goes frequently to the Bath, is now laid up there with the gout in the feet'. By late July he was back in London trying unsuccessfully to clear up his confused marital affairs. While he was doing so, however, his mother moved into the last stages of her 68-year journey to another world. At the end of August she was at Sunninghill, near Windsor, taking the waters and suffering from a severe cold, and there on Saturday 28 August Hervey dined with her. Two days later her condition compelled her to return to her house in St James's and by the following Thursday she was dead. Her favourite son, her 'poor dear Augustus', was with her to the end and indeed, for reasons good and bad, the only member of the family at her bedside. Her last days are recorded in two letters that he wrote to George Grenville. On Tuesday 31 August, his emotions and concerns having an odd effect on his grammar, he wrote as follows:[22]

I can say no more at present, being in my Mother's Drawing Room, where she is in the next Room, most exceeding ill indeed, which I have not left these three days that she has been taken. James and Hawkins attend her, and she is in great danger, I fear; I do not leave her bedside but for meals, and took this opportunity to assure you again of my most sincere attachment. I am obliged to send to Ickworth to let them know of my poor Mother's situation, an Inflammation on her breast.'

I am, dear Sir
Your most faithful and obedient servant
A. Hervey

On the Thursday she died quietly in her bed. Later that day Lord Bristol arrived from Ickworth. On the following Sunday, by which time her will had been read, Hervey wrote again to Grenville describing his reactions, which do not seem out of character:[23]

As you will see the death of my poor Mother in the papers, I dare say you will be anxious to know how it may have affected my situation, since your last so kindly expresses your feeling obliged by any communication of what concerns me.

I dined with Lady Hervey, Saturday, at Sunninghill, where she had been complaining some days of a cold, which obliged her to come to town the Monday following late, and very much oppressed. She felt herself going some time before, as my brother tells me, in a letter she wrote him. She was blooded and blistered, and Mr. Hawkins and myself at last persuaded her to have a physician, when she consented, provided it was James.

I never left her, though but very indifferent myself, till she expired at 4 o'clock Thursday afternoon; in the course of her illness she never mentioned any one of her children or acquaintance, nor ever spoke to anyone but Mr. Hawkins or me, when we advised about the physician; only on Wednesday she squeezed my hand and said '*Poor dear Augustus*', and never spoke afterwards even to her maid. She felt, thank God! no pain whatever. I sent an express to my brother, Wednesday, who came up Thursday night, and with me went on Friday to the House, *he and I being reconciled* first entirely, and he has dined with me every day since.

My mother has left her house, plate, furniture, etc, and all her jewels, to my brother Bristol and his son;* then to me and mine; and then to my brother William for ever, cutting out the Bishop. Her money in these and other funds equally between William and myself; to my sister Mary a little ring, and never mentioned any other sisters at all. There were two wills, the one of 1763 that left all to me, and this of last May in the manner I tell you. Some small legacies to Lady Bute, Lady Jane Macartney, Lord and Lady Holland, Mr. Walpole, etc, whom (between you and I) I believe have in some degree influenced that opinion which may have occasioned the unexpected change, but which my brother saw had no effect, nor has it on me; he could not read the rest of the will for surprise, and I did without the least. I only know I have a satisfaction of having been the one here to continue that invariable filial affection and duty I had ever shown her, to her last sigh, and hope she is happy now. God knows how all these things are, or why anything is; I can only say, like Desdemona, ''tis strange, 'tis wondrous strange' and in any sense of the word our whole conditions and dispositions seem as she also says 'pitiful, 'tis wondrous pitiful'.

I thank God my health is surprisingly recovered, and if I have better success in *another point of life* I shall not let the disappointment of affluence affect me whilst I have the convenience as well as necessaries of life. I never loved money for the sake of money in my life, and as I have never wanted it less than at present, the lucre of gain could never induce me to follow

---

* Of course, neither brother had a legitimate son at this time, nor was destined to father one, so that the house and effects passed eventually to William Hervey

opinions that avarice might put other people upon undertaking; to be thought enough beloved by her to have distinguished me, and to be thought considerable enough by the friends I am unalterably attached to, and to receive distinction through them whenever they could, is what I own I have had pride and vanity enough to desire; but for the rest *fortunae caetera mundo*. Forgive this scrawl, and be assured I am, etc, etc.

A Hervey

There is much in this letter to ponder upon. Lady Hervey had to all appearances been a fond mother to her growing children, but at the end of her life had little if any contact with four of the eight – Frederick, by this time Bishop of Derry, Lepel, now Lady Mulgrave, and the two youngest daughters. Only Lord Bristol, Augustus and William were at her funeral. It was, however, with Augustus that she had the closest accord and about whose well-being she was constantly anxious. Perhaps in a perverse way this heightened maternal love arose from a feeling of guilt. While all her other children had grown up at home or had what might be termed a normal schooling for the day and age, Augustus had left home to join the navy at the tender age of 11. It needs little effort to imagine the heavy heart with which his mother must have accepted this separation, and much imagination to visualize the arguments that led her to do so. Augustus, for his part, had written to her regularly from sea and always came straight to her on his infrequent visits to London. Augustus, also, was the one who thought too highly of family ties to waste time and energy in family quarrels. He took care to avoid taking sides, though during his active naval career he had not been at home long or often enough to be able to pour oil on troubled waters.

Hervey comes well, in terms of character, out of his mother's testamentary sinuosities. He knew, clearly, of the will she had made in 1763, by which she left everything to him, but he did not know, neither did Lord Bristol, of the more recent will by which she left her house and personality to her eldest son and divided her money between Augustus and William. According to Lady Mary Coke[24] the well known letter and journal writer, Augustus's share amounted to £4000, enough if invested in the funds to bring £200 or so a year.

We shall never know with certainty the reason for the change. It has been attributed variously to advice from Horace Walpole and other friends, or to pressure from George William himself, any of whom might have feared that Augustus, with his irregular lifestyle and frequent absences from London, might not look after her house – regarded as one of the most gracious and most tastefully furnished in London – as well as it deserved. If this was the reason her spirit may have been disappointed, since Lord Bristol almost immediately let the property with all its contents to the Earl of Carlisle.

If Augustus was disappointed by the change in the will he did not let it show. He was already reasonably well off and was no longer so interested in ambitious and expensive entertainments or in spending large sums on the lady of the moment as he had been in his Mediterranean days. He had, moreover, other pressing matters on his mind in the shape of his confused, obscure and frustrating marital status, the subject to which his comment above on 'another point of life' refers.

Any suggestion that his marriage to Miss Chudleigh was more than a nominal one had come to an end in 1749. After their *de facto* separation in that year Hervey was for thirteen years seldom in England, so that their paths did not cross. They were both in marital limbo. Hervey made the best of his opportunities as they arose, while Elizabeth found herself in a position of some difficulty, without an acknowledged husband, to all appearances in the marriage market but unable to offer herself in marriage. She failed to hold the affections of her first Duke, James the 9th of Hamilton, who in 1751 married Elizabeth Gunning. In the same year, however, she met Evelyn Pierrepont, 2nd Duke of Kingston, and an association began which was to last with varying degrees of closeness until the Duke's death in 1773. The Duke seems to have been generous in the extreme so that she now became a woman of substance, able to build a house at the western end of Knightsbridge, then virtually open country, and also to own a house at Colnbrook, west of London, which provided a refuge for the discreet reception of her lover; but she could not marry.

In the late fifties, however, the considerations on which she calculated her future prospects took a different turn. The health of the delicate earl, still unmarried and then serving as ambassador in Madrid, was again causing concern. So, since on George William's death the Bristol title and estates would pass to Augustus, Elizabeth once again reconsidered her position. To be Countess of Bristol, with a call on her husband's most impressive revenues, could still be an attractive proposition, even if their marriage remained one in name only. This marriage, however, had never been acknowledged publicly by either husband or wife and though some suspected its existence few had any real knowledge of it. She needed to be in possession of proof, to be used in the event of her brother-in-law's demise, but had not even a marriage certificate or an entry in a register to provide it.

In the course of action that Elizabeth now took she appears to have confided in and had the advice of the Princess Dowager, to whom she was still a Maid of Honour and with whom she had a close relationship. The clergyman who had married her, Thomas Amis, at the time Rector of Lainston, was still living in Winchester, though an old man and in poor health. In February of 1759 Elizabeth went down to Winchester and with her relative Mr. Merrill went to Mr Amis, by now dying, and persuaded him through his wife that the marriage that he had performed fifteen years previously ought to be recorded in official form. There had at no time been a register of births, deaths and marriages for Lainston, so one was now created. A suitable book was bought and inscribed with the appropriate title and in it was recorded first the death in August 1742 of Mr Merrill's wife Susannah, then in the following form the marriage of Mr and Mrs Hervey:

> The 4th of August 1744 married the Honourable Augustus Hervey Esq to Miss Elizabeth Chudleigh, daughter of Colonel Thomas Chudleigh late of Chelsea College, deceased, in the parish church of Lainston, by me, Thomas Amis.

Elizabeth took a copy of the entry which Amis had duly signed and arranged that on the old man's death his wife should pass the register to Mr Merrill for safe keeping and production if occasion arose. Merrill died in 1767 and the register was then given to Mr Kinchin, at that time rector of the parish. Thus she assured, in the event of George William's death, her passport to riches and to noble status as Countess of Bristol. But soon after the visit to Winchester Lord Brisol's health recovered and his sister-in-law's stratagem was rendered nugatory.

Miss Chudleigh persisted in her irregular lifestyle, consorting more or less openly with the Duke of Kingston throughout the sixties. In June 1760 she gave an extravagant ball in honour of the birthday of the Prince of Wales, at which her attachment to the Duke was obvious and brazen. At the same time her life of dissipation went from strength to strength. When she visited Berlin in 1765 Frederick the Great remarked that she drank two bottles of wine and could hardly stand up on the dance floor. This, however, did not discourage him from paying court to her in an unenthusiastic way, and as far as is known without climax or sequel.

By then knowledge of her marriage was becoming more widespread, perhaps because her husband, growing increasingly frustrated at his inability to offer himself in marriage to any of his inamorati, was less than discreet about it. He had reached the age at which most men feel the need for a more settled life and must also have been conscious that neither he nor his elder brother had produced an heir – Lord Bristol himself, now well over 40, seems to have been remarkable for the number of eligible women to whom he offered his hand without eliciting a favourable response. Hervey's young son 'little Augustus' born in about 1764 of his liaison with Kitty Hunter, though a joy to him as a child of his body, could never solve the wider problem. For the younger brother the potential outcome was especially undesirable. In default of either of them producing a legitimate son the title would pass to the third of the four brothers, Frederick. Frederick stood reasonably well with George William but was anathema to Augustus, and keeping him from the succession provided a second weighty reason for wishing to produce an heir.

In 1768 matters came to a head when Hervey fell in love with Mary Moysey, the daughter of a Bath physician, and wished to marry her. By August of that year the whole scenario became common knowledge and the gossips went to work on it. They were, however, more intent on providing delicious items of scandal than in promulgating the truth. Lady Mary Coke wrote in her journal for 6 August:[25]

> Mr Augustus Hervey (I suppose at the desire of his brother, Lord Bristol) is going to prove his marriage as the first stage towards suing for being unmarried, and has sent the lady who goes by the name of Miss Chudleigh a letter to signify his intentions; to which she has returned this answer: That if he proves the marriage he will have £16,000 to pay, as she owes that sum of money. As this answer is looked upon to be intended to stop the proceeding, everybody is much surprised, as it was the general opinion that if She was at liberty the Duke of Kingston would marry her, which now seems to be doubtful

A few days later[26] she retracted one of the numerous inaccuracies in that entry:

> I am obliged to contradict in one journal what I have mentioned in another. Mr Hervey is really going to sue for a Divorce, but he told Lady Blandford that the answer which it was reported Mrs Hervey had sent to his letter was an invention, for he had received none.

On 20 Augustus Horace Walpole entered the fray, though he adds little to the inaccuracies reported by Lady Mary: [27]

> Augustus Hervey, thinking it the *bel air*, is going to sue for a divorce from the Chudleigh. He asked Lord Bolingbroke, 't other day, who was his proctor, as he would have asked for his tailor. The nymph has sent him word that if he professes her his wife he must pay her debts, and she owes £16,000. This obstacle thrown in the way looks as if she was not sure of being Duchess of Kingston. The lawyers say it will be no valid plea; it not appearing that she was Hervey's wife, and therefore the tradesmen could not reckon on his paying them.

It is not stated by either writer how Hervey was to show proof of the marriage. The register that Elizabeth had concocted in 1759 was in the hands of the new Rector of Lainston, Mr Kinchin, but it seems unlikely that her husband knew even that it existed. The only witness still living was Ann Cradock, whom he could readily have produced as a witness since she had married his servant William Cradock; though the unsupported evidence of a dependent might not have been sufficient in the face of Miss Chudleigh's denial. Perhaps, however, Hervey thought that Elizabeth would welcome a divorce and would therefore not deny the marriage.

While Lady Mary and Horace Walpole were for many a welcome source of gossip they seldom provide the most accurate of accounts. In this instance the most helpful statement of Hervey's intentions and Miss Chudleigh's response is given in Caesar Hawkins' evidence at Miss Chudleigh's trial for bigamy eight years later, in 1776. Hawkins, the surgeon who had delivered Miss Chudleigh's infant son in 1747, was chosen by Hervey to tell Miss Chudleigh of his intentions. It may be accepted that memory can be fitful after such a period, and that Hawkins may have sanitised the evidence that he gave in an attempt not to provide fuel for the scandal-mongers, but his statement has the appearance of being a considered report of events and is not subject in any important way to incontrovertible contradiction:

> To the best of my remembrance Captain Hervey met me in the street, and stopped me, telling me that he should be glad if I would call on him at his house the first morning I had half an hour to spare, and if I could then fix the time he would take care to be in the way, and that no other company should interrupt the conversation. He intimated that it was not on account of his own health, but on account of an old friend of mine. I named the time and went to him. I found Captain Hervey expecting me, Upon a table, at a little distance from his right hand, there lay two or three bundles of papers, folded up as these papers are [here the witness picked up some papers at the bar]. To these papers he often pointed in course of what he said afterwards. After making some polite apologies to me for the particular trouble he was then giving me, he told me it was on Miss Chudleigh's account; that he wished me to carry her a message upon a subject that was very disagreeable, but thought it would be less shocking to be carried by, and received from, a person she knew than from any stranger; that he had for some time past been very unhappy on account of his matrimonial connections with Miss Chudleigh; that he wished to have his freedom, which the criminality of her conduct, and the proofs which he had of it (which in pointing to the papers I before mentioned, he said he had for some time past, with intent and purpose to secure a divorce, been collecting) quite justified; that he believed they contained the most ample and abundant proofs, circumstances, and everything relative to such proof; that he intended to pursue his prosecution with the strictest firmness and resolution; but that he retained such a regard and respect for her, and as a gentleman to his own character, that he wished not to mix malice or ill-temper in the course of it, but that in every respect he would wish to appear and act on the line of a man of honour and gentleman; that he wished (he said) she would understand that his soliciting me to carry the message should be received by her as a mark of that disposition; that, as

most probably in the number of so many testimonial dispositions as were there collected there might be many offensive circumstances named, superfluous to the necessary legal proofs, that if she pleased I might inform her that her lawyers, either with or without herself, might, in conjunction with his lawyers, look over all the depositions, and that if any parts were found tending to indecent or scandalous reflections, which his gentlemen of the law should think might be omitted without weakening his case, he himself should have no objection to it; that, as he intended to act only on the principles of a gentleman and man of honour, he should hope she would not produce any unneccessary or vexatious delays to the suit, or enhance the expenses of it, as he did not intend to prosecute to gain by any demands of damages, I think, or to that purpose.

I delivered this message to Miss Chudleigh as well as I could. After a little time taken for consideration I do not recollect exactly what Miss Chudleigh desired me to report to Captain Hervey; but it was to this effect; that she was obliged to him for the polite parts of the message; but as to the subject of the divorce, she should cut that short by wishing him to understand that she did not acknowledge him as her legal husband, and should put him to the defiance of such proof; that she had then already, or should immediately institute a suit in the Ecclesiastical Court, which she called, I think, a jactitation of marriage; but as he had promised before that he would act upon the line of a man of honour and a gentleman in his own intended suit, she hoped he would pursue the same line now, and that he would confine himself to proofs of legal marriage only, and not to other proofs of connections or cohabitations; if he did, that he would make it a process of no long delay, and that either he would gain an equal freedom to himself by a sentence of that Court declaring them to be free, or he would the sooner be able to institute his intended suit. Captain Hervey received my message as one affected and struck by it, making no reply or answer for two or three minutes; then, not speaking to me, but rather seeming to express his own thoughts aloud in short sentences, [said] that he did not conceive he should have his equal freedom by that method. I believe I should have mentioned that Miss Chudleigh desired, in part of her message, that nothing might be brought forward which might be a subject of useless conversation or scandal. He said in reply; that he was no more inclined to bring forward anything for the lovers of scandalous conversation than she should be, and that if he could not establish the proof of legal matrimony (I do not remember the words, but to the sense of this), that he was too much of a gentleman to bring anything before the public relative to other connection with the lady'.

In all this there are two discrepancies from the story as put about by Walpole and Lady Mary Coke; Hawkins refers to a message, not a letter, and he makes no reference to the £16,000 of debts. The threat may have been gossip-writer's licence, or conceivably Miss Chudleigh's initial and unconsidered response to Hervey's message. When the exchange took place is not made plain, but the comments by Lady Mary Coke and Horace Walpole show that Hawkins must have given Miss Chudleigh her husband's message in July or at the latest early August 1768.

But legal affairs moved no faster then than they do now and two months later Hervey was still putting it about that he intended to sue for divorce, writing on 31 October to Grenville, from whom he concealed little, as follows:[28]

> I find this town has made me a much more intrepid person that I really am, for they have already given me another person for a wife, and such a one as I am sure I should never have thought of. Very likely the report may have reached you, and I am sure you will treat it as it deserves, but it has been very industriously put about here. My suit [presumably the intended petition for divorce] comes on this term, and I hope to have success, I am sure of you wishing me well.

But who was the wife that 'they' had given him? Can this be a reference to the young lady of Bath who he is said to have wished to marry? If so, was he deviously concealing that wish, or had he had second thoughts? No matter; within a few days of this letter we find Miss Chudleigh making good her intention to forestall the unsavoury disclosures inevitable in an action for divorce. In early November she brought her threatened suit for jactitation of marriage – the false pretence of being married to another, then an offence. In effect she petitioned in the Consistory Court of the Diocese of London for an order forbidding Hervey to make such a claim. Her petition was based almost entirely on statements that she was living and managing her financial affairs as a single woman without reference to Hervey; for example that she had had a bank account with the Bank of England for many years, that in 1757 she took a copyhold of her house in Knightsbridge from the Dean and Chapter of Westminster, that in 1766 she took a mortgage from John Drummond, banker, and so on; also that she was commonly addressed as Miss Chudleigh and that her aunt Mrs Hanmer and Mr Merrill wrote to her in that name; and that she still continued a Maid of Honour to the Princess Dowager.

All these actions, however, were equally open to her if she was married but had not disclosed the fact, so that her case was seemingly very easy to dispose of. All Hervey had to do was to give evidence himself that the marriage had taken place before witnesses and duly been consummated in Mr Merrill's house, and to produce the only surviving witness – Ann Cradock. Ann, however, was in Lincolnshire, and in the light of the defence actually offered there must be a strong suspicion that she had in effect been hidden by Hervey on the family estates in that county. The defendant chose instead to state that some kind of ceremony had taken place when they were both minors (they were in fact both of age at the time) and that they had only slept together in secret, though Ann Cradock could have been a witness to a rather different state of affairs.

Miss Chudleigh was much perturbed by the demand that she declare on oath that she was unmarried. She discussed the necessity with Caesar Hawkins who in his evidence at the bigamy trial reported, as we have seen, that she had told him words to the effect that: 'Oh for that matter the ceremony as done was such a scrambling shabby business and so much incomplete that she would have been fully as willing to have taken a positive oath that she was married as that she was not married'. Nevertheless, she did swear that she was unmarried and in February 1769 the Court had no difficulty in declaring her a spinster and in ordering Hervey not to assert otherwise.

The way was now open again for the gossip-makers. In Lady Mary Coke's Journal for 17 February she comments:[29]

> Miss Chudleigh has taken an oath that she is not Mr Hervey's wife; and though everyone knows that she is, as the witnesses to the marriage are all dead, she intends marrying the Duke of Kingston. 'Tis said she has bespoken a white gown to be presented in at Court, that is to be trimmed with point lace and pearl.

Later in the month Horace Walpole's pen delivered another broadside, though so much imagination did he use, and so ill-informed was he that much of the fire was wide of the mark:[30]

> After a marriage of twenty years, Augustus Hervey, having fallen in love with a physician's daughter at Bath, has attacked his spouse, the maid of honour, the fair Chudleigh, and sought divorce for adultery. Unfortunately, he had waited until all the witnesses of the marriage and of her two deliveries are dead, as well as the two children. The provident virgin had not been so negligent. Last year she forced herself into the house of the parson who had married them, and who was on the point of death. By bullying, and to get rid of her, she forced the poor man to give up the certificate. Since then she has appeared in Doctor's Commons, and swore by the Virgins Mary and Diana that she never was married to Mr Hervey. The Ecclesiastical Court has admitted her corporal oath, and enjoined silence to Mr Hervey. Next week this fair injured innocence, who is but fifty, is to be married to the Duke of Kingston, who has kept her openly for almost half that time, and who by this means will recover half his fortune which he had lavished on her. As a proof of her purity and poverty her wedding gown is white satin, trimmed with Brussels lace and pearls, Every work of this

history is extremely true. The physician, who is [a] little more in his senses that the other actors, and a little honester, will not give his daughter – nay, has offered her five thousand pounds not to marry Mr Hervey; but Miss Rhubard is as much above wordly decorum as the rest, and persists, though there is no more doubt of the marriage of Mr Hervey and Miss Chudleigh than that of your father and mother . . .

Miss Chudleigh now moved quickly and within a month of the Court's decision went through a form of marriage with the Duke. By avoiding the scandal of a divorce she had retained the favour of the Court, which she had enjoyed and profited from for many years. Lord Masham was excused from attending on the King so that he could give the bride away and after the marriage the Duke and his new, 49-year-old Duchess were presented to the King and Queen. It has been stated that Hervey was there. Countess Temple's account, which we may believe or disbelieve as we choose, is as follows:

> The King hardly spoke to the bride, the Queen little more, Lord Bristol did not appear, Augustus chose to be there, and said he came to take one look at his widow.

The marriage lasted for little over four years. The Duke died in September 1773 and dissension over the terms of his will was to lead in 1776 to the trial of his Duchess for bigamy before the House of Lords.

Thus Miss Chudleigh's success in the jactitation suit persuaded her, in spite of the qualms of conscience evident in her conversation with Caesar Hawkins, that the ceremony at Lainston had no legal standing. It also persuaded the Archbishop of Canterbury, for it was by his special licence that the wedding took place. For Hervey, however, matters stood rather differently. It is clear from Caesar Hawkins' evidence that Hervey was convinced that Miss Chudleigh was his legal wife and that no declaration by the Consistory Court could make things otherwise. He had not married before the case because of this belief and he did not marry after the Court ruling in effect allowed him to do so.

The two principals in this will-o'-the-wisp of a marriage had had very different objectives and had followed conflicting paths in their efforts to reach them. Miss Chudleigh's proceedings have at least the virtue of consistency. The thought of a divorce case was most unwelcome to her, because of its effect on her place as a Maid of Honour and the repercussions on her standing at Court. She therefore anticipated Hervey's suit by bringing the action for jactitation of marriage, a course which had not been open to her until her husband's claims to be married to her had become open knowledge. By bringing the action she deflected his divorce suit and in addition placed herself in a position to marry the Duke her lover.

Hervey was less adroit and less consistent, and some of his actions have never been satisfactorily explained. His objective in the summer of 1768 seems to have been clear; he was married and wanted a divorce, but would not seek one unless his wife concurred with this course of action. She did not, and he did not press the matter. Later, when the Consistory Court ruled that he was not married to her he still appears not to have accepted that he was free to marry; certainly he took no further steps in relation to Miss Moysey, neither does he appear to have considered marrying Mrs Nesbitt, who he took up with two years or so later.

The inconsistency lies in his attitude during the jactitation case. Knowing he was truly married he could have affirmed his marriage and brought forward the one remaining witness – Ann Cradock. Mrs Amis, the widow of the parson who had married them, was also still alive; she could in principle have been a witness to the existence of the register whose production Miss Chudleigh had masterminded in 1759 . He did none of this. Instead he made an indeterminate statement effectively denying that the ceremony which they had gone though was a valid one, and it is not surprising in the light of his half-hearted evidence that the court ruled in his wife's favour.

Why Hervey failed to fight his corner is a mystery. The suggestion that he had taken money from his wife as an inducement can be disregarded, essentially because he was a man of honour with a high regard for his position as a gentleman, but also because he was not in financial difficulties and his freedom would have been a more important consideration than money. That his wife might have threatened him with her £16,000 debts is irrelevant since such a claim from a wife who had consistently denied her marriage would not have been easy to enforce. More persuasively, he may as a matter of delicacy or from some residual grain of affection or respect have found it distasteful to oppose his wife in public; or perhaps by a temporary failure in resolve he surrendered his principles in favour of an apparently easy route to freedom. Or did Lord Bristol, of whose attitudes he always took due note, put pressure on him not to expose too much scandal to the light of day?

Contemporaneously with the proceedings in the Consistory Court there are anomalies in Hervey's attitude to Miss Moysey. If as is generally assumed it was in order to marry her that in midsummer he sought a divorce, by late October he was denying to Grenville any intention to marry 'such a one as I am sure I should never have thought of',[31] a peculiar remark, and one to which it is impossible to fit any name except that of the young lady of Bath. Yet the belief that he had designs on her survived until at least the following February, when Walpole, always unreliable when retailing gossip, reports that he was still intent on marrying Miss Moysey, and that the intention was reciprocated.

There is little further hard evidence on the relationship, but in its place it is possible to erect a structure of events which would fit the known facts and the characters of the participants. At the age of 44 Hervey's desire for a real wife is entirely credible. Miss Moysey was at this time 24 years of age,[32] a personable and apparently virtuous young woman, and to accept that she was attracted to the gallant and amiable captain needs no suspension of disbelief. Though the social status of the Moysey family was perhaps two rungs below that of the Herveys a marriage between them would not have run foul of the social conventions of the day.

There was, however, a further problem, that of Hervey's prospective father-in-law, Dr Abel Moysey. Moysey was an Oxford graduate in medicine who had been settled in Bath for fifteen years and was an accomplished and fashionable physician of good family. According to Walpole, quoted above, he was unfavourably impressed by his daughter's intended. And who will blame him? Hervey was then a sick man well into his forties, a man with the poorest of reputations for constancy in his relations with women, the younger brother and heir presumptive, certainly, to an unmarried Earl, but a member of a family with the most peculiar range of habits imaginable. The poor father may well have taken the view that a respectable marriage to a young man with prospects in her own station of life would be much more likely to assure his daughter's happiness than the possiblity that she might one day be Countess of Bristol.

There may indeed have been yet another influence at work. Frederick Hervey, by then Bishop of Derry, was the next heir after his brother Augustus and could not be expected to welcome a marriage which might deprive him of the succession. He was in Bath during 1769 and what more likely than that he should have spoken warning words to Dr Moysey about his prospective son-in-law; or indeed that he should attempt to provide proof that his brother was already married and so obstruct Miss Chudleigh's jactitation suit.

How much these factors affected the outcome is unclear, and indeed it may be that Hervey's doubts of conscience on his marriage to Miss Chudleigh were enough to bring the affair to an end. No marriage took place and Miss Moysey went on to marry, with her father's full approval, a Dorset parson of good family.

References

1. Namier & Brooke, 1964, p617
2. Ibid.
3. Ibid., p618
4. Lewis, 1937–83, (31), p125
5. Smith, 1852, (3), p382
6. SRO(B), 941/50/5, p517
7. Ibid., p523
8. Ibid., p537
9. Ibid., p413
10. Ibid., p419
11. Ibid., p553
12. Ibid., p559
13. Namier & Brooke, 1964, p618
14. Smith, 1852, (4), p24
15. Ibid., p29
16. Namier & Brooke, 1964, p618
17. Smith, 1852, (4), p67
18. SRO (B), 940/50/5, p571
19. Ibid., p577
20. Smith, 1852, (4), p180
21. SRO(B), 940/50/5, 579
22. Smith, 1852, (4), p352
23. Ibid., p356
24. Hume, 1889, (2), p371
25. Ibid., p330
26. Ibid., p347
27. Lewis, 1937–83, (39), p105
28. Smith, 1852, (4), p393
29. Hume, 1889
30. Lewis, 1937–83, (23), p93
31. Smith, 1852, (4), p393
32. Gainsborough's House Society, 1984

CHAPTER XV

At the Admiralty

'Augustus Hervey's Navy'

While these legal adventures were in train Hervey's political campaigns seem to have taken second place. In March 1768 he had written an open letter to the Duke of Grafton, still nominally Prime Minister, which appeared in the *Gazetteer* upbraiding him on the weakness of his government and on 'abandoning' office. He repeated these sentiments in October.[1] In October also he wrote to Grenville the letter quoted earlier as an example of his action as a source of court gossip, ending effusively:[2]

> How can a Grafton supply the seat of a Walpole or a Grenville? Indeed, my dear Sir, you are universally prayed for by all sets now, except a few dependent hirelings that surround the gilded Pagod, God knows whether one can wish you at such a time [to be] in such a crazy sinking vessel, though it can only be such a pilot that can conduct us to safety.

Nevertheless, he had since the general election earlier in the year been member for the family borough of St Edmundsbury and his obligations to his brother, still a follower of Pitt, continued to compete with his support for Grenville. Before the end of the year, the Privy Seal being still vacant from Pitt's resignation, it was offered to Lord Bristol who was quick to accept the office which had formerly been held by his father. The way in which it came to him is told by Hervey, who wrote to Grenville from his dead mother's house in Park Place on the last day of October:[3]

> . . . this will be a little surprise for you, when I tell you Lord Chancellor wrote to my brother by the King's desire to offer the Privy Seal, which my brother is come to town to accept, having sent to Lord Chatham to know his inclinations about it. My brother sent immediately to tell me of this, and that he would be in town directly; he came yesterday and tells me it is now all settled . . . every individual thinks of his own situation, and therefore as one I find I must now take a different part from what I intended, and support my brother as long as I can, and wherever it is not absolutely contrary to those opinions I have already given. You have recommended this so strong and so repeatedly to me, that it would be ill

paying my court to you not to follow your advice in it, had I not even other calls. But, however that may be, I can never alter my wishes nor my opinions. It makes me very tired indeed of the whole, as I see very little good to arise from these arrangements, nor shall I ever expect any 'till the reins are again placed in your hands, . . . however, the D of Grafton must not like this, as he had no naming, nor any one appearance in it. How then is he the master? . . .

So Hervey continued to give tacit support to Grafton's government, though no office or other advantage came to him and he continued to write to and consort with Grenville. His pro-Grenville letters also continued; in December 1768 one signed 'To my King and Country a True Friend', believed to be from Hervey's pen, appeared in the *Political Register*. Its title was 'The Man who thinks himself Minister', and it takes up the theme of the last quoted sentence in his letter above: was Grafton really Prime Minister (he was certainly First Lord of the Treasury) when he was so inactive and so ignored by the King and those about him? It inveighs against Rockingham's repeal of Grenville's Stamp Act and again sighs for the return to office of a Walpole or a Grenville.

Hervey appears to have gone abroad little in the years after his retirement from sea service but towards the end of 1769 he visited Portugal. The visit is recorded in a letter to Grenville from Lisbon, dated 14 December. Its burden is a description of an attempt made ten days earlier to assassinate the King of Portugal and it may thus be categorized as one of Hervey's 'informative' letters to his patron. It begins:[4]

Dear Sir,
I scarce think I could have been tempted to have troubled you with a letter from this remote melancholy corner of the globe . . .

This, the only personal comment in the letter, suggests that he was not finding the solace or pleasure in the new Lisbon that he had enjoyed there during his naval service. The city was still being rebuilt after the disastrous earthquake of 1755, and the political state of the country and in particular of the aristocracy with whom Hervey had been accustomed to mingle was, under the dictator Pombal, to say the least unhappy. But he stayed there for some time, returning in the spring of 1770. His health was still giving him much trouble and a letter to Grenville dated from London on 4 August 1770 shows the constraints that it put him under:[5]

. . . but I have such frequent flying pains, and am so constantly obliged to have recourse to Dr Ingram, that I have not yet ventured to quit this dismal, hot and forlorn town, even for a night, since my return from Lisbon; though I have not been better these four years, yet I am thinking to sail for Lisbon next month, in order to bathe in some particular baths there . . .

However, the projected visit did not take place, probably being overtaken by the quickening pace of political events described below.

At about this time also Hervey's personal affairs took a turn for the better. We do not know precisely when he first met Mrs Mary Nesbitt, or when their relationship developed into that of protector and mistress. It must, however, have been some time between his return from Portugal in the first half of 1770 and 1772, when Walpole makes a comment on the liaison in one of his letters. Further than a liaison it could not and did not go; Hervey's continued refusal to accept that Elizabeth Chudleigh was not his wife precluded any thought of marriage. By all accounts, however, the relationship with Mrs Nesbitt was a close and affectionate one, and it was certainly one which was to last to the end of Hervey's life.

Mrs Nesbitt's origins are obscure. One scurrilous magazine article[6] gives an unflattering description of her, a description which is certainly not supported by the decorous and enterprising nature of her life with her protector and after his death:

[a lady] whose exploits in the republic of gallantry have made some noise east and west of Temple Bar. This lady, whose origin may be traced to a wheelbarrow, made acquaintance to Mr Nesbitt, a worthy young gentleman then in partnership in the banking business. [They married and the husband shortly after became bankrupt and insane]. No sooner had she thrown off the shackles of connubial restraint than she ran riot at every man that pleased her eye. Among the rest the Captain particularly attracted her; his athletic form, his generous disposition, his rank, in the fine *tout ensemble* impressed her so forcibly that she relinquished a long catalogue of lovers to be blessed in the arms of Augustus . . .

Perhaps the author of the passage was using the degree of freedom with exactitude often claimed by the more sensational press. If not, here is a description of Augustus, at an age when many men of the period would be developing a certain redness of face and shortness of breath, and a less than upright figure, suggesting that he had retained the physical stance and presence that must have formed one of the supports of his remarkable attractiveness to women.

It seems to have been her exceptional beauty, coupled with intelligence and personality, which enabled Mrs Nesbitt to make her way in the world, or at least in the *demi-monde*, through which she rose to gain acceptance as the chosen and permanent partner of one of the more rank-conscious members of the nobility. Born in obscurity probably around 1740, by 1762 she was married to Alexander Nesbitt, a partner in a city banking firm, and in that year was painted by Sir Joshua Reynolds as Circe. Nesbitt appears to have been putty in her hands and established her in a house at Norwood, the house in which she subsequently lived with Hervey.[7] She, however, was roundly unfaithful to her husband and it may be surmised that there was a series of liaisons before she took up with Augustus. At this time her husband was still alive, though insane, but he died in 1772, leaving the house at Norwood to his widow.

Such are the few known facts about the origins of the liaison. At first it must have appeared to onlookers to be as unpromising as all Hervey's previous affairs – one with a woman of beauty, certainly, and of character, but with a poor record for constancy. Mrs Nesbitt, however, had now 'captured' one who had captivated dozens of attractive women, a man who might one day find that circumstances allowed him to marry her, and indeed to make her Countess of Bristol; while Hervey had reached an age at which what he wanted most from a female companion was the comfort and security of love and affection with which Mrs Nesbitt seems to have been successful in providing him.

Hervey's letter to Grenville of 4 August 1770, already referred to,[8] continues with a lengthy diatribe against the Government. He attacks in particular the conduct of the Admiralty, where Sir Edward Hawke had been First Lord since December 1766. Hervey deplores the great fire that had recently destroyed much of the dockyard stores at Portsmouth – a result perhaps of poor management rather than neglect – and the genuine neglect which had led to the silting up of the Medway at Chatham. He criticizes the stewardship of the First Lord in the following terms:

> . . . I would go down there [to Portsmouth] to be a judge myself, but that I have sometimes seen and felt that no attention in our profession can avail the public any more than [it can] the individual who shows it; I do assure you my dear Sir, 'tis a ruined service . . . I have the particulars of many instances of neglect very alarming to this country, but when ignorance and obstinacy are predominant at that Board, it is of little consequence to [make representations] . . . Sir Edward Hawke will not go out without the peerage, and, however wished, they cannot obtain it for him.

He goes on to suggest that Lord North (who had succeeded Grafton as First Lord of the Treasury earlier in the year) no longer intended Grafton as Hawke's successor, as some had earlier suggested, but that in the event of Hawke's death, which he thought not unlikely, Lord Sandwich would return to the Admiralty for a third period of office.

The burden of Hervey's complaints is a true one, for Hawke with all his qualities as a sea commander had little administrative ability and was by this time so ill that he had difficulty in reaching the Admiralty Board Room. The

Admiral, however, had never been one of his favourite colleagues, in spite of their grand co-operation before Brest in 1759; witness, for example the coldness of a letter from Hervey to Hawke in 1763:[9]

> Sir
>
> I have received the Honor of your letter; my intentions for standing for Bury were only told you in Confidence as my friend – Your son shall always Command any Interest I have at Saltash or any where else.

Some factor unknown must have served to negate the good relationship they had enjoyed during their splendid co-operation before Brest four years previously. One possibility is that Hawke's relatively humble background made him less than acceptable to Hervey, who always had grandiose ideas of what was due to him as a son, grandson and brother of members of the House of Lords. But Hervey can hardly have expected that a letter to Grenville would have any useful effect, for he also had been in failing health for some time and died in November that year; yet another example to add to the lengthening list of naval and political patrons whom Hervey lost over the years by death or illness.

Hervey was also in correspondence with Sandwich, as he had been on and off for many years. From this time on their relationships were so close, at first in friendship and later in enmity, that some account must be given of this most able but controversial man. In 1770 John Montagu 4th Earl of Sandwich was 52 years of age. He had been close to the centre of affairs for twenty-five years, having as a young man successfully carried out the negotiations for the Treaty of Aix-la-Chapelle which brought to an end the War of the Austrian Succession. In 1749 he became First Lord of the Admiralty and introduced many useful reforms. He was First Lord again for a few months in 1763 before becoming Secretary of State for the remainder of Grenville's administration.

His great period in office, however, was his third term at the Admiralty, which lasted from 1771 to 1782. During it he bore the heat of the day throughout the American war and has often been blamed for Britain's poor naval performance at that time. In fact the navy that he took over had been neglected by the previous Board, its ships were in a poor state and the dockyards were in bad order; in particular the fire at Portsmouth referred to above had destroyed most of the reserves of spars and rigging while the shortage of seasoned timber resulting from the demands of previous wars meant that ships were being built of unseasoned oak, a recipe for continual trouble. He was a meticulous and hard working First Lord, with a deep knowledge of naval affairs, and did much to set the management of the dockyards, the maintenance of the navy's ships and the naval shipbuilding programme on a firm and effective basis. If he can be criticized it is for his political bias in promotions and appointments, and this was a major reason for his unpopularity with many serving officers. Add to that his reputation as a rake, the prominent part he had taken in the early sixties in the prosecution of John Wilkes for sedition and the undoubted fact that for much of the American War the navy was overstretched and unsuccessful, and it is not surprising that many historians have taken a jaundiced view of his tenure of the Admiralty, a view that has only been challenged successfully in last few decades.[10]

In his private life Sandwich had gained a reputation as a rake and a seducer. His marriage was troubled and in 1757 he separated from his wife, who was by that time of unsound mind. Thereafter he seems to have gone through a period of riotous promiscuity until he took up with the young Martha Ray, who was his acknowledged mistress from the early sixties until her untimely death in 1779; though the arrangement did not prevent him from straying as opportunity offered. He was a member of the Medmenham Monks, a group of aristocratic playboys who met at the pleasure gardens of Sir Francis Dashwood in the Thameside village of that name, where they were reputed to have indulged in nameless orgies; but how much of what has been written about Sandwich's vices is true and how much sinister imagination it is difficult to assess. His general relationships with women were, however, so similar to Hervey's life as described in his *Journal* that it is unsurprising that they saw much of each other and corresponded fairly frequently throughout the sixties.

Hervey's first official contact with Sandwich was the confrontation on the Navy Bill in 1749, described in Chapter V. It was not a fortunate beginning but did not prevent them from becoming close friends. By 1751 Hervey was, as indicated by his *Journal*, much in Sandwich's company at balls and sharing with him a pleasure-seeking and perhaps dissipated life. They seem to have kept up this friendship whenever Hervey was in England and certainly by 1763, when he returned from the West Indies, it had taken on the political dimension recounted in Chapter XIII.

During the sixties the friendship between the two men blossomed, in its political as well as its personal manifestations. Thus when Hervey wrote the Letter to Lord Bute of 1 August 1765 Sandwich was one of the few people to whom he showed the draft; and he did this without being a close political ally, for Sandwich was still a Bedfordite. A series of letters[11] from Sandwich to Hervey in 1765–66 shows that they were in friendly discussion on political matters, one dated 4 July 1765 (shortly after the fall of Grenville's government) suggesting an alliance between Sandwich's friends and Lord Bristol's. In December Sandwich writes that he was glad to have talked to Lord Bristol at the Inn at Huntingdon. Later, after the formation of the Grafton/Pitt government in 1766, Sandwich resigned himself to lack of office and enquired about the possibility of joining forces with the Grenvillites.

The letters show a more personal side. Sandwich describes his involvement with Huntingdon races. He commiserates on the state of Hervey's health, writing from Hinchingbroke on 15 July 1766 in a boldly sympathetic style:

> . . . I flatter myself I need not tell you how unhappy I am to hear of your indisposition, but you see the consequences of sedateness and regularity, when you were here you could dance and sing, eat and drink, walk in the wet and labour at an oar with impunity but as soon as you grow wise and serious you are laid up probably for the rest of the summer . . . be assured that tho' I laugh at your illnesses sometimes, I feel them when they are serious as much as you do yourself.

Sandwich was undoubtedly trying to jolly his friend out of despondency, but it was in the nature of gout in the then state of medical knowledge to show great fluctuation in the severity of its symptoms.

Hervey was a frequent visitor to Hinchingbroke, as was his sister Lady Mary Fitzgerald, whose marriage to the unsatisfactory George Fitzgerald had broken down in the late fifties. Sandwich was enamoured of her and they carried on a long and flirtatious relationship, starting as early as 1759 and continuing until some time after 1766.[12] Though her letters are coquettish and seem to be intended to lure him on she was in fact one of the few women who successfully resisted his advances. Their association must have been a fillip to his friendship with Augustus. For example, in a letter to him from Woburn dated 17 July 1766 Sandwich wrote:

> . . . I sent some verses to Ickworth supposed to be wrote by the crimson bed at Hinchingbroke, please tell me whether the person to whom they were sent has mentioned them to you.

Presumably the addressee was Lady Mary and equally it may be supposed that she had been the occupant of the crimson bed, and Sandwich had not.

By 1770 much water had passed beneath the bridge but the terms on which Sandwich and Hervey corresponded had altered little. Sandwich had since January 1768 held the relatively junior position of joint Postmaster General, but under Lord North, was hoping for better things, specifically the Admiralty. In the first week of August Hervey wrote to him from London[13] advising him to come up to town for his own good, pointing out that there were competitors for Sir Edward Hawke's post when he resigned, and ending on a more personal note 'Adieu; my best compliments to Mademoiselle [Martha Ray] and all her parrots, dogs etc'.

He followed this with a stronger warning on 13th August, written from Bury and saying that both Grafton and Lord Rochford, then Secretary of State, were hoping for the Admiralty, and that Rochford might well be appointed; he advised Sandwich to write to Lord North setting out his claim.[14]

Again there was a personal slant to these letters which demonstrates the terms of easy familiarity on which they corresponded; Sandwich had clearly reproved Hervey for an excess of obscurity in his references to individuals, and Hervey in turn commented on his:

> . . . venerable reproof of my *puerile* custom of writing so mysteriously; but as I happen not to have so good an opinion of the clerks of the Post Office as I have of their *chief* [Sandwich] I do not wish to be communicating to them what I had only intended for him. On the other hand I judged too favourably, I find, of you, as I did not apprehend that time had yet robbed you of your former alertness and penetration, when an initial letter or a dash required no dictionary. Alas I am as sorry for Miss R as I am for all your friends, lest age should have made the same havoc in you from head to foot; though perhaps she has yet the consolation in not having been long enough acquainted with your Lordship's great parts to regret the difference . . .

With the increasing incapacity of George Grenville Hervey can be perceived to be transferring his support towards the most suitable alternative patron. He must have given up any thought of the First Lordship for himself, and have fallen back on the hope that Sandwich would find a place for him on the Board, for which his long experience of naval life and affairs made him a suitable choice. In January 1771 Hawke gave up his struggle and Sandwich was appointed for the third time to preside over the Commission for carrying out the duties of the Lord High Admiral. The only other naval member of Hawke's Board was Admiral Francis Holbourne, who retained his position until early February. On his resignation Hervey was appointed a Lord Commissioner of the Admiralty in his place. His patent is dated 2 February. At last he had obtained the stake in the direction of naval affairs that he had striven for since 1763.

Hervey first attended a meeting of the Board of Admiralty on 15 February 1771. He was the only naval member of the Board and all but one of the other Lords were essentially placemen. The exception was John Buller, a Cornish borough-owner and member for East Looe, who spoke for the Board in the Commons and is described[15] as an 'office drudge' for the Admiralty; coincidentally he was a nephew of Governor Trelawney, Hervey's old friend from his days in Jamaica over twenty-five years previously.

In the First Lord, however, although he was a civilian, the Board and the Government were fortunate to have a politician of much experience and of considerable industry, and one whose previous tenures of the post had given him as deep an understanding of naval affairs as it was possible for one who had not been a sea-officer to acquire. Many civilian First Lords were figureheads lacking in knowledge and application, an extreme example being the

Duke of Bedford, who in the forties had avowedly left the whole management of the navy to Anson, the senior naval member of that Board. Sandwich, however, was a man of different mettle. He had done the job twice before, he knew or took trouble to find out what needed to be done, he kept in touch with officers at all levels and knew what they were thinking, he was prepared to spend time on administrative matters and after seven years out of high office he was keen to get to grips with what had become a neglected department of state.

Because Sandwich so controlled and dominated his Board it is his name that has become synonymous with its actions and achievements, and with the criticisms that were levelled at its performance later in the decade. What contribution Hervey made is not easy to establish, but his attendance at Board meetings tells us something of the course of events. During the eleven months of 1771 for which he was a member of the Board it met 159 times and Hervey was present on 112 occasions (70%), only Sandwich himself and Buller being there more often. Board meetings were slightly less frequent in subsequent years, but Hervey's attendance fell away, to 56% in 1772, 44% in 1773, 27% in 1774 and 40% in the two months or so of 1775 for which he was a Board member.[16] The reasons for this decline are not spelt out but can be deduced from circumstantial evidence. Health was undoubtedly a predominant factor. It is clear that Hervey continued to suffer periodically from incapacitating attacks of gout. A comment from the King himself (with whom Hervey continued to be in close contact as a Groom of the Bedchamber) paints the picture as vividly as any. Writing to Lord Bristol in July 1773 he says:[17]

> . . . I saw your brother yesterday who seems more shattered than after any former confinement, and even more mortified at his not being able to appear at Portsmouth than I expected; he seems to attribute his state of relaxation to the continually taking James's powders which he has now abandoned, I hope his example will deter you from medicines . . .

There was in fact a pattern to Hervey's absences which tells the same story. In all the winters from 1772 to 1775 there were periods of over a month in which he did not attend, a state of affairs clearly showing that winter weather in London had a bad effect on his health. Location also seems to have had a great influence and he frequently notes a significant improvement when he was able to leave London for a spell at Ickworth. In the late summer of 1774 he tried to do even better by going abroad. Details are sparse but in October when Bury Corporation re-elected him to Parliament they minuted that he was at the time in France for the benefit of his health. He was not at the Admiralty between 27 August and 31 October. Where he went is not recorded – two months including travelling seems too brief a period for a worthwhile stay in Nice, a favourite location for him in later years.

What part Hervey took in those Board meetings at which he was present cannot be evaluated in detail. Sandwich was a 'hands-on' First Lord and did not delegate, so that the other Board members had influence, not power. Board minutes define the subjects under consideration and the decisions taken but do not describe the nature of the discussions or particularize on which members contributed. Hervey, however, was the only naval member and must have had much to say on essentially maritime matters; but he was not dominant in those subjects as Anson and Hawke had been. Lord Chatham's sarcastic reference[18] in a letter to the Earl of Shelburne to 'Augustus Hervey's fleet' is very far from the truth.

That he gave Sandwich the benefits of his naval experience informally is shown by the limited correspondence between them which survives. One example concerns the revision of the guardship arrangements which Sandwich's Board was quick to introduce. It was customary in peacetime for 'guardships' to be kept in commission at each port, in principle to provide against sudden attack but also to provide a nucleus of ships which could be quickly mobilized in case of need. In practice, however, and particularly in the last years of Hawke's tenure of the First Lordship, the condition of the guardships had been allowed to deteriorate. The ships were not kept in a good state of repair or readiness and the crews were inadequate to take them to sea – so that, for example, when the Spanish attitude to the Falkland Islands caused a crisis in 1770 it took many weeks to get together a fleet. Sandwich's Board was very conscious of the need for change. An undated letter from Hervey to the First Lord, probably written in April or May 1771, shows him giving the benefit of his sea experience on this subject:[19]

Some thoughts concerning the Regulations
about the Guardships

I would propose that only two guardships, and those of 60 or 64 guns, should be at Chatham. They are of no use there but for rowing the night guard; and the water is too shallow there for larger ships to lay conveniently with such stores, and so fitted as your Lordship, I hope, will have the guardships in future to be.

I would think three at Sheerness are necessary, as the essential post for guarding the River Medway and the readiest to fit out on any occasion.

The ships at Portsmouth and Plymouth, in my opinion, ought to be so manned that they can be sent immediately on service without turning over people from any other ships, the most disgustful service to a seaman of any, and is the occasion of more desertion than any other motive.

The ships so manned to be fitted also, that they should have little to do but what may be done whilst receiving on board the provisions to complete for the service they are intended for. The topsails, small sails of all kinds, and one pair of courses, always on board ready to bend, as they can be more conveniently aired than when on shore and always as well preserved in the ships' storerooms. Orders for two thirds of the officers always to lie on board the ships, and the people let to go on shore as many as convenient and at the discretion of the captain.

I wish to recommend to your Lordship that the Portsmouth and Plymouth guardships should by turn rendezvous at Spithead from the month of May to the beginning of September; and if they were to cruise for six weeks in the mouth of the Channel, and so relieve each other half and half, it would be no kind of detriment to the ships, but on the contrary, in my opinion, tend to their preservation by their being kept much cleaner, constantly washed with salt water, and by the people always on board the little defects constantly repaired, which would more than over-balance the wear and tear by being at sea, as in those summer months and on such service there would be no occasion to strain the ships by over pressure of sail. This would exercise their people, and especially the young officers.

I would wish the commanders-in-chief of each port to have very strict additional orders to repair frequently on board the several ships under their command, and without any previous notice to muster their people and examine the state and condition of the ships, reporting to the Admiralty every time and every ship they do so, by which means, I am persuaded, many abuses and many neglects will be prevented.

I would have the guardships have all their spare masts, yards, and booms, on board, to be kept under good cover, which would ease the storehouses on shore very much, and in case of fire in the yard make the loss much less to the public.

The large ships of the line in ordinary, I would have them all have their standing masts in, their standing rigging etc on board, lashed up under their decks to the beams, constantly tarred or pitched, with one set of topmasts and topsail yards etc for their booms, which would be kept constantly pitched also or tarred, and will be full as well preserved as on shore, being all summer under awnings, and will have the same good consequences as above in case of fire in the yards.

I would have the commander-in-chief of each port, as well as the commissioner of the yard, now and then visit all the ships in ordinary and know from the different officers on board them the state etc of them, reporting also to your Board he does so.

Many other things at leisure may be thought on; but as you seem so intent on putting the Navy on a proper foot, you'll forgive my offering my thoughts when they recur . . .

In this letter can be seen the genesis of the new approach to the guardships. Hervey rightly puts much emphasis on proper management and training of both officers and men; his approach is practical and seamanlike, drawing on his long experience afloat and his first-hand knowledge of what could go wrong. Most of his suggestions were put into effect, so that the next time a fleet was ordered to sea the guardships were in a much more satisfactory state of readiness.

Sandwich's reply shows two things: that at this stage there was a dialogue between the First Lord and his principal naval adviser and that Sandwich was taking note of Hervey's advice and information; he was also doing his best to familiarize himself with naval problems and personalities. Indeed, he wrote his reply[20] in a spare moment during his summer tour of the dockyards:

Augusta at anchor in a calm off Dunnose June 13 1771

Dear Sir

I take this opportunity to thank you for your letter which I received at Plymouth, and hope to thank you in person on Sunday or Monday next, possibly sooner.

No one will make me alter my opinions about the ships going to sea for a summer cruize, unless there should be any political reasons against it, which will be better removed, if there are any, when I am on the spot; and I thing it will be easy to fix on the ships when at a distance; and perhaps more so than if I had declared it to be the determined resolution of the Board while I was among them, as I should then have had application for some to go and for others to be excused and therefore might not have had so much choice as I shall when I name them without asking their consent, I must however do the captains the justice (some of whom had got scent of our intention, and questioned me a little about it), to say, that they all of them seemed to approve of the plan, and that the competition will be who shall go, and not who shall stay behind.

I believe you will find the reductions have in general been made according to your idea, and that a considerable number of landsmen are continued in the service; and I perceive it to be the opinion of many of our best officers that a ship so filled is better manned than if she had nothing but able seamen on board.

I do assure you that I have not been idle since I have left you, as you perceive when I communicate to you the several observations I have made during this visitation, all of which is reduced into writing, and on which I shall be very happy if your opinion coincides with mine, and I shall be greatly obliged to you for any further hints which your experience in and knowledge of naval matters may suggest.

Many thanks for your news of various kinds; if you pick up anything fresh it is very probable an answer to this might catch me in the Downs

or at the Nore . . .
  I am etc
    Sandwich

Sandwich certainly gave Hervey much of the credit for the revision and improvement of the arrangements for the guardships, acknowledging in the Lords in July 1775[21] (three months after Hervey had left the Admiralty) his great assistance in the matter, and more generally 'and though I still have his private assistance I must confess I have much reason to regret his absence from that board'. On Sandwich's other new policies, especially his annual inspections of the dockyards and his insistence that the Navy Board adopt a planned approach to ship building and maintenance and to procurement of materials, in particular seasoned oak, there is little evidence that Hervey was much involved. It would indeed have been uncharacteristic of him to have been interested in complex administrative detail of that nature.

Hervey did, however, concern himself with operational matters and questions of personnel. One such occasion was the First Lord's dockyard visitation in 1773, which was combined with the King's review of the fleet at Spithead. The review had its origin in a mobilization of the fleet in May of that year. Though the mobilization was aborted within a few days the fact that ships had been brought to a high state of readiness provided Sandwich with an opportunity to display the navy's improved condition to the King. Hervey had no executive responsibility but gave Sandwich advice on both operational and personnel aspects. On 29 May he wrote [22] to Sandwich with advice on the layout of the fleet and on the susceptibilities of some of the senior officers: Sandwich should have the ships so disposed that those which were intended to return to Plymouth were easternmost, with the Summer Squadron next to them, so that they could weigh and sail in front of His Majesty without risk of going aboard the Portsmouth ships; and he should let Rear-Admiral Spry set sail in command of the Plymouth ships, not Vice-Admiral Lord Edgcumbe, Spry having done well as Commander-in-Chief Plymouth and much disliking Edgcumbe, who was being brought back for the review only.

In early June Hervey went down to Portsmouth, where Sandwich had arrived in the yacht *Augusta*. Together with Thomas Bradshaw they constituted a quorum of the Board and assembled in the Port Commissioner's yacht under the Hope and Anchor flag of Admiralty, one of the few occasions, perhaps the only one, on which Hervey would have seen the old flag of the Lord High Admiral hoisted on board ship. Sandwich led a thorough inspection of the dockyard and the new hospital at Haslar, and on 22nd of the month the King came down and inspected the assembled fleet. It was an occasion of some splendour and marked a degree of regal interest in the navy that had not been exceeded since the time of James II.

Though Sandwich had very clear ideas on naval policy he had not lived among the naval community and his first-hand knowledge of the naval officers of the day was to begin with limited. Hervey knew them all, at least by reputation, and Sandwich called on him for opinions and advice. Though little of this advice has survived its tenor can be judged by a letter from Sandwich to Hervey,[23] obviously in reply to suggestions which the latter had recently made. Its substance was as follows:

1   Sandwich could be depended upon to recommend Admiral Hughes for one of the foreign stations.

2   He would contrive that Hughes should know of Hervey's interest in Captain Robinson.

3   It was unreasonable that Admiral Amherst should wish to nominate the captain of one of the guardships at Plymouth and Sandwich had refused him.

4   In no way would Sandwich appoint Admiral Gayton to the American command. [This was the Clark Gayton whom, when he was Admiral Osborne's flag captain in 1757, Hervey had described as 'a poor creature, tho' good boatswain he would have made'. In 1776 Sandwich appointed him C-in-C Jamaica].

5   'Your nephew [Constantine Phipps, 2nd Lord Mulgrave] does not leave me 'till tomorrow. I hope and believe we are very well satisfied with each other'.

This exchange of views cannot have been the only one and from the number of officers mentioned it may be assumed that Hervey was prolific in his recommendations (both positive and negative), and that Sandwich took note of much of his advice.

Hervey had never been a prolific speaker in the Commons and his membership of the Admiralty Board did nothing to change his reserve. It was John Buller who spoke for the Board in the House on such matters as the Navy Estimates. In January 1772 Buller asked for an increase from 16,000 to 25,000 in the number of seamen and on this occasion it was Hervey in seconding the motion who explained the need for the increase; in Jamaica there was danger from the large Spanish force in the Caribbean who might attack the island before reinforcements could be sent; there was tension in East Indian waters, requiring stronger forces there; and the reorganization of the guardships, which were in poor condition and required larger standing crews, was a response to experience during the recent period of peace.[24] Later Hervey appears not to have taken any large part in Commons debates on the estimates, for example in December 1772 he seconded the estimates and 'entered into no explanation whatever.[25] It was Lord North himself who provided the strategic justification.

In February 1773 Hervey took no part in the debate on a petition from the captains of the navy to increase their half-pay. This attitude was in marked contrast to the leading part that he had taken on the similar petition for the naval lieutenants; but at the time of the debate on captains' pay he was not attending Board meetings, which suggests ill-health, and as a captain himself he could well have thought it wrong to participate. His only other reported speech in the Commons while he was a Lord of the Admiralty was in February 1775, shortly before he left the Board, on the relationship between Britain and the American colonists, in which he declared, reflecting his consistent attitude on the matter, that he would never consent to any abnegation of British legislative control over them.[26]

For most of Hervey's time at the Admiralty Britain was at peace, albeit a peace that was increasingly threatened by the increasing unrest in the American colonies. Thus strategy and operational matters entered little into the decisions with which he was concerned. The Board had, however, to cope with several periods of elevated international tension, as when in 1771 the Spanish authorities in the Caribbean took a British auxiliary schooner in dubious circumstances. Rodney, then Commander-in-Chief at Jamaica, took a high-handed attitude to obtain her release and for a time the Admiralty was concerned that he might drive the Spanish towards war – a war which it was well recognized the C-in-C (whose financial embarrassments were well known) would welcome on account of the prize money he might expect to gain. However, the crisis simmered down and in February 1772 Hervey wrote to Rodney congratulating him on his handling of the situation, though it may be that the main purpose of the letter was related to the supply of certain tropical delicacies:[27]

Admiralty Office, February 25, 1772

. . . I am very glad to find the affair of the *Hawke*, Schooner, terminated so well. We were all very sour here I assure you by it, and I hope the Spaniards will be more cautious for the future

I beg you will not give yourself the trouble to send me any Madeira, Capt Robinson [one of Hervey's followers, see later] got me some, admirable he says, when he was at Madeira, and will send it me the first opportunity. But if you will send me some fresh limes and chaddocks I shall thank you and readily accept them. Or some pineapple roots, well done up, for my Hot House.

I am better than I have been for many years owing to James's powders which I have taken regularly now eight months every night, and have surprised everyone by so great a recovery . . . Naval news there is none, all goes quietly – many suitors and little to bestow.

Adieu, I envy you nothing but your sun, Oh! I always loved Jamaica's sun – I spent much time there and very happily – but most of my old friends are no more – but I shall ever retain the highest sense of their hospitality and kindness to me . . .

There was, however, one occasion when he must have looked forward to a more active role. In the Spring of 1773, in response to hostile French movements in the Mediterranean, it was decided to prepare the guardships for sea and to send out a strong reinforcement. On 22 April the Board resolved[28] that Sir Charles Saunders should be appointed Commander-in-Chief Mediterranean, that Sir Peter Denis (then commanding the small peacetime squadron already in place there) should be appointed his second-in-command and that Hervey should command the third division of the fleet with the rank of Commodore. Thus as in 1765 the prospect of an active command opened up before him, this time after an interval of ten years since he had last served at sea.

As in 1765, however, his hopes were dashed. The political situation simmered down and on 5 May it was decided that the fitting out of the guardships should be suspended, that Saunders should strike his flag and Hervey his broad pennant. For the second time he must have been bitterly disappointed.

The course of events while Hervey was at the Admiralty shows that he gradually became disenchanted with his position there. His less frequent attendances at the Board provide one measure of this, though an indirect one. His absences were mainly due to illness, and the fact that he was so frequently incapacitated was itself enough to inhibit his enthusiasm for a say in naval affairs. Clear evidence for this is provided by a downhearted letter he wrote to Sandwich in August 1773:[29]

Norwood, 5 August 1773

My Dear Lord

. . . I am much obliged to you for your hint about the elder-Brother-Ship of Trinity House, but 'tho I had an ambition of making one of seven, where your Lordship presided uncontrolled, I cannot say that I have any left to be one of thirty one where I must suppose you are controlled, or I should have flattered myself I should have been one long ago, as I remember a kind of promise in former days of it; which believe me I do not mean to reproach your Lordship about, because that would seem as if regretted, which I now decline. My repeated lameness is a cheque to every pursuit which the activity of my mind might have prompted, and I find myself so seldom [able] to do anything I wish to do, and so often unfit for everything I ought to do, that I do assure you, my dear Lord, 'tis with some restraint that I keep what I have, in hopes of soon being better able to do the duties of them; tho' I confess were [I] rich enough to afford it, I believe, I should not even wait for so uncertain a prospect, my ambition having nearly kept pace, in subsiding with my strength, and I should scarce repine at throwing away the fruits of thirty eight years service.

I have been so lame these three days past, that I have not been able to attend your Board, 'tis some consolation in knowing how little I am wanted there.

There was, however, more to this lack of enthusiasm than poor health. After years of frustration Hervey had joyfully taken his seat at the Board, and as the only sea officer on it could reasonably have expected to have a powerful say in all those deliberations and decisions that bore directly on the organization and disposition of the fleet. Under civilian First Lords such as Winchilsea, Bedford, or Halifax the senior sea-officer on the Board would willy-nilly have carried this responsibility. As we have seen, however, Sandwich was of a different stamp and needed no dog to bark for him. Thus Hervey found himself with less power and less influence than he had hoped for and as time went on was consulted less frequently, even when he was well enough to take his part.

In consequence Hervey had gradually become disillusioned with Sandwich. The friendship that had been so close in August 1770 was gradually eroded, a process in which two factors can be seen at work. Sandwich in office, with all his knowledge of what needed doing and his energy in carrying it out, was not an easy man to work with, particularly for a sea-officer of Hervey's long experience. The First Lord was also purposefully developing a coterie of supporters, men of ability but many with none of the background of aristocratic privilege that Hervey enjoyed and thought essential to high office. With his strong views on naval matters Hervey was an unlikely candidate for membership of such a group and seems to have felt that his experience and abilities were being ignored. Underlying his attitude, also, was an increasing dissatisfaction with his subsidiary position at the Admiralty, where he had long had an ambition to be First Lord.

Contemporaneously with this change in attitude a radical alteration in Hervey's position and prospects was foreshadowed in November 1774, when George Earl of Bristol's long history of illness culminated in what would today be termed a severe stoke, which left him paralysed. He lingered for several months, dying at Bath on 18 March 1775. Augustus thus succeeded at the age of 50 to the title and the extensive and wealthy Bristol estates, becoming a very rich man. Some idea of his wealth can be obtained from the estimate that has been made of the income that the next Earl, Frederick the Earl-Bishop, enjoyed from them, which was of the order of £20,000 per annum. This was an enormous sum in the currency of the day and made the official salaries that Hervey was drawing inconsiderable.

The Dictionary of National Biography curtly describes Hervey's response in the following terms:

. . . on succeeding 18 March 1775 to the earldom of Bristol and to considerable wealth, he resigned all his offices.

The offices surrendered were his Lordship of the Admiralty and his positions as Groom of the Bedchamber and as Colonel of Marines. As far as the Admiralty was concerned, however, there was much more to his resignation that the *DNB* suggests. The weariness, disillusion and disappointment shown in his letter about the Elder Brother-ship had not gone away, while his new wealth made him in financial terms entirely his own man. He therefore moved immediately to better his position. With Sandwich well established there was no immediate prospect of the First Lordship. He therefore confined himself to asking for promotion to flag rank and to the second position on the Board, effectively to the unofficial position of senior naval lord. But this demand for seniority seems to have been essentially a reflection of his convictions on the privileges due to a peer – a peer, he maintained, could not be expected to place his signature on letters and instructions below that of a commoner. A letter of 28 March to Sandwich[30] shows him trying to find precedents for this attitude:

My Dear Lord

I can only tell your Lord what I had from Lord Vere [Beauclark] himself three days ago, and which he particularly repeated to me last night, that the Duke of Newcastle told his Lordship from the K, H M would not let a peer sign under a Commoner, & that Lord Vere had acquiesced under that . . .

Such matters of procedure were, however irrelevant to the position taken up by the First Lord, who appears to have wished for a change in naval representation on the Board. Perhaps Hervey's gout, and consequent frequent absences from Board meetings, was a factor, though it is as likely that Sandwich wanted as a member one of his own new men who would be able to speak for the Admiralty in the Commons. He discussed the matter with the King and his letter of 27 March to His Majesty, reporting (in the third person) his subsequent discussion with Hervey, makes his attitude plain:[31]

Ld Sandwich told Ld Bristol that he thought the King listened to the idea of a promotion, but that he did not fully explain his intention; and that upon the whole it was Lord Sandwich's opinion that if he confined himself to the single object of the flag, and agreed to vacate the Admiralty, he would prevail upon your Majesty to gratify him . . . Ld Sandwich told him that he thought it would be very awkward for him to come over all the other Lords of the Admiralty to sign second, to which he answered that he could sit at the Board on no other conditions, and if there was any difficulty on that point he must at once determine to quit, whether he had his flag or not.

From this it can be construed that Sandwich knew what he wanted, while the new Lord Bristol had conflicting and unreconcilable objectives. The outcome was inevitable. Bristol resigned and was promoted to Rear-Admiral of the Blue. Sandwich at once filled his place with Rear-Admiral Sir Hugh Palliser, one of his group of supporters, a man of considerable ability whose advancement by the First Lord was perversely to bring much trouble upon the navy.

References

1. SRO(B), 940/50/50/5, pp 583 & 683
2. Smith, 1852, (4), p383
3. Ibid., p393
4. Ibid., (3), p488
5. Ibid., p524
6. *Town & Country*, January 1775, p9
7. PRO, C 12/433/30
8. Smith, 1852, (3), p488
9. NMML, PST/5/D
10. Rodger, 1993, passim
11. NMML, Sandwich Papers, F41/17–24
12. Marillier, 1910, passim
13. NMML, Sandwich Papers, F41/51
14. Ibid., F41/54
15. Namier & Brooke, 1964, (2), p232
16. PRO, ADM3/78–81
17. Fortescue, 1927–28, (3), p2
18. Taylor & Pringle, 1838–40, (4), p107
19. Barnes & Owen, 1972–78, (1), p26
20. NMML, Sandwich Papers, F/2/24
21. Cobbett, 1806–20, vol XVIII, col 671
22. NMML, Sandwich Papers, F4/43
23. NMML, Sandwich Papers, F4/93
24. Cobbett, 1806–20, vol XVII, col 238 et seq
25. Ibid., col 538 et seq
26. Namier & Brooke, 1964, (2), p618
27. PRO, 20/20
28. PRO, ADM3/80
29. NMML, Sandwich Papers, F4/77
30. Ibid., F41/78
31. Barnes & Owen, 1972–78, (1), p xii

CHAPTER XVI

Earl of Bristol

Marital victory, professional defeat

With his resignation from the Admiralty the new Earl of Bristol was left without official or professional duties, except for those incumbent on him as a member of the House of Lords. He did in due course become a regular participant in the Lords' proceedings and spoke much more often there than he had in the Commons. He usually spoke, his health permitting, in any debate concerning the navy or the place of Britain in world affairs. At first he continued to support the Government and remained on friendly terms with Lord Sandwich, though as will be seen his relations with both Government and First Lord became very different with the passage of time.

Bristol had succeeded to considerable estates, with land in Suffolk and Lincolnshire and two principal houses, the London house in St James's Square and Ickworth Lodge. He had for many years watched his brother oversee their management and now had that task himself, though this was done through capable stewards and did not absorb much of the earl's time. His annual income was in excess of £10,000, so that he was no longer under any financial constraint.

Both before and after Bristol came to the peerage he spent much time with Mrs Nesbitt at the house at Norwood which had been settled on her by her husband.[1] The house is described by Sir John Thomas Stanley (later Lord Stanley of Alderley)[2] who was at school with Hervey's illegitimate son Little Augustus. Between them Bristol and Mrs Nesbitt had transformed it from a cottage into a spacious and comfortable villa with stables, while Bristol had purchased several surrounding acres so that it lay within a ring of garden, woodland and pasture. When Augustus succeeded to the earldom and to two great houses of his own (he had up to then had a small house in Chesterfield Street, north of Piccadilly) the couple seem to have moved from one to another of the three houses – Norwood, St Jame's Square and Ickworth – to suit their convenience.

Mrs Nesbitt was accepted in 'bachelor' society and among those with similar irregular unions, but not in the highest circles. She was thus almost but not quite chatelaine of both the Hervey family houses. As far as is known she had no children of her own, but she took on the position of 'stepmother' to

Mrs Mary Nesbitt. From the picture by Sir Joshua Reynolds, reproduced by courtesy of the Trustees of the Wallace Collection.

Little Augustus. Bristol had accepted the lad as his own, and with the disappearance of the errant Kitty Hunter from the scene brought him up, a task which appears to have given him considerable pleasure and satisfaction.

Little Augustus is thought to have been born about 1765, so that at the time of Hervey's accession to the title he was 10 years old or so. In the seventies he was at school at Loughborough House, Lambeth, where several future peers were among his fellow pupils. The fees, £52 a year, were high and the accommodation correspondingly, and for a school unusually, palatial, the boys having separate beds and eating off plate. In a later description by Lord Stanley of Alderley,[3] who had been a particular school friend of Little Augustus, the boy is said to have been warm-hearted, passionate and intrepid. He remained there several years but later moved to a school at Bury, which he was attending when his father made his will in May 1779. He was destined for the navy and soon after, at the age of 14 or so joined *Courageux*, whose captain was his cousin Constantine Phipps, 2nd Lord Mulgrave.

There is little direct information about the terms on which Bristol and Mrs Nesbitt lived together – no letters between them, and little in the way of comment from third parties. Sir John Stanley describes visits by Bristol to Loughborough House in which he was accompanied by Mrs Nesbitt and the couple took him and Little Augustus to St James's Square. Mrs Nesbitt certainly accompanied her protector to Nice in 1775,[4] but how closely she followed him from house to house in England is not clear, though Bristol's use of the word 'us' in referring to his presence at Ickworth in June 1776 seems telling.[5] That they lived in considerable intimacy is also shown by a comment[6] which she made during the administration of Bristol's will, to the effect that the linen at St James's Square was hers, it having travelled between Norwood and the London house as needed. Moreover, the will makes it clear how high a regard he had for his mistress, not only in the generous provision that he made for her but also in some of the wording and the fact that he desired that she should be buried with him in Ickworth church.

Bristol, however, in his own opinion and in the judgement of history, and in spite of the ruling of the Consistory Court in 1769, was still married to the woman then known as the Duchess of Kingston, the former Elizabeth Chudleigh. The existence of the marriage was widely suspected; Horace Walpole had his ear well to the ground and with his penchant for scandal and intrigue had been one of the first to appreciate the implications of George Earl of Bristol's illness, writing on 11 November 1774 to Sir Horace Mann as follows:[7]

The bigamist duchess is likely to become a real peeress at last, Lord Bristol has been struck with a palsy that has taken away the use of all his limbs. If he dies, and Augustus should take a fancy to marry again, as two or three years ago he had a mind to do, his next brother, the bishop, may happen to assist the Duke of Kingston's relations with additional proofs of the first marriage. They now think they shall be able to intercept the receipt of the Duke's estate; but the law is a horrid liar, and I never believe a word it says before the decision.

Though there is no evidence to support his comment on the Bishop of Derry

Walpole had indeed correctly highlighted the continuing saga of the so-called Duchess of Kingston's marital affairs, a saga from the trammels of which Hervey could not hope to escape. For if it was true that she had been married since 1744 to the new Earl of Bristol she now gained a second or alternative title. She was not in law the widowed Duchess of Kingston but was presumably Countess of Bristol, and the wife of a very rich man. It was, however, too late. Even if she had wished to claim Augustus as her husband, and a share of his income as hers, she had negated such a move by her marriage to the Duke and by the claims to his estate that she had made when he died in 1773.

The Duke's death and the testamentary arrangements that he had made left her in full control of his estate and in the benefit of the income from it. She was not, however, to remain for long in their undisputed enjoyment. Though the Duke had died childless there were nephews, children of his sister Lady Frances Meadowes. The eldest of them, Evelyn Meadowes, had been entirely disinherited by the Duke (according to the Duchess for a number of venal social offences, including mistreatment of a young lady and attempting to avoid service in the recent war), though the younger brothers were named as heirs after the death of their uncle's presumed widow.

Evelyn, knowing of the doubts about the legality of the Duke's marriage, contested the will by asserting that Miss Chudleigh was not the Duke's wife. To do this he did not rely on civil proceedings but sought evidence for a criminal charge of bigamy. Though the Consistory Court had ruled in 1769 that Miss Chudleigh was not married to Augustus Hervey, the decision was one on which many had had doubts. Hervey had made a weak and as some thought collusive defence and appeared himself, by not marrying elsewhere, not to accept the Court's ruling. Meadowes therefore began to look for witnesses who could support his case.

There were three, none of whom had given evidence before the Consistory Court. They were Ann Cradock, Caesar Hawkins and Judith Phillips, formerly the wife of Thomas Amis the clergyman who had performed the marriage ceremony in 1744. Meadowes and his lawyers continued with the preparation of their case and in the early summer of 1775, nearly two years after the death of the Duke and shortly after Hervey had succeeded to the earldom, a bill of indictment was presented to a Middlesex grand jury, charging the so-called Duchess with bigamy. The jury found that there was a case and the Duchess hastened back from Rome to answer it, since if she did not appear she was liable to a process of outlawry which would forfeit her property to the Crown.

Our knowledge of events is obscured by drama and gossip, much of the latter of the usual half-informed nature, leading to conflicting accounts of events preceding the trial and of the attitudes and motives of the witnesses and others closely involved. No matter; biographers of the Duchess are legion and the course of events only of indirect interest to the affairs of Augustus Earl of Bristol. In summary, the Duchess surrendered herself to the Sheriff of Middlesex, whereupon the Middlesex judiciary, aided by claims made by the Duchess, found that she was a peeress, and therefore could not be tried by the ordinary courts but only by the House of Lords. Occasions for the Lords to exercise their judicial power were infrequent, but as recently as 1760 they had tried Earl Ferrers for murder and condemned him to death. For bigamy, however, the penalties were less extreme, and there was no precedent for the trial of a peeress for this offence.

There was a further complexity in that, the charge being bigamy it followed that the prosecution did not believe the lady to be Duchess of Kingston at all and could not charge her as such – though if the charge was proved on the ground of her previous marriage to Hervey she would indisputably be Countess of Bristol. Naturally this perplexity provided the lawyers with material for extensive deliberation from which it eventually emerged that she might rightly be charged in the Lords as Elizabeth wife of Augustus John Hervey Esq., now Earl of Bristol.

These and other matters had taken time to resolve. The indictment was first brought to the Lords in November 1775 but it was not until 15 April 1776 that the trial began. It was a stately affair. To accommodate the lawyers and their hangers-on and more particularly to make room for the multitude of eager spectators the Lords had transferred themselves from their own chamber to Westminster Hall. The Queen and the Prince of Wales were present, together with a large representation from London society. One person who was not there was the Earl of Bristol, the man who the prosecution urged was the prisoner's true husband, and who as a member of the House of Lords was technically entitled to sit in judgement on his alleged wife. Bristol had gone abroad to Nice in the autumn of 1775 and remained there until after the trial, thus avoiding the problems which might have beset him if he had been called to give evidence – for who was more competent to do so than the true husband of the lady whom Walpole named the Countess-Duchess, and who could give a better account than any of the Lainston wedding and of its consummation at Lainston house?

When the proceedings opened the Lord High Steward read the indictment, to which the Duchess pleaded not guilty. The Solicitor-General stated the prosecution case and the Duchess immediately offered her defence, the findings of the Consistory Court in 1769, which concluded that she was not at that time married to Augustus Hervey. Since this Court had been competent to deal in marital affairs her argument had some force. There followed two days of protracted legal pleading on her claim, at the end of which the Lords decided that they were not bound by the lower court's findings, and that the case should continue.

The first witness was Ann Cradock, now an old lady. Her evidence was succinct and to the point: the marriage had taken place as described previously and had been consummated. The only uncertainty about her evidence was as to how much inducement she had been offered and by whom. It is probable that both the prisoner and Meadowes had at various times offered her financial support, and that she accepted it from Meadowes. Tainted therefore, her evidence may have been, but it has every appearance of being the truth. Caesar Hawkins gave evidence about the negotiations between Hervey and Miss Chudleigh before the jactitation case, evidence which can readily be considered unbiased and to the point – to the effect that the prisoner knew she had gone though a ceremony of a kind in 1744 and that there had been a baby which she had registered in the name of Hervey.

The third important witness was the widow of the clergyman Thomas Amis, since remarried to a man named Phillips, at one time steward to the Duke of Kingston. Mrs Phillips recounted Miss Chudleigh's visit to Winchester in 1758 or 1759 to fabricate a register and was then asked by the Solicitor-General, producing a book 'Can you be sure whether that is the book you have been speaking of?' There was no doubt in her mind, and the then rector, Mr Kinchin, was called to confirm that this was the register that he had been given after the death of the accused's relative Mr Merrill.

The defence did not produce anything of substance to contradict these witnesses and at the conclusion of the case the Lords gave their verdicts individually. All but one, when asked by the Lord High Steward, rose and said 'Guilty, upon my honour'. The exception was the Duke of Newcastle, one of the prisoner's closest supporters, who varied his verdict to 'Erroneously, but not intendedly guilty, upon my honour'.

The punishment for bigamy of branding on the hand was waived, the prisoner claiming 'benefit of clergy' as a peeress (presumably in her real title of Countess of Bristol) and the farce and farrago were over. As a matter of record she retained the Duke's estates and continued to be known as Duchess of Kingston. She lived abroad until her death in Paris in 1788.

The outcome of the bigamy trial left Lord Bristol apparently married to Elizabeth Chudleigh, and therefore to all appearance free to bring the suit for divorce for which he had been seeking an opening for nearly ten years. However, he made no immediate move to do so. His lawyers appear to have taken a cautious view of the Lords' decision, which seemed to overturn that of the Consistory Court in 1769. But the latter was an ecclesiastical court, not previously considered to be amenable to decisions by the royal courts, and there was still a danger that a suit for divorce would be thwarted by a claim, based on the 1769 decision, that the marriage had never existed.

Soon after the Lords' verdict, therefore, they gave notice to the countess to appear before the London Consistory Court and show cause why the ruling of the Court in 1769 should not be set aside. Bristol would then be free of any hindrance to asserting his marriage and the way would be open for him to sue for divorce. His Countess was by this time at Calais, where she was served with the notice on 26 June. This she ignored and on 3 July the case came before the Court, no defence being offered. The judge, however was reluctant to grant the request, since the Lords's verdict seemed to render such a revocation unnecessary, and also perhaps because the couple's affairs had been dragged, often with more than a whiff of collusion, though so many suits that he feared the same in this instance. There was considerable delay, therefore, and it was not until 22 January 1777 that the Court granted the request.

Though this declaration removed the last barrier to a suit for divorce no suit was brought. The reasons are unclear. Perhaps Bristol was still afraid of the legal process, or of the risk of a charge of collusion. Alternatively he may have had problems of conscience of a deeper nature. When in 1768 he had asked for a divorce and his wife had taken him to the Consistory Court he had offered an unnecessarily slender answer to her case, as if conscience would not let him abandon a marriage unless the other partner agreed with his course of action. If this was so it may be that the same qualms beset him in 1777; whatever the reason he remained locked into a meaningless and loveless marriage for the short remainder of his life.

The possibility of collusion, or even bribery, has been mentioned several times and seems to have hung like a miasma over the whole series of matrimonial cases between Bristol and his wife. The comment that 'Hervey lost reputation through his relations with his wife' in the *Dictionary of National Biography*[8] shows how widely the suppositions were given credit at the time. There were suggestions in 1769 that he had been threatened by 'Miss Chudleigh' that if he proceeded with his attempt to divorce her she would compel him, as her husband, to pay her debts of £16,000; later it was said that she had paid him a similar sum to mute his defence at the Consistory Court. In April 1776, at the time of the bigamy trial, Walpole wrote to Mann with an even wilder story:[9]

> . . . But if it is true that he [Bristol] has given her a bond of £30,000 not to molest her, and that this bond is in Lord Barrington's hands either she will recriminate, and collusion proved prevents a divorce; or his silence will speak a collusion.

Barrington was in fact called as a witness at the bigamy trial and at first refused to speak, on grounds of conscience and honour. Asked directly whether he knew anything about a bond he said he did not.

There seems, however, to be neither evidence that collusion occurred nor reasonable motive for Bristol to have engaged in such activity. As far as bribery goes, the 1769 rumours are readily explained by 'Miss Chudleigh's' empty threats about her debts. Bristol, for his part, was under no financial pressure at that time, having two official salaries, his half-pay and a substantial recent legacy from his mother. Suspicion of collusion at that time seems to derive solely from his half-hearted rebuttal of the jactitation case. This hesitation is equally well explained by his known desire, as expressed to Caesar Hawkins in 1768, not to force his wife into any action that was not acceptable to her.

In 1775–76 Bristol was abroad and the most he can be accused of is an unwillingness to expose himself to the embarrassment, as a peer, of being required to give evidence against his wife before the House of Lords. The existence of a £30,000 bond requires that his Countess had a massive hold of some kind over him, something for which there is no evidence or logical substance; indeed, the bond rumours seem to be put to flight by Barrington's evidence to the Lords. It may be concluded that irregular as Bristol's marital and extra-marital situations were it is difficult to accuse him of anything more than irresolution – both in 1769 in his answer to the jactitation charge and in 1777 when he failed to bring an action for divorce. Even a charge of irresolution is mitigated by an apparent reluctance to take any steps about his legal relationship with his wife without her full consent. If this amounted, in legal terms, to collusion, then it was an honourable variation on the offence.

Politically, in the meantime, Britain's relations with her American colonies and with the European powers had taken a turn for the worse. The quarrel with the Americans is well documented. It may be said to have begun in 1764 with Grenville's attempt to tax them by means of the Stamp Act. By March 1775, when Bristol left the Admiralty, the Tea Act of 1773 had given rise to the Boston tea party and in the following month further repressive measures resulted in fighting between British troops and the colonists at Lexington and Concord.

From this time there was a seeming inevitability in the increasing deter-mination of the colonists to assert their independence and the efforts of Lord North's government to prevent them doing so. British troops had their share of successes, capturing New York and Philadelphia, and throwing back an American attempt to invade Canada. The colonists, however, did quite enough to convince the French, who delighted in every British reverse, that they were a force to be reckoned with and in February 1778, nineteen months after the Declaration of Independence, the infant United States and France came to a formal alliance. Spain followed and it became only a matter of time before Britain was at war with both powers.

Such was the background to the last few years of Bristol's life, a period in which he passed from the support for Government implicit in his place as a Lord Commissioner of the Admiralty to downright and outspoken opposition. At the same time his long term friendship and co-operation with Lord

Sandwich became transmuted into an almost unbecoming antagonism, an antagonism which showed itself in persistent criticism of naval policy, dissatisfaction with the state of the navy and progressively harsher criticism of the First Lord. Though his campaign was conducted in a polite fashion as between two gentlemen it inevitably resulted in a permanent breach in their personal relationship.

As always it was on the navy that Bristol's thoughts were directed. When he left the Admiralty he had had some considerable responsibility for its direction and policies for over four years. It is not surprising, therefore that at that time he had a confident view of its state of preparedness, a view that is well expressed in the speech he prepared for the Commons debate on 13 February 1775 on additional supply for the navy.[10] He compliments Sandwich on his achievements and says that the ships are almost all repaired and in good condition, that the guardships are ready for service at short notice, that the strength of the navy exceeds that of France and Spain combined and that 'never was the navy of England in better condition'.

In May of the same year, two months after his resignation, he made his first speech in the Lords.[11] In a debate on repeal of the Quebec Government Act which had been sidetracked into a discussion of an apparent naval and military mobilization by Spain, he asked Sandwich for an assurance, which was duly given, that the navy was in a position to defend Gibraltar from a Spanish attack. In doing so he refers to 'the noble earl at the head of the Admiralty, who has, much to his honour, done more than any man who has resided at that board for upwards of a century . . .' and Sandwich in reply acknowledges Bristol's contribution to naval affairs.

Thus there was no immediate bitterness between them. However, Bristol now appears to have withdrawn for a period from public life as well as public office and no correspondence has survived for the next twelve months. The reasons for withdrawal were almost certainly of a private nature; perhaps it was his wife's forthcoming trial by the House of Lords as much as his health which later in 1775 led him to withdraw to Nice, where he appears to have remained until the early summer of 1776.

An indication of his state of mind on his return to England is given by a letter he wrote to Sandwich on behalf of Peter Foulkes, one of his oldest naval colleagues. It gives a strong impression that he was happy in his 'retirement' and had no ill feelings about the manner of his resignation:[12]

Ickworth Park June 17 1776

My Dear Lord

I was in hopes my retirement here, and my little consequence anywhere, would have freed me from any solicitations but I find that in spite of the many proofs of how little use I am to serve any of my followers at sea that some will still persist, and tho' I resist many, yet there is one who in justice to my own self I cannot help begging leave to your Lordship's favour. Tis one who many years ago I begged your Lordship to employ and serve, you made him my first lieutenant (which he also was in the year 1746 in the *Princessa*) when I was going out with Admiral Saunders [a reference to the mobilization against Spain in 1765] – Lieut Peter Foulkes, one of the oldest Lieuts in the service, and was one of the best officers, many disappointments of preferments has had, tho' appointed to command [a] frigate but never confirmed from the irregularity of the appointment, or more properly speaking the want of interest – he now asks to be employed . . . I wish your Lordship would set him down quietly at Greenwich Hospital some day, if he will consent, as I have little hopes now of ever giving or procuring for him that rank he had once a right to expect from his very long and good services – not only from me but from many flag officers he has served with . . . I am here in perfect health and retirement and shall be very happy when you have leisure and inclination to look upon us – for I always feel myself particularly wishful to believe your friendship . . .

During his naval service Bristol had of course acquired the usual collection of followers, officers and others who had served under him and who looked to him to use his influence to their advantage. There is little record of the use he made of the influence while at the Admiralty – it was not a period in which much patronage of this nature could be brought into effect – but now in 1776 there was at least one man who had not received the recognition that his long service suggested was his due. Foulkes had in fact been very unlucky, having twice been promoted into frigates 'by order', i.e. on the authority of the local Commander-in-Chief; once by Byng after the Battle of Mahon, when Bristol himself was moved into the 60-gun *Defiance* and Foulkes made captain of his former command *Phoenix*; and again by Rodney at Martinique. Neither appointment was confirmed by the Admiralty.

Sandwich replied in friendly terms, saying he would do what he could for Foulkes as soon as there was a vacancy, probably in a guardship. In due course he was appointed first lieutenant of *Queen* and Bristol was emboldened by this to ask in a letter to Sandwich dated 26 April 1777[13] to ask for his promotion. The letter ends 'If he cannot be made a Master and Commander he has only to lament having for his friend and patron . . . etc . . . Bristol.'

Sandwich refused, on the grounds that there were many other claimants and that a precedent would be set, and Bristol immediately reiterated his request. Nothing happened until the following December, when Sandwich wrote to Bristol[14] to tell him that Foulkes had at last been promoted. Bristol's letter of thanks[15] says all that was needed but there is a tinge of dissatisfaction in it that seems to reflect the increasingly critical attitude that he was by then taking to the actions and policies of the First Lord:

St James's Square Dec 13 1777

My Lord

I have just received the honor of your Lordship's letter and am very happy that your Lordship has at last rewarded Lt Foulkes' long and very good services: I confess that after finding 13 or 14 Lieutenants had been promoted here, it would have much mortified me, on his account, to have him still remain on the List of Lieutenants on mine.

Foulkes was eventually found a place a Greenwich Hospital and died about five years later.

In June 1776, then, Lord Bristol appeared after fifteen months retirement to be happy with his lot. However, the onset of war in America and the increasing tension with France and Spain soon brought him back to the centre of affairs, the adrenalin running again in his veins as after fourteen years ashore he sought a sea command. By October he is to be found at St James's Square writing to Sandwich offering his services. In his first letter,[16] after an appeal for employment for a Mr Lawrence 'an able and clever storekeeper at Woolwich' he continues without much sense of immediate purpose:

. . . you will be surprised to see me grown so young and active again after all my accidents [he had recently had a fall from his horse at Ickworth] but I am perfectly well and ready for any commands of yours, either to attack Brest or Ferrol, whenever *they* give you offence.

Six days later rumours of war stimulated him to a noticeably more purposeful request:[17]

St James's Square, October 30 1776

My Lord

I cannot sit still to hear that in consequence of France and Spain arming H M has been pleased to order an augmentation of his Naval Force, without offering my service thro' your Lordship to his Majesty, if it shall be thought that forty three years service [it was actually forty one] has entitled me to any consideration.

Wherever His Majesty thinks I can be of use to him I shall always be happy to obey, if my health permits.

So in becomingly friendly style began Bristol's long, persistent and ill-fated campaign for sea employment, a campaign which became increasingly ran-corous and intertwined with his developing opposition to the policies of the Admiralty and disillusionment with the person of the First Lord. Both sagas can be followed from Bristol's correspondence with Sandwich and from the proceedings of the House of Lords. The two earls were well matched. Bristol brought to the tussle his long experience of naval matters, his membership of the House of Lords, his access as a long-serving former courtier to the King, his rank – he was promoted to Rear-Admiral of the White in April 1777, to Rear-Admiral of the Red in January 1778 and to Vice-Admiral of the Blue later the same month – his facility with words, both written and spoken, and a certain dogged resolution which persisted almost to the end of his life, and which was only partially diminished by the ill health which continued to trouble him and to frustrate his ambitions; and there is no doubt that, his health set aside, his record gave him a good claim to employment as a flag officer. Sandwich knew this and said as much in the Lords in one of the later debates on naval affairs,[18] as late as February 1778, when the relationship between them was no longer a warm one. Indeed he was not at first against employing Hervey, but later opposed him with his equally long and deep knowledge of naval affairs and procedures, with delicate and oblique responses to his requests and with the power of his office, supplemented in the end, to Bristol's chagrin, by the support of the King. The First Lord's weakness was that he had already fallen out with several senior Admirals, some of whom refused to serve; not only was it important for him not to alienate any more but he was in fact short of suitable candidates for the more onerous commands.

Bristol's pursuit of sea employment is best told all of a piece. In following it the fact must be borne in mind that it was contemporaneous with the campaign of opposition to and criticism of the Admiralty in which he took a leading part in the Lords and elsewhere; it may indeed be thought that the careful way in which Sandwich handles his end of the correspondence reflects his desire not to exacerbate his former colleague. After his request of October 1776, which was ineffective, Bristol continued as a candidate for employment, though the matter did not come to a head until war with France became almost certain in the early spring of 1778. But before this Bristol's follower Captain Robinson had been appointed to *Queen*, suggesting that Sandwich had in mind to ask his lordship to hoist his flag in her in the event of mobilization. Such intention is confirmed by the First Lord's remark in the Lords on 16 February[19] to the effect that there was a ship ready for him in the event of mobilization. Bristol, who was engaged in a dispute with Sandwich on the navy's state of readiness, somewhat ingenuously denied knowledge of any such agreement. He went on to say that while he was obliged to the first Lord he would refuse to go on board. It appears that he considered her to be undermanned and in a poor state of repair, hardly fit to go to sea.

In early March Bristol seems to have been given an indication, apparently through his nephew Lord Mulgrave, by then a Lord of the Admiralty, that he might be given *Royal George*. Later in the month, however, Sandwich offered him *Queen* as his flagship,[20] the ship to which he had taken exception in the Lords just over a month previously:

Admiralty March 17 1778

My Lord

As all the ships in readiness for service are ordered to assemble at Spithead without delay I take the liberty to ask you without an official notification whether your health will allow you to hoist your flag on board the *Queen* as soon as she arrives at Portsmouth, her destination will probably be to cruize to the westward under the command of Admiral Keppel for the protection of the Home Seas.

I flatter myself that your Lordship will be convinced that my reason for asking whether your health will permit you to go to sea at this time, is, because I think it my duty to point out to His Majesty the ablest and best officers in his service as those most proper to be employed in the present important crisis; and that I might not make any arrangement with regard to the Admirals that are immediately to go to sea, 'till I knew your determination upon this subject.

This was a crucial letter as far as Bristol's naval future was concerned. Sandwich was in fact offering him the second position in the fleet that was preparing under Keppel, the position that was held later (including at the Battle of Ushant in July that year) by Sir Robert Harland. Both Keppel and Bristol were aligned with the First Lord's political opponents, and it is consistent with Sandwich's policies in making critical sea appointments (as distinct from filling shore or Admiralty posts) that the best available man should be given the job. If this were the only factor it might be concluded that Sandwich had a high opinion of Bristol as a sea-officer, high enough to appoint him over many other flag officers of repute including his own supporter Sir Hugh Palliser, whom he appointed to the third position. The problem, of course was Bristol's health. Was Sandwich in reality giving him a free decision on whether he felt that his health would allow him to take up the command? Or did he judge when he wrote the letter either that Bristol was suffering from such a severe attack of gout that he had no choice but to refuse, or that he would so object to *Queen* that he would not accept her? The answer is surely that Sandwich, manipulator of men as he was, was acting in a clearcut and straightforward manner, which coincided with his own and the Government's interest; there can be little argument that Bristol, if in good health, was the best man, or one of the best men, available, and that Sandwich acknowledged him to be so − witness his many encomiums on his naval abilities throughout the period in which they were in dire disagreement on political and strategic matters. It is equally true that if Bristol went to sea one of the Government's principal critics would not have an additional grudge to nurse against the First Lord and would have been absent from his place in the House of Lords. It may be noted, also, that a certain level of disability was accepted in senior officers, and that illness was not necessarily a bar to success. Two years after these events Rodney destroyed a Spanish squadron blocking his approach to Gibraltar while incapable of rising from his cot below decks; and Howe won the Glorious First of June seated in an arm chair on his quarterdeck.

Bristol, however, was in doubt. He replied the same day from 'my bed to which I am at present confined with the gout'.[21] The key sentence reads as follows; 'I return my thanks for your Lordship's attention; at the same time [I] acquaint your Lordship that my health at present obliges me to decline undertaking a cruize of that sort'. To this he appended a fervent declaration of his desire to serve as soon as his health permitted. Perhaps he was having a bad day, or it may be that he was hoping for a command in waters and under a sun that would be kinder to his gout. Indeed, only four days later he felt able to ask Sandwich for just that, writing from St James's Square[22] and after asking a favour for a Lieutenant Fraser in terms suggesting he thought he still had a lien on *Queen* continuing.

> I hope in a few days to be able to pay my duty to His Majesty but before I do so, shall endeavour to see your Lordship and acquaint you of my wishes, of being appointed to the Mediterranean Command, as I have long pointed out to your Lordship if a French war took place, I flatter myself I could be of as much service as anyone to his Majesty in that Command, having long considered and digested the various Objects and Services relative thereto.

In the light of Bristol's refusal of *Queen*, Sandwich clearly considered that both requests were completely unreasonable and was quick to reply in no uncertain terms:[23]

Admiralty, March 22 1778

My Lord

Your Lordship having in your former letter signified that your health would not permit you to cruize to the westward in the *Queen* I considered that ship as disposable, and have offered her to Sir Robert Harland . . . I should think the command in the Mediterranean could not be in better hands than your Lordship's, but as there is a senior officer now in possession of that command, I should fear this will be a difficulty not easily removed.

The only crumb of comfort that he offered was that Bristol might have Lieutenant Fraser as one of his officers if he went to sea.

In retrospect it can be seen that Bristol's refusal in his letter of 17 March was fatal to his hopes of further sea service. His motives may have been pique at being offered *Queen* after the comments he had made about her, or that he thought he had a lien on an alternative command, perhaps *Royal George,* or the stated one of gout. His downfall may be said to be his characteristic impetuosity in replying to Sandwich so precipitately. The First Lord would have waited a day or two for a considered reply, and by delaying Bristol would have given himself opportunity to consider his option. But he did not do so and the rest of the tale is one of obstinate pertinacity on his part against a diplomatic but equally obstinate First Lord.

Queen had been given to Harland and in the normal practice of the day the officers appointed earlier when she was tentatively chosen to fly Bristol's flag were removed and replaced by those chosen by Sir Robert. Naturally this was a cause of anxiety to the removed officers and in late April Bristol wrote to Sandwich asking that they be appointed to *Royal George*, relying presumably on the communication that he had had with Lord Mulgrave in March:[24]

St James's Square April 25 1778

My Lord

The Captain [Robinson] of His Majesty's ship *Queen* acquainting me, that the six lieutenants and master of that ship being superseded, and that himself is to be so, as soon as Captain Prescott arrives, and these officers being very uneasy at their present distressful situation, having no orders relative to their appointment to the *Royal George*, I hope your Lordship will give immediate directions therein, that what I am persuaded has been omitted by the great Hurry of Business . . .

To this Sandwich had an immediate and adequate reply:[25]

Admiralty April 29 1778

My Lord

I am honoured with your Lordship's letter of 26th instant to which I can only say in answer that as you had declined going to sea in the *Queen*, it was according to the constant usage necessary to remove her officers for the convenience of the Admiral who is to hoist his flag in her . . .

With regard to the *Royal George* I understand it will be many months before she can be ready for service; and I do not understand that anything that has passed between your Lordship and me has fixed any particular arrangement concerning her; as I apprehend that the mode and time of your being employed remains as you left it in your last letter, namely 'till you had an opportunity of laying your wishes before our Royal Master'.

In this letter a rather different view of Sandwich's wishes can be detected, a change of heart which surely derives from Bristol's refusal of *Queen*. He also shows his hand by using Bristol's appeal to the King to delay matters, probably in the full confidence that in the end His Majesty would accept his First Lord's advice. Bristol however, returned to the fray:[26]

St James's Square April 30 1778

My Lord

I had just last night the honor of your Lordship's letter and shall now only say, that when the *Royal George* was ordered to be fitted out for the reception of them I desired Lord Mulgrave (the 9th of March last) to acquaint your Lordship that I should be glad of that ship being fitted for me, and to have the officers, and my own immediate followers then in the *Queen* removed to the *Royal George*.

Lord Mulgrave brought me for answer – that I might certainly have the *Royal George*, and my officers in her, but the men I could not, as the *Queen* was wanted, and could not be dismantled, and added – that your Lordship had mentioned it to our Royal Master, who had been graciously pleased to approve. My health not permitting me to hoist my flag in the *Queen* for this cruize, I flattered myself the *Royal George*, according to my request and your Lordship's promise would have been appointed to receive those officers, when you thought proper to supersede them in the *Queen*.'

In response Sandwich gave no ground but continued to play for time while being as conciliatory as possible on the matter of employing Bristol's officers:[27]

Portsmouth May 3 1778

My Lord

The message I sent to your Lordship by Lord Mulgrave was, that I saw no objection to your Lordship having the *Royal George* when she was ready for sea, but that was at a distance; Lord Mulgrave very well recollects that this was all that passed between us on the subject

I now repeat to you what I then said to Lord Mulgrave, and shall add that the *Royal George* is still unengaged; but I understand that she wants much more repair than was at first expected, and that she will not be ready to be commissioned these five or six months.

By your Lordship's former letter I apprehended that everything relative to your having a Command remained in suspense 'till you had seen the King; therefore, had the above mentioned or any other ship been ready, I should not have thought of ordering her to be fitted for your reception, till I had heard from you again.

With regard to Captain Robinson and the late Lieutenants of the *Queen*, if they desire to be employed I will find them employment; and if they are within reach when your Lordship hoists his flag they or any other Captain and Lieutenants shall be appointed to serve under you.

Bristol had appealed unto Caesar, and to Caesar he should go.

There was a long and unexplained delay before he had an audience of the

King and when he did his understanding of the outcome was different to His Majesty's. Bristol wrote to Sandwich with his version:[28]

St James's Square July 9th 1778

My Lord

I was obliged to go out of town without having an opportunity of acquainting your Lordship that his Majesty was graciously pleased to honour me with an audience, and to accept my offers of service, my health being thoroughly re-established; at the same time I expressed my wishes, that the officers superseded in the *Queen* should be appointed to the *Royal George* as your Lordship had promised me – I understand that ship will be completely ready the 29th inst, but is now in a state for receiving them, and fitter than many others that have been commissioned in that situation – I hope your Lordship will therefore let those officers be appointed to her, and whenever his Majesty pleases I shall be happy to contribute my services when and where he pleases . . .

Bristol, however, had misinterpreted the King's attempts to mollify him without committing himself or Sandwich to giving him a command. Sandwich wrote back immediately, and whatever the rights and wrongs of the matter it is the men in charge who have the last effective word:[29]

Admiralty July 9th 1778

My Lord

I cannot agree that I promised your Lordship the *Royal George* when she should be ready for sea, I refer your Lordship particularly to my letter of the 29th of April last, in which I said that I did not understand that anything that had passed between us had fixed any particular arrangement concerning that ship, but that things were to remain as you had left them in your last letter, namely till you had had an opportunity of laying your wishes before our Royal Master; in that state they did remain 'till after your late audience, when I received the King's commands to give the *Royal George* to Sir Robert Harland whose officers are to be appointed to her without further delay.

Bristol made one last attempt, this time bypassing Sandwich and making an appeal to the King through the Earl of Suffolk, then Secretary of State, and using the actual declaration of war with France as the occasion:[30]

Ickworth Park August 7th 1778
To the King

Sir

Your Majesty having thought proper by your declaration to open hostilities with France, and my health being so perfectly re-established; I cannot resist throwing myself once more at Your Majesty's feet, to repeat my offer of service at this time to Your Majesty, in any manner, time or place Your Majesty shall think proper to employ me; Nor would I, Sir, trouble Your Majesty again on this occasion, could I resist the most anxious ardour which I feel, to devote my life and fortune to Your Majesty's and my country's service in that profession in which I have served forty-four years. The manner in which I have always served, and the justness and goodness of Your Majesty's heart, leaves me not the least doubt of Your Majesty's favourable reception of this my most humble and repeated request; and whatever may be the fate of my application to Your Majesty only I shall ever remain, what I hope I have ever been with the greatest respect and warmest attachment.

Sir, Your Majesty's most faithful and
dutiful servant and subject
Bristol

There is no record of a reply or of further correspondence on the subject, but the outcome was predictable; Lord Bristol did not serve at sea again. It makes a sad and sorry story and apart from Bristol's personal disappointment must have had a marked effect on his political relationship with Sandwich, which continued to deteriorate. Sandwich for his part, seems rightly to have been willing in March 1778 to appoint Bristol to a command suited to his experience and abilities, had his health allowed. When Bristol refused the First Lord seems to have decided against any further offer, but used soft words to drag out the discussions, hoping to avoid an irreparable breach with yet another senior naval figure. In this he failed, as can be seen in the long saga of Bristol's passage from his place in Government in early 1775 to downright opposition to Admiralty policies, and to the petition for the First Lord's removal from office.

References

1. PRO, C12/431/36
2. Quoted in Adeane, 1899
3. Quoted in Stuart, 1936
4. PRO, C12/431/36
5. NMML, Sandwich Papers, F9/8
6. PRO, C12/431/36
7. Lewis, 1937–83, (24\)0, p88
8. *Dictionary of National Biography*, (9), p730
9. Lewis, 1937–83, (24), p106
10. SRO(B), 941/50/5, p483
11. Cobbett, 1806–20, vol XVIII, col 667 et seq
12. NMML, Sandwich Papers, F9/8
13. Ibid., F10/85
14. Ibid., F11/108
15. Ibid., F11/109
16. Ibid., F9/70
17. Ibid., F9/77
18. SRO(B), 941/50/5, p721
19. *General Advertiser & Morning Intelligencer*, 18 February 1778
20. NMML, Sandwich Papers, F13/25
21. Ibid., F13/26
22. Ibid., F13/38
23. Ibid., V13
24. Ibid., F13/118
25. Ibid., V13
26. Ibid., F13/136
27. Ibid., F14/15
28. Ibid., F15/21
29. Ibid., F15/22
30. SRO(B), 941/50/5, p759

CHAPTER XVII

The Declining Years

A death too soon

The political dimension to Bristol's campaign against Sandwich and the Admiralty had been slow to develop. Indeed, it seems wrong to describe his attitude as entirely 'against', and thus negative, when his speeches in the Lords mark him as having two very positive objectives – a deep care for the prosperity of his country and for the well-being of the navy which he regarded, rightly, as its prime defence. Nevertheless, his attitude cannot have been unaffected by his personal transactions with Sandwich, nor by the thought that the First Lord had let him down.

After Bristol left the Admiralty in 1775 he was at first careful to make comments and ask questions which did not imply criticism of the Department in which he had so recently served. An example of this nature is provided by his contribution to the debate in the Lords on 17 May 1775 – peculiarly, a debate on the Quebec Government Act which had been sidetracked into a discussion on the recent Spanish mobilization of troops and ships in and around Cadiz.[1] Bristol was concerned that they might be intended for a surprise attack on Gibraltar, in which case, he asked Sandwich, had the Admiralty enough ships in readiness to send out a squadron. Sandwich indicated that the guardships would provide seventeen of the line for immediate service (a state of affairs for which Bristol himself could claim some of the credit) and all passed off in friendly fashion. Bristol paid compliments to Sandwich – 'who has, much to his honour, done more than any man who has presided at that board for upwards of a century' – and Sandwich returned them – 'I must confess I have great reason to regret [Bristol's] absence [from the Admiralty]'.

For the next year Bristol took little part in Lords affairs, being abroad or retired at Ickworth for much of the time. Illness also played a part in keeping him from Parliament when he dearly desired to make a case. In October 1776, however, he closed the debate in the Lords on the motion for an address in reply to the King's speech, normally an opportunity to support Government, with an account of the good state of the navy and the high qualities of the First Lord. He did this, moreover in a period during which the Admiralty were accused more than once by extreme members of the opposition of neglect of the navy and of having an insufficient number of ships available. Though this insufficiency was only marginal so far as the navy's commitments to the war in America were concerned the shadow of war with France and Spain as well as with the Americans became more threatening during 1777 and 1778, and alarm about the navy's ability to cope with this wider range of commitments became more audible.

It was at this difficult stage – difficult largely because of the economies which Lord North's government had found expedient – that Bristol became actively engaged. He spoke in the Lords on 16 February 1778 in a debate on the state of the nation, a speech[2] in which he gave a dolorous assessment of government policies towards America, of their ineffectiveness and of the waste of money – vast sums of money – attending their execution. He was at pains, however, to emphasize that he had no connections with either Government or Opposition and that at this stage he still did not consider himself a party man. He praised Sandwich for his abilities and for the assiduity with which he had carried forward his duties at the Admiralty, but continued with a sombrely eloquent warning on the tasks ahead, one of the most striking examples of the eloquence of which he had always been capable.

> . . . when this great fleet . . . is to be put in motion and all its detail attended to; the different proper dispositions made of it, with proper Commanders-in-Chief to the different stations. I say, my Lords, when all this is to be put properly in motion, when the calm in which his Lordship has so long presided is ruffled and the storm begins to blow from every quarter, his Lordship must excuse me if I do assure him, that old and experienced as he may think himself in that office, he has yet an apprenticeship to learn in that profession.

A stern warning indeed, but of a future which in the next two years Sandwich met with tolerable competence, even if he did not cover himself with glory.

The speech concluded with an offer from Bristol to serve King and country in any position offered without taking a penny in pay or emoluments. When next he spoke, three days later[3] questioning Sandwich's account of the number of ships in readiness it was evident from his exchange with the First Lord that Bristol's sources and contacts gave a very different view of the navy's readiness, both in numbers and state of ships, to the public Admiralty account.

A fortnight later, on 2 March 1778 the Duke of Bolton, one of the more forthright if not more intelligent of the 'retired' admirals of the day, instigated a debate on the state of the navy,[4] accusing the Admiralty of incompetence and of mis-representing the fleet's degree of preparation. Bristol supported Bolton, saying that the Duke had 'fully convinced me of the [poor] state of our forces at home and abroad and of the enormous expense it has already been to this country these last three years to so little purpose'.

In defending his record Sandwich threw the blame for the deficiencies onto Hawke, his predecessor as First Lord, saying that he had found the guardships to be rotting away. Bristol immediately sprang to Hawke's defence and said that there were other reasons for reorganizing the guardships that did not reflect on Hawke's period in office. He seems to have been satisfied that he had defended Hawke's name adequately for he wrote to the Admiral[5] saying:

I wish to let you know particularly how happy I have been again in the opportunity of doing justice to your Lordship's most valuable name in every respect, when I thought Lord Sandwich threw out insinuations . . .

But the two earls remained on superficially congenial terms. To Bristol Sandwich was emollient, referring to the noble Earl whose professional qualities he highly extolled and whom he could assure that he need not be afraid to trust himself aboard Queen, in which as already shown he appeared to intend that Bristol should raise his flag. Bristol, however, queried the state of Queen and her manning saying that a crew of 600 men was entirely inadequate for a 74, and that '. . . I shall always be ready to serve my king and country when I am wanted; but I will ever persist in my determination not to go aboard any ship so manned . . .'

In spite of his comments on 16 February Bristol was clearly already beginning to turn towards and give comfort to the Opposition. The debate on 2 March was acrimonious, but the Government won the vote by 64 to 38 (though 16 of the majority were bishops). Nevertheless, as recorded earlier none of this put Sandwich off offering Bristol Queen a few days later.

Bristol's next public expostulation on the state of British naval affairs was in a debate in the Lords on 25 May,[6] initiated by the Duke of Richmond, one of the principal members of the opposition. In the interval Augustus Keppel, by then an Admiral of the White, had been appointed Commander-in-Chief of the Channel Fleet which in May was reviewed, thirty-one strong, by the King at Spithead. Also in the meantime the French Toulon squadron had sailed, passed through the Straits of Gibraltar unhindered and was either making for Brest to join the considerable squadron there or was on its way to America, where its presence would have grave implications for British naval operations.

Bristol, weak and lame from gout, dragged himself to the Lords and supported Richmond's attack. Why had no squadron been sent to Gibraltar to bar the Toulon squadron's way? Why had no proper watch been kept on either Toulon or Brest? Why, if as Sandwich said forty-nine ships of the line were ready, had it only been possible to assemble thirty-one at Spithead? Why indeed bring them to Spithead, which was much inferior to Plymouth or Torbay as a base for watching the French at Brest? And what had happened to the eighty-one ships of the line fit for service in 1771 when Bristol himself first became a member of the Board? It was a speech which did not lack for critical content, though in fact it may be thought that the policy of economy and the time needed to develop a long term dockyard and shipbuilding programme were more important underlying problems than mismanagement by the First Lord.

Bristol spoke again on 2 June[7] when the Duke of Bolton moved to defer Prorogation of Parliament because of the parlous and dangerous state of the nation's affairs. His contribution was again to deplore the freedom allowed to the Toulon squadron and to bandy numbers of ships with the First Lord. He was profuse with praise for Keppel as Commander-in-Chief but criticized Sandwich for limiting his control of the fleet. He had by this stage dropped any pretence of geniality and referred to Sandwich's 'Machiavellian policy', accusing him of endeavouring to ridicule arguments and facts that he could not contravene.

In spite of the protests Parliament was prorogued and Bristol spent much of the summer at Ickworth. Before he returned to the parliamentary fray in November much had happened at sea and much dissent had been aroused in the navy by the repercussions of events. To understand the background to his actions later in the year and in the early months of 1779 it is necessary to describe Keppel's action off Ushant in July and the quarrel that developed between the Commander-in-Chief and Vice-Admiral Sir Hugh Palliser, who commanded one of the divisions of the fleet.

Politically, Keppel was one of the principal followers of the Marquis of Rockingham and thus an opponent of the Government. His appointment had been queried on these grounds but can be justified by his experience as a young commodore in the previous war and by the scarcity of other suitable candidates. Nevertheless Keppel was encouraged by his political friends to treat Sandwich as an opponent who might sacrifice him to save the face of the Administration, and comparisons were even made with Byng's fate twenty years earlier. Keppel may even have been tempted to believe that a modest failure at sea might be blamed on Admiralty and Government negligence and lead to a change of government and to his own advancement to First Lord.

There was thus a lack of harmony in naval affairs and when Keppel took the fleet to sea in June and quickly returned to Portsmouth on the grounds that the French appeared to be stronger (an eventuality covered in his orders) Government and Parliament were much disturbed. Sandwich went down to Portsmouth and exerted himself to get the fleet to sea again. When in July Keppel did so his numbers were close enough to those of the French to encourage him actively to seek an engagement. Late in the month in light winds off Ushant he came near to the French fleet under the Comte d'Orvilliers and manoeuvred to join battle.

It was not easy, however, to bring a cautious enemy to an engagement.

British tactics were almost always to engage the enemy, the British aim to destroy the enemy fleet. The French, in contrast, placed the emphasis on maintaining a fleet in being and were only ready to engage in particularly favourable circumstances. Their circumspection was aided by the limitations of the naval tactics of the day. The only approved method of engagement was to form in line ahead and approach the enemy's line, which would normally have adopted the same formation. A formed line, however, was a formidable organization, in approaching which considerable damage might be expected from its gunfire. Moreover, even if the attacking fleet had the weather gage (i.e. was approaching from the windward side) it was comparatively easy for the other fleet to slip away and avoid battle.

So on 27 July Keppel gained the weather gage and approached d'Orvilliers' line. It was a slanting approach, however, and only one of Keppel's divisions, that commanded by Palliser, came near to engaging the enemy. There was a short, sharp, inconclusive exchange of fire in which several of Palliser's ships suffered considerable damage to masts and rigging before the French fleet drew off and disappeared into the haze. The battle of Ushant was over. Keppel retired to Plymouth for necessary repairs to his damaged ships and the French went back into Brest.

Though the British government and public opinion were disappointed it was generally considered, at least at first, that Keppel had done his duty and that no blame attached to him for failing to win a great victory. There were, however, those who cast doubts on Palliser's part in the battle, suggesting that commanding the leading division of the fleet he had not done enough to bring the French to battle. But any failure in this respect could be attributed to damage to Palliser's flagship and to signalling difficulties and Keppel had not sought to throw any blame on his subordinate. It was not until October, while the fleet was at sea, that an offensive letter from one of Keppel's officers (thought to have been his nephew Lieutenant Berkeley) cast all the responsibility for the French escape on Palliser, who immediately took the view (probably wrongly) that the letter reflected Keppel's own views. There developed a bitter row, which the 'friends' of each protagonist did their best to exacerbate, and early in December Palliser was moved to ask formally for a court martial on his Commander-in-Chief, alleging negligence in the face of the enemy; the same charge as that laid against Byng twenty years earlier, and the same confrontation between two admirals as had been allowed to develop after the inconclusive Battle of Toulon over forty years beforehand.

Since Keppel was a prominent member of the opposition while Palliser was a supporter of Sandwich, a Lord of the Admiralty and very much a government man the quarrel spread out into the body politic and throughout the politicized corps of naval officers. Bristol had immediately taken Keppel's part and in a speech in the Lords on 26 November[8] supported the

Commander-in-Chief, asked why Sandwich had not ordered a Court of Enquiry on the 'National Disappointment' (as he described Ushant) and castigated Palliser for attacking Keppel. When after Palliser's request Sandwich ordered a court martial on Keppel Bristol is to be found organizing a petition to the King asking for the withdrawal of the charges. He was particularly active in this and persuaded many peers and senior naval officers including Hawke, who was by this time very much a father figure of the navy, to sign; some of them it is said subsequently regretted their actions. The petition was duly presented to the King and as duly ignored. Keppel was tried at Portsmouth amidst great exitement and acquitted on all charges. When the news reached London Bristol's house in St Jame's Square was brightly illuminated in approval of the verdict, though on the other side of the coin some of Keppel's supporters showed their approval in a less savoury way by rioting and attacking Palliser's London house.

As a sequal the opposition moved in Parliament for a court martial on Palliser. He was acquitted of cowardice but reprimanded for failing to inform Keppel of the damage to his ships; opinion ran so strongly against him that he was forced to resign his offices and his seat in Parliament.

Illness then kept Bristol from the House until 24 March 1779. On that day Sandwich defended himself by accusing Bristol, in his speech of 26 November, of asking for a court martial on Keppel and Bristol refuted the allegation,[9] saying that Keppel (a member of the Commons) had asked him to draw the attention of the Lords to Palliser's comments and publications about him and to say that the Commander-in-Chief would no longer be prepared to serve with the Vice-Admiral. He did not, he said, ask for a court martial but for a court of enquiry. (The draft of his speech of 26 November,[10] however, does mention a court martial as well as a court of enquiry, but surely refers this to Palliser, not Keppel.) Bristol's whole tenor throughout this speech of 24 March shows how his exasperation with and antipathy to Sandwich were increasing almost daily.

The next step in the saga, indeed its climax, came in the following month. The Opposition decided to move in both Houses for the removal of Sandwich from office, a dire step even in the acid politics of this stage of the war. Bristol, who by now had become a prominent member of the Rockingham Whig Opposition led for them in the Lords. The debate was set for 16 April but in the meantime Sandwich suffered a dire and entirely unexpected bereavement. His long term mistress Martha Ray was murdered in London. In this personal disaster we see a brief return to the old friendship between the two earls, when Sandwich writes to Bristol asking for a postponement of the debate[11] and Bristol willingly accedes:

Ickworth Park, 12 April 1779

My Lord

I have this moment the honour of receiving your Lordship's letter of yesterday; and though I had not such an application from your Lordship, yet, from the very instant I heard of your misfortune, I felt too much for it not to have determined that no consideration should induce me to bring on any business that might be disagreeable to your Lordship to attend to till it was more convenient for you. I am at present not very well with a touch of the gout, and shall therefore desire some of my friends to give that as my reason to the House for desiring to put off the business alluded to till I am able to attend.

I must also beg that your Lordship will do me the justice to believe that there is no man in this world who felt more for you on this occasion nor who can be more concerned than I am for any interruption to your domestic felicity, I have etc.

On 23 April Bristol opened the debate. It was a long speech[12] in which he reiterated his charges that the Admiralty (and the noble Lord at its head in particular) had mismanaged the country's naval affairs since the outbreak of hostilities with France the previous year, had by its own account exaggerated the numbers of ships available (as shown by comparison with Bristol's numbers for those in service on the various stations) and since 1771 had spent over £17 million to little effect. Sandwich was berated as 'the . . . baneful influence [which] prevails, and the same baneful ignorance, fallacy and obstinacy [which] presides over that department . . .', and much more. Bristol ended by moving for the First Lord's removal from office, the least punitive measure, he said, that was available to deal with the situation.

Sandwich defended himself by retreating behind the doctrine of cabinet responsibility and by bandying numbers of ships and availability of supplies with Bristol and others. He came out of the argument well enough to retain the support of his political friends in the House, the motion being lost by 78 votes to 39.

The tenor of Bristol's speech was such as to make it obvious that all his friendship and past association with Sandwich had fallen away to nothing – or at least to nothing but remote memories of better times. It is not difficult to list the reasons behind this attack on Sandwich, reasons which include Bristol's patriotism, his political *rapprochement* with the Opposition and his personal disappointment at his treatment by Sandwich in the previous year, but it is not easy to apportion his motivation among them. It has sometimes been suggested that he was activated by designs on the First Lordship for himself, and this may well have entered his thoughts. He cannot, however, have thought in April 1779 that removing the Government's First Lord –

Lord North and the King's First Lord – would have led in itself to his elevation in this way. For this to happen would have required the whole Government to be so unstabilized by the First Lord's removal that it was replaced by Rockingham and his Whig supporters.

There is in fact evidence[13] that Bristol had by this time come closer to Rockingham's group and in particular to his principal lieutenant the Earl of Shelburne, though the correspondence does not indicate any incisive meeting of minds. It does, however, suggest that he had found a successor to Grenville and Sandwich as his chosen political patron, though too late for anything to come of it. He had in any case only a few more months to live, and the rather scrappy correspondence with Shelburne suggests that the sharpness of his mind was no longer what it had been.

Bristol was to speak in two further debates in the Lords. On 2 June Shelburne introduced a motion deploring the current state of Ireland, a genuine subject for debate and one on which there was much scope to suggest necessary improvements. Bristol while agreeing with the need for Government action characteristically made a forthright speech about the navy and the dire state of national affairs, with war against Spain expected daily, and attributed all Britain's and Ireland's woes to Government mismangement,[14] a fine example of irrelevance and of the introduction into the Lords of King Charles's head.

He spoke again on 25 June[15] in a debate on two bills, one for doubling the militia and the second for the better manning of the navy. Predictably, he considered it more important that the navy should get the men it needed, but in his principal speech – he made at least five interventions – he went once again over the ground which he had covered in asking for Sandwich's dismissal on 24 April. It is again evident from the general lack of incision in his comments that he was less capable than he had been of making good debating points. The debate was in fact the last occasion on which he spoke.

There is little to say about the last few months of Bristol's life. His gout was increasingly troublesome, with pain in his feet making him lame at times, or confining him to bed. Apart from severe colds there is no mention of any illness other than gout, to which seems to have been attributed the weakness and the severe pains in the intestinal regions ('gout in the stomach') to which he was also subject. He suffered also from fits of some kind which may or may not have been associated with his gout.

After speaking in the Lords on 25 June he went to Ickworth, always his favoured residence, and probably spent most of the summer there. He still travelled, however, and in September he was south of London on a round of visits which included Horace Walpole at Twickenham[16] and in December, for the last sad and painful days, was at St James's Square. The desultory correspondence with Shelburne continued, while among his long-standing friends Lord Pembroke continued to write to him and in his kindness encouraged his son Lord Herbert to do so as well.

In the four years and eight months that Bristol enjoyed the title and estates he seems to have made few changes. In 1778 he made a number of improvements to Ickworth church, which stands in the centre of the park and had been the burial place of the Hervey family for many years. He provided additional burial space at the east end, laid a grey marble floor in the chancel and built the red brick tower.

Most of the landed property had been entailed by the 2nd Earl. This entailed property would willy-nilly pass on Augustus's death to the next heir and could not be diverted to the benefit of his own dependents, his mistress Mrs Nesbitt and his son Little Augustus. Fortunately, however, after making his will George William had bought several lots of land in Suffolk and Lincolnshire, and these had come to Augustus without entail. To this free estate Augustus added in 1778 a substantial estate at Evedon in Lincolnshire which brought in a net income of between £600 and £700. He thus had enough free property to enable him to make provision for those he loved.

In the last cold days of 1779 the ill health which had dogged him for so many years at last overcame him. At three o'clock in the morning of 22 December he died at the family's London house in St James's Square. William Hervey was at his bedside, as was Mrs Nesbitt, faithful to the last; but a few hours later she left the house, giving all the keys to the dead Earl's brother, never to enter it again. The reported cause of death was 'gout of the stomach', that widely reported but not readily identifiable condition which affected so many in that day and age. A strong possibility however, is that death was due to kidney failure, often associated with long-term gout. On the 28th of the month Augustus Earl of Bristol was buried with his ancestors in the vaults of Ickworth church, which he had renovated only a year previously. He left instructions in his will that Mrs Nesbitt should in due course lie beside him.

Walpole was as usual quick to make a flippant but appropriate comment.[17]

> Lord Bristol has outran me, and leaves an Earl-Bishop and a Countess-Duchess.

Augustus, 3rd Earl of Bristol was indeed succeeded by his brother Frederick, Bishop of Derry since 1768 and to be known to posterity by Walpole's soubriquet. The enmity between the two brothers had, however, persisted and the new Earl inherited only that upon which the law insisted. The property – St James's Square, Ickworth and the older estates – was subject to entail, but Frederick is on record as complaining that Augustus had so rigorously worded his will that he deprived him even of the deer in Ickworth Park. Frederick, however, held the title and estate for twenty-four years, much of the time as an absentee, and was responsible for the building of the great house that stands in the centre of Ickworth Park today. It is from him that all subsequent holders of the Bristol title are descended.

Augustus's will dated 20 May 1779 was in essence a simple document, its objectives being to ensure that Mrs Nesbitt and his son Little Augustus were well provided for, and that his legal heir received only his minimum legal entitlement. To ensure that his wishes were carried out in spirit as well as letter the executors were Mrs Nesbitt, his brother Colonel William Hervey and the Earl of Coventry.

All the free landed estate in Lincolnshire and Suffolk was left to Mrs Nesbitt (whom he describes as his dear, valuable, best friend) for her life and then to Little Augustus, while all monies and personal estate were left equally to these two. Little Augustus was also left an income of £300 from the estate until he came of age, and then £400, a rather more generous provision than the £50 made for Augustus by his grandfather, though the 1st Earl did have many more descendants to provide for. There were a number of personal bequests and pensions — to his 'worthy friend Thomas Pennington my steward', his bailiff at Ickworth Robert Freeman, his mulatto servant and his *valet de chambre*. All his papers relative to the sea were left to his nephew Lord Mulgrave, who had one of the best naval libraries of the time. Unfortunately, it seems to have been dispersed on his death and almost all Bristol's papers disappeared from view — the only important exceptions being his *Journal* and the account of his part in the attack on Cartagena.

Two unsigned codicils were written on the will. One gave 'my gold box set round with diamonds which the Emperor gave me with his and the Empress' picture set on the top' (given to him in 1748 for services rendered, in particular for saving the Emperor's port of Leghorn from damage when *Caledonia* caught fire the previous year) to Little Augustus with the wish that he should leave it within the family. Little Augustus left the box to William Hervey. Several years after the young man's death it was seen in Mrs Nesbitt's house at Norwood but its further history is unknown. It is not mentioned in William Hervey's detailed will.

The second codicil left all his father's papers to Little Augustus and then to his brother William, with instructions never to let his brother Frederick near them. The ban caused some curiosity at the time, but appears to have been intended to prevent Frederick giving publicity to John Lord Hervey's memoirs, with their revealing comments on George II and the royal family.

Augustus left behind two much loved members of his family circle and a wife in name only, but one from whom he had never been divorced. Elizabeth Hervey continued to be known as the Duchess of Kingston and to enjoy the revenues from the Duke's estate. She lived abroad in a rather scandalous fashion and died abroad in 1788.

Mrs Nesbitt in contrast continued to live at Norwood. She was a woman of considerable intelligence and charm, as well as retaining her good looks, but was inhibited from taking a normal place in society by her questionable early life. She did, however, develop a wide circle of friends, including Lord Mulgrave and Sir John Stanley (who had been at school with Little Augustus). His accounts of visits to her show that she had retained many items of Augustus's personal property, including his portrait and that of Lord Mulgrave by Gainsborough and one of Little Augustus. The house also contained the clock given to Augustus by Admiral Byng just before his execution and a great bell brought back from Havana after the capture of the city in 1762.

Later Mrs Nesbitt travelled much and lived abroad. Her travels in Germany and Switzerland were in the best circles and there were at one time rumours that she was married morganatically to the Duke of Wurtemburg. It was also said, but denied in London, that she acted as a British agent in setting up royalist activities directed against the revolutionary government in France. She died at the age of 90 at Montreuil, France, in 1825. Forty-six years after Augustus's death there was nobody to care that his wish that she be buried with him at Ickworth was carried out and she was buried in France. Her house at Norwood was sold and its contents dispersed.

Little Augustus makes a brave figure during his short life, saddened by our foreknowledge of its shortness. Sir John Stanley describes him as noble spirited and with the character of a Hervey – impetuous, eager, clever and fascinating. He joined the navy in c. 1780 and went to sea as a midshipman in *Courageux*, commanded by his cousin Lord Mulgrave. During the relief of Gibraltar in 1782 he was fatally injured by a shot from one of the French blockading ships, and so all his father's hopes for him came to an early end.

Finally, what can be said about Augustus Hervey's character and the mark he left on the world? His character has in fact been summarized by someone who knew him better than we can ever do, his nephew Constantine Phipps, Lord Mulgrave. In the sad quarrel that Hervey had with Sandwich Mulgrave had been on Sandwich's side. However, though he had been Sandwich's man, both professionally and politically, Mulgrave had maintained a friendly relationship with his uncle and it was Mulgrave who provides the best contemporary assessment of Hervey's character and achievements.[18] His assessment can be summarized in four words – brave, intelligent, impetuous and loyal.

Brave he certainly was. His naval career shows overall and in detail that he never shied from personal danger and provides numerous examples of occasions on which he actively sought it out. From his description of the first time he came under fire, in a small boat off the coast of Portugal in 1739, to the attack on the Moro fort over twenty years later it seems that he positively enjoyed the experience of danger and the thrill that ran through him when the adrenalin began to flow.

Neither is there any doubt about his intelligence and judgement of events. Two admirals (Byng and Osborne) turned to him for advice when he was a comparatively junior captain and he exercised his several detached commands with aptitude and aplomb. Later when ashore his writings and his speeches in Parliament show a grasp of their subjects and a felicity with words which do more than justice to the unconventional education that he had received at sea. In politics he was perspicacious enough to see the need for economic and social measures to help the poor in Britain and to shore up the whole social fabric in Ireland. Any thoughts that he might have had about the rights and wrongs of self government or independence for the American colonies were overshadowed by his total belief in the rights and powers of the British Crown and Parliament.

His instinct for loyalty was dominant but sometimes tested to the limit. In spite of the tests to which his wife's behaviour put him he seems to have retained a firm feeling that she was indeed his wife and he should not divorce her without the full consent of both parties. In family matters it was Augustus who showed the greatest love for and comfort to his mother and who refused to become embroiled in the quarrels which divided some of his siblings. In political matters, however, loyalty to his brother clashed with loyalty to his chosen political mentor George Grenville. Hervey's attempts to reconcile these conflicting demands did not serve his own best interests and in fact lost him at least one opportunity of office.

That he acted as he thought right without regard for the consequences is undoubtedly true. No better example can be found, in low key, than the way he stood up to General Blakeney in Minorca in early 1756; and on a grander scale than in his efforts on behalf of Byng during and after his court martial, when his own best interests with Government and Admiralty would best have been served by a discreet and respectful silence. On occasion and in his political career it may be suggested that he allowed his impetuosity to draw him into inconsistency. But was he inconsistent when he broke with Sandwich in 1775 and allowed the relationship to deteriorate gradually into open conflict? Or was he responding to the pressures put upon him by a First Lord who had become manipulative to an unacceptable degree and who had taken into his own hands many of the functions and decisions on which a professional as well as a political input was appropriate?

Let Lord Mulgrave have the last word: '. . . his failings were those of a warm temper and unguarded disposition; his virtues those of a heart formed for every thing amiable in private, every thing great in public life.'

References

1. Cobbett, 1806–20, vol XVIII, col 667
2. *General Advertiser & Morning Intelligencer*, 18 February 1778
3. Ibid., 20 February 1778
4. Cobbett, 1806–20, vol XIX, col 818 *et seq*
5. Mackay, 1965, p347
6. Cobbett, 1806–20, vol XIX, col 1145
7. Ibid., col 1257
8. SRO(B), 941/50/5, p777
9. Ibid., p781
10. Ibid., p777
11. Barnes & Owen, 1972–78 (2), p257
12. Cobbett, 1806–20, vol XX, col 427
13. The Bowood Papers, *passim*
14. Cobbett, 1806–20, vol XX, col 674
15. Ibid., col 975 et seq
16. Lewis, 1937–83, (28), p488
17. Ibid.
18. *Gentleman's Magazine*, 1783, (53), p1007

Principal Sources

The manuscript sources quoted are identifed as follows:

BL:	British Library, Manuscript Collection
NMML:	National Maritime Museum Library.
PRO:	Public Record Office, Kew.
SRO(B):	Suffolk Record Office, Bury St Edmunds.
SRO(I):	Suffolk Record Office, Ipswich.

Bibliography

ADEANE, *The early married life of Josepha Maria Holroyd (Lady Stanley)* with extracts from Sir John Stanley's Praetorita. London, 1899

BARNES G R & OWEN J H (Eds) *The private papers of John, Earl of Sandwich* (4 vols). Naval Records Society Vols 69, 71, 75, 78, 1972–78.

BLEACKLEY, M (Ed.) *Casanova in England, being the account of the visit to London in 1763–64 as told by himself.* London, 1923.

BROOMFIELD J H *Lord Sandwich at the Admiralty Board: politics and the British Navy, 1771–1778.* Mariners Mirror, 51, p6, 1965.

CHARNOCK, J *Biographia navalis* (6 Vol.) London, 1794–98

CHILDE-PEMBERTON, W S *The Earl-Bishop. The life of Frederick Hervey, Bishop of Derry, Earl of Bristol.* London, 1924.

COBBETT, W *Parlimentary History (Hansard)*, vols 15–20. London, 1806–20

CORBETT, J S *England in the Seven Years War.* London, 1907

DICTIONARY OF NATIONAL BIOGRAPHY. Oxford, 1937–38.

ERSKINE, D (Ed.) *Augustus Hervey's Journal* London, 1953.

FORTESCUE, SIR J (Ed.) *The correspondence of King George III from 1760 to December 1783.* London 1927–28, 6 vols.

GAINSBOROUGH'S HOUSE SOCIETY *The Moysey family.* Sudbury, 1984

GENTLEMAN'S MAGAZINE, *passim.*

HERVEY, A J *his Midshipman's logs and an account of his part in the attack on Cartagena in 1741.* BL, Add. MSS 12129

HERVEY, A J *Manuscript notes, 1746–79.* SRO(B), 941/50/5.

HERVEY, A J *Notebook of Augustus John Hervey as Secretary for Ireland, 1766–67.* SRO(B), 941/50/7.

HERVEY, JOHN (1st Earl of Bristol) *Diary and expenses* (MS). SRO(B), 941/46/13 and 14.

HERVEY, LADY M *Letters of Mary Lepel. With a memoir and illustrative notes.* London, 1821.

HERVEY, S H A (Ed.) *Letter books of John Hervey, 1st Earl of Bristol.* Wells, 1894.

HUME, J A (Ed.) *The letters and journals of Lady Mary Coke.* Edinburgh, 1889–96.

KEPPEL, T *Life of Augustus Viscount Keppel.* London, 1842

KETTON-CREMER, R W *Horace Walpole. A biography.* London, 1964.

LEWIS, W S et al. (Eds) *Horace Walpole's correspondence.* New Haven, Connecticut, 1937–83, 48 vols.

MACKAY, R F *Admiral Hawke.* Oxford, 1965

MARILLIER, H C *A Bit of eighteenth century romance*. London 1910.

MUNDY, G B *Life and correspondence of Admiral Lord Rodney*. London, 1830.

NAMIER, SIR L and BROOKE, J *The history of Parliament: the House of Commons, 1754–90* (3 vols). London, 1964.

PACK, C J *Admiral Lord Anson*. London, 1960

PALMER, C J *The perlustrations of Great Yarmouth, with Gorleston and Southtown*. Great Yarmouth, 1872.

PEARCE, C E *The amazing Duchess*. London, c 1910.

POPE, D At 12 *Mr Byng was shot*. London, 1962.

RICHMOND, H W *The navy in the war of 1739–48*. London, 1920.

RODGER, N A M *The Admiralty*. London, 1979.

RODGER, N A M *The insatiable Earl. A life of John Montagu, 4th Earl of Sandwich*. London, 1993.

SEDGWICK, R (Ed.) *Lord Hervey's memoirs*. London, 1952.

SEDGWICK, R *The history of Parliament: the House of Commons, 1715–54*. London, 1970.

SMITH, W J (Ed.) *The Grenville Papers*. London, 1852–53

SPINNEY, D *Rodney*. London, 1969.

STUART, D M *Molly Lepel*. London, 1936.

SYRETT, D *The siege and capture of Havana 1762*. London, 1970.

TAYLOR W S and PRINGLE J H (Eds) *The correspondence of William Pitt Earl of Chatham*. London, 1838–40, 4 vols.

TUNSTALL, B *Admiral Byng and the loss of Minorca*. London, 1928.

WALPOLE, H *Memoirs of the reign of George II*. New Haven and London, 1985.

WALPOLE, H *Memoirs of the reign of George III*. London, 1894.

WALPOLE, H *Journal of the reign of King George III from the year 1771–83*.

    (1) Edited with notes by Dr Doran, 2 vols. London 1859.

    (2) Edited with an introduction by A F Steuart, 2 vols. London, 1910

Index